Unearthing childhood

THE AUTHOR

Robin Derricourt received his MA and PhD in archaeology from the University of Cambridge. His career has included appointments as a university lecturer in archaeology, as a director of a national heritage commission, as an archaeology publisher and the director of a university press. He is a Fellow of the Society of Antiquaries of London, a Fellow of the Australian Academy of the Humanities and an Honorary Associate Professor in the School of Humanities, University of New South Wales.

His previous books include *Inventing Africa: History, Archaeology and Ideas* (2011) and *Antiquity Imagined: The Remarkable Legacy of Egypt and the Ancient Near East* (2015).

UNEARTHING CHILDHOOD

Young lives in prehistory

ROBIN DERRICOURT

MANCHESTER UNIVERSITY PRESS

Copyright © Robin Derricourt 2018

The right of Robin Derricourt to be identified as the author of this work has been asserted by him in accordance with the Copyright, Designs and Patents Act 1988.

Published by Manchester University Press
Altrincham Street, Manchester M1 7JA

www.manchesteruniversitypress.co.uk

British Library Cataloguing-in-Publication Data
A catalogue record for this book is available from the British Library

ISBN 978 1 5261 2893 5 hardback

ISBN 978 1 5261 2808 9 paperback

First published 2018

The publisher has no responsibility for the persistence or accuracy of URLs for any external or third-party internet websites referred to in this book, and does not guarantee that any content on such websites is, or will remain, accurate or appropriate.

Typeset in Warnock Pro by R. J. Footring Ltd, Derby
Printed in Great Britain
by Bell & Bain Ltd, Glasgow

CONTENTS

List of illustrations	ix
Key references, with abbreviations	xv
PREFACE	xvii
Aims and scope	xviii
Comparisons and analogies	xx
Structure of the book	xxi
Terminology and usage	xxiii
Acknowledgements	xxiv
Notes	xxvi
1 UNDERSTANDING *The deep past of childhood*	1
Who are children, what is childhood?	4
The missing children	10
The use of analogy	14
Recent hunter-gatherers	16
Higher primate relatives	21
The framework of hominin prehistory	22
The deep past	26
Notes	27
2 BEING *Birth, motherhood and infancy*	33
Primate dependency and independence	34
Evolution of the hominin family	38
Mothers and babies	44
Notes	50
3 GROWING *The child in the family*	55
Visual impressions of the prehistoric family	56
The 'traditional' family	63
Carrying a young child	66
Questions and answers	71
Notes	71

4	FEEDING *Weaning, eating and health*	75
	Great apes	76
	Prehistoric forager weaning and after	78
	Food provision and diet in modern small-scale societies	82
	Weaning and food preparation in agricultural groups	85
	Diet and health	88
	Conclusions	91
	Notes	91
5	WEARING *Clothing, adornment and body shaping*	97
	Ornamentation and clothes	98
	Prehistoric foragers' body covering and body ornamentation	100
	Prehistoric agriculturalist clothing and adornment	110
	Body shaping	116
	Conclusions	118
	Notes	118
6	LEARNING *Knowledge and skills*	123
	Learning and tool use among the great apes	125
	Hominin evolution and knowledge transmission	129
	Learning and work in recent small-scale societies	130
	Stone tools and apprenticeship	135
	Children's involvement in rock art	141
	Pottery and crafts in prehistoric farming communities	143
	Conclusions	147
	Notes	148
7	PLAYING *Fun, games, toys and culture*	156
	Primates at play	157
	Foragers and farmers, ancient and modern	159
	Games, toys and miniature items	162
	Children's dolls and adult figures	165
	Conclusions	171
	Notes	172
8	FIGHTING *Conflict and violence*	176
	Archaeological evidence of conflict	178
	Conflict and violence among prehistoric foragers	180
	Conflict and violence among prehistoric farmers	184
	Sacrifice	189
	Toy and real weapons	190
	Conclusions	192
	Notes	193

9	DYING 1 *Death and burial in forager societies*	198
	The death of children	199
	Great apes	203
	Australopithecines	204
	Early *Homo*	208
	Neanderthals and the Middle Palaeolithic	209
	Homo sapiens and the Upper Palaeolithic	213
	Advanced foragers of the prehistoric world	217
	Modern hunter-gatherers	220
	Conclusions	223
	Notes	224
10	DYING 2 *Death and burial in Old World farming societies*	233
	Neolithic of the Middle East and Europe	234
	Copper and Bronze Ages of the Middle East and Europe	238
	Iron Age Europe	245
	African farmers	248
	Other regions	251
	Conclusions	254
	Notes	255
11	PROGRESSING *The future of childhood's deep past*	262
	Notes	267
	Index of places	268
	General index	272

ILLUSTRATIONS

Museum artist's image of a European Upper Palaeolithic family   3
© National Museums NI. Collection: Ulster Museum

Child and adult from the Mesolithic rock art of Cuevas del Engarbo, Spain   7
M.yM.G.L. Soria, *Los Abrigos con Arte Rupestre Levantino de la Sierra de Segura*, Jaén: Arqueología Monografías, 1999

Kalahari San woman with her child in a sling   17
Photo Romas-Vysniauskas / Shutterstock.com

Neanderthal family scene: reconstruction at Krapina Neanderthal Museum, Croatia   23
Tromber / Wikimedia under Creative Commons License 4.0

Gorilla mother with her infant   35
Flickr / Kwita UIzina under Creative Commons License CC BY-ND 2.0

Child with two adults from the Mesolithic rock art of Lucio o de Gavidia, Spain   42
L. Dams, *Les Peintures Rupestres du Levant Espagnol*, París: Picard, 1984

Sculpture of an apparently pregnant woman from the Upper Palaeolithic of Kostenki, Russia   45
Thilo Parg / Wikimedia under Creative Commons License CC BY-SA 3.0

Woman possibly giving birth, a sculpture from the 4th millennium BC, Ħaġar Qim, Malta   47
M. Gimbutas, *The Language of the Goddess*, London: Thames & Hudson, 1989, p. 106, fig. 176

Ivory sculpture of mother and child from predynastic Egypt, in the Neues Museum, Berlin   49
Anagoria / Wikimedia under Creative Commons License 3.0

Plan of the footprints of an archaic *Homo* family from Happisburgh, England   57
N. Ashton et al., *PLoS ONE* 9 (2014), e88329

Stencilled hands of children and adults from Upper Palaeolithic cave wall art at Gargas, France   59
Jean Clottes

Infant hands or lizard feet? Stencils in rock art at Wadi Sura in the
Western Desert of Egypt 60
E. Honoré et al., *Journal of Archaeological Science: Reports* 6 (2016), p. 243

Possible initiation scene from the Later Stone Age of Sevilla, South
Africa 61
J. Parkington, *Antiquity* 63 (1989), p. 17; traced by Royden Yates

Later Stone Age rock paintings from Zimbabwe depicting two young
children with two adults, and a mother with a child, alongside
two adults 62
Redrawn after C. Thorneycroft copy, Rock Art Research Institute,
Johannesburg, ZIM CBY1 and ZIM BNR3

Engraved plaquette from Upper Palaeolithic Gönnersdorf, showing a
procession of four women. The third from the left is suggested to
have on her back a cradle with an infant 67
G. Bosinski & G. Fischer, *Die Menschendarstellungen von Gönnersdorf
der Ausgrabung von 1968*, Wiesbaden: Steiner, 1974

Drawings of a clay model, from Tennessee, USA, of an infant bound
to a flat carrying board 69
N. Morss, *American Antiquity* 18 (1952), p. 164

Unbaked clay figures interpreted as babies, from Ancestral Pueblo
site of Waterfall Ruin, Arizona 70
D.S. Byers & N. Morss, *American Antiquity* 23 (1957), p. 82

Chimpanzee suckling her young 77
Primate Research Institute, Kyoto University

Pottery vessels interpreted as infant feeding bottles, from the Late
Bronze Age and Iron Age of France, Germany and Austria 87
A.D. Lacaille, *Proceedings of the Royal Society of Medicine* 43 (1950),
p. 566

Australian Aboriginal family near Sydney, early 19th century 99
Louis de Freycinet, *Voyage autour du monde: atlas historique*, National
Library of Australia, NK1725/A

Statuette carved from a mammoth tusk showing a close-fitting
garment, from the Upper Palaeolithic of Buret' in Siberia 103
I. Gilligan, *Journal of Archaeological Method and Theory* 17 (2010), p. 57

Burial of an adolescent ('The Prince') in the Gravettian era, at Arene
Candide, Italy, with elaborate shell bead headdress 104
© Libor Balák – Antropark, http://www.liborbalak.wz.cz

LIST OF ILLUSTRATIONS

Reconstruction by Libor Balák of a burial of an adolescent ('The Prince') in the Gravettian era, at Arene Candide, Italy   105
© Libor Balák – Antropark, http://www.liborbalak.wz.cz

Perforated teeth and beads accompanying the burial of an Upper Palaeolithic child aged between 2 and 4 years, at La Madeleine, France   106
M. Vanhaeren & F. d'Errico, *Paléo* 13 (2001), p. 6

Reconstruction by Libor Balák of two lavishly decorated Upper Palaeolithic child burials at Sunghir, Russia   108
© Libor Balák – Antropark, http://www.liborbalak.wz.cz

Decorated pottery from the US Southwest showing the 'butterfly' hair decoration of young women   111
K. Hays-Gilpin in *CPPS*, p. 204

Reconstruction of woollen clothing and a bronze disc found on a Bronze Age girl from Egtved in Denmark   113
FinnWikiNo / Wikimedia under Creative Commons License CC BY SA 3.0

Copper diadem from the grave of an 8-year-old child of the Bronze Age at Abbekås, Sweden   114
F. Hansen, *Skanska bronzaldershogar*, Lund: Gleerupska univ.-bokhandeln, 1938, p. 78, fig. 44

Bead necklaces on children at burials from the 4th millennium BC, Adaima, Egypt   115
B. Midant-Reynes; Photo A. Lecler, IFAO

Figurines with artificially flattened heads, from Chalcolithic Choga Mish, Iran   117
A. Daems & K. Croucher, *Iranica Antiqua* 42 (2007), p. 9, after P. Delougaz, H.J. Kantor & A. Alizadeh

Chimpanzee mother demonstrating tool use to her young in Bossou, Guinea   126
Primate Research Institute, Kyoto University

Children's finger fluting on the cave walls of Upper Palaeolithic Gargas, France   142
Jean Clottes

Reconstruction by Libor Balák of children involved in craft in a Neolithic village of the Danube valley   144
© Libor Balák – Antropark, http://www.liborbalak.wz.cz

Figurines from the Sinagua culture of Lizard Man village, Arizona, USA 146
K.A. Kamp, *Journal of Anthropological Research* 57 (2001), p. 435; art by Amy Henderson

Pottery vessel with fingerprints of the child who made it, from the Bronze Age of Kamennyi Ambar-5, in the Trans-Urals, Russia 147
Natalia Berseneva; photo: Andrey Bersenev

Possible children's items in clay from the Czech Republic: Bronze Age animal from Prague Vinoř and Iron Age rattle from Prague-Střešovice 164
J. Turek, 'Being a beaker child: the position of children in Late Eneolithic society' (2000), available at http://www.kar.zcu.cz/texty/Deti/deti.htm

Clay doll found in 2017 at the Kori burial mound site of the Yayoi period, Japan, dated between around 300 BC and 300 AD 166
Asahi Shimbun via Getty Images

Doll's house or cultic objects? Miniature ceramic items from Neolithic Ovčarovo, Bulgaria 167
M. Gimbutas, *The Language of the Goddess*, London: Thames & Hudson, 1989, p. 72, fig. 112, after H. Todorova, Kultszene und Hausmodell aus Ovčarovo, Bez. Targovişte, *Thracia* 3 (1974): 39–46

Model house from Neolithic Platia Magoula Zarkou, Greece 168
OREA- Institut für Orientalische und Europäische Archäologie, Project Platia Magoula Zarkou in Thessaly/Greece, Austrian Science Fund FWF P 27159-G18; photo: Mario Börner

Grave of a newborn from Iron Age Sanga, Democratic Republic of the Congo, with long bones probably used as dolls 170
P. de Maret, *Journal of Field Archaeology* 41 (2016), fig. 6

'Fertility doll' from Guinea Bissau: an ethnographic parallel to the Sanga find 170
P. de Maret, *Journal of Field Archaeology* 41 (2016), fig. 4; photo: Udo Horstmann

A 13-year-old soldier from Vietnam, 1968 177
Under Creative Commons License CC.BY.2.0

Skull of a 13- or 14-year-old with fatal wound from a macehead blow, from Chalcolithic Shiqmim, Israel 186
L. Dawson, T.E. Levy & P. Smith, *International Journal of Osteoarchaeology* 13 (2003), p. 116

Miniature bow made from deer antler, and presumed to be for a child, from the Middle Bronze Age of Isleham, England 192
Cambridge University Museum of Archaeology and Anthropology

LIST OF ILLUSTRATIONS   xiii

Kindertod (*Death of a Child*), woodcut by Ernst Barlach, 1919   199
   http://www.artnet.com

Ibex horns surrounding a Neanderthal child's body at Teshik-Tash,
   Uzbekistan   202
   H.L. Movius, *Bulletin of the American School of Prehistoric Research* 17
   (1953), fig. 5

Reconstruction at the University of Padua of the Taung Australopithecine child   205
   Arc-Team Open Research under Creative Commons License BY

Cranium of a Neanderthal child   210
   Smithsonian National Museum of Natural History: Ryan Somma under
   Creative Commons License BY-SA 2.0

Bronze Age infant from Lake Itkul, Russia, buried with figurines and
   a cap with copper decoration   241
   A. V. Polyakov & Y. N. Esin, *Archaeology, Ethnology and Anthropology of
   Eurasia* 43 (2015), p. 46, fig. 4

Figurines with the Bronze Age infant from Lake Itkul   241
   A.V. Polyakov & Y.N. Esin, *Archaeology, Ethnology and Anthropology of
   Eurasia* 43 (2015), p. 50, fig. 9

Bronze fibulae and pendants from an Iron Age child's burial at
   Bettelbühl, Germany   247
   Landesamt für Denkmalpflege im RP Stuttgart, Y. Mühleis

Petroglyph of a family from the Mojave desert, Nevada, USA   264
   trekandshoot / Shutterstock

Every effort has been made to obtain permission to reproduce copyright material, and the publisher will be pleased to be informed of any errors and omissions for correction in future editions.

KEY REFERENCES, WITH ABBREVIATIONS

JOURNAL

CitP   *Childhood in the Past*

SINGLE-AUTHOR BOOKS

Baxter, *Archaeology*   J.E. Baxter, *The Archaeology of Childhood: children, gender and material culture*, Walnut Creek, CA: Altamira, 2005

Lancy, *Anthropology* 1ed, 2ed   D.F. Lancy, *The Anthropology of Childhood: cherubs, chattel, changelings*, Cambridge: Cambridge University Press, 1st edition 2008; revised and extended as 2nd edition 2015

Lewis, *Bioarchaeology*   M.E. Lewis, *The Bioarchaeology of Children: perspectives from biological and forensic anthropology*, Cambridge: Cambridge University Press, 2007

Wileman, *Hide and Seek*   J. Wileman, *Hide and Seek: the archaeology of childhood*, Stroud: Tempus, 2005

EDITED VOLUMES

AAA   W. Wendrich (ed.), *Archaeology and Apprenticeship: body knowledge, identity and communities of practice*, Tucson, AZ: University of Arizona Press, 2012

AOC   G. Coşçunsu (ed.), *The Archaeology of Childhood: interdisciplinary perspectives on an archaeological enigma*, Albany, NY: SUNY Press, 2015

BRIPP   K. Bacvarov (ed.), *Babies Reborn: infant/child burials in pre- and protohistory*, Oxford: Archaeopress, 2008

CCLA   P. Romanowicz (ed.), *Child and Childhood in the Light of Archaeology: studies*, Wrocław: Wydawnictwo Chronicon, 2013

CCS   S.E.E. Crawford & G.B. Shepherd (eds), *Children, Childhood and Society*, Oxford: Archaeopress, 2007

CIA *Children in Action: perspectives on the archaeology of childhoods*, special issue of *Archeological Papers of the American Anthropological Association* 15(1) (2015)

CMC J. Sofaer Derevenski (ed.), *Children and Material Culture*, London: Routledge, 2000

CPPS K.A. Kamp (ed.), *Children in the Prehistoric Puebloan Southwest*, Salt Lake City, UT: University of Utah Press, 2002

CSI M.S. Romero, E.A. Garcia & G.A. Jimenez (eds), *Children, Spaces and Identity*, Oxford: Oxbow, 2015

HGC B. Hewlett & M.E. Lamb (eds), *Hunter-Gatherer Childhoods: evolutionary, developmental and cultural perspectives*, New Brunswick: AldineTransaction, 2005

IPP J. Moore & E. Scott (eds), *Invisible People and Processes: writing gender and childhood into European archaeology*, London: Leicester University Press, 1997

RLA M. Lally & A. Moore (eds), *(Re)thinking the Little Ancestor: new perspectives on the archaeology of infancy and childhood*, British Archaeological Reports International Series 2271, Oxford: Archaeopress, 2011

TCBI J.L. Thompson, M.P. Alfonso-Durruty & J.J. Crandall (eds), *Tracing Childhood: bioarchaeological investigations of early lives in antiquity*, Gainesville, FL: University Press of Florida, 2014

TCIN G.E. Cunnar & A. Högberg (eds), *The Child Is Now 25*, special issue of *Childhood in the Past* 8(2) (2015)

PREFACE

If time travel took us to visit a prehistoric community – a small-scale farming village, perhaps, or a foraging band of early humans, or even earlier hominin ancestors – what could we expect to encounter? Mothers playing with their infants (grandmothers too), small children breaking off from their play to look at us (or running off in fear), older children learning and practising the skills which will make them full contributors to their society; more confident adolescents would perhaps be off with their elders hunting or fishing or herding or tending the fields. We could expect about half the community to be the young; in the home base (whether a temporary campsite or a permanent village) they might form the majority during the day.

This book surveys what we know and can learn about the lives of children in the societies that preceded the emergence of civilisation: the world of prehistory. While we cannot yet write a comprehensive history of prehistoric childhoods, the information derived from archaeology and associated studies shows there is much to reveal of the 'hidden half' of past humanity.

In the broad sweep of historical evidence, as in descriptions of more recent societies, we see that children represent around half of most human groups. It is reasonable to suggest that in our deeper prehistoric past also, only one of every two members of a community was an adult. We learn and acquire our culture, knowledge, skills and beliefs during childhood and when we are adults we pass them on to our own children and our grandchildren, and establish that continuity we call society, the human world. Children reflect and absorb tradition: culture in the broadest sense. The young may also feature as agents of change: as populations grow, it may be the young adults who question and innovate, and who shift their residence, making those movements in settlement which brought *Homo sapiens* to occupy and dominate the globe.

Despite their numbers and importance, children have been significantly under-represented in narrative accounts of the past. Although social and behavioural sciences pay substantial attention to the young, their presence in the work of historians has been a specialised if not marginal area. And archaeologists, especially those working on prehistoric societies (those without written records), have given relatively little attention to children and childhood. Most of their colleagues in social and cultural anthropology have similarly focused on the adult world and the social patterns it represents, rather than the life stages and processes in which those social patterns are transmitted to the next generation. Anthropologist Lawrence Hirschfeld asked baldly 'Why don't anthropologists like children?', noting this as 'A curious state of affairs given that virtually all contemporary anthropology is based on the premise that culture is learned, not inherited.... The marginalisation of children and childhood ... has obscured our understanding of how cultural forms emerge and why they are sustained'.[1]

In the 1960s French philosopher Jean-Paul Sartre criticised his fellow left intellectuals: 'Today's Marxists are concerned only with adults; reading them, one would believe that we are born at the age when we earn our first wages. They have forgotten their own childhoods'.[2] The situation has begun to change, as the importance, interest and potential of these topics are realised.

A parallel can be drawn from other 'missing' and recovered groups in the development of archaeology as a discipline. After an initial focus on the high elites of civilised cultures and the supposed ethnic identity of non-literate societies, archaeology expanded through the 20th century with the study of the common *man*: worlds of prehistory and history seen through dominant male perspectives. A movement that gained pace from the 1980s saw the emergence of studies of the missing gender, as the theme of women in prehistory and in the archaeological record was taken up, and this has continued to develop and strengthen. However, children and childhood are still only modestly represented in discussions of our deep past.

AIMS AND SCOPE

In this book I survey what we know of children and childhood in the prehistoric past, and by implication what more we could know when we ask new questions of old data, and develop new lines of enquiry. Such evidence can come from figurative sculptures or finger daubs in art on cave walls, from footprints, from finds of toys and dolls. It can come from the trial pieces of a young apprentice potter or maker of stone tools. Much of our archaeological evidence comes from the burials of those who did not survive into adulthood: their bodies show us something of the health and diet of the young, and their different status by age and family group, and material goods found with their bodies include clothing, personal decoration and the objects associated with daily life. We can attempt to improve our understanding by comparing prehistoric remains with our observations of more recent societies; and when we consider the earliest hominin ancestors and relatives of our species, comparison with living great apes can also provide illumination. But the core of our expanding knowledge of children in prehistory arises when researchers ask questions they had not asked before.

I hope to show that archaeology itself benefits from a broader sweep, encompassing the young as well as the old. But of no less importance, looking at prehistoric periods and the deep past can illuminate the perspectives on children and childhood that come from widely different areas of interest: social sciences, humanities, biological and behavioural sciences and from parenthood. The narrative therefore focuses on information and images of the prehistoric past in a framework intended to make sense to those who are not themselves archaeologists. But equally I hope this text will stimulate archaeologists to be ambitious in looking further at children and childhood in the context of their own regional and temporal interest. The main text does not, therefore, focus on interpretative debates between specialists (it is a book about archaeology, not archaeologists), but the extended list of detailed bibliographical references with some comments on them in the notes allow those topics to be followed up, and I hope will stimulate both further questioning and the re-examination of existing data. References to websites were accurate at the time of completion of the text of this book in August 2017, unless otherwise noted.

The developments and debates around archaeological theory have significantly strengthened and stimulated the subject over the last 50 years. We have escaped the straitjacket which suggested empirical descriptions of sites and finds gave an adequate, unbiased and reliable account of the past. The present book, however, is not designed to argue a set of interpretations or theoretical positions about children or childhood in the past, but to provide a reminder of the wealth of material on which such debates, interpretations and understanding can and should be based.

Understanding and analysis of infancy, children, childhood and adolescence come from specialists in biology and genetics, from psychology and education, from sociology and related applied areas, from anthropology, from history and cultural studies, as well as archaeology. All can and should borrow from each other and much of the archaeological discussion of children has sought to use the insights of other disciplines, as literature I cite shows. Few if any of us have the background to critique confidently the arguments and diverse views of all these different disciplinary perspectives. In presenting a more descriptive account rather than advancing a specific viewpoint I am certainly not downplaying the importance of vigorous theoretical debate about what all this means. In fact, I suggest that the images of children and childhood in prehistory, and from archaeology more generally, can and should be used by those in other disciplinary areas.

Perhaps the most important perception that has emerged in archaeology is this: the answers provided are limited by the questions asked, and these have been determined by issues of context – national, ethnic, religious, gender, class and so on. Self-awareness in the interpretation of the past over two centuries has moved us away from an intrinsic racism; we have subsequently sought to distance ourselves from the limitations of elitism. We have seen challenges to the use of ethnocentrism in prehistoric reconstructions and the ongoing movement against sexism in archaeological interpretations. Perhaps ageism is the next frontier to be broken, the unwritten assumption that only those of mature age matter in our study of the deep past.

A survey like this must be selective, and this book focuses primarily on examples from the Old World, especially Europe, the Middle East and Africa, extending with lesser detail into the Americas, Asia and Oceania. The category of prehistory covers the spread of time from early hominins more than 3 million years ago until the emergence of civilisations or the impact of these through processes such as colonisation. The longest stretch of time and fullest discussion here is of forager groups (hunter-gatherers and fishers) followed in most regions by pastoralists and crop farmers. Alongside the archaeology I discuss what we can gain from studies of the great apes and from ethnographic accounts of more recent communities worldwide.

COMPARISONS AND ANALOGIES

We can try to make sense of childhood in prehistory by comparisons across time and space, but we need to resist too much reliance on assumptions and images from later urban civilisation, whether historic or modern.

Archaeologists working on historical periods such as the Classical world of the Mediterranean inevitably use a mixture of historical, artistic and archaeological evidence in their discussions, an option not available to prehistorians. In a valuable survey of childhood in the smaller-scale societies studied by anthropologists, David Lancy has stressed how different, how anomalous, are the patterns of parenting and child rearing in modern western urban society compared with the great sweep of other societies.[3] When we move step by step back through 'our' history, we are looking at worlds whose complexity, ideologies and structures were quite different from those of our deeper prehistory. We may think back from the present, and indeed archaeological excavations strip away layers from now to then to before. But human history (and human prehistory) are not focused journeys aiming step by step towards the goals of modernity, progressive steps in a one-directional human journey. There are dangers in using the present, and using our knowledge of historical societies, to impose the assumptions and models of western society and the history of western (or eastern) civilisations backwards in time onto prehistoric worlds. History can stimulate questions and it may amplify interpretations, but we should avoid suppositions that what we see in one context can be tracked back in time to the deep past.[4]

Put simply, what we trace and study in the archaeological record is *tradition* (behavioural, technological, spiritual or ritual, demographic) and it reflects what went *before*, not what it will lead to in future generations, societies and cultures some centuries or millennia closer to our own time.

Despite this comment, the human species of today has largely the same essential biology, the same biological needs, the same power of body and the same power of mind as the first *Homo sapiens* who were spreading out of Africa by about 60,000 years ago. The primary difference is cultural, not biological. Foragers (hunter-gatherers), pastoralists and farmers in prehistory were the same people facing the same issues as those in more recent small-scale societies before these were affected by modernity and the impact of the global economy. With care and caution, we can consider issues such as childhood in prehistory by comparison with childhood in such small-scale societies. But as emphasised throughout this book, even a preliterate forager group recorded by 19th- or early-20th-century ethnographers is not a relic of prehistory. The use of analogy is limited, yet it may still be useful. In each chapter of this book I consider some of what we know from more recent groups whose economy and society had elements similar to those of some prehistoric groups.

The other source of evidence 'looking back' is to consider our earliest biological ancestors and relations in our superfamily: other great apes. We can do this only with living great apes. As often noted, we share almost 99% of our DNA with chimpanzees. In considering the biological basis of motherhood, infancy and childhood, we can compare our own species with our fellow great apes. When we look at early hominins – Australopithecines and members of the *Homo* and *Australopithecus* genera – and consider the biological underpinnings of our own species' earliest prehistory, the lives of juvenile great apes help stimulate our thoughts. We are not descended from these great apes but we share common ancestors; their patterns can suggest elements of what we have emerged from. In the following chapters I look at aspects of the pattern of parenting and child learning among our biological relatives.

STRUCTURE OF THE BOOK

In Chapter 1 I review the question of what childhood means: the different biological criteria and the very different social criteria by which a newborn progresses to social recognition as an adult. I explore in more detail the question of how much we can use information from history, anthropology and the study of great apes in understanding the prehistoric past. I note the kinds of valuable archaeological work undertaken in researching, writing on and the interpretation of prehistoric childhoods. I include a brief review of the chronological framework of earlier prehistory, with readers from outside archaeology in mind.

Chapter 2 discusses birth, motherhood and infancy through the evolutionary stages of hominins and what we know from prehistoric archaeology. While much of our knowledge of prehistoric children comes from burials and skeletal remains – those who experienced an early death – there is nevertheless much we can say about their early lives. The emergence of visual art – small sculptures as well as painted surfaces – gives us some direct images of children and childhood, discussed in Chapter 3, which also looks at the means by which infants could be carried by others during their daily activities.

In subsequent chapters I consider aspects of the lives of prehistoric children and how they fitted into their societies. Chapter 4 considers diet: from weaning through changes in children's food before they adopt the full adult diet of their families. In Chapter 5 I examine what we can see of the clothing and personal decoration of children in prehistory. Inevitably, some kinds of evidence are available to us only for later prehistoric periods.

The key question of learning is discussed in Chapter 6: the acquisition of knowledge and skills and how we can seek to track these in the archaeological record, and in particular the materials of apprenticeship and the gradual development of essential skills. Chapter 7 addresses the question of play: toys, dolls and recreational play, which contributes to the processes of socialisation. As shown in Chapter 8, conflict in human prehistory affected the young as well as the old: violence against children is nothing new, and includes sacrifice alongside the impacts of war and intra-group conflict.

In Chapters 9 and 10 I consider our most frequent source of knowledge for prehistoric children: their burials or other disposal of the dead. The death of children was an expectation throughout human prehistory and history; indeed, it has remained so in many societies of modern times. The burials of children give us much of the evidence that informs the previous chapters about their lives; but in death we see how the young who did not survive were treated, noting differences in cultures, sex, rank and ritual. Study of the death of the young is also a reminder of social practices such as infanticide alongside death by illness and misadventure. Chapter 9 considers the issue of childhood death among forager communities worldwide, past and present. Chapter 10 gives an account of childhood death and burials in prehistoric farming communities, primarily of Europe and the Middle East but with some comparative examples from elsewhere.

Finally, Chapter 11 notes how much more there is to learn before we can write a comprehensive prehistory of childhood.

TERMINOLOGY AND USAGE

This book draws primarily on the methodology and information of the scientific discipline of archaeology, together with approaches of palaeoanthropology, primate biology and ethology, bioanthropology and genetics, social and cultural anthropology, historical sciences and more.

To suit the needs of readers with different interests and backgrounds I have sought to limit the use of technical and specialist terminology as far as possible. This is especially so where it contributes neither brevity nor clarity: for example, 'newborn' has the same meaning, and length, as 'neonate'. Specialist language does not always seem to add value, as when we read that newborn primate infants 'show a strong negative geotropism': that is, they do not like to be held upside down![5]

I have sought to gloss essential technical terms for non-specialists. Technical terms can be indispensable, especially in chronology and the classification of prehistory cultural identity. Despite their limitations, classificatory terms for archaeological units in time and space (what we traditionally called 'cultures') remain valuable tools. This is true whether we are referring to the Palaeolithic hunter-gatherers of the Pleistocene (Ice Age); or more specialised Mesolithic/Epipalaeolithic hunter-gatherers of the subsequent Holocene epoch (geologically dated from about 9700 BC); or the farming communities that archaeological tradition in the Old World commonly (but not universally) subsumes under the term Neolithic; or the often more complex societies whose identity we shorthand by reference to one aspect of their technology in the terms Copper Age (or Chalcolithic or Aeneolithic), Bronze Age, Iron Age.

Dates are presented as *calendar dates* (AD, BC or just as years ago). Most radiocarbon dates, which are calculated as years Before Present (BP), are calibrated to calendar years, as presented by individual sources, or otherwise by using the online calibration tables of OxCal from the University of Oxford's Radiocarbon Accelerator Unit.[6]

In this book I use the terms 'forager' and 'hunter-gatherer' interchangeably. The latter term can be misleading as it is often taken to imply the dominance of non-agricultural and pre-agricultural societies by 'man the hunter'. Studies of modern foragers show a wide range in the relative food contribution of females and males, and a broad variety in both the mix of their food resources and their foraging techniques – gathering plants, collecting insects and other small animals, hunting larger animals, collecting shellfish, and both inland and coastal fishing. 'Forager' avoids implying the priority of any one economic resource. In addition, foragers may supplement food gathering and hunting with varying degrees of farming activity – gardens or herding, for example – just as farmers may also hunt, fish and collect wild foods. I also use the terms 'farmers' and 'agriculturalists' interchangeably and unless otherwise indicated I apply the term to include those engaged in animal husbandry as well as crop farming.

In many chapters of this book there are discussions of foragers and some agriculturalists from the recent and modern era: communities we know best from accounts by outsiders who may be professional anthropologists or other social scientists, or earlier generations of observers. Such descriptions of 'traditional' societies by definition reflect a time when they were already in contact with a wider world, and sometimes already radically transformed by such contact. No society is unchanging, but in the context of this book it has proved most convenient to adopt the language of 'the ethnographic present', to describe these societies as 'modern' and as communities of 'the modern world', and to use the present tense when referring to accounts of such groups, whether these descriptions were made in the later 19th century, or in the 1960s, or even very recently. Individual sources make clear when the individual studies took place and it should be emphasised that a statement such as 'The !Kung do X' or 'the Yanomami do Y' does not imply that they do (or do not) behave in a particular way today. The present tense implies the time a study or observation was made and when I use the term 'traditional' I am not implying some kind of unchanging society.

Alternative terminologies can exist according to context (e.g. Ju/'hoansi for !Kung San, also called baSarwa and previously called Bushmen) and vary according to the usage of different disciplines. Some traditional ethnographic terms are now seen as dated, inaccurate or even occasionally as cause for offence, but it has seemed best to retain the terms familiar in the scholarly literature and references.

On the occasions where I have been unable to access an original publication I have cited both the reference and the secondary source which I have used. This is especially so for literature in languages unfamiliar to me, and I acknowledge that this survey is biased towards information from publications with text or abstract in European languages.

ACKNOWLEDGEMENTS

A volume like this rests on the shoulders of giants and giantesses who pioneered the study of children and childhood in archaeology in recent years. A number of key collections are highlighted on pp. xv–xvi ('Key references, with abbreviations') and the spread of references throughout the book pays direct tribute to many individuals who have contributed important work to this still emerging field; I apologise if I have misinterpreted any of their views, especially when summarised in the interests of brevity.

I am grateful to a number of friends, colleagues, specialists and others who have provided specific advice, stimulated questions or thoughts. In particular, I thank Harry Allen, Natalia Berseneva, Pierre de Maret, Robin Dennell, Brian Fagan, Catherine Frieman, Clive Gamble, Linda Gilaizeau, Misato Hayashi, Jody Joy, Phillipa McGuinness, Nana Nakayama, David Phillipson, Laurel Phillipson, John Shea, Kirsty Squires, Sofija Stefanović, Peter White and others who have sent me their papers. It was instructive that a number of other people I consulted could bring to mind few or no works in their field addressing childhood and children specifically. Contributors to sessions on the archaeology and bioarchaeology of childhood at the 2016 World Archaeological Congress in Kyoto provided stimulating ideas. I am especially grateful for the suggestions from anonymous publisher's reviewers. None of these shares any responsibility for my errors and omissions. While I have not adopted all their suggestions of how I might further expand the coverage and discussions in the book, they do indicate the strong potential for much more work in this field.

For encouragement and stimulation I thank Marguerite Derricourt, Tim Derricourt, Madeleine Hawcroft, Frances Mayall, Jonathon Mayall and the frequent if unaware research assistance of Evie and Rufus.

I am pleased to acknowledge the interest and support of the staff of Manchester University Press, especially Meredith Carroll, Bethan Hirst and Alun Richards. I am particularly grateful for the invaluable professional copy-editing by Ralph Footring, who was also responsible for the interior design of the book.

Especial thanks are due to those who responded generously and promptly to requests and supplied images or granted permission for the use of illustrations in this book, including Libor Balák, Natalia Berseneva, Jean Clottes, Aurelie Daems, Pierre de Maret, Francesco D'Errico, Yuri Esin, Ian Gilligan, Misato Hayashi, Kelley Hays-Gilpin, Emmanuelle Honoré, Udo Horstmann, Kathryn Kamp, Dirk Krausse, Beatrix Midant-Reynes, John Parkington, Patricia Smith and Jan Turek. If there are any images for which I have been unable to locate the copyright holder I will appreciate their contact.

The staff and facilities of a number of libraries have provided invaluable help in the research for this book. In particular, I am indebted to the exceptional online facilities of the University of New South Wales Library, and also to the University of Sydney libraries, the State Library of New South Wales and Australian National University Library, not forgetting the invaluable resources of Google Scholar and the useful news feed from David Meadows's *Explorator*.[7]

As a reader, publisher and author I know well that every book contains errors: I welcome advice on where these might be. Attempting a broad survey like this carries the necessity and risk in making some generalisations over a very broad and diverse range of evidence, from which I would expect and accept some challenges; I hope the book stimulates dissent and debate. To the non-academic friend who suggested I was working on rather a narrow topic I would say that if a survey of 50% of humanity for 98% of human time over the larger part of the world is narrow, I am relieved not to have addressed something more ambitious.

NOTES

1. L.A. Hirschfeld, 'Why don't anthropologists like children?', *American Anthropologist* 104 (2002): 611–627, p. 611.
2. Jean-Paul Sartre, *Search for a Method*, New York: Vintage Books, 1968, p. 62.
3. D.F. Lancy, *Anthropology* 1ed, 2ed.
4. For example, the influential work by medievalist historian Philippe Ariès, *Centuries of Childhood: a social history of family life*, London: Penguin, 1962, argued that childhood emerged as a category in Europe only in the 15th century.
5. C.L. Coe, 'Psychobiology of maternal behavior in nonhuman primates' in N.A. Krasnegor & R.D. Bridges (eds), *Mammalian Parenting: biochemical, neurological, and behavioral determinants*, New York: Oxford University Press, 1990: 157–183, p. 170.
6. c14.arch.ox.ac.uk
7. exploratornews.wordpress.com

1
UNDERSTANDING
The deep past of childhood

Is the study of childhood and children in the past an irrelevant sideline? Is it marginal to the real human story? Is prehistory itself of little relevance to modern society or to those whose interests in childhood are limited to the very recent past?

The narrower our perspective on the past, the narrower will be our understanding of the world we live in, or the future we design or seek to design. Our senses show us the world in three dimensions; our study and understanding of the past gives us the fourth dimension of time and, with archaeology, that understanding is not limited by our own memories, the often faulty oral testimony of others, or even the selectivity, redaction and elite authorship of written documents.

The danger of 'presentism' is that we assume the world we know and see is how the world must be. Studies of past societies remind us that members of our species – with the same physical and mental powers as ourselves – could and did live very different lives in different social and cultural frameworks. As the rate of change in our social world seems to increase, and even the physical environment in which we operate is said to have entered the 'Anthropocene', we need awareness of the subjectivity of our assumptions of human and societal norms. In this, understanding the broadest sweep of human history is essential – across the preliterate societies we call prehistory, as well as the historic societies which we know primarily through the written records of their literate minority.[1]

Taking this further, if we want to gain awareness of the past to help our thinking about the present and future, we are ill served by being selective. If we concentrated only on the ruling groups as in a history textbook of 100 years ago, we would be severely limited. If we looked only at the male half of society we would miss so much of the picture. When we look at the past, we need to see a total society of children and infants, adolescents, adults and the old, men and women, work and family, economic life, cultural life and more.

It is basic to say that children are half of humanity and to emphasise both the role of motherhood in the lives of women and the central part in men's personal, economic and social lives that lies in raising a family. But children are more than this. Without children, culture and knowledge die. Without the company of their elders (and peers), children cannot acquire knowledge and share in culture and be equipped to transmit these during their own older lives. A culture without children ceases to exist, as much as a shipwrecked community of males on a desert island.

Human culture is a learned suite of accumulated abilities and behavioural patterns, which complement the limits of biology and instinct. The human story is that of substantial continuity and gradual change. Continuity means that practical skills, forms of knowledge and ability to operate in a group are passed on from individual to individual, from generation to generation. During the many years of human childhood, an individual acquires the means to operate as part of a social group, within which he or she will continue to pass on the society's accumulated culture to children and grandchildren. Even when knowledge is not formally taught, most of that knowledge is learned during the childhood years.

Because so much of our lives as the most advanced species on earth depend on cultural rather than biological factors, our period of dependency, of 'childhood', is longer than that of other mammals. Many animals gain their skills of movement, safety and independent feeding well before they reach their own reproductive age. Human children appear the slowest of mammals when judged by the time they take to gain the abilities required for adult social life. They start more helpless than a whale or a rabbit or a monkey; it takes them longer to learn what they need to become an adult; then they end up able to dominate every other form of known life. The length of childhood may appear to disadvantage young infants, making them dependent on their mothers for an extended period, but the investment in a long period of childhood has its rewards.

So in understanding childhood in history, in the prehistory of our species and in the evolutionary history of Australopithecines and other early hominins, we emphasise the place of culture over the limits of biology and emphasise the value of a long childhood over a quick spurt to independent adulthood. Children are not just a part of society whom we might choose to study if the data were available; they could be described as central to social and cultural tradition because the transmission of culture is the core of humanity, distinguishing ours from other species. And it is culture which is studied and revealed by archaeology and (for prehistoric societies) only by archaeology: material culture, settlement patterns and

Museum artist's image of a European Upper Palaeolithic family
(© National Museums NI)

economic life, social structures, as well as the impact of non-material beliefs and patterns.

Within the discipline of archaeology, we need to be constantly pressing the boundaries of what we investigate, describe, interpret and think. Each generation creates new questions as well as new techniques for investigation, and recognises the limits as well as the achievements of earlier scholarship. There are many topics studied which are far less significant than the processes of giving birth, raising and weaning infants, training and integrating children into the practical skills, economic lives, beliefs and social roles of society. Examining the burials of children, the artistic representation (and output) of children, the trial works of apprenticeships and the demography of early societies contributes to the central theme of making sense of the human past and interrogating its complexities and variability.

Awareness of children and childhood can also help to avoid oversimplifications that occur in archaeological interpretation. A figurine may not be a religious cult object but a child's doll. Daubs on a wall may be a child's addition to adult artwork. Items buried with a child could reflect a formal set of ritual beliefs, or just be the tender sentimental offering of a family member or age mate. An unfamiliar assemblage of stone artefacts may just be the work of an early learner. And the puzzling but apparently deliberate association of objects in a domestic setting might just be the result of a young child playing.[2]

In this book I consider what we can say, know and interpret about children in times and places before written records, what we conventionally call human prehistory: the deep past of childhood. Much of this information comes from the work of archaeologists, but is complemented by that of other scientists. Physical anthropologists and biologists reveal what we can tell from the skeletal remains (bioarchaeology), environmental scientists put the archaeological evidence in context and professionals in other human sciences extend the debate. In periods of written records, historians and archaeologists (and often art and architectural historians) work hand in hand, and historical studies can feed back into interpretations of prehistory. In studies of recent small-scale and sometimes non-literate societies, cultural and social anthropologists and (to use an older term) ethnographers have provided pictures that can be compared, with caution, to societies of similar scale from the prehistoric past. When we consider the emergence of our species, *Homo sapiens*, and its distant relatives we rely on the work of palaeoanthropologists, and in turn this stimulates questions raised by comparison with other great apes and the contributions of different branches of the biological sciences.

WHO ARE CHILDREN, WHAT IS CHILDHOOD?

Although we are a biological entity, we are one dominated by social patterns ('culture'), and so our definition of childhood and its stages can vary, depending on whether we use biological or social criteria. As the narrative in this book suggests, there are widely different concepts of childhood and its stages in human societies across time and place, and there is no direct and consistent correlation between social category and biological age or category.[3]

The ambiguity can be a challenging one in archaeological interpretations of the prehistoric past.[4] Inevitably, citations using terms such as 'perinatal', 'infant', 'child', 'adolescent' and 'young adult' are likely to encounter these difficulties. In this book I typically use the terms 'children' and 'childhood' to include all who have not reached full biological and socially recognised adulthood.

A biologically fully mature male may still be considered a child in society for some years and subject to the rules, limitations and expectations of that role. A girl who has not yet reached menarche may have left the parental home and be married.

Reaching reproductive age makes us a biological adult: able to bear children or to father them. When does full adulthood begin? The literature on childhoods past and present has no consistent usage. Infants can be anyone from the newborn to the fully weaned, or may be applied only to those under 1 year, or under 2. An 'adolescent' is someone whose puberty has begun but is not yet considered an adult: this is therefore a mixture of social and biological categories. Biologists use indicative criteria in relation to skeletal remains from archaeological sites to determine age and group age ranges for analysis.[5] They often use the term 'juveniles', while physical anthropologists sometimes apply the ungainly term 'sub-adult' (or 'pre-adult') to a broad range of ages.

In studying the bones retrieved from archaeological contexts, bio-archaeologists applying the techniques of osteoarchaeology typically classify a population by age group. Common categories are *Infans 1*, *Infans 2* and *Juvenilis*, together with *Adultus*, *Maturus* and *Senilis*. But different researchers may use slightly different age breaks between these categories, and in the present survey it is simpler to indicate specific ages and age ranges.[6]

The age of puberty has changed significantly with changes in health, diet and environmental factors. A European girl may typically experience her first period at the age of 12 or 13 today, notably earlier than her ancestors. A study applying new osteological techniques to 1000 skeletons showed that in much of medieval England menarche occurred around the age of 15, but in London (perhaps reflecting poor health and poor diet) it was estimated to be as late as 17.[7] Although puberty now starts earlier, the average age at first pregnancy has not moved with it. Similarly, reductions in the typical age of male puberty are seen over time, falling recently by up to an estimated year every 50 years according to one study, but do not correlate with changes in male status in society.[8] Medieval males from the same English study seemed to continue their physical adolescence until around 21 years, a surprising conclusion.

Stages of growth appear different too when we consider the brain of modern humans. The all-important neural connections in the cortex increase rapidly in the foetus and briefly in early infancy until about 6 months. The cortex volume increases until the age of 10 or 11 years in boys, 8 or 9 in girls, with a slow decrease thereafter.[9] Analysis of brain development also shows a neurochemical basis for the level of risk-taking seen in adolescence, which might alternatively be considered innovative explorative behaviour.[10]

Whatever the approach of bioarchaeologists and bioanthropologists in their analysis of skeletal remains, cultural perceptions of age groups will differ widely. Children become adults when society says they do – not when biology does. Different societies have classified in very different ways the stages of childhood: infants, children and youths of the adolescent years.[11] Changes in the highly variable age of *social* adulthood of males and of females are certainly not in one direction in historical development. Adulthood is cultural, and may be indicated in archaeological evidence alongside what we know from history and the observation of recent and modern communities. Social patterns (time, place, class, belief, social practice and family situation) vary the definitions of infancy, childhood, adolescence and even the adult stages, certainly to the point before a person is expected to acquire a partner and raise a family.

Judging from current trends in my own city, my grandchildren will probably continue their education well into their 20s and not become parents themselves until well into their 30s. My English maternal grandmother (born in Lancashire in 1886) finished her schooling soon after reaching the age of 12, then the legally stipulated minimum to leave school, and was soon employed back at the same rural English elementary school as a school teacher, where she was working by the age of 15, until marriage at 21 and producing the first of five children at 22, before she died aged 37.

In every community, past and present, the key question is how society (and family) consider the stages of life. When does an infant begin to have a new status as a young child? Is an intermediate classification as adolescent/young adult recognised between childhood and adulthood? Must an adult male pass through further stages of social life before being eligible to take a partner? Is a daughter typically betrothed (even married) before puberty, or soon after, or does she remain as a dependent child for much longer? These are social and cultural, not biological, questions.

The English language terms 'toddler' and 'teenager' are relatively recent. The *Oxford English Dictionary* records the present meaning of 'toddler' only from 1876 (with an early possible use in 1837) and tracks 'teen-age' back to 1921 and 'teenager' from the 1950s, though to be 'in one's teens' is dated back to 1664. More recent still is the use of the phrase 'young adult' by publishers, bookshops and libraries to categorise books intended primarily for teenagers.

In pre-modern times, children often moved into the workforce well before they became marriageable adults, while European aristocrats might marry off their daughters at or before puberty. Most variable has been the period between being a child dependent on its parent for food, shelter, protection and learning skills, and a full adult, with an independent economic role and marriageable status. In Byzantium, legal responsibility for criminal actions began at the age of 7 years, when the strongest penalties were applicable, at least in theory. A child may become formally an adult at 10 or 12 (as in early Anglo-Saxon England),[12] at 13 (as in Jewish tradition), at 16,

Child and adult from the Mesolithic rock art of Cuevas del Engarbo, Spain

18, even at 21 (as in some very recent western contexts). In Britain, the legal age of adulthood was changed from 21 to 18 only on 1 January 1970. Before that date most university students would have been minors, the university having authority over their lives *in loco parentis.*

Culturally complex societies involve longer periods for the acquisition of the knowledge needed for participation as fully adult members of society, but they may also require their young to engage in economic activity or (for males) in war well before the age at which they are expected to marry and have children of their own. Within many hunter-gatherer societies no intermediate 'adolescent' stage is perceived between childhood and adulthood.[13] Among the Nayaka foragers of South India the concept of 'childhood' as an age stage between infancy and adulthood appears not to be recognised; adults have their own children, of course, as a family relationship, but society does not have 'children'.[14] In the Classical and post-Classical world of the Mediterranean, childhood (especially of the elites) ended much sooner for girls than for boys. Girls might be betrothed before puberty, married at or soon after puberty to older males, and already be mothers when boys of the same age were still in dependent roles and far from being considered of marriageable status. In some traditional Australian Aboriginal societies, girls could be promised at birth to older males.[15] Such a model reflects the social role of girls as future mothers: a role in which the selection of the husband and therefore the father of their children are all-important. In different societies, young men have other roles: not least, in military service and defence, as well as in their contributions to the labour economy of the family before they have established economic status enough to support a family.

While modern western democracies may think of child marriages as something from distant times or places, over 160,000 under-age marriages were reported as allowed by courts in the USA between 2000 and 2010, including some of children aged 12 or 13.[16]

The importance of these distinctions shows up in the archaeological record of prehistoric societies, as we note in the chapters of this book on the life cycle of birth, growth and death. The distinction between infancy and childhood in archaeological narratives is complex. Newborn infants may not be recognised as established members of the family until they have shown they can survive the initial threats of illness – or indeed the frequent human pattern of infanticide, discussed in later chapters. Such infants may not be buried with the formality or structure of older children: this is a matter of the specific culture of their society. Neither biological analyses of juvenile burials nor more complex discussions of children in prehistory supply consistent views on where infancy ends.[17] It is social norms, very different between societies of the past, that determine whether the family member who dies during childhood (but after infancy) is given burial rituals and associated grave goods similar to those of adults, or is buried in a different style or location.

An imaginative, but not entirely convincing, proposal by psychologist Mark Nielsen argues that childhood itself emerged relatively late in the sequence of development of our fossil hominin ancestors, well after the break from the line which led to the great apes. If human childhood is defined as characterised by pretend play (which allows for cultural innovation) alongside careful imitation of adult activities, then, he suggests, it was absent from the era of Australopithecines, and of *Homo erectus*, with their conservative stone tool industries (characterised in Africa and Europe by the tradition of Acheulean handaxes). Instead, by this definition, childhood itself emerged only with the Neanderthals and the early hominins of the Middle Palaeolithic, from about 300,000 years ago.[18] This sounds like a perception from a modern world where change and innovation appear primary forces. Anthropology reminds us of the importance of acquiring, maintaining and transmitting traditions in human society, processes central to childhood, and that innovations exist for an adaptive purpose.

In many societies of the past, higher than modern birth rates were balanced by variable and commonly high rates of juvenile mortality from disease, accident and infanticide, as well as violence between (and within) communities. The rate of improvement in levels of infant and child mortality in recent years is remarkable, as is the fall in fertility to a global average of 2.5 live births per woman in 2014.[19] This is less than half the figure seen in modern hunter-gatherer groups (see Chapter 2). In western Europe and North America, a dramatic transition in fertility can be traced for the 150 years from 1820, though it is not uniform because events like the Great War had their impact and different social factors influenced the net figures.[20] In other regions, the decline in fertility rates was marked in the second half of the 20th century.

What proportion of prehistoric human societies fell into the category of children, juveniles, sub-adults? Both historical studies and information on different recent societies suggest that a figure not much less than 50% can be considered a reasonable pattern for the human species across different kinds of society, before the changes that mark our modern, western, urbanised and industrialised world.

For recent societies of food gatherers, hunters and fishers, formal statistical details are available to show the range in the proportion of children, although variation is affected by the use of slightly different cut-off points in the definition of childhood. In one compilation, children in sub-Arctic groups ranged from 31% to 48% of the community, children in Paiute and Shoshone in the US West from 21% to 39% and children in some San groups from Southern Africa from 30% to 46%, while among tropical forest groups in different regions the proportion of children was generally larger, with most in the range from 30% to 60%.[21] Such communities were measured at quite different times in the 20th century and at different levels of external influence and 'modernisation', so these figures need to be treated with caution.

In the communities of our agricultural past we can also assume children and adolescents represented something approaching 50%, depending on whether 14 or a slightly higher age is taken as defining the end of childhood. A sample of English communities from 1574 to 1821 gave an average of 43% as children, where these were defined as unmarried resident offspring, that is, excluding those already at work away from home in farms and domestic employment, but including older unmarried adults.[22]

Today's world of increased longevity, fast urbanisation, reducing family size and sometimes delayed parenthood has seen children become a smaller proportion of the total human population, but this varies, especially with poverty and wealth. The World Bank (using 2013 and 2014 figures) estimates that 26% of the world population is now 14 and under.[23] In sub-Saharan Africa the comparable figure is 43%, but up to 48% in some countries. But there is a wide differential to remind us of the position of children in more rural communities and developing economies: only 16% of people in the European Union are aged 14 and under, and 17% in China, where the 'one-child policy' applicable to the Han majority operated from 1979 to 2015. And of course in many advanced economies while the proportion of children of 14 and under may be dropping, the proportion of adolescents (over 14) not in the workforce is large. Without the impact of modern medicine and economic change, the figures suggest that in our study of children, adolescents and childhood in prehistory, we are studying half of the human world, a half too often hidden.

THE MISSING CHILDREN

Children may have been nearly half of past human societies, but they have been much less than half of the human story as presented by archaeologists and historians – or even by social anthropologists.[24] Why is this?

This book looks at the deep past of childhood, especially as revealed by archaeology for the eras before the historical evidence of written records. Children are represented in the archaeological record, but have rarely and only sporadically been reflected in the narratives of archaeology over the century and a half of its development. This is gradually improving, and there has been awareness of the gap.[25] A leading British prehistorian, Clive Gamble, in a volume reporting a major interdisciplinary research project on the deep human past, admitted 'children are an almost invisible category in archaeology' while noting that many have considered them 'uninvestigable'.[26] A Polish archaeologist echoed this: 'Children have been notably absent from archaeological narratives'.[27] A useful survey of US archaeology articles mentioning children noted that children are 'sporadic, uneven and quite rare' in archaeological interpretations of prehistory.[28] It has further been suggested that the whole category of 'age' in the human lifespan has been largely ignored in archaeological discourse.[29] As US scholar Kathryn Kamp recently observed: 'Archaeologists remain to be completely convinced that the child is central to archaeological theory or that without examining this aspect of the human experience, explanations of past cultural dynamics are invariably flawed'.[30] Jane Eva Baxter echoed this: 'It was not long ago that archaeologists held no concern for the value of children in the past, and archaeological research was undertaken with the unquestioned assumption that children were fundamentally unimportant to archaeological interpretation'.[31] Reflecting on 25 years since she published a pioneering article on childhood in archaeology, Grete Lillehammer wrote in 2015, 'Even today, when children's issues in general are higher on the agenda, the "archaeological child" continues to be a minority issue and not placed at the heart of archaeology'.[32]

The editor of one recent volume of conference papers on children in archaeology suggests several reasons why they have played such a small part in the discipline: the supposed intangible nature of evidence for children; the perceived socioeconomic unimportance of children; a universal stereotype of childhood; gender biases; cultural biases; and lack of interdisciplinary collaboration. The present book suggests that none of this is inevitable – or justifiable.[33]

Are children so under-represented in archaeological interpretation of the past because they are under-represented in the archaeological record? Or because they have often been unrecognised in that record? And how much does this reflect a bias in interpreting the prehistoric past, with a focus on cultural achievement, not on the stages of cultural learning?[34] Few research projects into a prehistoric site, complex or era have uppermost in mind the search for evidence of the younger half of those societies.

Despite their minimal visibility in the archaeological literature, they are reintroduced to the narrative in popular presentations: in museum dioramas and painted backgrounds to displays (for which young museum visitors are a primary audience), in novels set in the prehistoric past and especially in books written for children (non-fiction and fiction, including illustrated story books) – the only place where the child can take centre stage in prehistory.[35]

Children are not as obvious as adults in the archaeological record. Where their play involves more than intangible elements, these items may not survive. Toys made by (or for) children may be constructed from impermanent materials, not designed to last the day, let alone remain to be recovered and recognised in archaeological investigation. Random assemblages and unskilled products created by the young may not be readily recognisable as such, or not located by researchers. Items associated with children may be misinterpreted. Small items might be toys but could be given many other readings.

This is not a conspiracy. In a complex discipline, subjects rise and fall in popularity; as the scale of studies grows so can the range of topics being examined. But researchers in a subject like archaeology only seek to answer those questions that are being asked, and those questions derive from the ideology of the time and place within which the research is undertaken.[36] Those questions have changed substantially as archaeology has grown as a subject area whose practitioners may consider themselves scientists or social scientists or humanities specialists.

As archaeology emerged as a discipline in 19th-century Europe and North America, certain themes took precedence.[37] One was of national origins: the distant ancestry of European societies, often linked to questions of supposed ethnic identity. But another, reflecting the era of colonial expansion and imperial visions, was a fascination with the elites of ancient civilisations. Exploration, excavation, objects in public museums and private collections: these focused especially on the world of the rich, powerful and male. Well into the second half of the 20th century, standard histories of the ancient states of Mesopotamia, Egypt and elsewhere, even Greece and Rome, would examine these societies from the top down, or only as political history of the rulers. The social, economic, demographic and cultural histories, which helped reinterpret the broad range of medieval and modern societies, would take much longer to penetrate the world of the earliest history. Some historians took the lead in eroding the top-down paradigm. But archaeologists, who unearthed the physical evidence of settlement, economy and technology, played a major part in spreading the understanding that ancient civilisations were more than their rulers.

In descriptions and discussions of prehistoric society, even with the new approaches and methodologies of deep history and archaeology, 20th-century interpretations remained heavily influenced by biases of gender. It was *man the hunter* and rarely *woman the food gatherer*. Written texts as well as visual reconstructions of prehistoric and ancient societies appeared to reflect male perspectives developed by male archaeologists and historians. The growing numbers of female academic, professional and student archaeologists began to change this, often in a programmatic and polemical way, from the 1980s and early 1990s.[38] A sequence of conferences, articles, books and even organisations set out to modify what was seen as a heavily biased gendered perspective, and to give either a feminist or gender-neutral revision to studies, or focus specifically on the archaeology of women. It can be said that these perspectives have now been fully established in the discipline. Some have suggested the shift to a feminist archaeology stimulated the emergence of an interest in the archaeology of childhood; but the strong activist growth of a feminist archaeology paid proportionately little attention to this theme. Meanwhile, some early feminist interpretations of the deep past (though generally not from professional archaeologists) took a quite different line on the prehistoric roles of women and child-rearing, developing models of a matriarchal past undermined by male dominance when prehistoric agricultural societies were transformed into urban civilisations.[39]

The initial study of the earliest human ancestors by palaeoanthropologists was no less gender biased. As anthropologist Nancy Makepeace Tanner observed, 'A major gap exists in most reconstructions of the social life of our pongid and early hominid ancestors. Female and young are omitted.... Traditional Western beliefs are read back into the past'.[40]

Thus in the growth of archaeology, study of the elites was supplemented by attention to the ordinary people, and then the focus on males moved to interest in the whole adult society of men and women. What remained missing from much archaeology was a significant interest in children. Despite the vast number of new books in archaeology, there are remarkably few by a single author describing what we know of the archaeology of childhood; a short but approachable book by Julie Wileman is a notable exception.[41] There have been pioneering articles on archaeological aspects of childhood, for example by Kathryn Kamp, John Shea, Jane Eva Baxter, Penny Spikins and others.[42] These followed a 1989 article by Grete Lillehammer which discussed what an archaeology of childhood could represent, as a theoretical contribution to the discipline.[43] A welcome increase in individual studies is referenced throughout the chapters of this book. A small number of sessions in archaeological conferences and publications of edited volumes have sought to move the theme forward, with papers including useful case studies of prehistoric or historic periods and some papers discussing the needs, issues and gaps in the overall topic.[44] But attempts at syntheses of childhood in the past as revealed by archaeology are still rare. At the time of writing (August 2017), an edited reference book on the subject is in preparation.[45] A 2016 exhibition on childhood and children in archaeology at the University of Cambridge's Museum of Archaeology and Anthropology served to stimulate interest in the topic.[46]

Because so much of our evidence for prehistoric childhood comes from burials, the role of biological anthropology (bioanthropology, bioarchaeology) is of great importance to this field, using a range of scientific techniques to examine the skeletal remains that have been uncovered in archaeologically dated contexts, both prehistoric and historic. Bioanthropologists and bioarchaeologists can advise us on the age at death of an infant or child from the skeleton – itself not straightforward, given that the developmental age of an individual may not correlate exactly with chronological age, though dentition remains the most reliable indicator of age.[47] They remind us of the uncertainty in suggesting the sex of a juvenile skeleton. As there are even subjectivities and uncertainties in sexing archaeological remains of adults, the issue with those below adult age is substantial.[48]

DNA studies may fill the void here. Their use to determine the sex of juvenile human remains is a growing field; it can tell us about an individual, thus confirming or undermining assumptions based on grave goods.[49] On a larger sample, DNA studies can provide evidence of wider demographic issues such as age and sex distribution and kinship relationships.

Bioarchaeologists' contributions to the understanding of childhood death and studies of disease and trauma from children's bones is an expanding field and such evidence is discussed later in this book, especially in Chapters 9 and 10.[50] Understanding the health of children in life and the death of children in society gives us a more intimate feeling for the topic. The contribution of investigators from the biological sciences is providing stimuli that seem especially likely to drive forward interest in and interpretation of prehistoric childhoods.[51] But we can also compare and contrast using information from disciplines other than archaeology and bioanthropology.

THE USE OF ANALOGY

The study of childhood is a vigorous industry involving social scientists, behavioural scientists and medical scientists, with their own journals, conferences and numerous specialists. These studies are necessarily focused on the contemporary world. Our understanding of childhood in prehistory gains more from the cautious use of history, social anthropology and primate biology.

We need to be aware of our ethnocentric and modern biases in approaching the concept of children and childhood. Our moral precepts against infanticide, for example, are culturally bound. The practices and protective role of parents towards their children may have reached extremes in some modern western communities; the *Oxford English Dictionary* traces the phrase 'helicopter parent' back to 1989. Different styles of childcare need not imply different levels of emotional and practical commitment to a child.[52]

Historians have contributed a substantial literature of analysis and description of childhood in different eras where written texts, as well as artistic representations and material culture, have given us images of the younger half of society. There are now many studies and accounts of the changing patterns of childhood in medieval and modern European history. The study of childhood in the ancient Classical civilisations of Europe and the Mediterranean is becoming a very active field, involving archaeologists, although a heavy reliance on literary texts and the iconography of tombs and art makes much of this lean towards a discussion of the literate elites of society.[53]

We can use these studies to help us ask questions about the preliterate, prehistoric past as recorded by archaeology. But we need to avoid too confident an assumption that a phenomenon of the deep past was similar to (or on its way to becoming) a phenomenon of the better-known and more recent past. While there are commonalities shared across the human species and the human mind, history is not a one-way story of progress or change directed towards some future, more complex and supposedly improved world. It is safer *not* to be too influenced by what we know of childhood in historic urban civilisations, cities dominated by religious and political elites and occupied by citizens with specialist economic roles, when we seek to interpret evidence from prehistory. Civilisation is an anomaly in the human record: five millennia in a few parts of the Old World (less in the New World) within our own species' timescale of 200,000 or even 300,000 years, and the timescale of hominins making stone tools stretches 10 times longer. From our knowledge of history we may hold assumptions about infant care, childhood and adolescence, toys and play, clothing, learning, social roles, even children's roles in war and conflict, and transitions into adulthood. We should apply these to prehistory only with the greatest of care.

We can, though, generate useful questions to help us understand the prehistoric past by using, with appropriate care and reservations, what we know of small-scale and non-literate societies as observed and recorded in recent and modern times. Ideas can be raised and interpretations considered for prehistory which are inspired by studies and accounts when people from urban literate (and, often, colonising) societies encountered small-scale (sometimes described as 'indigenous') communities of farmers, herders, fishers or hunter-gatherer foragers. The work of social anthropologists and the 'ethnographic record' of recent communities can stimulate and assist us in understanding ancient groups with some apparent similarities in economy and environment. While this can be helpful in stimulating questions, it requires care in interpretation.

Many small-scale farming communities are and were, of course, part of a much wider economy dominated by town dwellers with whom they traded their surplus crops and livestock in exchange for specialised products. The more isolated a community and the more subsistence its traditional economy, then the more useful it may seem for comparison with sites of prehistoric communities of similar status.

An exceptional study of children from the perspective of a social/cultural anthropologist is *The Anthropology of Childhood* by David F. Lancy. This broad-ranging, thoughtful, informative and witty (if sometimes disturbing) survey considers traditional small-scale societies and historically documented communities alongside modern patterns of developed industrialised and post-industrial nations, and provides a sometimes dramatic reminder of the distance between our 'modern' perceptions and the very different social norms across the wider expanse of time and place. The range of experiences of children and childhood includes the sense of children as commodities, and the role of often quite young children as economic contributors, whether as participants in a foraging or peasant agricultural economy, or (more troubling to us) as wage labourers.[54]

Descriptive accounts of small-scale agricultural societies, whether from professional anthropologists or early accounts by travellers and colonial administrators, still deal mainly with societies in a relationship with the wider world. This relationship may have affected not only their food crops and economic patterns but also social norms, even religion and ideology.[55] But the range of experiences and dimensions of childhood we see in small-scale agricultural groups – even if their traditions were in process of change – can help us consider some aspects of prehistoric farmers, including childhood in those societies.

Agriculture itself (incorporating both animals and crops) – what was long described as a Neolithic revolution – has existed only over the last 10 millennia or so, a stretch of time over which agricultural societies have seen substantial development in economic and social change. The diversity emphasised by David Lancy and other anthropologists reminds us of the diversity that we might expect in the prehistoric record. But for the longest stretch of prehistory, when human society had only a foraging economy, information on living foragers (hunter-gatherers) can provide us with food for thought.

RECENT HUNTER-GATHERERS

Studies of recent hunter-gatherer societies can be used with caution to inform different areas of archaeological interpretation of the prehistoric past.[56] They can show the range of activities that involve children in non-agricultural communities: motherhood, infant weaning and transport, acquisition of skills, play and social interaction, and the transition stages to adulthood. We can also consider how physical evidence of these activities may show up in (or be missing from) the archaeological record of prehistory. They may also remind us of the importance of the non-material – the ritual and spiritual – that run through the lives of hunter-gatherer peoples and which are rarely visible from prehistoric sites.

The economic lives of past and recent forager societies vary substantially. Traditional groups in this category may have derived widely differing proportions of their diet from hunting, from fishing and from gathering plants, honey and small animals, including insects and shellfish. The commonly used term 'hunter-gatherers' appears to privilege a hunted meat (and by implication male) contribution to a diet, which was in fact often the minority of food.[57] Since there is major diversity between traditional non-agricultural groups encountered in the modern world, great care is needed in how we use analogies between prehistoric hunter-gatherers and those more recent societies in 'the ethnographic record'.

Such communities are not an anomalous remnant of some prehistoric peoples; they are a significant part of the world of modernity. 'As recently as AD 1500 hunters occupied fully one third of the globe, including all of Australia and most of North America, as well as large tracts of South America, Africa, and Northeast Asia.'[58] People have maintained a forager lifestyle well into recent times. I recently met a British woman whose late husband was born into a 'traditional' Aboriginal hunter-gatherer group in Australia's Great Sandy Desert; he had first encountered the modern world of European-dominated rural Australia only in his early teens, during the 1950s.[59]

Analogies between children in forager prehistory and in the ethnography of recent societies is limited by the relative lack of attention to them in studies of modern hunter-gatherers.[60] An exception was a 2002 interdisciplinary conference on forager childhoods with a valuable

Kalahari San woman with her child in a sling

subsequent publication, taking the subject as the period between weaning and becoming eligible to become a parent.⁶¹ The editors, Barry Hewlett and Michael Lamb, observed:

> Children represent more than 40 percent of most hunter-gatherer populations but anthropologists working with these groups seldom describe their daily life, knowledge, and views, thereby ensuring, in essence, that about half the population is omitted from most hunter-gatherer ethnographies.⁶²

And in a recent major reference survey of the field it is noted:

A compelling, comprehensive treatment of hunter-gatherer child-rearing and childhood has yet to be written. Yet, the formative experiences of children are crucial in constructing the gender roles informing adult behaviour in later years. More systematic attention to the corpus of play activities, lore and games, miniatures and toys, and adult supervision and mentoring of girls and boys in the early phases of work will reveal cultural expectations about gender in adulthood.[63]

One background factor that initially held back accounts of forager children may be the 19th-century prejudice (including from pioneers in anthropology) that 'primitive hunter-gatherers' were themselves analogous to children, so it would be almost tautologous to study their own young.[64] This reflected the colonial view that human society (and often human biological races) represented a hierarchy, from the untamed savage to the 'higher and greater' civilised educated Christian of metropolitan Europe or North America. Such a view fitted well the era of European empires, when the civilising mission was to help bring trade, administration, law and Christian religion to the heathen of occupied lands, with none so in need as the wild hunter reliant on natural resources to survive.

Englishman Edward Tylor, often named as a founder of social/cultural anthropology, wrote in his 1871 book *Primitive Culture* of the 'savage as a representative of the childhood of the human race … savage races, as the nearest modern representatives of primæval culture', before evolution through time from the primitive to the 'higher and greater grades of civilization'.[65] In an earlier work he had commented:

> The trite comparison of savages to 'grown-up children' is in the main a sound one, though not to be carried out too strictly. In the uncivilized [Native] American or Polynesian, the strength of body and force of character of a grown man are combined with a mental development not beyond that of a young child of a civilized race.[66]

Tylor's contemporary Sir John Lubbock focused his interests on the human past rather than the contemporary 'primitive'. He titled his 1865 book *Pre-historic Times, as illustrated by ancient remains, and the manners and customs of modern savages.*[67]

> Savages may be likened to children; and the comparison is not only correct, but also highly instructive. Many naturalists consider that the early condition of the individual indicates that of the race,—that the best test of the affinities of a species are the stages through which it passes. So also it is in the case of man: the life of each individual is an epitome of the history of the race, and the gradual development of the child illustrates that of the species. Hence the importance of the similarity between savages and children. Savages, like children, have no steadiness of purpose.[68]

This is an interesting contrast to countercultural ideas of recent decades that hunter-gatherers from 'traditional' societies and cultures have special spiritual insights and enviable social and personal strengths denied to western society ('the noble savage in New Age garb'): or at the very least represent a human harmony with nature lost to the rest of humankind.[69]

We rely on what narrative descriptions and discussions exist, despite the often limited information about children and childhood. The accounts we have for modern small-scale societies may have come from professionally trained social/cultural anthropologists, or ethnographers (to use an older term), or from other social, behavioural and medical scientists, or from colonial officials or missionaries or from travellers' descriptions. But by definition, such accounts by outsiders reflect a period when there was *already* contact between the indigenous and the outsider. These contacts may have changed lifeways, beliefs, economy and material culture. They may have been preceded by significant, even critical, shifts. For example, Aboriginal Australian nomadic groups, once commonly described as modern examples of Stone Age hunter-gatherers, have been most often studied in the arid marginal areas in which their separate identity and communities had survived following European expansion, rather than in the rich well-watered coastal environments which had supported denser populations.[70] Even the early 'classic' studies were possible only when indigenous groups were in contact with outsiders; as Australian anthropologist Les Hiatt observed, 'anthropologists have regularly worked on the frontiers, never beyond them'.[71]

There is a further problem with using recent communities of hunter-gatherers as an analogy for our pre-agricultural past. Most such groups – the majority of pre-modern Australian Aborigines are an exception – long lived in regular contact with settled agriculturalists, trading with them, sometimes playing other client roles (the San of Southern Africa or the Pygmies of the equatorial forests, for example), so were far different from the isolated economies of early human hunter-gatherers.[72] And some groups have shifted their economy from a partial reliance on farming to a greater reliance on hunting and foraging.

Nevertheless, with these cautions, this book presents some of the knowledge of the lives of children in such modern societies, as a tool in considering what the archaeological record of our modern human species in previous millennia might mean. Recent hunter-gatherers have tended to be mobile communities associated with a territory which provides them with shelter and food, often in a nomadic migratory cycle. Such a group may comprise as few as 15 people but typically number around 25 or 30, though the range may go as high as 70.[73] Since such groups are commonly linked by kinship, marriage may be favoured and often required outside of that band, and a mobile band will interact or even cohabit seasonally with other bands. It has been suggested that an inter-breeding group up to 200, and a larger classificatory unit of up to 500, gives a pattern that can be seen in different regions.[74]

Groups who are or were traditionally foragers in the modern world are widely spread, and the population identified as members of such groups may range from a few hundred people to many hundreds of thousands, with estimates differing according to the criteria used.[75]

Aboriginal peoples of Australia have been a major subject of anthropology for over a century, though, as noted above, with the expansion of European settlement in the early to mid-19th century much of this professional study and description was centred on communities living in remote areas. An intensive study of child rearing among Aboriginal people of Arnhem Land in the late 1960s showed substantial differences from European patterns, yet this study necessarily took place in a township of 1000 residents, Maningrida, created by the Australian government a decade before.[76]

Some of most widely cited studies of hunting and food-gathering communities are those of San ('Bushmen') such as the !Kung, who with the Khoe people (traditionally herders) number up to 100,000 within eight countries in Southern Africa.[77] There are also about 125,000 people in the different forager 'Pygmy' groups around the Congo basin, many of whom have long lived in patron–client relations with settled farmers. The Hadza people of Tanzania are a small forager group who have been the subject of study.

Numerous indigenous communities in Southeast and South Asia were considered to have been traditional foraging societies, even though some may have shifted between different economic roles. In Japan the indigenous Ainu, descendants of a hunter-gatherer group, are primarily on the northern island Hokkaido, with around 60,000 people of Ainu identity said to be in the traditional areas of their occupation.

The northern-most regions of both Europe and North America hold communities for which fishing and hunting were traditionally dominant modes: Inuit, Sami and different Siberian groups, as well as Siberian communities further south. And while isolated northern Eurasian groups may be classified as foragers, some also herd domesticated reindeer.

In North America the ethnographic studies of the Native Americans of California and the smaller numbers in the Great Plains (Paiute, Shoshone, Ute and others) have a classic status. The peoples of the Pacific north-west, though not agriculturalists, were not nomadic but settled in permanent communities. By contrast, many Plains peoples were farmers who turned to a hunting economy after the introduction of the horse to North America by the Spanish.

South American hunters and gatherers range from the communities of the upper Amazon basin, still subjects of study today, to the former forager groups whom Europeans encountered in Tierra del Fuego at the southern tip of the continent. Between these are other hunter-gatherer communities spread primarily through the eastern lowlands, including tropical groups who shifted from farming to a foraging life, and may still supplement foraging with seasonally planted gardens.

Thus the sample of peoples who have exercised non-agricultural lifestyles in recent times is substantial, and provides some basis for a cautious reference when we consider hunter-gatherer communities of the past. Note that discussions of modern people are often in the tense of an 'ethnographic present', as if these were unchanging societies, which is far from the case. As noted in the Preface, references to modern groups in this volume may refer to recent times, or to a study period very many decades back.

HIGHER PRIMATE RELATIVES

The deepest prehistory is that which precedes our identity as a species. We can consider human infants and the young, the stages to adulthood, by examining their skeletal remains, material culture and environment. But we can also raise questions relevant to earlier prehistory and consider parallels and differences by observing the other great apes of the modern world, and how the young in those groups live, learn and move to adulthood.[78] The big difference between humans and other great apes is, of course, the role of culture and the dominance of culturally learned patterns over those attributable to 'nature'. Chimpanzees may learn new ways to acquire foodstuffs and their offspring may observe and imitate these, but the social, economic and mental lives of humans – and we assume our recent hominin ancestors – see learned and socially imposed structures balancing instinct in a unique way.

We humans share with chimpanzees some 98–99% of our DNA and we share a similar percentage with bonobos (pygmy chimpanzees). The date when the ancestry of humans and chimpanzees diverged was long considered to be over 4 million years ago, though specialist opinions vary and recent fossil finds could push the date earlier than 6 million years.[79] We have to go back around 14 million years to find the common ancestor we share with the other living great apes – the gorillas of Africa and the orangutans of Southeast Asia – and even longer since the line split off which led to the gibbons, known today only in Southeast Asia. But in examining the evolution of human society, looking at great ape life has interest and value. It should be noted, however, that it appears likely that some of the specialised behaviour of chimpanzees and bonobos – including their adeptness in tree climbing – has developed since the split from their common ancestor with humans.[80]

Several of chapters in this volume consider aspects of infancy and the young among these biological relatives. In Southeast Asia, orangutans (as well as gibbons, the closest relatives to the great apes) have been carefully observed and their life cycles analysed. Orangutans today live only on the islands of Borneo and Sumatra, and these populations are considered to be two separate species.

Gorillas have been studied in detail in their natural African habitats. There are separate western and eastern species; the eastern species – living in Rwanda, Uganda and the Democratic Republic of Congo – has been intensively recorded at Karisoke in Rwanda, where Dian Fossey in the 1960s initiated a programme of research on mountain gorillas which has been continued by many others since.[81]

Chimpanzees have been widely recorded in their African habitats of Equatorial Africa (Gabon, Democratic Republic of Congo, Cameroon as well as westernmost Tanzania) and in parts of coastal West Africa. The lengthy field studies led by Jane Goodall in the Gombe area of Tanzania are complemented by the extended researches of Japanese scientists such as those at Mahale, also in Tanzania, and in Bossou in Guinea. Important, though of less relevance here, are the many studies of chimpanzees in captivity, including those who have been raised from infancy with human families for purposes of experiment with their potential abilities.[82] Bonobos, whose habitat is now restricted to tropical forests of the Democratic Republic of Congo, have been subject to far less research.

Scientists have closely observed primate infancy and have compared patterns of early child rearing in modern human societies with that of different primate species in the wild. Where there are similarities, we can confidently attribute these also to our early hominin ancestors; where there are differences, we must consider whether the earliest ancestral hominins may have had social, biological or environmental characteristics more like our species, or comparable to aspects of the great apes, or neither. Reconstructions of Australopithecine family life, in movies, museum dioramas and painted scenes, or text descriptions, frequently reflect influences from observations of chimpanzee or other great ape groups.

In considering the nature of childhood in human prehistory, the young of our great ape relatives may help to raise questions, if not parallels, and show us a range of behaviour which can help us think about our earliest hominin ancestors.

THE FRAMEWORK OF HOMININ PREHISTORY

For early prehistory, most of our knowledge of childhood is from the physical remains of those who did not survive into adulthood, complemented by reconstruction of the environment in which they lived. The further back we go in time, the less information we can present about social life, including

Neanderthal family scene: reconstruction at Krapina Neanderthal Museum, Croatia

children, except by cautious comparison with later species and with our closest primate relatives.

Our knowledge of the earliest hominins comes from their fossilised skeletal remains, the majority of which are of adults, but an important minority of fossil hominin remains are of juveniles. There is bias in the preserved record: bones from an infant are small and brittle, and we are far less likely to find them than the preserved and fossilised bones of an adult or older juvenile.

The term 'hominins' rather than the broader 'hominids' is now commonly used for primate genera, including Australopithecines and *Homo*, after the split from the line which led to chimpanzees. In fact, the majority of hominin finds are classified as different Australopithecine or *Homo* species. Here the term 'Australopithecines' is used to include species described as *Australopithecus*, *Paranthropus* and *Ardipithecus ramidus*, dating from 4 million years ago until possibly as late as 1.4 million years ago, all in Africa. The growing sample of fossil materials is subject to diverse classifications by different scientists, who may tend to be 'splitters' (seeing differences as representing a range of different species) or 'lumpers' (who argue for fewer species with greater variation within a species). The different classificatory systems may also reflect national or personal prejudices.[83]

When we consider the material culture of prehistory, we begin by relying on stone tools and the waste products from their manufacture, which are known from finds in Africa dated around 2.6 million years ago (with a recent find in Lomekwi, in Kenya, dated to perhaps 3.3 million years ago).[84] With the early pebble tool technology (sometimes called Oldowan, or Mode 1) it is somewhat more difficult than with later technologies to distinguish the product of young apprentices from the artefacts produced by experienced adults. We see our first glimpse of our early ancestors themselves in footprints, some of which may include those of children in a family group.

Homo habilis, associated with a pebble tool technology, lived in Africa from around 2.3 to 1.4 million years ago. The subsequent evolution and then the expansion out of Africa into Asia of our ancestral species, *Homo erectus*, and its relatives present a long period of continuity, with dates from about 1.8 million years, and possibly surviving up to as late as 143,000 years ago in parts of Asia.[85] They were the creators of the stone tool culture dominated by the familiar 'handaxe' of the Lower Palaeolithic (Acheulean, also called Mode 2) found throughout Africa, Europe and the Middle East but we can reconstruct relatively little of their society. Within East Asia, a different technology is found, rather than handaxes, and there appears to be continuity across the periods elsewhere called Lower Palaeolithic and Middle Palaeolithic, with gradual evolution of material culture.[86]

Homo erectus developed into new archaic human species called *Homo antecessor* (from around 850,000 years) and *Homo heidelbergensis*, seen until about 250,000 years ago, and they maintained the handaxe tool tradition in Europe. Fossilised skeletal remains are still our main source of information on the children of the period, though footprints from the English coast represent a family of *Homo antecessor*.

From this group developed the Neanderthals (*Homo neanderthalensis*) of the Middle East and Europe (from around 250,000 to maybe 40,000 years ago), whose tool technology marked another step forward (the 'Middle Palaeolithic' of archaeological terminology, sometimes called Mode 3). With the emergence of Neanderthals, our record becomes a little fuller. Many burials of children, even of the very young, have been found from the Neanderthal world, and it seems that some of these were associated with simple grave goods, such as animal bones. We start to see examples where the care of the youngest members of society was marked by the deliberate disposal of their bodies.[87]

We know much more about the early members of our own species, *Homo sapiens*. Anatomically modern humans may have originated in Africa by around 300,000 years ago, and were subsequently responsible for the more sophisticated and specialised artefact technologies classified as Middle Stone Age.[88] The expansion from the African continent by around 60,000 years ago (and from a recent Australian date, perhaps earlier) brought anatomically modern humans by water and land crossings to colonise the Middle East, Asia, Australia then Europe (and eventually, of course, the Americas and the Pacific).[89] The spread through mainland Asia had its impact on settlement patterns and technology, though the survival of other

Homo species has been shown in the Indonesian island of Flores and in probably also in south-west China.

Newer technologies again, with sophisticated specialised toolkits, went alongside complex social organisation and language as well as what we may distinguish among modern human behaviours: symbolic and belief systems. Scattered evidence has contributed to fierce debates on just when forms of modern human behaviour emerged: the use of personal decoration and of non-functional markings on artefacts, the development of sophisticated language which allowed forward planning in human groups, and, later, art and non-subsistence items such as musical instruments. Some emphasise the adaptation to maritime and freshwater foods, especially shellfish, as a major economic transition, one which may also have stimulated the development of the brain by the contribution of omega-3 fatty acid.[90] An alternative view sees population pressures as the major driver for social progress.[91]

African cultural development transformed into further new technologies and social patterns of the Later Stone Age: a term which continues to be applied to the very latest pre-modern hunter-gatherer communities. Occupied rock shelters in Africa provide a chronological sequence showing changes in material culture and economy (although many coastal sites of today were a distance from the sea during some parts of the Pleistocene).

Anatomically modern humans came to replace the Neanderthals in Europe from about 45,000–40,000 years ago; these were the users of the advanced blade stone tool technology of the Upper Palaeolithic (in some terminologies, Mode 4). This era has provided us with a rich source of archaeological evidence for their lifeways, including those of children. Burials of children with sometimes lavish clothing and grave goods, footprints of children in caves, finger daubs and handprints of children in rock art, all give us images of the early children of our own species, while small sculptures include women apparently at different stages of pregnancy.

Major excavations in Europe and Asia have revealed details of sites of occupation and other areas of activity to give us more of a human 'feel' of the Upper Palaeolithic, such as a complex campsite with hearths and shelters, human burials, engravings and personal ornaments. The archaeological record of children is variable in the subsequent cultural and social developments typically described as Mesolithic in Europe, Epipalaeolithic in the Middle East and North Africa, or Later Stone Age in sub-Saharan Africa.

In the post-glacial climate of the Holocene, which followed the end of the Pleistocene around 11,700 years ago, we see human settlement in all continents except Antarctica. Within the latter part of the Pleistocene, it was possible for humans to cross the Bering Strait to begin populating the Americas at a date long thought to be around 15,000 years ago, but with emerging evidence for a somewhat earlier date, and a dramatic and controversial claim for a human presence as far back as 130,000 years ago.[92] Excluding that latter date, humans appear to have spread rapidly across the Americas. Development of agriculture and the cultures of agricultural societies were more localised, as was the appearance of state-based urban civilisations.

The emergence of agriculture early in the Holocene marks very different societies, in which the economic roles of children had also begun to change. We know that there was not one single invention of agriculture, spreading out from a single region, but diverse and gradual local adaptations in different Old World and New World localities, as well as the spread of domesticated plants and animals from their original regions. Nevertheless, the emergence of agriculture remains one of the most significant changes in human history: the importance of the 'Neolithic revolution' has not diminished with our growing knowledge of the transition.[93]

There was significant diversity in early farming communities, reflected in settlement patterns, social patterns, burial patterns and of course the different patterns of childhood. Acquisition of further new technologies was accompanied by further political, social and economic changes and variability, in periods with archaeological labels such as (for Europe and the Middle East) 'Chalcolithic period' or 'Copper Age', 'Bronze Age' and 'Iron Age'.

As subsequent chapters of this book indicate, the kinds of evidence we can retrieve from these agricultural and metal-working societies may be fuller than for hunter-gatherer groups, but the vast majority of prehistoric human time is that of hunter-gatherers.

THE DEEP PAST

This chapter has argued the importance of studies of the young in the human (and hominin) past, with optimism about the scope available for research and interpretation. While there are limitations in the data, there have also been limitations created by past assumptions: that investigating children in prehistory was irrelevant, or too difficult. Subsequent chapters of this book look at the kinds of information which can start to illuminate prehistoric childhoods. New approaches, new questions are reinforced by the kind of questions that arise when we look at childhood in history, or at the lives of recent small-scale societies or even (for the earliest hominins) at our higher primate relatives. What we now know may be modest; what we could know with new research and thought could be much less modest. We can begin this survey by considering the stages of growth, from pregnancy and infancy onwards.

NOTES

1 Where history has relied on a small number of written sources, archaeology can reveal a fuller and quite contrary picture. For the early medieval centuries of post-Roman Britain 'the discoveries of archaeologists in the past thirty years are profoundly transformative, not least because they are so often at odds with our texts': R. Fleming, *Britain After Rome: the fall and rise 400–1070*, London: Penguin, 2010, p. xi.
2 G. Hammond & N. Hammond, 'Child's play: a distorting factor in archaeological distributions', *American Antiquity* 46 (1981): 634–636.
3 Lillehammer notes the unproductive division in which 'children' means biology and 'childhood' means the social: G. Lillehammer, '25 years with the "child" and the archaeology of childhood' in *TCIN*: 78–86, p. 82.
4 R. Gowland, 'Ageing the past: examining age identity from funerary evidence' in R. Gowland & C. Knusel (eds), *The Social Archaeology of Funerary Remains*, Oxford: Oxbow, 2009: 143–154, pp. 143–144.
5 M. Lewis, 'The osteology of infancy and childhood: misconceptions and potential' in *RLA*: 1–13.
6 F. Fahlander 'Subadult or subaltern? Children as serial categories' in *RLA*: 14–23, Table 1.
7 M. Lewis, F. Shapland & R. Watts, 'On the threshold of adulthood: a new approach for the use of maturation indicators to assess puberty in adolescents from medieval England', *American Journal of Human Biology* 28 (2016): 48–56.
8 J.R. Goldstein, 'A secular trend toward earlier male sexual maturity: evidence from shifting ages of male young adult mortality', *PLoS ONE* 6 (2011): e14826.
9 S. Greenfield, *A Day in the Life of the Brain*, London: Penguin, 2016, p. 64, citing N. Gogtay et al., 'Dynamic mapping of human cortical development during childhood through early adulthood', *Proceedings of the National Academy of Sciences* 101 (2004): 8174–8179.
10 Greenfield, *A Day in the Life*, pp. 135–138.
11 Biological, rather than cultural definitions of the stages of childhood are discussed in Lewis, *Bioarchaeology*, pp. 4–8.
12 The age of criminal responsibility seems to have varied between 10 and 12: H. Cunningham, *The Invention of Childhood*, London: BBC Books, 2006, p. 24.
13 *HGC*, pp. 8–9.
14 N. Bird-David, 'Studying children in "hunter-gatherer" societies' in *HGC*: 92–101.
15 A. Hamilton, *Nature and Nurture: aboriginal child-rearing in North-Central Arnhem Land*, Canberra: Australian Institute of Aboriginal Studies, 1981, p. 6.
16 www.unchainedatlast.org/child-marriage-shocking-statistics
17 M. Lally & T. Ardren, 'Little artefacts: rethinking the constitution of the archaeological infant', *CitP* 1 (2009): 62–77.
18 M. Nielsen, 'Imitation, pretend play, and childhood: essential elements in the evolution of human culture?', *Journal of Comparative Psychology* 126 (2012): 170–181.
19 A graphical presentation of the impact of fertility and other factors on population is at www.gapminder.org/videos/dont-panic-end-poverty
20 T.W. Guinnane, 'The historical fertility transition: a guide for economists', *Journal of Economic Literature* 49 (2011): 589–614.

21 R.L. Kelly, *The Foraging Spectrum: diversity in hunter-gatherer lifeways*, Washington, DC: Smithsonian Institution Press, 1995, pp. 206–208, Table 6.1. I have translated Kelly's child/adult ratios to proportions. Analyses of Hadza people in eastern Tanzania gave a figure of 40.3% under 15 in 1967, shifting to 39.1% in 1985: N.G.B. Jones et al., 'Demography of the Hadza, an increasing and high density population of savanna foragers', *American Journal of Physical Anthropology* 89 (1992): 159–181. Yengoyan's hypothetical Aboriginal 'tribe' of 100 people with 62% aged 14 or under does not seem to be based on empirical statistical evidence: A. Yengoyan, 'Demographic and ecological influences on Aboriginal Australian marriage sections' in R.B. Lee & I. DeVore (eds), *Man the Hunter*, Chicago: Aldine, 1968: 185–199, p. 195.

22 P. Laslett, 'Size and structure of the household in England over three centuries', *Population Studies* 23 (1969): 199–223, p. 217.

23 data.worldbank.org/indicator/SP.POP.0014.TO.ZS

24 Baxter, *Archaeology*, p. 7.

25 K.A. Kamp, 'Where have all the children gone? The archaeology of childhood', *Journal of Archaeological Method and Theory* 8 (2001): 1–34.

26 F. Coward & C. Gamble, 'Big brains, small worlds: material culture and the evolution of the mind' in R. Dunbar, C. Gamble & J.A.J. Gowlett (eds), *Lucy to Language: the benchmark papers*, Oxford: Oxford University Press, 2014: 461–480, pp. 465–467.

27 M. Pawleta, 'An archaeology of childhood – a new subfield of study' in *CCLA*: 9–28, p. 9.

28 B.E. Roveland, 'Archaeological approaches to the study of prehistoric children: past trends and future directions' in H.B. Schwartzman (ed.), *Children and Anthropology: perspectives for the 21st century*, Westport, CT: Bergin & Garvey, 2001: 39–56, p. 39.

29 S. Lucy, 'The archaeology of age' in M. Díaz-Andreu, S. Lucy, S. Babić & D.N. Edwards, *The Archaeology of Identity: approaches to gender, age, status, ethnicity and religion*, Abingdon: Routledge, 2005: 43–66.

30 K.A. Kamp, 'Children and their childhoods: retrospectives and prospectives' in *TCIN*: 161–169, p. 161.

31 J.E. Baxter, 'The devil's advocate or our worst case scenario: the archaeology of childhood without any children' in *AOC*: 19–36.

32 Lillehammer, '25 years with the "child"', p. 82.

33 A useful survey of the topic is G. Cosçunsu, 'Introduction: children as archaeological enigma' in *AOC*: 1–16.

34 Pawleta, 'An archaeology of childhood', p. 15, suggests that the discipline's lack of interest in 'the human being' rather than in socio-cultural processes may be a background cause.

35 K.A. Kamp & J.C. Whittaker, 'Prehistoric Puebloan children in archaeology and art' in *CPPS*: 14–40; B.E. Roveland, 'Child the creator: children as agents of change in juvenile prehistoric literature', *Visual Anthropology Review* 9 (1993): 147–153.

36 The post-processual critique of archaeology and its subjectivities was especially inspired by the work and students of Ian Hodder from the 1980s. An early manifesto was in a book in the series 'New Directions in Archaeology': D. Miller & C. Tilley (eds), *Ideology, Power and Prehistory*, Cambridge: Cambridge University Press, 1984; this was followed by M. Shanks & C. Tilley, *Re-constructing Archaeology*, Cambridge: Cambridge University Press, 1987.

37 Archaeology as ideas rather than discoveries is well surveyed in B. Trigger, *A History of Archaeological Thought*, 2nd edition, Cambridge: Cambridge University Press, 2006.
38 For example, M.W. Conkey & J.D. Spector, 'Archaeology and the study of gender' in M. Schiffer (ed.), *Advances in Archaeological Method and Theory, Vol. 7*, New York: Academic Press, 1984: 1–38; J.M. Gero & M.W. Conkey (eds), *Engendering Archaeology: women and prehistory*, Oxford: Blackwell, 1991 (a collection derived from a 1988 US conference).
39 Thoughtfully critiqued by C. Eller, *The Myth of Matriarchal Prehistory: why an invented past won't give women a future*, Boston, MA: Beacon Press, 2000. These myths have still not vanished: see for instance J. Foster & M. Derlet, *Invisible Women of Prehistory: three million years of peace, six thousand years of war*, Adelaide: Spinifex Press, 2013.
40 N.M. Tanner, *On Becoming Human*, Cambridge: Cambridge University Press, 1981, p. 1.
41 Wileman, *Hide and Seek*, gives brief but good thematic coverage of historic and some prehistoric archaeology. Another rather general discussion of what an archaeology of infancy should consider (with some brief discussion of individual sites) is E. Scott, *The Archaeology of Infancy and Infant Death*, British Archaeological Reports International Series 819, Oxford: Archaeopress, 1999. Baxter, *Archaeology*, includes a useful literature review and theoretical survey of what such an archaeology could look like, drawing on anthropology and other disciplines.
42 Notable articles include K. Kamp, 'Where have all the children gone? The archaeology of childhood', *Journal of Archaeological Method and Theory* 8 (2001): 1–34 (a useful, broad-ranging survey); J.J. Shea, 'Child's play: reflections on the invisibility of children in the Paleolithic record', *Evolutionary Anthropology* 15 (2006): 212–216; J.E. Baxter, 'The archaeology of childhood', *Annual Review of Anthropology* 37 (2008): 159–175; P. Spikins et al., 'The cradle of thought: growth, learning, play and attachment in Neanderthal children', *Oxford Journal of Archaeology* 33 (2014): 111–134. In 1981 Norman Hammond published an article on the effect play can have in mixing up archaeological deposits: G. Hammond & N. Hammond, 'Child's play: a distorting factor in archaeological distributions', *American Antiquity* 46 (1981): 634–636.
43 G. Lillehammer, 'A child is born: the child's world in an archaeological perspective', *Norwegian Archaeological Review* 22 (1989): 89–105, was a pioneering outline of possibilities, whose 25th anniversary was marked by a US conference and subsequently published papers – *TCIN*; see in this Lillehammer, '25 years with the "child"'.
44 For edited collections focusing on archaeology, see the list under 'Key references, with abbreviations' (pp. xv–xvi). Most of the collections noted there include theoretical discussions and studies of historic as well as prehistoric sites, but inevitably papers in these volumes are of variable importance.
45 S. Crawford, D Hadley & G. Shepherd (eds), *The Oxford Handbook of the Archaeology of Childhood*, Oxford: Oxford University Press, forthcoming 2018.
46 J. Joy et al., *Hide and Seek: looking for children in the past*, Cambridge: Museum of Archaeology and Anthropology, 2016, is a catalogue of the exhibition.
47 M.A. Perry, 'Redefining childhood through bioarchaeology: toward an archaeological and biological understanding of children in antiquity' *CIA*: 89–111, p. 90.

This article provides a good survey of issues in the study and interpretation of children's remains in archaeological contexts.

48 Gowland, 'Ageing the past', p. 147.
49 K.A. Brown, 'Placing children in society: using ancient DNA to identify sex and kinship of child skeletal remains, and implications for gender and social organisation' in *AOC*: 129–148.
50 S.E. Halcrow & N. Tayles, 'The bioarchaeological investigation of children and childhood' in S.C. Agarwal & B.A. Glencross (eds), *Social Bioarchaeology*, Malden: Wiley-Blackwell, 2011: 333–360, reviews practical and theoretical issues in bioarchaeological studies, especially of child skeletal material and pathology. Lewis, *Bioarchaeology*, includes a review of the development of this sub-field.
51 A review of the contribution and recent development of the field is S. Mays et al., 'Child bioarchaeology: perspectives on the last 10 years', *CitP* 10 (2017): 38–56.
52 Lancy, *Anthropology* 2ed, pp. 396–410. A 2006 documentary film directed by Thomas Balmès, *Bébés* (also *Babies*), presenting the first year of life of four babies in Namibia, Mongolia, Japan and the USA, is informative here.
53 Major studies include J.E. Grubbs, T. Parkin & R. Bell (eds), *The Oxford Handbook of Childhood and Education in the Classical World*, Oxford: Oxford University Press, 2013; L. Beaumont, *Childhood in Ancient Athens: iconography and social history*, London: Routledge, 2012; M. Golden, *Children and Childhood in Classical Athens*, 2nd edition, Baltimore, MD: Johns Hopkins University Press, 2015.
54 Lancy, *Anthropology* 1ed, pp. 12, 24; 2ed, pp. 12, 27.
55 As one example of such a relationship, the 'classic' ethnographic survey of the Torres Strait Islands by anthropologist A.C. Haddon, from 1898 to 1899, took place 27 years after the arrival of Christianity, which is celebrated there today as a transformative event, 'the Coming of the Light'.
56 V. Cummings, *The Anthropology of Hunter-Gatherers: key themes for archaeologists*, London: Bloomsbury, 2013, discusses the value of anthropological analogy to prehistory, including non-material aspects, and also the limitations. She also notes that the classificatory boundary between foragers and farmers is porous. A useful debate on the limits of using modern hunter-gatherers (the San people) to make inferences from Pleistocene prehistoric finds in southern Africa is in *Antiquity* 90 (2016): 1072–1089.
57 Kelly, *The Foraging Spectrum*, pp. 67–69, 337–338.
58 R.B. Lee & R.H. Daly (eds), *The Cambridge Encyclopedia of Hunters and Gatherers*, Cambridge: Cambridge University Press, 1999, pp. 1–2.
59 She has published an account of her husband's life: Pat Lowe, *In the Desert: Jimmy Pike as a Boy*, Melbourne: Penguin, 2007.
60 V. Cummings, P. Jordan & M. Zvelebil (eds), *The Oxford Handbook of the Archaeology and Anthropology of Hunter-Gatherers*, Oxford: Oxford University Press, 2014; Lee & Daly (eds), *The Cambridge Encyclopedia*, include case studies of 53 communities. Neither of these major surveys gives much space to children, except for mention in the *Oxford Handbook* of how little has been said on the subject.
61 *HGC*.
62 *HGC*, p. 3. Case studies included or referred to in this volume differed in the age groups of the children of interest to individual researchers. The absence

of children from the hunter-gatherer ethnographic literature, despite their importance to hunter-gathers themselves, is discussed in *HGC* by N. Bird-David, 'Studying children in "hunter-gatherer" societies, pp. 92–101. One explanation for the omission of children is that field ethnography is often done by young people without children of their own.
63 R. Jarvenpa and H.J. Brumbach, 'Hunter-gatherer gender and identity' in Cummings et al. (eds), *The Oxford Handbook*, p. 1257.
64 H. Montgomery, *An Introduction to Childhood: anthropological perspectives on children's lives*, Chichester: Wiley-Blackwell, 2009, p. 18.
65 E.B. Tylor, *Primitive Culture: researches into the development of mythology, philosophy, religion, art, and custom*, London: John Murray, 1871, p. 257.
66 E.B. Tylor, *Researches into the Early History of Mankind and the Development of Civilization*, 2nd edition, London: John Murray, 1870, p. 108.
67 J. Lubbock, *Pre-historic Times*, London: Williams & Norgate, 1865. The book ran to many subsequent editions.
68 Lubbock, *Pre-historic Times*, 7th edition (1913), p. 564.
69 L. Aldred, 'Plastic shamans and astroturf sun dances: new age commercialization of Native American spirituality', *American Indian Quarterly* 24 (2000): 329–352.
70 The limits of using recent Australian Aboriginal society to interpret early archaeological materials are well addressed in P. Hiscock, *Archaeology of Ancient Australia*, London: Routledge, 2008. The recency of many apparently traditional belief systems is discussed by T. Swain, *A Place for Strangers: towards a history of Australian Aboriginal being*, Cambridge: Cambridge University Press, 1993. See also comments in C. Gamble, *The Palaeolithic Societies of Europe*, Cambridge: Cambridge University Press, 1999, pp. 16–18.
71 L. Hiatt in R.B. Lee & I. DeVore (eds), *Man the Hunter*, Chicago, IL: Aldine, 1968, p. 211.
72 R.K. Hitchcock, 'Hunter-gatherer research traditions in Southern Africa' in Cummings et al. (eds), *The Oxford Handbook*: 918–935. W.C. McGrew, *Chimpanzee Material Culture: implications for human evolution*, Cambridge: Cambridge University Press, 1992, pp. 123–126 (see also pp. 198–202) notes the limitations of using either chimpanzee groups or modern hunter-gatherers in analogies with our early human ancestors.
73 Gamble, *The Palaeolithic Societies*, pp. 62–63; Kelly, *The Foraging Spectrum*, p. 205. The oft-quoted norm of 25, and wider group of 500, derive mainly from J.B. Birdsell, 'Some predictions for the Pleistocene based on equilibrium systems among recent hunter-gatherers' in R.B. Lee & I. DeVore (eds), *Man the Hunter*, Chicago, IL: Aldine, 1968: 229–240.
74 Kelly, *The Foraging Spectrum*, pp. 209–213.
75 For example, 550,000 people identified themselves as Aboriginal or Torres Strait Islander in the 2011 Australian census, with one-third living in major cities, and this increased to 650,000 in the 2016 census. This self-identification includes many individuals with partial biological descent from indigenous peoples.
76 Hamilton, *Nature and Nurture*.
77 Hitchcock, 'Hunter-gatherer research traditions', p. 919.
78 Interestingly, a complaint was voiced over two decades ago about the lack of attention in primate studies given to juveniles: M.E. Pereira & L.A. Fairbanks (eds), *Juvenile Primates: life history, development and behavior*, New York:

Oxford University Press, 1993, p. vii. This too has begun to change, as references in subsequent chapters of this book show.

79 Z. Alemseged, 'Early hominins' in C. Renfrew & P. Bahn (eds), *Cambridge World Prehistory, Vol. 1*, Cambridge: Cambridge University Press, 2014: 47–64.

80 C.O. Lovejoy et al., 'The great divides: *Ardipithecus ramidus* reveals the postcrania of our last common ancestors with African apes', *Science* 326 (2009): 73, 100–106.

81 M.M. Robbins, P. Sicotte & K.J. Stewart (eds), *Mountain Gorillas: three decades of research at Karisoke*, Cambridge: Cambridge University Press, 2001.

82 See for instance J. Goodall, *The Chimpanzees of Gombe: patterns of behavior*, Cambridge, MA: Harvard University Press, 1986. Results of 45 years of research at Mahale are in an excellent account by T. Nishida, *Chimpanzees of the Lakeside: natural history and culture at Mahale*, Cambridge: Cambridge University Press, 2012.

83 R. Derricourt, 'Patenting hominins: taxonomy, fossils and egos', *Critique of Anthropology* 29 (2009): 193–204.

84 S. Harmand et al., '3.3-million-year-old stone tools from Lomekwi 3, West Turkana, Kenya', *Nature* 521 (2015): 310–315.

85 *Homo erectus* is used here *sensu lato*, to include *H. ergaster*.

86 C. Seong & C.J. Bae, 'The eastern Asian "Middle Palaeolithic" revisited: a view from Korea', *Antiquity* 90 (2016): 1151–1165.

87 R.M. Rowlett & M.J. Schneider, 'The material expression of Neanderthal child care' in M. Richardson (ed.), *The Human Mirror*, Baton Rouge, LA: Louisiana State University Press, 1974: 41–58.

88 D. Richter et al., 'The age of the hominin fossils from Jebel Irhoud, Morocco, and the origins of the Middle Stone Age', *Nature* 546 (2017): 293–296.

89 J. Allen & J.F. O'Connell, 'Both half right: updating the evidence for dating first human arrivals in Sahul', *Australian Archaeology* 79 (2014): 86–108; C. Clarkson et al., 'Human occupation of northern Australia by 65,000 years ago', *Nature* 547 (2017): 306–310.

90 See for example A. Jerardino & C.W. Marean, 'Shellfish gathering, marine paleoecology and modern human behavior: perspectives from cave PP13B, Pinnacle Point, South Africa', *Journal of Human Evolution* 59 (2010): 412–424; C.W. Marean, 'The origins and significance of coastal resource use in Africa and Western Eurasia', *Journal of Human Evolution* 77 (2014): 17–40.

91 A. Powell, S. Shennan & M.G. Thomas, 'Late Pleistocene demography and the appearance of modern human behavior', *Science* 324 (2009): 1298–1301.

92 L. Bourgeon et al., 'Earliest human presence in North America dated to the Last Glacial Maximum: new radiocarbon dates from Bluefish Caves, Canada', *PLoS ONE* 12 (2017): e0169486; S.R. Holen et al., 'A 130,000-year-old archaeological site in southern California, USA', *Nature* 544 (2017): 479–483.

93 Among many discussions of this topic, Andrew Sherratt's Boston University lectures *Between Evolution and History: long-term change in human societies* are invaluable, though never formally published; available at usheffield.academia.edu/SusanSherratt

2
BEING
Birth, motherhood and infancy

We can see something of birth and motherhood in prehistory from the evidence of archaeology, and by examining the fossil remains of early hominins we can discuss how they may have changed through time. The human child is dependent, especially on the mother, longer than most other mammals: for food, protection and the first stages of learning. When considering these topics, we can bear in mind what we know from history, the anthropology of recent small-scale forager and farming groups, and the lives of other higher primates.

The mother–infant bond is the norm observed in all types of human society. 'The love of a mother for her infant is one of the strongest of which the mind is capable' emphasised Charles Darwin in his 1872 book on emotions in humans and animals.[1] It reflects the necessity to provide food and protection. From his or her mother the infant learns language, food preferences and first skills (and language learning seems to begin in the first six months of life).[2] The bonding of the newborn to her or his mother is not reduced by the important role learning and culture are to play in the development of the human child. But one emphasis in village communities and forager bands is on the shared involvement of the broader community in raising children.

In the modern 'developed' world we are used to seeing birth as a private family affair: the mother, in the presence of a midwife and now (unlike a generation or two past) the father, with a medical specialist on hand. The infant and mother may then receive sequential visits at a maternity ward and home from relatives and friends, before the nuclear family returns to its relative domestic isolation. But through almost all of past time and still today in much of the world, family norms have been quite different from what occurs in the segment of the contemporary societies tellingly described by the acronym WEIRD ('western, educated, industrialised, rich, democratic').[3]

The model of parenthood in the modern developed world is thus very different from that of prehistoric communities, and also different from that of other societies until very recent times. Today we see the widespread trend to have a small number of children, with the expectation that all will probably survive into adulthood. The human norm, however, in historic and prehistoric society, was of a larger number of pregnancies. We can presume for most prehistoric societies what we see in historical records until very recently: a higher than modern fertility rate, accompanied by a higher than modern urban rate of death before adulthood. As the figures cited in Chapter 9 remind us, until quite recently there was a high probability that some would be stillborn, while others would die during infancy or early childhood, or if they survived their childhood they ran a high risk of death in early adulthood – males perhaps in conflict, females perhaps in an unsuccessful pregnancy. Such a pattern remains true of many of the poorest areas of the world today.

In prehistory we can see continuities more often than we can see dramatic change. When high fertility is accompanied by high survival rates, the growth of population puts pressures on society and the environment. When fertility rates are low, and the common pattern of infant death takes its toll, a society shrinks its footprint in the archaeological record. Continuity in prehistory is evidence for broad continuity in population size with the impact of high juvenile death rates on high fertility rates. Mobile forager groups of recent times had fertility rates of 5 or 6 live births with attrition which limited population growth.

Greater wealth in the modern era, perhaps paradoxically, has produced lower fertility. Wealthy families in the developed world consider how many children they can 'afford', assuming each will be raised with an acceptable level of care and material comfort. World fertility rates (live births per adult woman) have been estimated by the World Bank as falling from 3.3 births per woman in 1990 to 2.5 in 2014, and with low-income countries moving from 6.3 children in 1990 to 4.8 in 2014.[4] China, with its policies to limit family size, had a 2014 rate of 1.6 births. Different and sometimes conflicting cultural, practical, medical and economic factors influence fertility rates.[5] In the poorest sections of the poorest societies, high fertility often remains. For families, for mothers and for the young, the past was in marked contrast to our present.

PRIMATE DEPENDENCY AND INDEPENDENCE

We see Australopithecine and other early hominin children almost only in their fossilised bones, but the lives of the modern great apes help us consider questions and possible aspects of their lives.

Gorilla mother with her infant

A striking feature of primates is that they mainly give birth to a single young. This means that the mother–infant bond is direct and not affected by the competition that comes with a multiple birth. It also means the mother can carry her infant around – or that the infant can grip its mother's fur – changing from continuous contact in the early stages of life to a mechanism for safety and mobility as the infant grows.[6] The evolution of the opposable thumb is especially important in allowing an infant to grasp and cling to its mother's fur for a longer period than the mother herself will hold and carry her baby. In turn, this frees up the mother's arms (something essential to hominin cultural development).

In Southeast Asia, gibbons, which can live up to 30 years in the wild, are primarily tree-dwellers, though they descend to the ground to search for food. Females have their first offspring when around 9–11 years of age. A monogamous pair with children is a common pattern, which means the offspring are much more influenced by an adult male than is the case with the other apes (none of which are monogamous). Infants are weaned relatively young – typically at around 2 years, even earlier in some gibbon species – and the interval between offspring is around 3 years, depending on species.[7]

The orangutan of Southeast Asia is also largely tree-dwelling, though occasionally their foraging brings them to ground level in the forest. They have a longer lifespan than the African great apes – 50–60 years – and females have their first offspring at the age of about 15 or 16 years. They may have a 6- to 8-year gap between births. They do not operate in social groups, but the mothers travel with their own offspring, sometimes into the territory of others.[8] This means that all the upbringing of children is undertaken by the females but, as their older offspring stay with the mother, sibling play and influence are important too. Infants stay in bodily contact with their mothers for four months and become gradually more autonomous. Scientists describe an adolescent phase from 8 to 15 years, after which age they lead fully independent lives.

By comparison, the gorilla groups of Africa live mainly on the ground, and in small social groups (typically around 8 but up to 20 individuals) led by one adult 'silverback' male, which means other adult males live a separate existence.[9] This silverback male may play with the offspring, which he can assume are his own.[10] Infants are born singly, never leave their mothers for the first 4 or 5 months of their lives and rarely leave body contact for their first 6 months, by when they travel either on the mother's belly or on her back. Gorillas stay very close to their mothers for the next year or more, then gradually spend more of the day in independent play but nest with their mother at night. Once infant mountain gorillas are weaned, by 3 or 4 years, the mother may become pregnant again, though the arrival of a new sibling may encourage jealous older ones to increase their proximity to her.[11] By the age of 10 years a female gorilla is fully adult and able to give birth herself; the male reaches reproductive adulthood a couple of years later.

The bonobo or pygmy chimpanzee of the Congo is generally more omnivorous than the common chimpanzee, but is seen to have a social behaviour more conciliatory than them. Mothers undertake all the care of offspring in bonobo society.[12] The young stay close to their mothers until they are about 3 years old, and they are only weaned at about age 4 or 5. Their lifespan is about 40 years.

The most studied of the great apes is our closest living relative, the common chimpanzee. They have a primarily vegetarian diet (especially forest fruits), supplemented by insects and occasional meat from successful hunts. They live in social groups of largely interdependent individuals. These groups are larger than is typical of human hunter-gatherers, but they separate temporarily into smaller groups for food-gathering purposes.[13] In these groups there are likely to be several females with their offspring, the latter at different levels of dependency. Chimpanzee females have their first offspring at the age of 13–14. While the mothers are feeding their own milk to their infants they tend to stay in association with other nursing mothers, and a gap of 3–5 years between births is normal, so that they will have a maximum of 6 births in their lifetime.[14] The dominant male in the group may not have fathered all these children and aggression by adult males against infants (and between males) is common.[15]

Careful long-term studies undertaken on chimpanzees in the wild have revealed the early life of the infant and its mother. Where modern humans in small-scale societies and these closest living primate relatives exhibit similar patterns in infancy and child rearing, we can assume that our early hominin ancestors too may have shared those patterns.[16]

At birth, the infant chimpanzee cannot hold on to its mother's hair: it needs the support of her arms, whether she is sitting or walking, and guidance to find the nipples and to feed. It will whimper to show its need for milk, or in anxiety to appeal to its mother. If she is climbing up into the forest trees, as she does to sleep at night, she may use her rear limbs to hold the baby to her belly. After the first few weeks, the young infant can hold on to the mother's hair but will still be supported, for safety. It is in touch contact with its mother for the first three months of life, and the first efforts at crawling will be over its mother. One feature of chimpanzee mothers and their newborn infants is that they spend a lot of time gazing at one another.[17]

Gradually, the infant will develop the confidence to ride on its mother's back, increasingly from the age of six months, clinging on to the hair when travelling and climbing back on after a tumble. This position gives it a view of the world and a safer ride over the ground. But right through its first year the infant will rarely move away from reach of its mother, whimpering if it feels the distance is too great; nor will the mother choose to lose sight of her infant, until it is around a year old, when the infant will takes more initiative, although still staying within a safe distance.[18]

The mother must still protect her infant for many more months, including guarding it from the risk of attack by adult males. Mothers with small infants put a priority on protecting them, both in daily activity and in the night-time sanctuary of arboreal nests. Mothers with babies in a study of wild chimpanzees at Gombe (in Tanzania) were alone much of the time and could control access to others when their infants were very small.[19] As the mother greets other adults with pant-grunts, the infant may copy her and learn to make these social noises in the group. The risk of attack from adult males is real and potentially fatal (see Chapter 9). An interesting example of devoted foster mothering was observed at Mahale in Tanzania, to care for an orphan.[20] An unexpected observation also in the chimpanzee group of Mahale was a mother's care for her severely disabled infant daughter over 2 years, aided to survive with the additional help of a sister.[21]

Detailed observation of very young chimpanzees at Gombe allowed comparison with the development of human babies, and a striking similarity can be noted in many developmental stages of the very young of both species.[22] One notable difference is that human infants sit, crawl and stand much later than chimpanzees, a phenomenon attributed to modern child-rearing practices rather than nature.[23]

Play is important, and up to the age of 2 years play is mostly between the infant and its mother: being tickled, rolling and experimenting with foods. But the 2-year-old is more adventurous, able to stand on the ground, even to stand while riding on its mother's back. Play is more boisterous: play with the long-suffering mother or with other young at a further distance from the mother (although the mother is still watchful, rescuing her offspring from risk or danger). In their second year chimpanzee infants supplement their mother's milk with fruit, sometimes already chewed by their mother; now they can tackle leaves and more independent eating. From the age of 3 years they are more independent still (though still watched by their mother) and can walk independently as part of the chimpanzee troop on the move.[24] As discussed in Chapter 4, their diet becomes more varied and their suckling much more intermittent. Between the ages of 4 and 5, despite resistance and protests, weaning begins and the mother may become pregnant again during the next year.[25]

The young chimpanzee increasingly interacts with other members of the group. Much of the learning by the young chimpanzee, both social and practical – including tool use – is from copying the mother. Puberty at around 8–10 years marks the point at which they associate much less with their mothers. Chimpanzees in the wild can be regarded as full adults at 16 for males and 13 or 14 for females (figures not very different from historical perspectives within human society); their lifespan is typically 40–45 years.[26] But with both gorillas and chimpanzees, unlike most monkey species, adolescent males may remain in the social group while females migrate.[27] The mother–child bond of chimpanzee society may have echoes of human societies yet the social differences of chimpanzee groups from any human social group are marked.

EVOLUTION OF THE HOMININ FAMILY

In a classic paper published in 1981, physical anthropologist Owen Lovejoy reviewed different ideas about what distinguished the development of the human line from that of other higher primates.[28] He concluded that it was not biological features such as bipedalism, nor cultural developments such as tool making, so much as changing social factors, especially the nuclear family, and the intensive parenting role of the family in raising the young in human ways and human culture with human learning. Human society as we know it was not a development of humankind but a necessary creator of humankind. It is hard to state at what stage in human evolution this change in the family was found. Lovejoy pushed this back to the earliest hominins, as the major distinction from other great apes. However, as shown by studies of modern forager groups, the community as a whole, not just the nuclear family, may be involved in the rearing of children.

The understanding of motherhood and infancy in different early hominin species raises challenges: which aspects were closer to chimpanzees, which more like us and which like neither? The natural biological interval between being born and becoming a mother for the first time is estimated at 18 years for humans, 14 years for chimpanzees and just 4–6 years for monkeys. Human babies are large and their birth passage more difficult than for our primate relatives: a human baby weighs about 6% of its mother's weight, compared with 3% for a chimpanzee. Comparison of the different stages of evolution towards our modern species shows this change, with *Ardipithecus* of 4.4 million years ago closer to the pattern of chimpanzees, and the subsequent *Australopithecus* already about 5% of mother's weight at birth.[29] The increase in relative birth weight over hominin evolution placed biological penalties on the process of birth, especially with the emergence of upright gait and terrestrial residence.

Open to debate are why human childbirth is so difficult and historically so dangerous to mother and baby, and when it evolved this way.[30] If we are searching for the earliest specialised skills in human society, it is hard to look past midwifery. The most common interpretation is that the hominin development of bipedalism reduced the area for the birth canal, with a pelvis designed for upright running and walking rather than for pain-free childbirth. But evolution also gave us a large brain. The main growth of the human brain is after birth – although the phenomenon of significant brain growth after birth is also noted in chimpanzees.[31] If our brain and its containing skull grew more in the womb, we would not be born at all, so brain growth in the months immediately after birth is all-important, and provides one explanation why humans are initially more helpless as young infants than are many other advanced mammals. One view is that dietary changes, especially since the invention of agriculture and even more with the diets of prosperous modernity, have increased the physical difficulty of giving birth to a full-term baby. On the other hand, a sedentary rather than permanently nomadic lifestyle could be seen to present other advantages in childbirth.

The development of an upright gait and bipedalism in our hominin ancestors, notably in *Australopithecus afarensis* from before 3 million years ago, can be linked to the birth of young whose large brain develops *after* birth, with a longer period of dependency and a longer period of learning the skills required for adulthood.[32] But anatomical examination of the young of *Australopithecus afarensis* has suggested that birth was already far from easy this early in the hominin line. The size of the head as well as of the shoulders seems to imply that a safe birth would require a partial rotation after the baby's head had emerged.[33] The full rotation seen in modern births had not yet arrived; there is no implication that Australopithecines had midwives!

Confirmation that the species walked upright comes from remarkable evidence in the form of footprints of the same (or closely related) Australopithecine species at Laetoli in Tanzania, dated at 3.6 million years ago.[34] Here the steps of two adults (one male, one smaller and provisionally interpreted as an adult female) were captured in hardened volcanic ash; these imprints were discovered by Mary Leakey in 1978. Some interpreters of the find suggest that the woman was accompanied by a child who followed her and stepped into her prints in the mud. Ancient footprints have since been found at other African sites.[35]

It is in fossilised skeletal remains that we see the young of our early ancestors and their relations in the hominin line after the split from the ancestors of the great apes. These fossils tell us a little about their lives and a little more about their deaths: evidence discussed in Chapter 9. The finds of the 'First Family' are discussed there: an Australopithecine group of 13 adults and young who are thought to have died together in a flash flood some 3.2 million years ago.

But one important point needs to be made. Our closest great ape relatives show the central or exclusive roles played by mothers in the raising of children: in protection, in food provision (which is mainly or entirely foraged fruit and vegetation), in guidance of play, in demonstrating skills which the young can imitate. The male plays little or no role until the offspring are themselves young adults. This contrasts with the traditional view of 'man the hunter' leading the family and group in the iconic image of our ancestry and development. If we start with these ideas of the present and trace back, we may impose such an image on the deep past; but if we consider our hominin ancestors emerging within the family of the great apes, then a more feminised, matrocentric model presents itself, with at least equal claims. As discussed in Chapter 6, growing children later learn from each other, from slightly older children, and by observing and imitating their fathers and other members of their social group.

US anthropologist Nancy Makepeace Tanner applied the analogy of chimpanzee society to the earliest human ancestors.[36] The bond between mother and child is central to the social life, upbringing and training of chimpanzee young, and the mother guides the child in its food acquisition, including the use of tools for vegetable and insect foods. Tanner prioritised the role of mothers in those developments of culture which mark the movement towards human rather than ape existence. For what she calls 'transitional hominids' – our earliest ancestors after the lineage separated from that of the great apes – mothers' food-gathering strategies, sharing of food and tool use would be the essential drivers of the evolution of modern humans.[37] Mothers developed the new strategies in food gathering which marked the steps on the way from ancestral great ape to early hominin. Such a model also has implications for mate selection: a female choosing a mate not because of his physical strength, prowess as a hunter or his ability in food provision, but on other grounds.[38]

An alternative argument would suggest the increasing period of dependency in hominin evolution put social pressures on the mother as the primary caregiver, and this continuing role of the mother in hominin groups could inhibit her availability as a food gatherer, favouring therefore the role of the males and of hunting over food gathering, and helping reinforce male dominance in the group.

Yet primate society shows us that females are effective food providers and caring mothers. And there are more than enough examples in recent and contemporary rural societies of women as primary carers, home makers and dominant economic providers while their men discuss politics, plan or engage in war and exercise their authority in different ways. Among living primates, humans are the only species with lifelong links to adult offspring, which is perhaps related to the importance of grandparents in human groups, guiding, caring and making social, economic and non-material contributions.

Just as the brains of modern humans grow significantly after birth, it has been suggested that the same was true of *Homo erectus*, who spread from Africa into Eurasia after about 1.8 million years ago: the small pelvis limiting the size of the infant's cranium at birth.[39] A detailed study argues, nonetheless, that the early post-natal brain growth of *Homo erectus* was significantly less than that in modern humans.[40]

While our direct knowledge of children among Australopithecines and early species of *Homo* is limited, we have a stronger image of Neanderthal children. This visibility is from excavated sites, and their location in Europe has given them a greater presence in the archaeological literature and also in popular culture ever since the later 19th century.

It appears that the Neanderthal female pelvis was not much easier for childbirth than it is in our modern species.[41] However, studies of Neanderthal female skeletons have led to suggestions that the Neanderthal full-term foetus presented differently from a modern foetus and this may have made their births easier. A Neanderthal pregnancy was probably of much the same length as that in modern humans.[42]

It seems very possible that Neanderthal babies were born larger than a newborn of our species. In a society whose life patterns had developed to resist the colder climates of the European ice ages, a larger infant would be more likely to survive, and even modern humans have larger babies in colder climates.[43] The demands on a feeding mother were substantial,

Child with two adults from the Mesolithic rock art of Lucio o de Gavidia, Spain

especially through the winters of colder areas.[44] But overall body size need not mean greater height: one study suggests that Neanderthal infants were the same height as modern humans at birth, and from the age of five months their height grew less than modern humans, because of nutrition or perhaps metabolism.[45] Evidence from the dental enamel at Neanderthal burials in France suggests there were periods of serious physical stress in childhood, arising probably from dietary challenges in the coldest periods of the year, stress from which the young were not protected.[46]

They would also require a significant calorific intake to live and thrive in the European winters: the protective role of their community would have been all-important. Neanderthal babies, like modern humans, would have been very dependent when young. After birth, the growth of their infant brain was at a greater rate than for other hominins, perhaps at a faster rate than in modern humans.[47] There is evidence that, in the Middle Palaeolithic, Neanderthals reached biological adulthood sooner than *Homo sapiens*.[48]

As noted in Chapter 7, a shorter period of childhood implies a briefer stage in which to acquire the cultural knowledge achieved through childhood play.[49] We should not follow the cliché of minimising Neanderthal abilities: they adapted to the challenges of variable climatic zones, made striking advances in tool technology and provide occasional evidence of non-material activity such as formal burials and decorative items.

Nevertheless, their culture was less complex than that of *Homo sapiens*: Neanderthal children might therefore have needed less time to acquire the full range of adult skills and capabilities.

Most of what we know of Neanderthal young is from their skeletons, sometimes buried by their community in what appears to be a caring and ritualised manner, as discussed in Chapter 9. Such attention given within Neanderthal society to the burial of infants and children suggests a similar care for them in life.[50] But excavated sites of Neanderthal settlement do not create the same image we see in later prehistory: of a central hearth and seating area around which adults would sit and talk and children play.[51]

There are many imaginative reconstructions of Neanderthal social life (including those in museum dioramas and in fiction) but there is much we cannot know.[52] Indeed, the climatic changes in Ice Age Europe may have meant that the size and nature of Neanderthal groups fluctuated and varied significantly, as did the overall population of the species. We should not be surprised that a Neanderthal society which had made skilled and dramatic improvements to the stone tool technology of its handaxe-making predecessors, and which had economic strategies that saw it survive the harshest of European Ice Age climates, should have developed a caring approach to the death of children (and to the survival of some of the unfit adults, as indicated by some of the skeletal remains).

Changes over time in pregnancy, birth, motherhood and infancy can be discussed with greater clarity as the assemblage of fossil hominin remains increases, and we apply new techniques of analysis to the bones and to the genetic makeup of prehistoric individuals. We will be able to distinguish more clearly the differences between Australopithecine birth and development in the first years of life and those of early *Homo* species, including our own.

The anatomically modern humans of the Upper Palaeolithic who gradually supplanted (and at times bred with) the Neanderthals from around 45,000–40,000 years ago used a diverse technology, and new economic strategies and uses of the landscape, represented by settlement and workshop sites uncovered in archaeological work.

Many (but by no means all) archaeologists would locate the origins of language with the emergence of our own species; others argue for at least some aspects of language in Neanderthal culture. Archaeologist Steven Mithen has speculated and argued for an earlier scenario, when sounds and music, rather than the language of our modern species, formed a central part of the interaction between mother and baby, a hypothesis which may contribute to the picture of Neanderthal family life. Mithen suggested this phenomenon may have been a characteristic of even earlier hominins.[53] Certainly Neanderthal family life can be pictured as one of deep interdependency of children with mothers, and of both within a small community of mobile foragers in command of the resources of diverse European and Middle Eastern landscapes.

The planning skills of Upper Palaeolithic society were certainly enhanced by language, and they possessed new approaches to the non-material aspects of life. These can be seen in the archaeological record of deliberate human burials and the clothing and decoration applied to these, but they are seen most dramatically in the art which developed as sculptural objects, engravings and paintings, some of which have been recovered, typically those in hidden caves and shelters, sites which also give us direct evidence of children. In the advanced forager cultures of the Holocene, new skills in stone tool technology and specialised exploitation of resources developed but the classic cave art of the European Upper Palaeolithic is no longer seen.

We can look to accounts of recent societies whose economy is largely reliant on foraging to help us gain some insights into the lives of children in advanced prehistoric hunter-gatherer communities. As noted in Chapter 1, this approach has limitations and too much reliance on analogy has dangers, since the societies under study were already, by definition, in touch with the 'modern' world, and their pattern can therefore be expected to include adaptations to it. There are trends seen across forager groups, but of course much variability too: contrasts have been noted in patterns of fertility and more so in patterns of child rearing, as discussed below.

Although they represent a minority of time in human prehistory, agricultural societies provide new kinds of evidence about prehistoric lifeways and the role of children in those societies. Ethnographic studies of recent small-scale pastoralist and arable farming communities have shown the vast diversity of their approaches to childhood and children.[54] High fertility rates need not reflect high wealth: children may be an economic cost but may also be an economic benefit in their provision of labour. When changing regimes of health and diet may reduce infant and child mortality, this need not automatically reduce the number of live births a family desires.

MOTHERS AND BABIES

The rich and well documented traditions of European later Upper Palaeolithic art give us some direct images of motherhood. The 'female' characteristics of these carvings are often exaggerated: large breasts, large buttocks and large thighs, together with representation of the sexual organs. Some of the sculptures suggest stages of pregnancy and others appear to represent the process of birth. But as Patricia Rice observed in a classic article, the female figurines of the European Upper Palaeolithic seem to include all stages of an adult woman's life, and so do not particularly emphasise fecundity and motherhood.[55] Yet the tradition remains one showing adults (including

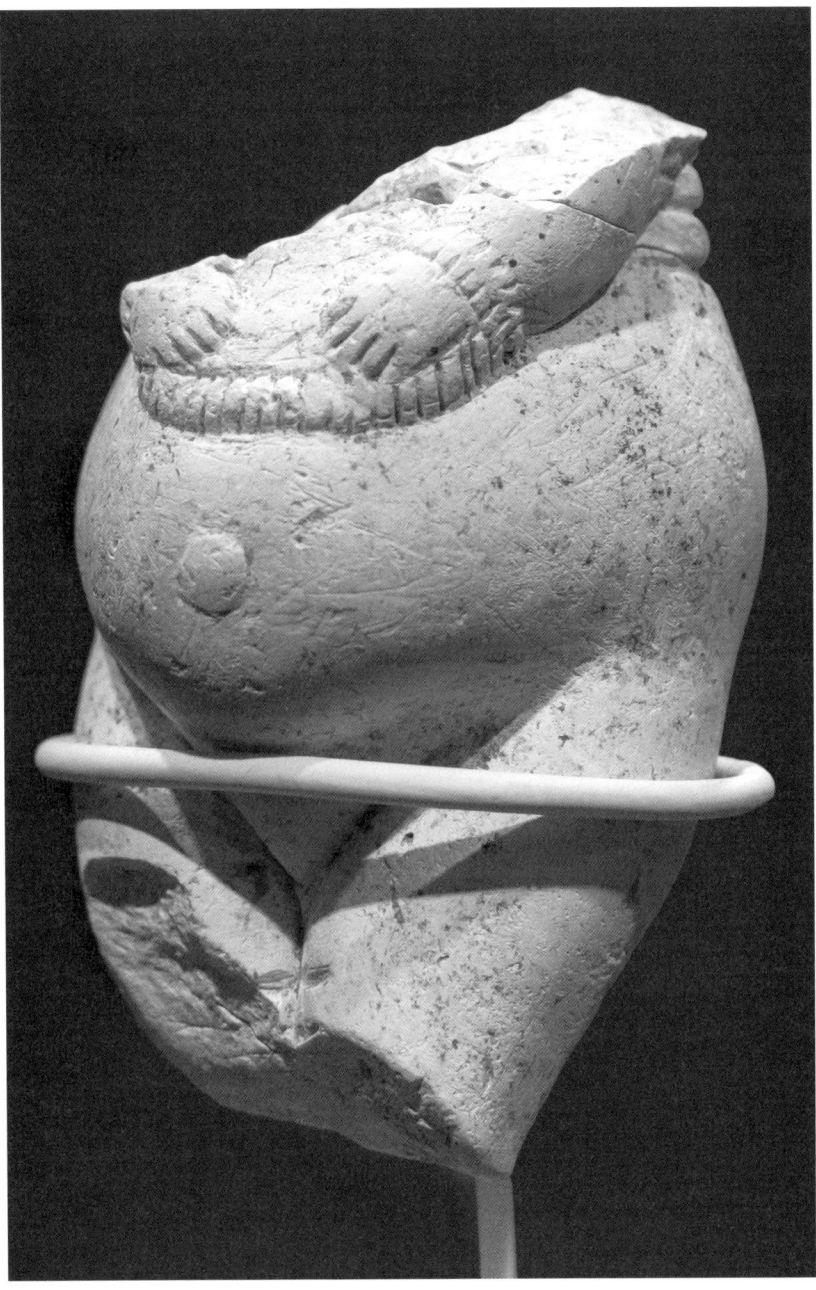

Sculpture of an apparently pregnant woman from the Upper Palaeolithic of Kostenki, Russia

young women), not younger girls, which does lend support to an emphasis on sexual or reproductive aspects. Sculptural images of children are a rarity in the Upper Palaeolithic; the Siberian sites of Mal'ta and Buret' are notable for the presence of statuettes with childlike bodies.[56]

Did these sculptures represent a male fascination with the female body, things created by lonely hunters? Was there a ritual intention, perhaps to encourage fecundity? Were some of these just dolls for children, or even educational? Multiple theories and multiple explanations will remain.

At Kostenki on Russia's River Don, excavations of living areas dated around 26–21,000 years old revealed a wide range of sculptures, including limestone and ivory figures of pregnant women.[57] Strangely, some of these had been deliberately damaged before disposal. Finds from Kostenki, from Zaraysk (south-east of Moscow) and from Avdeevo (near Kursk) include sculptures of women clutching their abdomen, which have been interpreted as denoting stages of pregnancy.[58] The female figurine tradition seen elsewhere in Russia includes images of naked women who are not pregnant.

Carved figures from the Grimaldi caves in Italy are considered to show a woman giving birth.[59] That from the Grotte du Prince on the French coast near Italy is a fine steatite carving, just 5 cm or 2 inches tall, with an ill-defined baby partly emerged – though the earlier identification of the sculpture as a hermaphrodite shows how subjective such an assessment can be. Another steatite sculpture from the neighbouring Barma Grande cave is also thought to be a woman about to give birth.

Some of the same themes can be found in two-dimensional art: incised marks which have survived because they were made on flat pieces of mammoth ivory or bone. Engravings on the surface of bone from Laugerie Basse in France combine the image of a reindeer with a very pregnant woman.[60] The association of the two has led to some imaginative suggestions. There may be a ritual or totemic link between them, or the conventional perspective, with her lying down, could even be mistaken: perhaps she is standing and beside her waits dinner.

There are other engravings from this later period of the Upper Palaeolithic that combine images of women with images of animals. Particularly interesting are engraved plaquettes at the German Magdalenian site of Gönnersdorf, on the Rhine, including an example showing a procession of females, one of whom has a cradle on her back, possibly holding an infant (see p. 67).[61] Another has been interpreted, somewhat controversially, as a woman giving birth, linked by an umbilical cord to a foetus shown without limbs (if correct, this interpretation would make it the oldest known representation of childbirth). The detail of the woman giving birth suggests she was doing so in an upright and supported position. We can still only surmise whether the presentation of such a scene on an engraved plaquette was for magical, educational or other purposes.

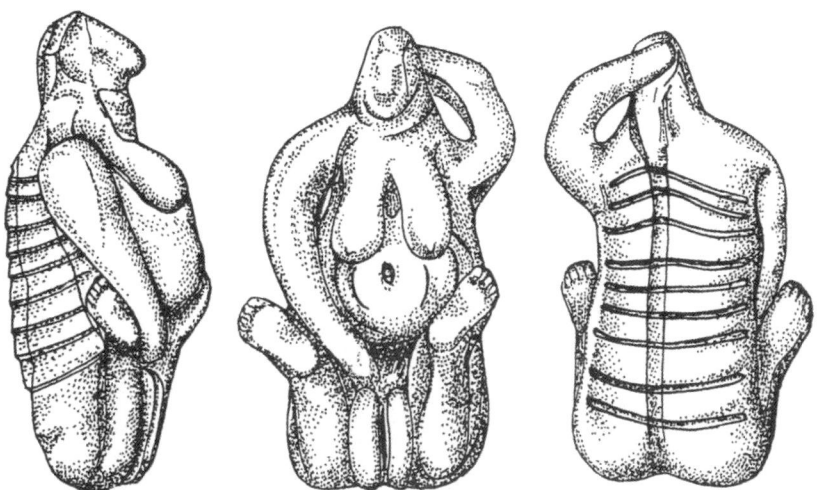

Woman possibly giving birth, a sculpture from the 4th millennium BC, Ħaġar Qim, Malta

In addition to such images of pregnancy and childbirth, we may find a burial of a woman with a newborn which suggests a death in childbirth, as discussed in Chapters 9 and 10. One example of such a death is from a late hunter-gatherer find from Lokomotiv (Raisovet) in southern Siberia, dated to the Mesolithic of 5000–6000 BC.[62] The burial of a 20–25-year-old woman in a community cemetery contained the unborn full-term foetuses of twins. Fifteen decorated marmot teeth buried with the woman represented personal decoration, probably from attachment to clothing, and there were no other grave goods. Examination of the position of the twins suggested that one was in the early stages of a breech birth (the other twin being in a normal position *in utero*), representing a high danger for the death in childbirth that ended the life of mother and babies.

We can complement our partial image of prehistoric forager children by noting what has been observed in more recent groups. Although childhood and motherhood were not central to most ethnographic descriptions and anthropological studies of small-scale hunter-gatherer communities, the diverse information available to us is a reminder of the even greater diversity in prehistoric forager groups.

Compared with modern urban societies, women in such forager communities tend to a later menarche (often about 15–16 years) but an earlier first birth (about 19) with longer periods of nursing infants and an earlier menopause (in the early 40s).[63] For mobile hunter-gatherers, there are generally advantages in a longer interval between births: a typical interval between births being 3–4 years, with an average of five or six live births over a woman's lifetime.⁶⁴ Such a fertility rate among forager groups is lower than among farmers.⁶⁵ A higher figure of fertility, eight children per mother, was recorded in the 1970s among the Yanomami of the Amazon rainforest.⁶⁶ Low or marginal fat storage in the body may influence fertility and the spacing of infants.⁶⁷ The prehistoric development of agriculture is commonly thought to have increased the number of surviving children.

The !Kung San (from the arid Kalahari region of Southern Africa) have been among the most studied of hunter-gatherer groups, especially in the 1960s and 1970s. Almost all !Kung San mothers have their first child between the ages of 17 and 22.⁶⁸ They were noted in the 1970s to have an average fertility of five live births per woman, with a late first menstruation and early menopause. Extended nursing and other factors served to space children about 36 months apart.⁶⁹ Perhaps a quarter of the babies did not survive their infancy.

A pattern of infanticide was traditional in many forager groups, as discussed in Chapter 9, as well as in agricultural societies. David Lancy's survey of the anthropology of childhood references evidence of infanticide as common across numerous societies, past and present.⁷⁰ Communities known to have practised infanticide did so not only as a response to disabled newborn, and also to twins, but also to manage the gender ratio in the community, with newborn females more often the subject of infanticide than males.⁷¹ In a harsh environment infanticide was a social mechanism to limit dependants, one of the means to establish intervals between children in the family and defer weaning of a current infant. The ancient Roman practice of exposing babies may have anticipated that they would be found and nurtured by another family, and the 'foundlings' institutions of European countries into the modern era reflects such an approach.

When we move to consider evidence from prehistoric farming communities, as well as burial finds, we can see rare images of motherhood in art. Artistic images have generated controversy in their interpretation: whether a sculpture represented an ordinary woman, a powerful individual within society or a 'mother goddess' figure, an idea stimulated by writers such as Lithuanian/American archaeologist Marija Gimbutas. The idea of the prehistoric mother goddess influenced the model of a matriarchal society in prehistory preceding the emergence of patriarchal complex urban civilisation.⁷² One feature within the 'matriarchal prehistory' narrative is the proposition that prehistoric societies pooled their children: that all women were mothers to all children, and that collective child-rearing rather than the individual mother–child bond was the core of the prehistoric community.

Today 'goddess tours' are an established part of the international travel industry.⁷³ Because of the site's artistic images, excavations at Çatalhöyük in Turkey have received regular visits from such groups, visits that have

Ivory sculpture of mother and child from predynastic Egypt, in the Neues Museum, Berlin

stimulated debates about multiple approaches to the past by the archaeologists involved in the site. Current research tends neither to accept the goddess hypothesis for the site, nor the specific identification by the earlier excavator James Mellaart of a female figure as a women giving birth. The discovery of a complete female figurine of stone announced in late 2016 adds to the debate: is this a pregnant female, or is the exaggerated body shape symbolic of fertility, age or carrying other significance?[74]

When we approach the eve of civilisation we begin to find new kinds of evidence. An ivory model of a mother and child from predynastic Egypt (now in the Neues Museum, Berlin) shows the artist's humanity and particular sensitivity to the theme.

Birth may be familiar to mothers but not always to artists. There are direct but unrealistic images of birth on decorated pots from villages of the Mimbres period in New Mexico, USA, dated about 1000 AD.[75] On each design, the baby is painted emerging face forward with its arms up. While this biologically incorrect view could suggest the paintings were by men or someone ignorant of birth, it might also be intended as a non-representational portrait of such an important life event, and not too much should be read into the form shown in the paintings.

It is unusual to find an image of motherhood as direct as the painted pottery figures from the site of Knight Mound in Illinois, USA, probably of the early agricultural Hopewell tradition.[76] One is of a woman naked above the waist and holding a naked infant, and another is a woman suckling her naked infant.

Through such data, alongside selective analogy, we can get some images of motherhood in prehistory: pregnancy, birth and babies. We can consider what changed over the long stretch of time in hominin development, and what remain as absolutes and continuities. Chapter 4 considers the process of weaning, which marks a change in the physical relationship between mother and infant. We now consider our perceptions of children developing as active members of family and social groups.

NOTES

1 C. Darwin, *The Expression of Emotion in Man and Animals*, London: John Murray, 1872, p. 215.
2 J. Choi, A. Cutler & M. Broersma, 'Early development of abstract language knowledge: evidence from perception–production transfer of birth-language memory', *Royal Society Open Science* 4 (2017): 160660.
3 Lancy, *Anthropology* 2ed, pp. 2–3.
4 wdi.worldbank.org/table/2.17
5 Lancy, *Anthropology* 1ed, pp. 59–63; 2ed, pp. 115–119.
6 C.L. Coe, 'Psychobiology of maternal behavior in nonhuman primates' in N.A.

Krasnegor & R.D. Bridges (eds), *Mammalian Parenting: biochemical, neurological, and behavioral determinants*, New York: Oxford University Press, 1990: 157–183, p. 160.

7 pin.primate.wisc.edu/factsheets/entry/siamang/behav
8 pin.primate.wisc.edu/factsheets/entry/orangutan/behav; G. Kaplan & L.J. Rogers, *The Orang-Utans*, Sydney: Allen & Unwin, 1999, ch. 4.
9 pin.primate.wisc.edu/factsheets/entry/gorilla/behav. A silverback male was observed to adopt an orphaned infant whose mother had died: D. Fossey, 'Development of the mountain gorilla (*Gorilla gorilla berengei*): the first thirty-six months' in D.A. Hamburg & E.R. McCown (eds), *The Great Apes*, Menlo Park, CA: Benjamin/Cummings, 1979: 139–184, pp. 177–181.
10 K.A. Bard, 'Primate parenting' in M.H. Bornstein (ed.), *Handbook of Parenting*, Vol. 2, 2nd edition, Mahwah, NJ: Erlbaum, 2002, p. 110; Fossey, 'Development of the mountain gorilla'.
11 A. Fletcher, 'Development of infant independence from the mother in wild mountain gorillas' in M. Robbins, P. Sicotte & K.J. Stewart (eds), *Mountain Gorillas: three decades of research at Karisoke*, Cambridge: Cambridge University Press, 2001: 153–182; A.H. Harcourt & K.J. Stewart, *Gorilla Society: conflict, compromise and cooperation between the sexes*, Chicago, IL: University of Chicago Press, 2007.
12 pin.primate.wisc.edu/factsheets/entry/bonobo/behav
13 pin.primate.wisc.edu/factsheets/entry/chimpanzee/behav
14 Although one study recorded an average of 5.5 years after the first child had survived. T. Nishida et al., 'Demography, female life history, and reproductive profiles among the chimpanzees of Mahale', *American Journal of Primatology* 59 (2003): 99–121.
15 Although three examples of males adopting orphaned infants were observed in the Taï Forest of Côte d'Ivoire. C. Boesch & H. Boesch-Achermann, *The Chimpanzees of Taï Forest: behavioural ecology and evolution*, Oxford: Oxford University Press, 2000, pp. 82–83.
16 Chimpanzee developmental stages are well summarised in T. Nishida, *Chimpanzees of the Lakeside: natural history and culture at Mahale*, Cambridge: Cambridge University Press, 2012, pp. 86–124; see also Bard, 'Primate parenting'.
17 Bard, 'Primate parenting', p. 107.
18 F. X. Plooij, *The Behavioral Development of Free-Living Chimpanzee Babies and Infants*, Norwood, NJ: Ablex, 1984, p. 124.
19 Plooij, *The Behavioral Development*, p. 17.
20 Nishida, *Chimpanzees of the Lakeside*, pp. 176–182.
21 T. Matsumoto et al., 'An observation of a severely disabled infant chimpanzee in the wild and her interactions with her mother', *Primates* 57 (2016): 3–7.
22 Plooij, *The Behavioral Development*, p. 77.
23 Plooij, *The Behavioral Development*, p. 143.
24 Coe, 'Psychobiology', p. 174, cites evidence that chimpanzee mothers begin to show rejection of their young aged 2–3 years, forcing them into more independence, as a function of the resumption of sexual activity rather than as part of the weaning process as such.
25 T. Matsuzawa, M. Tomonaga & M. Tanaka (eds), *Cognitive Development in Chimpanzees*, Tokyo: Springer, 2006, p. 8.
26 M. Shimada & C. Sueur, 'The importance of social play network for infant or

juvenile wild chimpanzees at Mahale Mountains National Park, Tanzania', *American Journal of Primatology*, 76 (2014): 1025–1036; pin.primate.wisc.edu/factsheets/entry/chimpanzee/taxon

27 Coe, 'Psychobiology', p. 159.
28 C. O. Lovejoy, 'The origin of man', *Science* 211 (1981): 341–350.
29 J.M. DeSilva, 'A shift toward birthing relatively large infants early in human evolution', *Proceedings of the National Academy of Sciences* 108 (2011): 1022–1027.
30 H. Dunsworth & L. Eccleston, 'The evolution of difficult childbirth and helpless hominin infants', *Annual Review of Anthropology* 44 (2015): 55–69, takes issue with some of the conventional assumptions.
31 S.R. Leigh, 'Brain growth, life history, and cognition in primate and human evolution', *American Journal of Primatology* 62 (2004): 139–164.
32 S. Sutou, 'The hairless mutation hypothesis explains not only the origin of humanization from the human/ape common ancestor but also immature baby delivery', *Human Genetics and Embryology* 3 (2013): 111.
33 J.M. DeSilva et al., 'Neonatal shoulder width suggests a semirotational, oblique birth mechanism in *Australopithecus afarensis*', *Anatomical Record* 300 (2017): 890–899.
34 M.D. Leakey & R.L. Hay, 'Pliocene footprints in the Laetolil Beds at Laetoli, northern Tanzania', *Nature* 278 (1979): 317–323; T.D. White & G. Suwa, 'Hominid footprints at Laetoli: facts and interpretations', *American Journal of Physical Anthropology* 72 (1987): 485–514.
35 Summarised in N. Ashton et al., 'Hominin footprints from Early Pleistocene deposits at Happisburgh, UK', *PLoS ONE* 9 (2014), e88329. Footsteps at Ileret in Kenya included adults and a possible juvenile; those at Koobi Fora were of an adult, as were those at Langebaan; in Europe footsteps at Roccamonfina in Italy were of individuals 1.5 m (5 feet) high; a Neanderthal footprint at Vartop Cave Romania was made by an individual of a similar height.
36 N.M. Tanner, *On Becoming Human*, Cambridge: Cambridge University Press, 1981: one of the minority of studies of hominin evolution to treat it as a human rather than a natural science topic.
37 Tanner, *On Becoming Human*, pp. 11, 89–93, 267–271.
38 Some scientists, including Lovejoy, 'The origin of man', have argued from the comparison of hominin males and females to suggest a pattern of monogamy; see discussion by G.C. Conroy, *Reconstructing Human Origins: a modern synthesis*, 1st edition, New York: Norton, 1997, pp. 227–237.
39 D.C. Johanson & B. Edgar, *From Lucy to Language*, New York: Simon & Schuster, 2006, p. 78.
40 Z. Cofran & J.M. DeSilva, 'A neonatal perspective on *Homo erectus* brain growth', *Journal of Human Evolution* 81 (2015): 41–47.
41 Dunsworth & Eccleston, 'The evolution of difficult childbirth', p. 57.
42 T.D. Weaver & J.-J. Hublin, 'Neandertal birth canal shape and the evolution of human childbirth', *Proceedings of the National Academy of Sciences* 106 (2009): 8151–8156; R.G. Franciscus, 'When did the modern human pattern of childbirth arise? New insights from an old Neandertal pelvis', *Proceedings of the National Academy of Sciences* 106 (2009): 9125–9126; S.E. Churchill, *Thin on the Ground: Neandertal biology, archeology and ecology*, Hoboken, NJ: Wiley Blackwell, 2014, p. 343.

43 M. Cartmill & F.H. Smith, *The Human Lineage*, Hoboken, NJ: Wiley-Blackwell, 2006, pp. 383–384; Mellars, *Neanderthal Legacy*, p. 3; Churchill, *Thin on the Ground*, p. 92.
44 Churchill, *Thin on the Ground*, pp. 94–97.
45 J.A. Martín-González et al., 'Differences between Neandertal and modern human infant and child growth models', *Journal of Human Evolution* 63 (2012): 140–149.
46 Churchill, *Thin on the Ground*, p. 98.
47 M. Dean, C. Stringer & T. Bromage, 'Age at death of the Neanderthal child from Devil's Tower, Gibraltar and the implications for studies of general growth and development in Neanderthals', *American Journal of Physical Anthropology* 70 (1986): 301–309, pp. 307–308.
48 P. Spikins et al., 'The cradle of thought: growth, learning, play and attachment in Neanderthal children', *Oxford Journal of Archaeology*, 33 (2014): 111–134; T.M. Smith et al., 'Dental evidence for ontogenetic differences between modern humans and Neanderthals', *Proceedings of the National Academy of Sciences* 107 (2010): 20923–20928.
49 A. Nowell, 'Childhood, play and the evolution of cultural capacity in Neanderthals and modern humans' in M.N. Haidle et al. (eds), *The Nature of Culture*, Dordrecht: Springer Netherlands, 2016: 87–97.
50 R.M. Rowlett & M.J. Schneider, 'The material expression of Neanderthal child care' in M. Richardson (ed.), *The Human Mirror*, Baton Rouge, LA: Louisiana State University Press, 1974: 41–58.
51 Clive Gamble, *The Palaeolithic Societies of Europe*, Cambridge: Cambridge University Press, 1999, pp. 206–201; P. Mellars, *The Neanderthal Legacy: an archaeological perspective from Western Europe*, Princeton, NJ: Princeton University Press, 1996: 295–301.
52 Lewis Binford suggested he could distinguish male and female areas in the Neanderthal levels of the rock shelter of Combe Grenale in the French Dordogne. See L.R. Binford, 'Hard evidence', *Discover*, February 1992: 44–51.
53 S. Mithen, *The Singing Neanderthals: the origins of music, language, mind and body*, London: Weidenfeld & Nicolson, 2005; Cambridge, MA: Harvard University Press, 2006.
54 Lancy, *Anthropology* 2ed.
55 P.C. Rice, 'Prehistoric Venuses: symbols of motherhood or womanhood?', *Journal of Anthropological Research* 37 (1981): 402–414.
56 R.G. Bednarik, 'The Pleistocene art of Asia', *Journal of World Prehistory* 8 (1994): 351–375.
57 J. Cook, *Ice Age Art: arrival of the modern mind*, London: British Museum Press, 2013, pp. 78–84.
58 Cook, *Ice Age Art*, pp. 83–84.
59 Cook, *Ice Age Art*, pp. 94–95.
60 Cook, *Ice Age Art*, pp. 227–228.
61 B. Roveland, 'Footprints in the clay: Upper Palaeolithic children in ritual and secular contexts' in *CMC*, p. 34, citing Bosinski & Fischer (1974); F. d'Errico, 'The oldest representation of childbirth' in P. Bahn (ed.), *An Enquiring Mind: studies in honor of Alexander Marshack*, Oxford: Oxbow, 2009: 99–109; A. Marshack, 'Exploring the mind of Ice Age man', *National Geographic* 147 (1975): 65–89; G. Bosinski et al., *Die gravierten Frauendarstellungen von Gönnersdorf*, Stuttgart: Franz Steiner, 2001.

62 A.R. Lieverse, V.I. Bazaliiskii & A.W. Weber, 'Death by twins: a remarkable case of dystocic childbirth in Early Neolithic Siberia', *Antiquity* 89 (2015): 23–38.
63 S.B. Eaton & S.B. Eaton, 'Hunter-gatherers and human health' in R.B. Lee & R.H. Daly (eds), *The Cambridge Encyclopedia of Hunters and Gatherers*, Cambridge: Cambridge University Press, 1999: 449–456.
64 K.M. Weiss, *Demographic Models for Anthropology*, Memoir Series no. 27, Washington, DC: Society for American Archaeology, 1973; F.A. Hassan, 'The growth and regulation of human population in prehistoric times' in M.N. Cohen, R.S. Malpass & H.G. Klein (eds), *Biosocial Mechanisms of Population Regulation*, New Haven, CT: Yale University Press, 1980: 305–319, p. 311.
65 R.L. Kelly, *The Foraging Spectrum: diversity in hunter-gatherer lifeways*, Washington, DC: Smithsonian Institution Press, 1995, pp. 244–246. An older study suggested the main contrast was between high fertility of intensive farmers and lower for others (garden cultivators and foragers alike): G.R. Bentley, T. Goldberg & G. Jasieńska, 'The fertility of agricultural and non-agricultural traditional societies', *Population Studies* 47 (1993): 269–281.
66 Also called Yanomamo; M.N. Cohen, 'Speculations on the evolution of density measurement and population in *Homo sapiens*' in Cohen, Malpass & Klein (eds), *Biosocial Mechanisms*, p. 295; N. Howell, 'Toward a uniformitarian theory of human paleodemography', *Journal of Human Evolution* 5 (1976): 25–40, p. 33.
67 Cohen, 'Speculations', pp. 280, 290–291.
68 M. Konner, 'Hunter-gatherer infancy and childhood: the !Kung and others' in *HGC*: 19–64, p. 29. While long referred to as !Kung in the literature, they are also named Ju/'hoansi in recent literature.
69 N. Howell, 'Toward a uniformitarian theory'; N. Howell, 'The population of the Dobe area !Kung' in R.B. Lee & I. DeVore (eds), *Kalahari Hunter-Gatherers: studies of the !Kung San and their neighbors*, Cambridge MA: Harvard University Press, 1976: 137–151; H. Harpending, 'Regional variation in !Kung populations' in Lee & DeVore (eds), *Kalahari Hunter-Gatherers*: 152–165.
70 Lancy, *Anthropology* 1ed, pp. 86 ff.; 2ed, pp. 29–37, 92–94.
71 Kelly, *The Foraging Spectrum*, pp. 232–244.
72 C. Eller, *The Myth of Matriarchal Prehistory: why an invented past won't give women a future*, Boston, MA: Beacon Press, 2000.
73 An internet search for terms such as 'goddess tour' links to thousands of web pages.
74 www.dailysabah.com/history/2016/09/13/neolithic-figurine-over-7000-years-old-unearthed-at-turkeys-catalhoyuk
75 M. Hegmon & W.R. Trevathan, 'Gender, anatomical knowledge, and pottery production: implications of an anatomically unusual birth depicted on Mimbres pottery from southwestern New Mexico', *American Antiquity* 61 (1996): 747–754; S.A. LeBlanc, 'A comment on Hegmon and Trevathan's "Gender, anatomical knowledge, and pottery production"', *American Antiquity* 62 (1997): 723–726; C.T. Espenshade, 'Mimbres pottery, births, and gender: a reconsideration', *American Antiquity* 62 (1997): 733–736.
76 W.C. McKern, P.F. Titterington & J.B. Griffin, 'Painted pottery figurines from Illinois', *American Antiquity* 10 (1945): 295–302.

3
GROWING
The child in the family

Information from archaeology, including prehistoric art, gives us images of the child within the family, as he or she passed from infancy through the stages of childhood, before transition into the adult world. Early hominins are thought to have developed to biological adulthood faster than anatomically modern humans, though slower than the great apes. One main impact of our slower maturation and later onset of reproductive age in both males and females is a longer gap between generations.[1] Whatever the biological significance of becoming an adult later, there are cultural advantages. A lengthy infancy, childhood and adolescence mean an extended education and a more 'educated' adult.[2] There is a longer period in which a human can continue to acquire the full range of practical and social skills needed to operate in the group as a full adult with offspring to feed and support.

The modern urban pattern of the developed world can be very different from the impact the arrival of a new baby has on a village of interdependent three-generation farming families, or in a mobile band of 25 nomadic foragers. While the bond between mother and infant is universal and biological, the context and upbringing of the newborn child is culturally determined. In different societies, various aspects of raising infants may involve the father, other mothers, older siblings, unrelated older children and that phenomenon almost unique to humans: grandparents, especially women who survive for years beyond their reproductive age.[3]

Kinship terms in different societies, cultural contexts and languages can have quite different applications from that of the modern urban west; even 'father' is a term whose meaning can change.[4] Terms such as 'brother', 'sister', 'uncle' and 'aunt' may have even broader application. While the biology of parenthood may be fixed, the question of who is defined by a relationship term can be very variable.

While the prehistoric family generally presents itself indirectly through archaeological evidence, we sometimes see it more directly, as in the Neanderthal group found in the El Sidrón cave in northern Spain. This may have been a mobile group killed together. The site had a radiocarbon date around 48,500 years BP (beyond the range of calibrated calendar years).[5] The skeletal remains appear to include three adult males, three adult females, three adolescents, two children (one aged 9 years and the other 5 or 6 years) and an infant. Genetic studies suggest two of the women were mothers of the children and two of the men were brothers. We thus have dramatic evidence for a mobile group of closely related individuals which resembles in many ways the mobile hunters seen in historic times.[6] It was initially suggested that the group died together as the result of a rock fall. Further analysis of the bones, with cut marks and bones split to obtain marrow, suggested, however, evidence of cannibalism, probably of both children and adults, which may have been ritual in nature rather than an act of aggression.[7] Their deposition was thus not accidental but deliberate; they were placed there by others and the rock fall came after the bones were abandoned.[8] Stone tools of the same period were recovered from the site.

By contrast, at a much later stage of prehistory, the early agricultural settlement of Çatalhöyük in Anatolian Turkey provides an unexpected challenge to our image of the family unit in the past. People lived in very close proximity in this early urban community: homes built and rebuilt close together, entered by ladders from above and with burials found under floors. It is hard to imagine a closer form of daily life, yet analysis of the dental remains of the burials show that the people living (and buried) in these houses were not close kin. A domestic unit had taken precedence over a biological unit.[9] In this most complex of early societies, our expectations of a norm have been undermined by new methods of analysis.

VISUAL IMPRESSIONS OF THE PREHISTORIC FAMILY

In the archaeological record we have some direct sightings of prehistoric children and their families in their marks on the earth and in their marks in art. Footprints at the site of Ileret in Kenya dated about 1.5 million years ago include those of adults and a probable child from *Homo erectus/ergaster*, with feet shaped for bipedalism much like those of our species.[10] New scientific studies have demonstrated they walked with an upright gait, like *Homo sapiens*.[11] The foot and gait of the Ileret child suggested he or she was aged about 9 years. We have the image of a mobile family trekking across the savannah.

Archaic *Homo* also literally walks into prehistory at another site: Happisburgh (pronounced Haze-burra) at a coastal estuary in Norfolk,

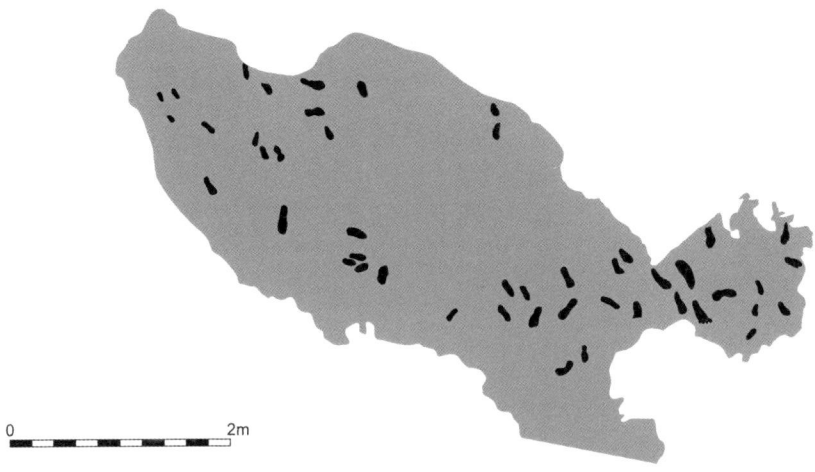

Plan of the footprints of an archaic *Homo* family from Happisburgh, England

eastern England, and dated to before 780,000 years ago.¹² Here in 2013 were found the oldest footprints known outside Africa: 50 prints of a group of pre-modern humans, five separate individuals including children, walking southwards on the mudflats at the edge of a river (or maritime estuary) in a landscape setting of pine, spruce and birch, with some open heath and grassland. The footprint sizes suggested both male and female adults and children (the smallest being about 1 m or 3 feet 3 inches in height): our first vision of a nuclear family group in prehistory. The media announcement presenting the find said 'They were a British family on a day out – almost a million years ago'. This was a trek across a muddy reach: they were probably searching the waterside for foods such as shellfish and crabs.

The caves visited by the Upper Palaeolithic hunter-gatherers of Western Europe, locations best-known to us for their rock art, provide us with the living imprints of children. Here can be found small footprints embedded in the surface deposit of cave floors, alongside those of adults.¹³

The French Pyrenees site of Le Tuc d'Audoubert is a small cave with a low roof on which are modelled fine clay relief sculptures of bison, 'slug' shapes and more, all dated to the Magdalenian period of the Upper Palaeolithic, around 13,500 BC. In the clay floor are footprints interpreted as those of children (probably in their early teens) walking on their heels. This is not a cave for living and the children's footprints have stimulated the suggestion they were there as part of an initiation ceremony: a possibility we cannot test.¹⁴ Finger holes around the clay bison modelled at the site have also been seen as children's activity, perhaps just the result of play.¹⁵

Also from the Magdalenian of the Pyrenees are the footprints of two young children on the floor of the art-rich cave of Niaux, whose walls carry outlines of horses and bison. In the nearby cave of Réseau Clastre are footprints of three children together, lightly calcified in the sandy floor. The art in this cave shows bison, a horse and – rather unusually – a weasel.[16]

In the site of Fontanet, in the same region and from the same era, the complex of prints – a left foot, hand and knee prints on the clay floor of a cave with rock art on the wall, as well as pawprints – suggests a young child walking and kneeling in pursuit of a canine, presumably a dog, the very first animal to be domesticated.[17]

Chauvet in southern France is one of the most celebrated sites of Upper Palaeolithic art, not least because of claims for its relatively early date. Images include lions, rhinoceros, hyenas, bears and panthers. The footprints found on the cave floor are considered to be those of a child about 1.3 m (4 feet 3 inches) tall, which might suggest an age of 8–10.[18] The painters' necessarily torch-lit walk into the cave (charcoal stains mark the route and are dated around 26,000 years ago) ended abruptly, perhaps when encountering a water-filled basin. This was a serious adventure for a child, as the cave floor also shows footprints of wild animals: a wolf-like animal and a bear.

In Chapter 6 we address briefly the question of whether children themselves contributed elements of the cave art. But the presence of these marks of children in caves featuring sophisticated adult paintings and engravings encourages us to imagine the young accompanying their parents (conventionally assumed to be their fathers) on a painting excursion. We may not be certain of the context and the reasons why this art was created, but the presence of the artists' children in caves used for purposes other than occupation brings an additional human image to the scene.

Handprints of adults and children are a common element in the Upper Palaeolithic cave art of Europe. The cave of Gargas, in the Haute-Pyrenees region of France, is notable for its art objects and the art on the cave walls, which uses some similar stylistic elements. Fingers were used to paint on the walls, but a feature of the art is the use of numerous stencils, where colour had been applied to make negative images of hands. These are considered to be the hands not just of adults, but of adolescents, children and even infants.[19] Perhaps predictably, most were of left hands (assuming the right hand was used to apply the colour to the walls). Less predictably, many of the hands appear to be deformed or mutilated, with missing fingers.[20] Did the hand stencils at Gargas represent a ritual involving young and old, or was the ritual in the mutilation itself? It is notable that the thumb was not mutilated, but that the mutilation could be any of the other fingers or even more than one finger.[21]

Contemporary with the European Upper Palaeolithic but from the other side of the earth, human footprints have been uncovered at Willandra Lakes

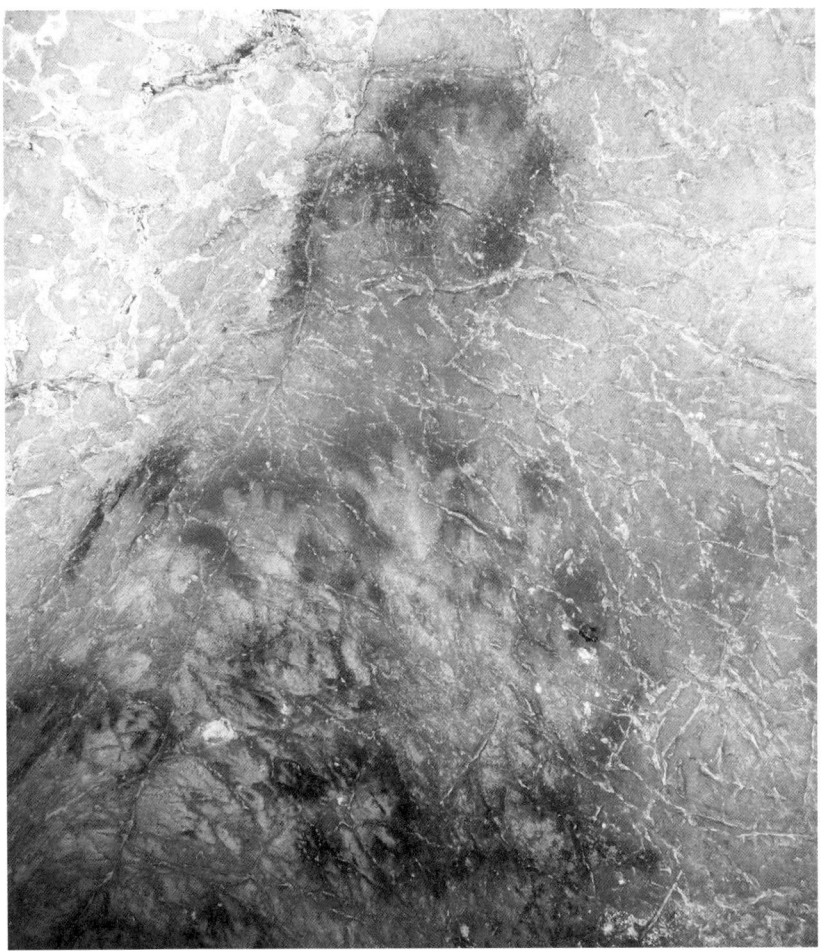

Stencilled hands of children and adults from Upper Palaeolithic cave wall art at Gargas, France

in Australia dated between 23,000 and 19,000 years ago.[22] These prints (more than 120) were spread over an area of 700 m^2 (840 square yards) on the exposed edge of a former lake or pan. From size of the prints it is clear that some were of adults, some of adolescents and some of children, moving along the pan edge, and usually running. It is possible to trace the tracks of a child just over 1 m (3 feet 3 inches) in height, running at 5 km (3 miles) per hour before slowing to 3 km per hour. Meanwhile, an adult's tracks suggest the individual was running at 17 km per hour (over 10 miles per hour), as in a hunting activity. The pan would have been suitable for fishing and collecting shellfish as well as hunting by this mixed-age community.

Infant hands or lizard feet? Stencils in rock art at Wadi Sura in the Western Desert of Egypt

From later hunter-gatherers in Engare Sero in Tanzania is one of the largest sets of footprints ever found, some 400 prints, which may be from anything between 19,000 and 6000 years ago. The prints were made in mud near a freshwater spring by an itinerant group of mixed age; the presence of footprints of zebra and unidentified bovids suggest a community following potential prey.[23]

Infants and children are seen in the rock paintings of eastern (Mediterranean) Spain, which are generally thought to date to the Mesolithic. In such scenes, young children are shown walking with women rather than men, and we may assume these are their mothers.[24] Some scenes have a child on a woman's back while another appears to be scenes of childbirth, and apparently pregnant females are also shown in the art. Representation of young children is not very different from that of adults, and personal decoration cannot be distinguished.

In Africa the arid Sahara provides archaeological evidence at settlement sites, tool manufacturing sites and rock art which represents the transition from foraging to animal husbandry and even to cultivating crops in the wettest areas. Art at Tassili n'Ajjer in Algeria shows children in family groups.

The rock shelter of Wadi Sura II in the Western Desert of Egypt has many thousands of paintings of different subjects and designs, positioned up to

Possible initiation scene from the Later Stone Age of Sevilla, South Africa

4 m (13 feet) above ground level with suggested dates of about 8000 years ago. They include negative images the size and form of human babies' hands. Their initial interpretation as babies' hands has been questioned, however, with the suggestion from careful measurement that the 'hands' might in fact be the imprint of the forelegs of a lizard or other reptile: presumably a lopped limb rather than a cooperative creature.[25] Despite this claim, an alternative possibility is that model hands were created just to represent babies' hands, and added to the adult prints made in the shelter art.

With an estimated date around 3000 BC, another rock painting site in the Western Desert of Egypt has been called 'the oldest nativity scene ever found'. That seems exaggeration: the content is a man, a woman and an infant positioned between them.[26]

The hunter-gatherers of the Later Stone Age dominated much of sub-Saharan Africa until their gradual replacement by farming communities over the past three millennia, but in parts of Southern Africa such communities continued into modern times, foraging inland, along the coast, or both in a seasonal pattern. These cultural ancestors of the San are reflected in a range of territorial markers, from coastal shell middens to montane rock shelters decorated with detailed paintings. Links have been made between the belief systems recorded from the San themselves and the imagery of the prehistoric art.

Some of the group scenes appear to represent initiation ceremonies: contexts which mark a formal transition from childhood to adulthood. In San society the timing of such a transition may be at the first menstruation for a girl, or the first kill of a specified animal prey by a boy. The eland form appears important in the art, carrying different meanings: symbolic, or as hunted animal or as a skin kaross. Paintings at Sevilla near Clanwilliam in south-west South Africa show one such initiation scene of eland and multiple young men, some of whom are carrying quivers, bows or sticks.[27]

 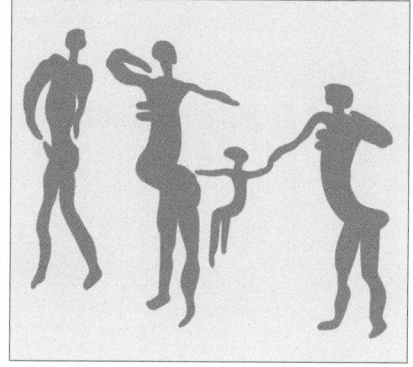

Later Stone Age rock paintings from Zimbabwe depicting two young children with two adults (left), and a mother with a child, alongside two adults (right)

Young children are seen on the backs of two adults in a rock painting in the Wedza district of Mashonaland East in Zimbabwe: they are part of a scene of about 40 humans together with animals and 'therianthropes' – humans in part animal form.[28] Two children kneeling next to a woman are seen in a rock painting in the company of a standing male and a therianthrope.[29] A woman holds the hand of a child in another Zimbabwean rock painting in a scene with other adults, a kudu and a warthog.[30]

Generally, children are rarely identified in the region's rock art. It is difficult to know which rock art individuals are children or adolescents: 'the depiction of children is not well substantiated, partly because the use of scale has not yet been adequately researched'.[31] The same may be true of prints of small hands: are they children or small San adults?[32]

Footprint sites – so important in our vision of early prehistory – continue in these later periods. One site near dunes in the south-west African nation of Namibia shows a whole group of children: about nine of them, and judging by size from 5 years old upwards.[33] A footprint site from the British Mesolithic was revealed by low tide in the Gower Peninsula of Wales, featuring the prints of both adults and children as well as the prints of deer and boar that they may well have been following.[34]

Handprints in the rock art of Australia can be of adults or children on the same site. At Middle Park Station in north Queensland, 139 stencils of children's hands have been recorded (compared with 1099 of adults), with no positioning specific to the juvenile prints.[35]

In all these signs of children in art, two questions remain. First, how much were they participants in creating the artistic representations? And second, how important was their role to adults? Among the diverse interpretations and debates on the roles and functions of prehistoric art, the indications of children's activity need to be carefully considered. Did they just come along as tolerated offspring of the adult artists, or were they seen as an essential part of a ritual activity, with deep community commitment to their participation?

THE 'TRADITIONAL' FAMILY

Studies of modern-era hunter-gatherers have emphasised the close physical bond between mother and baby; the extended period of breast-feeding by mothers in forager societies, with longer intervals between births than in agricultural or industrial societies; a common pattern of care of infants by older children; play taking place in groups of mixed ages; and varied levels of contribution by children to the work and economic life of the community. The roles of fathers, grandmothers and other adults do not diminish the strength of the mother–infant bond.

In !Kung society of the Kalahari region of Southern Africa, young children remain close to their mothers (literally so, in the mother's hold or fastened in by her kaross for much of the first year) but the mother is in the almost constant presence of other adults in the group. After the age of one, the infant gradually becomes more involved in groups of children, who will inevitably be of different ages, given the often small size of the !Kung band (25 being an often quoted average, although the range is broad). When a new sibling comes along, and the infant finds its mother's milk now belongs to another, association with other and older children may become the daily norm and a major source of acquiring social knowledge.[36] Compared with modern western society, young !Kung children thus have both more contact with their mothers and more contact with other children.

Women in !Kung society contribute about two-thirds of the community's food – a role which requires substantial ease of mobility. Infants and children under 4 years are typically with her on foraging trips, and from the age of 6 or 7 they walk independently if the group shifts camp. 'For the first 2 years of life a child is carried by the mother for a distance of 2400 km'. Gaps between pregnancies make this pattern of mobility a little less challenging.[37]

Among the Hadza foragers of Tanzania, if the parents become separated, the children remain with the mother, and family residence with the wife's mother is the most common arrangement.[38]

With the Baka Pygmies of Cameroon, older boys and well as girls care for young infants.[39] A study showed such older children were with the infants 20% of the time, with fathers or with grandmothers just 7–8%. However, the Baka have become increasingly sedentary in recent times so this pattern need not necessarily reflect traditional practice.

An exceptional group – described as 'unique by cross-cultural standards' in Barry Hewlett's anthropological study, which represented 15 years' fieldwork – is the Aka Pygmy forager community in the western Congo basin of the Central African Republic.[40] 'Aka fathers do more infant care-giving than fathers in any other known society.' It was calculated that Aka fathers can spend 47% of their day near their infants. Despite this, Hewlett considered the Aka was not specifically a child-centred community. In contrast with modern western fatherhood, fathers' attention to their offspring was seen as *quantity time* rather than our modern concept of 'quality time'. Fathers were not pursuing the boisterous physical play with their children seen in other communities.

Explanation for this unusual situation comes from the economic and social relationships between male and female. In Aka society women and men make almost equal contributions to the household diet, and this appears to be reflected in egalitarian relationships and ideology (an egalitarianism that extended to lack of respect for elders).[41] A relatively high fertility rate puts pressure on both parents in child rearing. The absence of violence and warfare between groups contributes to the context of this particular paternal role.[42]

The Aka serve to remind us that we should not make assumptions about prehistoric forager societies based upon some perceived norm derived from more modern communities. There is a broad range of economic, social and demographic variance in recent hunter-gatherer groups; over the very extensive prehistoric eras when foragers were the only residential humans in an area, we can project even greater variance from those of modern forager societies. The author of the Aka study hypothesised that an abundance of animal food available to Late Pleistocene hunter-gatherers would mean fathers then had more time available to be with their families, but such suggestions go beyond the realm of the testable.[43]

While young children are mainly in the primary care of their mothers, in some forager societies the daily care is spread across many different members of the community. This may be other mothers sharing childcare; it may be fathers or maternal grandmothers, or it may be older children. In a Brazilian Parakana Indian group, by age 3 or 4 a child may already be carrying a smaller sibling around. With the Efe foragers of the Ituri forest, in the Congo basin, childcare is described as a specific responsibility of older children.[44] Babies still breast-feeding may spend a third of their time in the hands of older (but commonly pre-adolescent) children. There is greater involvement by siblings than non-siblings, and generally greater by girls than boys, but elder brothers are still active childminders. When a nursing mother is out of the camp, as on a foraging expedition, the carer may have to follow with the infant. Older boys may be away from camp aiding in adult hunts so less available to childcare.

A study of childhood among Australian Aborigines at Maningrida in the late 1960s presented traditional attitudes in the changed setting of a government settlement.[45] The overwhelming impression was of a permissive approach to young children, indulging their wishes, paying attention whenever they cried or required food, but not watching closely or carefully over their activities. With a large degree of independence the young children developed physical abilities sooner and stronger than children in European society, but were also susceptible to accidents; thus the relaxed parenthood might be regarded as both positive and negative by western measures. The background of this was described as follows:

> Children must assert their rights for themselves.... The consequences for the population as a whole are obvious. Only those children who can tolerate physically and emotionally the conditions of camp life, and act independently in the feeding situation, are likely to survive. Children who cannot tolerate the demands placed upon these matters die at an early age, leaving behind those who are 'fittest' for their environment.[46]

Mobility is a feature of almost all forager groups. Ethnographic studies and archaeological analogy suggest that high fertility is not a barrier to high mobility: a forager group can expand its population and settle new areas rapidly, a model seen in the suggested relatively rapid human settlement within Australia and the Americas.[47]

The territory around a base camp is traversed daily for food supplies and when the distance required to obtain adequate supplies becomes too great it is time to move the whole community to a new base camp. A comparison of forager societies suggests that a 3 km radius (about 1.9 miles) is typically the ideal daily limit for a group – a total area of less than 30 km^2 (11 square miles), but not all of that would necessarily be accessible. When the resources of this area are exhausted, the group may be best served by moving camp. Indeed, there are narratives to suggest that it is women who often lead on the decision to move camp, since the resources they harvest are more likely to become locally depleted than those harvested by men.[48]

This is the pattern for those (including most women) who return home each night. Groups of hunters may of course go further, on hunting expeditions, eating some of their catch on route and bringing back the rest for their families and for distribution within the band. But depending on the resources of the land and the culture of economic exploitation, the number of moves in a year may range from two to four, aligned with the seasons, through to a shift of home bases every week or two. Such journeys may involve walks involving several hundred kilometres a year; an estimate for the Australian Aboriginal Ngadadjara people suggested an annual trek of 1600 km (1000 miles).

Moves to new home camp sites involve the whole forager band: mothers have plenty of help on hand to carry infants and young children alongside the material possessions of the group. The daily round of exploring for a family's food (plants, small animals) can place the greatest demands on a mother with an unweaned baby, but she will be aided by the practical solutions discussed below.

In reference to small-scale agricultural societies, anthropologist Tim Ingold has raised an interesting (if challenging) image: 'Growing plants and raising animals are not so different, in principle, from bringing up children'.[49] In this model, a woman in such farming communities nurtures and guards her young children, and at the same time nurtures and guards her garden of food plants, balancing the needs of both. Symbolic comparisons of plants and children can be found: Ingold noted that among slash-and-burn agriculturalists of the upper Amazon, planted manioc is seen as hostile to human infants, whose blood it can suck. In the Mount Hagen region of highland Papua New Guinea he noted a similar approach to the parallel between 'growing' children and growing plants. But this community lives in a landscape that can be threatening, although it does provide wild foods to supplement the cultivated. In this context, children and plants are part of the managed world.

We might see further contrasts between foragers and farmers (although bearing in mind that this is too simple a division for the broad span of prehistoric societies). While both are subject to natural forces and are dependent on the bounty of the land, the forager, with a nomadic pattern of moving, has continually to find water and plant and animal foods; planning is thus primarily responsive to the perceptions and realities of external resources. Gratification is (mainly) immediate: food is found, distributed and consumed. But the farmer lives in a world of forward planning: stock must be bred and only selectively slaughtered; crops must be planted and nurtured to provide future food. Climate can destroy as well as sustain. In such a context the ideology of child rearing may also be seen as part of the planned world. When a foraging economy is transformed to a planned farming economy we can expect different styles of motherhood, infancy and the development of an adult role in the community. The transition does of course have other dramatic impacts: a different and perhaps limited range of diet, the risks of famine from the failure of crops through drought or flood, and new diseases readily spread through larger and more densely located communities.

CARRYING A YOUNG CHILD

Across all forager groups, maintaining bodily contact with an infant is important. A sling is commonly used in tropical communities, and outside the tropics either heavy swaddling or a cradleboard is common. Infants

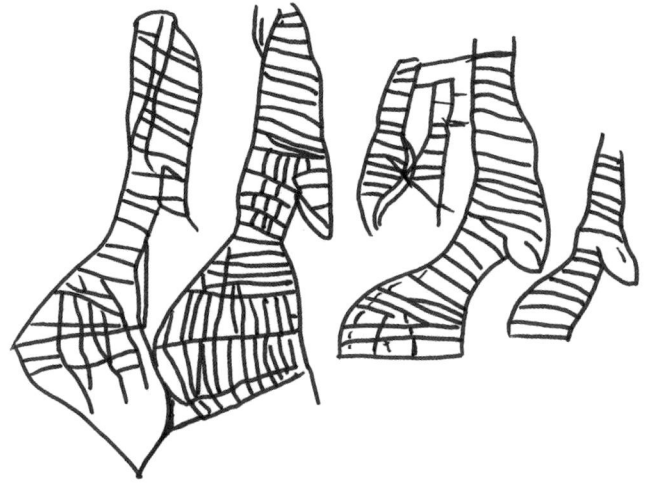

Engraved plaquette from Upper Palaeolithic Gönnersdorf, showing a procession of four women. The third from the left is suggested to have on her back a cradle with an infant

among Ache foragers of Paraguay are carried in a sling until about 18 months, after which they may ride in the mother's carrying basket, while clinging to her head.[50]

Richard Lee's study of the !Kung noted the restrictions on mobility imposed by an arid landscape.[51] An adult woman may walk up to 1500 km (950 miles) a year, with five of six changes of camp; her foraging trips may involve carrying 7–15 kg (15–35 lb). Use of a sling means children can be carried by their mothers for up to the first 4 years of life. In this context, having births at intervals of 3–5 years is a survival mechanism. When a !Kung baby cries, it is said to be with less intensity than a western child and for a shorter period.[52]

Far to the north, the Mansi people of western Siberia (also known as Voguls) had a traditional life of hunting, fishing, food gathering and reindeer herding. On food-gathering expeditions, a mother who went in search of berries or similar foods was reliant on a cradle to carry her infant, although the child was put in the care of older children while the mother was actually collecting food.[53] At home, the cradle and infant could be suspended within sight of the mother.

Such a consideration of the practicalities of nomadism raises an important question on the cultural apparatus of early humans. Unlike great ape babies holding a mother's body hair, young human infants do not simply cling on to their mothers: they must be supported until (if permitted) they can sit on a mother's shoulders, for example (a pattern reported among

Australian Aborigines at Maningrida), and perhaps hold on to her hair.[54] A woman carrying a baby in her arms is restricted in her active foraging. The economic value of a sling or wrap or swaddling cloth to hold the baby on her back is therefore substantial, allowing much fuller participation in the life of the group. Yet we cannot identify at what stage in human (or hominin) development such a sling (the earliest of which would have been made from animal skin) was first used.

Without a sling, a mother could only forage fully and adequately for food if someone else was caring for her baby, and then only after weaning. With a sling, a group of mothers could cooperate in the care of young children, or these could be left in the care of an older sister or a grandmother while their mothers foraged for food.[55] With the extended period of infancy before weaning seen in forager communities, and the important role played by women in food supply in most such groups, the mechanism for carrying an infant on a foraging trip is an essential part of material culture.

An interesting and imaginative, if complex, argument about the limits to foraging for nursing mothers came from a study of prehistoric Californian hunter-gatherers.[56] As this group became more sedentary in the 2nd millennium AD, the foods collected by women are presumed to have moved to a focus on acorns, as they could be stored over winter. This reduced the need for mothers to undertake distant foraging trips and thus increased their ability to care for their young children.

In settled agricultural societies, where the mother is likely to be involved in daily economic production, the role of other carers for young children is important. Infants may be the responsibility of older siblings, or be collectively cared for by a group of mothers, but grandmothers are of widespread importance.[57] As noted above, the human species is unusual in the extended period of post-reproductive life for women, which provides a major social benefit to a community. Grandmothers can allow mothers to undertake economic activities untrammelled by the care of small children.

A sling or other support to carry a small child is an essential tool if a child is to accompany the mother in agricultural and other economic activities. Very different devices have been noted in different communities.[58] As well as support to carry a child, there are the cradleboards of Native Americans to which a child could be fastened, with the cradleboard moved and suspended in different places. Baskets have been found in a wide range of societies, designed to hold a child safely without maintaining physical touch with an adult.

Direct evidence for the transport of prehistoric infants in the Old World is rare but they do exist. In Bronze Age Beaker burials from Britain, some burials show flattening at the back of the skull: possibly the result of infants being carried against a hard cradleboard, although deliberate reshaping of the skull by binding is not ruled out, as discussed in Chapter 5.[59]

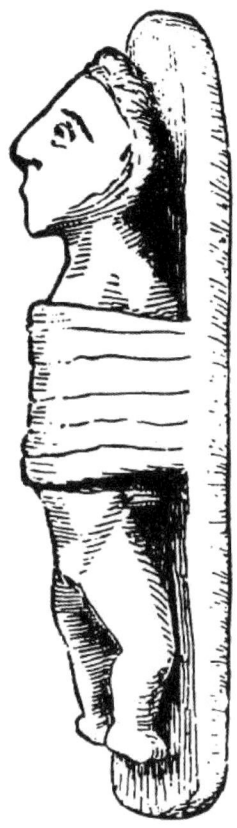 

Drawings of a clay model, from Tennessee, USA, of an infant bound to a flat carrying board

Clear archaeological examples of cradleboard use come from the USA and Mexico. A Tennessee example is from a late but undated Native American grave of a child, in the form of a clay model of an infant strapped to a flat cradleboard. Of somewhat similar design, Mexican finds, one from a burial at Los Ortices, have a pillow below the head.[60]

While cradleboards are part of the tradition in the US Southwest from prehistoric to recent times, their survival in the archaeological record of the Basketmaker period (before about 500 AD) is patchy.[61] Skulls provide the evidence for later Pueblo prehistory: heads flattened at the back from being placed as an infant on a cradleboard designed with a hard back. Other prehistoric and ethnographically recorded cradleboards from the region have different structures, suggesting that the cranial deformation was

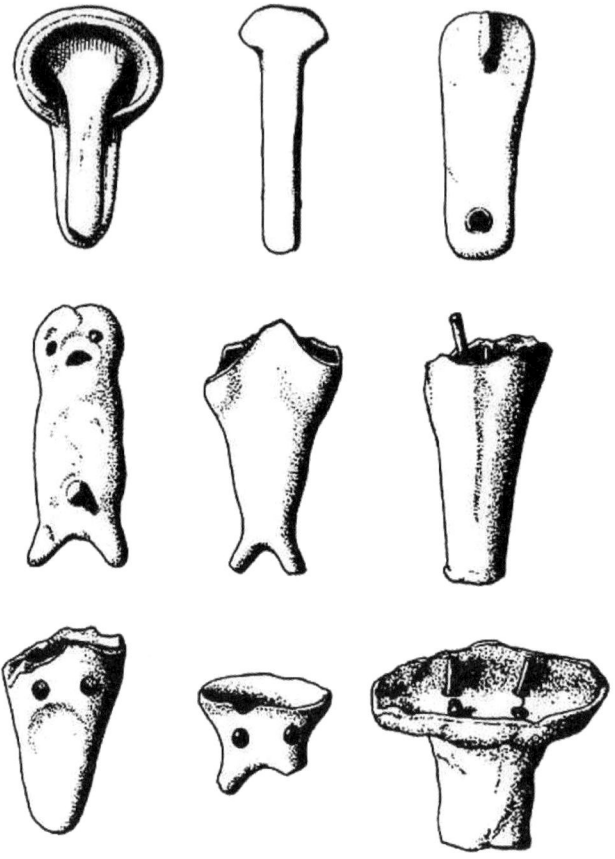

Unbaked clay figures interpreted as babies, from Ancestral Pueblo site of Waterfall Ruin, Arizona

not the kind of deliberate act discussed in Chapter 5. In the US Southwest another apparent means by which skulls were reshaped in infancy was a hard headrest on which a baby was rested.

Cradles of cane and other vegetable matter made for carrying can be found well preserved in archaeological sites from arid regions of the USA.[62] Carefully woven these would provide confident carrying of even older infants. It is particularly poignant when a baby cradle is found buried with the body of a woman.

Small unfired clay models of the Basketmaker tradition from Waterfall Ruin in Arizona may represent babies in carrying cradles, or in carrying baskets.[63] These items could have served as children's toys.

QUESTIONS AND ANSWERS

Fossil remains, footprints and artistic representations, baskets and cradles are images of prehistoric childhood in the prehistoric family. Our views on the origins of language impact our vision of family and social culture in deep time: was language associated only with anatomically modern humans, or did Neanderthals have language, and what was the equivalent in earlier *Homo*? When we observe the lives of young higher primates we can envisage some aspects of early hominin family life, while the roles of children in recent forager and small agricultural communities remind us of the limits of our present picture from archaeology. But archaeological data can present us with information on specific activities of children: their diet, their clothing and personal decoration, their acquisition of skills, their play and their experience of conflict, while their burials show us more of their position in family and wider social group. These topics are reviewed in the chapters that follow.

NOTES

1 A.T. Chamberlain, *Demography in Archaeology*, Cambridge: Cambridge University Press, 2006, pp. 138–139.
2 D.C. Johanson & B. Edgar, *From Lucy to Language*, New York: Simon & Schuster, 2006, p. 78; P. Mellars, *The Neanderthal Legacy: an archaeological perspective from Western Europe*, Princeton, NJ: Princeton University Press, 1996, pp. 361–362.
3 Lancy, *Anthropology* 1ed, pp. 133–136; 2ed, pp. 141–144.
4 A. Wierzbicka, 'Back to "mother"and "father": overcoming the Eurocentrism of kinship studies through eight lexical universals', *Current Anthropology* 57 (2016): 408–429.
5 R.E. Wood et al., 'A new date for the Neanderthals from El Sidrón cave (Asturias, northern Spain)', *Archaeometry* 55 (2013): 148–158.
6 C. Lalueza-Fox et al., 'Genetic evidence for patrilocal mating behavior among Neandertal groups', *Proceedings of the National Academy of Sciences* 108 (2011): 250–253.
7 H. Rougier et al., 'Neandertal cannibalism and Neandertal bones used as tools in northern Europe', *Scientific Reports* 6 (2016): 29005.
8 A. Rosas et al., 'Paleobiology and comparative morphology of a late Neandertal sample from El Sidrón, Asturias, Spain', *Proceedings of the National Academy of Sciences* 103 (2006): 19266–19271.
9 M.A. Pilloud & C.S. Larsen, '"Official" and "practical" kin: inferring social and community structure from dental phenotype at Neolithic Çatalhöyük, Turkey', *American Journal of Physical Anthropology* 145 (2011): 519–530.
10 M.R. Bennett et al., 'Early hominin foot morphology based on 1.5-million-year-old footprints from Ileret, Kenya', *Science* 323 (2009): 1197–1201.
11 K.G. Hatala et al. (2016). 'Footprints reveal direct evidence of group behavior and locomotion in *Homo erectus*', *Scientific Reports* 6 (2016): 28766.

12 N. Ashton et al. (2014) 'Hominin footprints from Early Pleistocene deposits at Happisburgh, UK', *PLoS ONE* 9 (2014), e88329.
13 B. Roveland, 'Footprints in the clay: Upper Palaeolithic children in ritual and secular contexts' in *CMC*, pp. 29–38; L. Van Gelder, 'Counting the children: the role of children in the production of finger flutings in four Upper Palaeolithic caves', *Oxford Journal of Archaeology* 34 (2015): 119–138.
14 P.J. Ucko & A. Rosenfeld, *Palaeolithic Rock Art*, London: Weidenfeld, 1967, pp. 177–178, 225.
15 P. Bahn & J. Vertut, *Journey Through the Ice Age*, London: Weidenfeld, 1997, pp. 10–11.
16 J. Clottes & R. Simonnet, 'Le réseau René Clastres de la caverne de Niaux (Ariège)', *Bulletin de la Société préhistorique française: Études et travaux* 69 (1972): 293–323.
17 Bahn & Vertut, *Journey Through the Ice Age*, pp. 10–11.
18 G. Michel-Alain, 'Ichnologie générale de la grotte Chauvet', *Bulletin de la Société préhistorique française*, 102 (2005): 103–108.
19 A. Sahly, 'Nouvelles découvertes dans la grotte de Gargas', *Bulletin de la Société Préhistorique de l'Ariège* 18 (1963): 65–74; P.G. Bahn & J. Vertut, *Images of the Ice Age*, Leister: Windward, 1988, pp. 58, 90, 103–105.
20 C. Barrière, *L'Art Pariétal de la Grotte de Gargas* (2 vols), Oxford: British Archaeological Reports, Supplementary Series 14, 1976, pp. 78–84.
21 A. Leroi-Gourhan & A.Michelson, 'The hands of Gargas: toward a general study', *October* [MIT Press] 37 (1986): 19–34.
22 S. Webb, M.L. Cupper & R. Robins, 'Pleistocene human footprints from the Willandra Lakes, Southeastern Australia', *Journal of Human Evolution* 50 (2006): 405–413.
23 C.M. Liutkus-Pierce et al., 'Radioisotopic age, formation, and preservation of Late Pleistocene human footprints at Engare Sero, Tanzania', *Palaeogeography, Palaeoclimatology, Palaeoecology* 463 (2016): 68–82.
24 M. Bea, 'Representaciones infantiles en el arte Levantino' in D.J. Vicente (ed.), *Niños en la Antigüedad: estudios sobre la infancia en Mediterráneo antiguo*, Zaragoza: Prensas de la Universidad de Zaragoza, 2012: 31–55.
25 E. Honoré et al., 'First identification of non-human stencil hands at Wadi Sūra II (Egypt): a morphometric study for new insights into rock art symbolism', *Journal of Archaeological Science: Reports* 6 (2016): 242–247.
26 www.seeker.com/5000-year-old-nativity-scene-found-2161058490.html
27 J. Parkington, 'Interpreting paintings without a commentary: meaning and motive, content and composition in the rock art of the western Cape, South Africa', *Antiquity* 63 (1989): 13–26; J. Parkington & A. Manhire, 'Processions and groups: human figures, ritual occasions and social categories in the rock paintings of the Western Cape, South Africa' in M. Conkey et al. (eds), *Beyond Art: Pleistocene image and symbol*, Memoir Series no. 23, San Francisco, CA: Californian Academy of Sciences, 1997: 306–320.
28 Site ZIM LDS5 at www.sarada.co.za
29 Site ZIM CBY1 at www.sarada.co.za
30 Site ZIM BNR3 at www.sarada.co.za
31 Parkington & Manhire, 'Processions and groups', p. 310.
32 Site ZAM MUH1 at www.sarada.co.za from Mpika district, Zambia.
33 M.R. Bennett et al., 'Exceptional preservation of children's footprints from a

Holocene footprint site in Namibia', *Journal of African Earth Sciences* 97 (2014): 331–341.
34 www.cardiff.ac.uk/news/view/615550-rare-prehistoric-footprints-redefined-as-7,000-years-old
35 V. Wade & L. Wallis, 'Style, space and social interaction', *Australian Archaeology* 72 (2011): 23–34.
36 M.J. Konner, 'Maternal care, infant behavior and development among the !Kung' in R.B. Lee & I. DeVore (eds), *Kalahari Hunter-Gatherers: studies of the !Kung San and their neighbors*, Cambridge MA: Harvard University Press, 1976: 218–245, p. 220; M. Konner, 'Hunter-gatherer infancy and childhood: the !Kung and others' in *HGC*: 19–64. The replacement by a new baby is well expressed in the individual narrative of N≠isa recorded in M. Shostak, 'A !Kung woman's memories of childhood' in Lee & DeVore (eds), *Kalahari Hunter-Gatherers*: 246–278.
37 R.B. Lee, *The !Kung San: men, women and work in a foraging society*, Cambridge: Cambridge University Press, 1979, pp. 309–310.
38 J. Woodburn, 'Stability and flexibility in Hadza residential groupings' in R.B. Lee & I. DeVore (eds), *Man the Hunter*, Chicago, IL: Aldine, 1968: 103–110, p. 108. See also N. Blurton Jones, K. Hawkes & J.F. O'Connell, 'Older Hadza men and women as helpers' in *HGC*: 214–236.
39 A. Hirasawa, 'Infant care among the sedentarized Baka hunter-gatherers in southern Cameroon' in *HGC*: 365–384, p. 370.
40 B.S. Hewlett, *Intimate Fathers: the nature and context of Aka Pygmy paternal infant care*, Ann Arbor, MI: University of Michigan Press, 1991, pp. 5, 167.
41 Hewlett, *Intimate Fathers*, p. 35.
42 Hewlett, *Intimate Fathers*, p. 168.
43 Hewlett, *Intimate Fathers*, pp. 151–168.
44 P.I. Henry, G.A. Morelli & E.Z. Tronick, 'Child caretakers among Efe foragers of the Ituri Forest' in *HGC*: 191–213.
45 A. Hamilton, *Nature and Nurture: aboriginal child-rearing in North-Central Arnhem Land*, Canberra: Australian Institute of Aboriginal Studies, 1981, especially pp. 16, 37, 99, 149, 161.
46 Hamilton, *Nature and Nurture*, p. 127.
47 T.A. Surovell, 'Early Paleoindian women, children, mobility, and fertility', *American Antiquity* 65 (2000): 493–508.
48 R.L. Kelly, *The Foraging Spectrum: diversity in hunter-gatherer lifeways*, Washington, DC: Smithsonian Institution Press, 1995, pp. 112–115, 135–139, 141.
49 T. Ingold, *The Perception of the Environment: essays in livelihood, dwelling and skill*, London: Routledge, 2000, pp. 82–83, 86. This adapts an argument Ingold first presented in 1993.
50 Konner, 'Hunter-gatherer infancy and childhood', pp. 33–34, 53.
51 R.B. Lee, 'Lactation, ovulation, infanticide and women's work: a study of hunter-gatherer population regulation' in M.N. Cohen, R.S. Malpass & H.G. Klein (eds), *Biosocial Mechanisms of Population Regulation*, New Haven, CT: Yale University Press, 1980: 321–348, p. 324; R.B. Lee, 'What hunters do for a living' in Lee & DeVore, *Man the Hunter*: 30–48, p. 35.
52 H. Montgomery, *An Introduction to Childhood: anthropological perspectives on children's lives*, Chichester: Wiley-Blackwell, 2009, p. 33.
53 E.G. Federova, 'Women's role in Mansi society' in P.P. Schweitzer, M. Biesele

& R.K. Hitchcock (eds), *Hunters and Gatherers in the Modern World: conflict, resistance and self-determination*, New York: Berghahn, 2000: 391–398, p. 395.
54 Hamilton, *Nature and Nurture*, p. 14.
55 Kelly, *The Foraging Spectrum*, pp. 154–156.
56 C.S. Whelan et al., 'Hunter-gatherer storage, settlement, and the opportunity costs of women's foraging', *American Antiquity* 78 (2013): 662–678.
57 Lancy, *Anthropology* 1ed, pp. 133–136; 2ed, pp. 141–144.
58 Lancy, *Anthropology* 1ed, pp. 118–119; 2ed, pp. 126–128. A survey of different child-carrying devices by different authors is H.C. van Hout (ed.), *Beloved Burden: baby carriers in different countries*, Amsterdam: Kit, 2005.
59 M. Parker Pearson et al., 'Beaker people in Britain: migration, mobility and diet', *Antiquity* 90 (2016): 620–637, p. 625.
60 N. Morss, 'Cradled infant figurines from Tennessee and Mexico', *American Antiquity* 18 (1952): 164–166.
61 C. Piper, 'The morphology of prehispanic cradleboards' in *CPPS*: 41–70.
62 For example, S.C. Dellinger, 'Baby cradles of the Ozark Bluff dwellers', *American Antiquity* 1 (1936): 197–214.
63 D.S. Byers & N. Morss, 'Unfired clay objects from Waterfall Ruin, Northeastern Arizona', *American Antiquity* 23 (1957): 81–83.

4
FEEDING
Weaning, eating and health

Although stone tools and, later, pottery may be the most visible finds from archaeological excavations of prehistoric sites, food waste (the remains of meals and of preparation for meals) is a highly valued part of the archaeological record. Animal bones can survive well in many protected sites such as rock shelters; piles of broken shells mark the sites of innumerable coastal campsites; careful sifting and flotation of excavated soils can produce small fish and bird bones, insect remains and seeds; and microscopic examination reveals further evidence of plants, including those collected for food or other purposes. Burials may be accompanied by food, perhaps for use in an afterlife. But whereas archaeological evidence for food in prehistory is abundant, direct evidence of food appropriate to the transitional stages of early childhood is harder to identify. Where can we find solid foods prepared for younger children? At what ages were children moving to solid food and then to share an adult diet? Most societies (but not all) recognise the need for a special diet for a child being weaned, a gradual process of transition to adult food.[1] We can assume that the cereals of agricultural societies processed as gruel or porridge offered a suitable weaning food.

When in different prehistoric societies were infants weaned? New scientific techniques are starting to answer that question. Chemical analyses of trace elements in tooth enamel serve as indicators of diet.[2] The analysis of stable isotopes in samples from teeth in archaeological contexts has been used to help reconstruct aspects of diet.[3] This is expected to contribute to future study of the dietary patterns of infants and children, although these studies are not without their challenges.[4]

In most archaeological contexts, burials of infants and young children available for study are scarce, and interpretations of diet during the period leading up to death need caution. Nevertheless, studies have contributed significantly to bioarchaeologists' discussions of changes in weaning age through prehistoric and historic periods. As discussed in Chapter 2, an earlier age of weaning can correlate with higher fertility of a woman; and when an infant is no longer dependent on its mother's milk, the mother's mobility, social and economic roles can be affected. Weaning is thus cultural as much as biological.

GREAT APES

The patterns of infant care and weaning among the great apes may help us think about our earliest hominin ancestors: Australopithecines and their successors. As noted in Chapter 2, great ape mothers continue to provide milk to their infant offspring for longer than humans do. This serves to establish intervals between births, but also emphasises a dependency which provides continuing practical protection, including protection against other members of the group. Even when infants have begun to include solid foods in their diet, the continuance of maternal milk reinforces this relationship. An early age at weaning, between 24 months and 36 months, as often seen in traditional agricultural and hunter-gatherer societies, has been interpreted as a necessary move to the nutritious food required for the early brain growth that underlay hominin cultural and social development over the past 2–3 million years.[5] Thus an early move from reliance on mother's milk to a broader nutritious diet (such as plant foods and meat from hunted animals) supported the brain development of hominins and eventually *Homo sapiens*. The evolution of hominins may have been marked by a gradual lowering of the age of weaning, alongside the extension of the period of childhood dependency.

Whereas we are omnivores, the orangutan adult diet is predominantly fruit, with an extremely wide range of edible species, though insects provide a small supplement. Infants experiment with feeding beyond milk under the careful watch of the mother, starting from the second year of life. As with other skills, young orangutans learn how to obtain food and what to eat by observation and imitation. They can be considered weaned at about the age of 4 years. But orangutans continue to supplement wild foods with mother's milk until the age of 5, 6 or even 7 years. Gibbons by contrast wean their young at about 2 years.

The gorilla adult diet is also vegetarian, dominated by fruits and selected other parts of plants, although also with a small intake of insects and caterpillars. Gorilla infants continue to feed from their mother's milk until weaned at 30–40 months or a little later, though western gorillas were seen to be weaned at an average of 4.6 years.[6] Slowly gorilla young begin to explore other vegetable foods by joining in with the social group's foraging

Chimpanzee suckling her young

(encouraged not least by the mother occasionally rebutting access to her nipples) but staying within sight of their mothers.

Bonobos (pygmy chimpanzees) end their weaning period a little later than chimpanzees, and stay close to their mothers longer.[7] As with chimpanzees, their diet is dominated by fruit but extends to insects and honey and occasionally meat. The bonobo diet is overall less varied than that of chimpanzees.

Chimpanzee diet is dominated by plant foods, especially fruits, but regularly includes insects, and a minor proportion of their food is hunted meat.[8] At Gombe it was noted that hunting mammals was a male activity, while securing insect food was mainly a female activity.[9] Though chimpanzees hunt for meat, they rarely scavenge.[10] A study of chimpanzees at Ngogo in Uganda recorded in their diet 167 identified plants, mushrooms, honey, a range of invertebrates and the meat of 10 animal species – notably monkeys.[11]

Weaning of chimpanzees begins around the age of 4 years, mainly by the mother resisting feeding, which can lead the infant to a temper tantrum, or to signs of regression such as clinging to the mother's belly in an attempt to postpone the weaning process.[12] Chimpanzee infants progress from mother's milk to chewing some of the food a mother has pre-masticated, then to trying foods other group members are eating. Mothers watch carefully over their offspring's experiments with food to avoid harmful items, just as they will watch against dangers from other experimentation in daily life.[13] It seems that chimpanzee young learn what to eat by imitation: the mothers do not formally teach them about specific foods, but the young observe the adult and test trial by copying a little. They may eat a familiar food without hesitation, but they sniff and lick a less familiar item.[14]

Young chimpanzees observed at Mahale, in Tanzania, begin to take in fruit at 1 year; a 2-year-old can handle and manipulate leaf foods, and skills gradually develop. By age 5 most plant food techniques are mastered. Confidence to catch insects is slower, though by 4 or 5 most chimpanzee infants can 'fish' with a stick for insects yet are still learning how to avoid the bites of soldier ants.[15] In an experimental situation, chimpanzees learned just before the age of 2 the use of a tool to fish for honey.[16] Other learned behaviours involving tools are discussed in Chapter 6.

A mother sharing with her offspring (when demanded by the infant, rather than initiated by the mother) is common, but the practice of food sharing is broader than this among chimpanzees in the wild, with a hunt resulting in meat being widely distributed.[17]

PREHISTORIC FORAGER WEANING AND AFTER

The close relationship of chimpanzee mothers and their offspring may be paralleled in the evolution of our early hominin ancestors. We can suggest food gathering, food sharing and guidance of the young in their own feeding strategies as a female role.

The classic popular image of Stone Age society has been dominated by the concept of man the hunter: male groups securing food for the community by organised hunts using stone tools to kill and butcher. This is an oversimplification, for several reasons. Animal bones can survive well in the archaeological record of the deep past, while plant or insect foods are far less visible and are found mainly from later sites in well protected contexts. Early excavations from which the classic images of prehistory were constructed did not have the techniques developed since the late 1960s and 1970s to retrieve the remains of small items of food such as plant seeds and insect parts. Similarly, foraging for plant foods may not have required tools, or may have used tools shaped (or, as with chimpanzees, unshaped) from organic materials which have not survived. What we see and identify are commonly the stone artefacts shaped for functions in hunting or butchery of meat, which may have formed only a modest part of the diet of Palaeolithic societies.[18]

For early hominins – Australopithecines, *Homo erectus* and perhaps even Neanderthals – meat may have come from scavenging as well as from successful hunting: eating animals that had been killed by carnivores. What was brought back to a home base by hunters, and available to children, would be a selective sample of meat, and the interpretation of the bone sample is a lively area for debate.[19] We do not know how the food eaten by children may have differed from that of the adult, except to suggest that hunters consumed some meat while on their expeditions, and brought back to the camp only what it was economic to carry. In this model, the diet of male hunters and the diet of females and children would have been somewhat different. And, needless to say, the 21st-century healthy-food fad of a supposed 'Paleo[lithic] diet' is different again.

Isotopic studies on the bones of early hominins have begun to show more of their diets and how they differed from those of the great apes.[20] While the earliest hominins had a diet similar to chimpanzees, a change is found in Australopithecines starting from 3.5 million years ago, with the apparent presence of more grasses – which would explain some of the tooth wear – and of meat from animals who had consumed grasses (although unfortunately it is hard to distinguish between these). Robust Australopithecines (*Paranthropus*) may have had a diet focused far more on plant foods than on meat.[21]

Neanderthal environments and skeletal remains suggest a diet in which protein foods from meat dominated.[22] Isotopic evidence suggests that a carnivore diet was typical of Neanderthals settled across a broad range of time and space.[23] However, one study of the nutritional value of foods challenges the image of Neanderthal pregnant women consuming a diet mainly consisting of meat. This argument claims that such a diet with minimal carbohydrates would result in protein poisoning and toxic levels of vitamin A and minerals, which would have been fatal for the unborn Neanderthal child, and even the mother.[24]

Neanderthal children needed a high calorific intake to survive in often seasonally harsh climates and may have built up a high body mass. For this they would have consumed significantly more maternal milk than modern humans but they probably began some solid foods early, perhaps below a year. Teeth wear and other studies indicate a gradual weaning process, lasting up to the age of 4 years.[25]

The teeth of the Neanderthal family found at El Sidrón cave in Spain, mentioned in Chapter 3, provided valuable information. Study of the microwear of their teeth gave indications of their diet, showing a mixture of quantities of both meat and vegetable foods. There was substantial similarity in the diets of adults and young (three adolescents, two children and an infant) but greater difference between the adult males and adult females, though this may reflect the use of their teeth in mastication. The dental calculus (tartar) on their teeth showed up non-edible materials; wear on the teeth demonstrated that all these individuals, including the children, used their teeth as a tool, like a third hand; it seems, for instance, that they had to chew bark and other plant materials in order to soften them.[26]

Those groups of anatomically modern humans who migrated from Africa before about 60,000 years ago brought with them new economic strategies with new technologies to help achieve these. Animal bone food waste has survived well at many sites, alongside the ubiquitous stone artefacts attributed to the processing of hunted (or scavenged) animals. Plant foods have been much less retrievable in the archaeological record, despite our knowledge of their importance to recent hunter-gatherer societies. We can abandon the clichéd, cartoon image of European Upper Palaeolithic families in caves chewing on mammoth bones, and envisage a range of plant and non-plant foods suitable for gentle weaning of the young, suited to their milk teeth, and allowing their gradual adaption to adult diet.

The developing use of marine food resources – fish and shellfish – had a profound impact on human society, though our evidence is only partial (rising sea levels in the Pleistocene would have drowned many locations of earlier coastal occupation).[27] First seen in the Middle Stone Age of East and Southern Africa, with evidence as early as 164,000 years ago at the South African site of Pinnacle Point, this economic change is marked by changes in mobility, and the social organisation around mobility, allowing at least seasonal settlement, which was not the norm in societies hunting terrestrial prey.[28] These dietary changes may have had positive effects on the human brain, stimulating developments which increased aspects of human cognition, as marine resources provide long-chain polyunsaturated fatty acids, which are essential for advanced brain development.[29] The value of marine foods to the modern human brain seems strong, but it is especially important during pregnancy and in the early development of an infant.[30] 'Marine molluscs ... represent one of the best and most accessible sources of brain-selective nutrients available to modern humans living along the south-western Cape coast. Diets rich in shellfish meat may have been particularly beneficial for women and children, who are the regular participants in shellfish collection among contemporary hunter-gatherers, and who have the greatest demand for brain-selective nutrients.'[31] The iodine of marine resources is especially important to pregnant and lactating women.

Finding clear evidence of children's food remains a challenge, but some evidence comes from the Czech Upper Palaeolithic site of Dolní Věstonice. The site dates from about 31,000 years ago and is an open-air settlement of shelters, hearths and pits, set close to a stream, where foragers and hunters lived a complex social life. It is famous for the sculptures found there, as well as personal ornamentation and burials associated with elaborate ritual. The food resources in the area seem to have been diverse, including plant foods from a range of open and forested landscapes. Here was found a 'mush' of finely crushed plant materials, which would be suitable to feed the very young.[32] (Some might argue that a special diet for the elderly was also a possibility, though we can assume that the very young outnumbered the very old.)

Specialist study of occupation deposits can give us some impressions of infant foods. At a late Palaeolithic site from the later Pleistocene in the now dry Wadi Kubbaniya of southern Egypt, charred faeces were considered those of infants because of their size and nature. They were analysed and found to contain soft vegetable foods, including club-rush and three kinds of camomile seeds. This suggests evidence of weaning: transitional foods for children, as the infant faeces indicated food had been ground into a fine mush on the grinding stones found at the site.[33] The presence of faeces thrown onto the fire within the campsite was considered further evidence of their infant origin, echoing what has been observed among contemporary hunter-gatherer camps. Specimens of faeces from slightly less finely ground foods were attributed to older children.

The later site of Abu Hureyra in the Euphrates valley of Syria also has charred infant faeces of ground-up food, from an Epipalaeolithic settlement of early Holocene dated 11,000 years ago, early in the gradual transition to agriculture.[34] From the same site, but from the later agricultural (Neolithic) levels, the dental wear on a child aged 4 or 5 years suggested that the child's diet was still that of ground-up mush. This contrasted with adult food, which showed significant wear on the teeth of adults, evidence of the dietary changes that marked the agricultural economy.[35]

Can we find direct evidence of when prehistoric forager children were weaned? In an isotope analysis of bones from Mesolithic sites at Hoëdic and Téviec in French Brittany, the comparison of remains of children under 4 years with young adult females from the same sites showed the children had high nitrogen values, and these were interpreted as the possible sign of continued breast-feeding.[36] These techniques, as discussed below, have been most successfully applied to child remains of later date.

In the Later Stone Age at Matjes River in South Africa, isotope analyses of bone from different periods suggested breast milk was the normal diet until the age of 18 months, and full weaning took place between the ages of 2 and 4 years.[37] The area around this site would have been able to provide suitable soft weaning foods derived from shellfish and fish. Such communities are seen as the cultural predecessors of San groups such as the !Kung, discussed below, and reflect the longer period between births in such forager groups.

FOOD PROVISION AND DIET IN MODERN SMALL-SCALE SOCIETIES

The hunter-gatherers encountered in the modern era were often living in what outsiders would consider marginal environments: the extreme cold of the Arctic or at Tierra del Fuego, the dense (though admittedly species-rich) rain forests of the Amazon or the Congo basin or the arid regions of the Kalahari. Or colonial encroachment may have forced them out of areas of the richest resources: in North America and especially in Australia. By presenting foragers in the richest and most productive environments, archaeology can provide a broader picture of prehistoric diets than do some studies of modern hunter-gatherer groups.

The ethnography of modern foraging societies indicates that the contribution of women to a family's food may exceed that of the men in tropical and temperate regions. Women may collect plant foods to feed their families, they may bring insects or small animals to the diet and may even be hunters.[38] Often the meat from successful major hunts by the men is distributed across the whole group rather than just to a successful hunter's own family. Men may also forage for plant foods, in which case their contribution is likely to be only for their own families. In a comparison of a number of forager societies, the proportion of food procured by the men ranged from 100% down to 30% or even (with Hadza) 20%. One highly influential factor is not cultural but climatic: the colder the climate, the more dependent a society is on the kind of food the men acquire (by fishing or hunting), whereas in tropical climates the collecting of plant foods may be paramount.[39] Especially in those cold regions where fishing and hunting dominate the economy, if a family has only daughters and no sons the girls may be trained to hunt.[40]

But whatever the context, past or present, mother's milk provides the first food and the first protection of the infant. Demand feeding is common in forager groups. !Kung infants in the Kalahari region are said to be fed 'more or less continuously', but weaning may be sudden on the arrival of a new sibling, or once the mother knows she is pregnant.[41]

Weaning ages vary in different cultures and influences the period between births. Many forager mothers breast-feed until the infant is between 2 and 3 years old, and in some groups like the !Kung infants may breast-feed to even older ages.[42] This is later than in small-scale farming groups, who typically may wean their children at or soon after the age of 2 years and have children at intervals of 2 to 3 years. It contrasts further with industrialised societies, and in modern western urban life breast-feeding as a whole has been on the decline.[43]

And of course, as discussed in Chapter 3, if children dependent on their mother's milk they will accompany her on foraging trips unless another woman can serve as a wet nurse. The conflict between raising young children and acquiring food is a real one which different societies tackle in different ways.[44] Agta women in the Philippines are willing to leave their children with others and join the hunt, but generally the demands of a carrying and breast-feeding a young child control how much and how far a woman may forage for food. Older women, including grandmothers, may help the mother, either by foraging to provide their food (as with Hadza) or by minding their children (as among the !Kung). Such a pattern would seem to favour matrilocal societies, where the mother's mother is on hand.

After a new sibling is born, a young child may be required to take greater initiative in securing his or her own food. Studies of small-scale societies – farmers as well as foragers – emphasise the young age at which children can be expected to play a part in economic life.[45] Martu children of Australia's Western Desert are active in foraging and hunting, and groups of both sexes can locate and kill goannas and other lizards, maybe even cooking and eating them before the adults return to camp.[46] Alaskan children may collect their own shellfish to eat; children from the Tasaday foraging group of the Philippines can collect up to two-thirds of their own daily diet. By the age of 12, children in some forager groups, like the Tiwi of Australia or the Cree of North America, were traditionally close to self-sufficient in food. By complementing their mother's activities in providing food for her family, they may also be contributing to her ability to produce more children.[47]

Children's participation in the economic life of a community is, of course, influenced by the mix between different food sources, and the contrast between predominantly hunting, gathering and fishing groups. If a major source of food is fish or shellfish from near to a camp, young children can be involved. From an early age they will accompany their mothers in plant-collecting forays. But if hunting expeditions involve the absence of the males for many days at a time to secure meat from distant locations, the children may become involved only as adolescents; indeed, hunting may be a marker of the transition from childhood to adulthood.

The !Kung of Southern Africa have been noted as a group where the young contribute little to economic activity. Children tended not to accompany their mother in food gathering until aged around 14 years, and boys may be 16 before they participate in the men's hunt.[48] 'Children do amazingly little work.'[49] Several explanations exist: one is that in the arid area where !Kung hunt and gather food, foraging requires long distances and children could easily get lost. An exception is where a particular group comprises few adults and many children, so the children's help in food gathering is essential.

By contrast, in the Yora group from the Amazon basin of Peru, economic activities in the subsistence economy occupied 39% of children's time, a similar proportion to that given to leisure.[50] And Hadza children in East Africa forage widely and independently.[51] They can provide half their daily food needs by themselves, whether accompanying their mothers or in independent groups of children with no adults present, and this may include both plant gathering and hunting small game or birds. The richness of the forest ecology, however, means that such expeditions need not be far from the home camp (unlike the arid situation of the !Kung) and this location allows greater independence. Such a pattern correlates with earlier weaning for the Hadza children, who grow up more independent and with less maternal supervision.

Anthropologist David Lancy has noted the contribution children – often young children, and girls more than boys – can make to food gathering in small-scale societies, among foraging groups, but also with herders and crop farmers.[52] The family is an economic unit, and all members are likely to play a part in the household economy as soon as they are able, whether that involves guarding livestock or fields, weeding or helping to plant or harvest, or practical activities at the homestead which free up adult members for economic work.[53] Of these tasks, herding may be among the most common.[54]

Small farming communities demonstrate a wide variety of practices in weaning age and the migration to an adult diet. Some may make the transition a quick one, with adult food provided to a young child despite its apparent unsuitability; others make careful preparation of easily digested food. In many groups the best food is reserved for the adults, and specifically the older males, so that children will take many years before they achieve a full adult diet.[55]

An established view was that mothers in agricultural societies achieved greater levels of fertility than foragers because they weaned their babies earlier; and that this early weaning was stimulated by the availability of milk and milk products from domestic animals together with suitable starchy foods from domesticated crops. This assumption has been challenged in a compilation of data from over 100 different societies, which suggests the later weaning of foragers cannot be attributed to these specific domestic foodstuffs.[56] In that study, crop farmers on average stopped breast-feeding at 21 months, pastoralists at 24 months and foragers at 27 months. Animal farmers introduced solids and liquids to an infant diet earlier than either other category. While comparisons of prehistoric and modern small-scale societies can be valuable, they must also be used with caution.

WEANING AND FOOD PREPARATION IN AGRICULTURAL GROUPS

Careful sifting and flotation of the soil excavated from the settlements of prehistoric agriculturalists have shown us much more of the total diet of these groups. Seeds, plant fragments and insect parts complement the more readily visible animal bones and shellfish. Distinguishing any special diets of children remains more of a challenge. But dietary evidence shows up in the analysis of skeletal remains, as do signs of malnutrition and of childhood diseases, which can be linked to the diets of pregnant and nursing mothers, infants and young children.

Evidence for the age at weaning (i.e. the starting of an infant on solid foods) can be obtained from analysis of the stable isotopes (especially but not exclusively nitrogen) of the bone collagen of infant skeletons, a technique whose early applications were in the north-eastern USA and on Maya remains from Mesoamerica.[57] Isotope ratios are indicative of diet. If we can reliably estimate the age at death of the individuals being studied, then we can judge whether they have reached or passed the stage of weaning. These studies are done on the remains of individuals of all ages: foetuses and nursing infants reflect the diet of their mothers, and changes visible in young children indicate the stage of weaning or the transition to solid foods. We should remember that we are studying the skeletons of those children who did not survive into adulthood, for causes which can include malnutrition alongside disease or injury.

Such a study of infants in the earlier Basketmaker cultures of Arizona and adjacent areas of the US Southwest, dated to the late 1st millennium BC, showed stages of infant weaning: infants appear to have had mother's milk supplemented by maize meal, and a total reliance on solid foods was interpreted as a possible contributor to the early deaths of some infants.[58]

A detailed study of bone and teeth samples from burials of different periods from California demonstrated the changes in diet across the life cycle as well as through time.[59] Immediately after weaning, children had a diet similar to that of adults. However, between the ages of five and nine they then progressed to a diet specific to themselves. The sample was small: six individuals, of whom four were dated to the 1st millennium AD; the other two were more recent. This result suggested that as young children they were determining their own food and perhaps even doing so by some of their own foraging, selecting food that required minimal processing.

Stable-isotope data from dental tissue of Late Woodland burials at a site in Ontario, Canada, suggested an unusually early weaning and transfer to solid diet, in this case dominated by maize.[60] This showed that an infant diet of foods derived from maize was similar to that of older children, up to 12 years of age, or even of adults. The economy of the community was based on maize cultivation and on foraging and fishing; early weaning may have made it easier for women to contribute to this strategy of harvesting diverse foods.

Moving to Old World studies, comparison of children from Mesolithic and Neolithic periods in Serbia's Danube Gorges suggested that children were breast-fed for shorter periods after the arrival of the agricultural Neolithic.[61] The latter saw a shift from protein (especially fish) to carbohydrates (derived from cereals) in the diet. Apart from negative health impacts from earlier weaning, this pattern would have allowed greater fertility – a possible explanation for population growth in agricultural societies compared with their forager predecessors. Neolithic children had much the same stature as modern children in the region but a lower body weight for their age.[62] What appear to be spoons carrying teeth marks have been found in the Neolithic of the Balkans, which suggested their use in feeding solid foods during weaning. Dental caries found on the teeth of infants at several sites indicated the use of a weaning food of porridge made from ground cereals (probably mixed with milk).[63]

At Neolithic sites in Turkey the weaning process was seen at the age of 1 year at Aşıklı Höyük but at Çayönü Tepesi at the age of 2 years and even later (2 to 3½ years) at another nearby site.[64] Here, the earlier weaning seems to have had a positive rather than negative impact on infant survival rates.

Evidence from the Neolithic in Poland shows gradual introduction of food between 6 months and 3 years. At Belgian sites in the Meuse Basin, only slight changes in weaning patterns were traced over time.[65] Mesolithic foragers and early Neolithic farmers both weaned their children by about 2 years.

Studies of remains from the Neolithic Linearbandkeramik of Europe suggested that young men who bore a special status symbolised by grave goods of polished stone adzes had received different diets in childhood. Overall, while diets appear to have been the same in infancy for males and females, with weaning probably around the late age of 3 years, there was a difference in diet for older children, with girls having a more plant-based diet than males.[66] Poorer health in females than males may reflect sustained differences in diet which began in childhood.

Evidence from several Bronze Age sites in Europe suggests solid foods were introduced from 4–6 months and weaning was completed by 3 years. An unexpected result came from skeletal remains from Wetwang Slack British Iron Age site in Yorkshire, with solid foods (or possibly milk from

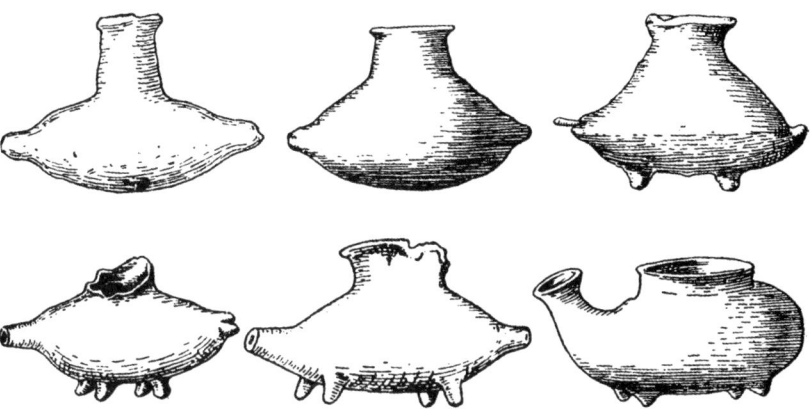

Pottery vessels interpreted as infant feeding bottles, from the Late Bronze Age and Iron Age of France, Germany and Austria

domestic animals) appearing to have been fed to the infants before 1 year of age, and with foodstuffs similar to those of adults at 2½ years.[67]

Another Iron Age study, on the Swedish island of Öland, showed a variety of weaning times and infants' diets of solid foods, with the analysts even suggesting there were some infants who seem not to have been breast-fed at all.[68] Was this a social pattern or specific to the individuals whose remains were found?

If prehistoric agriculturalists were weaning their children at an earlier age than forager women, this may reflect both positive and negative factors. The nature of physical work in the fields undertaken by women in agricultural societies makes transporting breast-feeding infants challenging. A woman foraging for plant or insect foods can carry a child on her back and rest him or her while harvesting the foodstuffs once she is at a suitable location. But farming can require continuous work in the fields and lengthy processing of crops for food in the homestead, which can be inhibited by a carried infant. However, farming also increases the predictability and control of foodstuffs, so that food suitable for young children can be safely selected, processed and fed to the child.

Direct evidence of food or of feeding practices specific to children in prehistoric agricultural societies can occasionally be identified. The soft-food diet of a 4- or 5-year-old at Abu Hureyra in Syria in the period of transition from foraging to incipient agriculture was noted above. Later in the Middle East, examination of bodies from a predynastic cemetery at Hierakonpolis in Egypt, from the mid-4th millennium BC, showed the difference between adult and child diets.[69] The adults ate a coarse food in which grain husks remained. But for two children (aged under 5 and 10) the wheat had been cleaned of its husks and ground into a fine flour before being made into a food.

Since the human body decays in most archaeological contexts, the chances of finding direct evidence of whatever constituted a last meal is limited. An unusual find of a 9-year-old boy's body in Salts Cave, Kentucky, USA, preserved by desiccation, was dated to the Woodland agricultural period at the beginning of the 1st millennium AD. Faecal material was still present in the child's lower intestine and colon and showed evidence of food, including hickory nuts, marsh elder (a type of sunflower) and grubs.[70]

Pottery vessels at widely different locations have been interpreted as feeding bottles for infants: from Neolithic France, Iron Age Germany and Neolithic Sudan.[71] The common element to these claims would seem to be a drinking channel for children too young to manage a cup or beaker.

Isotope analysis of skeletal remains can make an interesting contribution to the question of mobility, helping to trace long-distance movement at different stages of life, because a childhood diet shows up in adult teeth. Studies of Bronze Age burials near Stonehenge in England, dated to 2500–2000 BC, have shown that the individuals had left a distant area (Wales, Scotland, or even further) in their early adolescence before moving later in life to the Stonehenge area.[72] A wider study of Bronze Age Beaker burials suggested such mobility within Great Britain was not uncommon and continued over several centuries.[73] Childhood diet tells us not just about weaning, food and health but about migration too.

DIET AND HEALTH

Childhood diet and childhood health are tightly interwoven, and can be traced not only in the bones from children's burials but in those of adults too. Adult bones as well as teeth can bear indications of stress events in childhood: periods of illness or periods of poor nutrition. Comparative studies of human remains can demonstrate social rather than just individual changes – periods of conflict or famine, and periods of social and economic transformation.

Before the development of sophisticated newer techniques of analysis, the examination of bones was able to indicate the incidence of poor health and how the transition from a forager to a predominantly agricultural economy affected children's health and life expectancy. There are many examples to show a negative impact of this change.

A comparison of the skulls of children's burials at hunter-gatherer and maize agricultural sites in the US Southwest showed that 76.5% of children at a maize-dependent site had signs of the condition of porotic hyperostosis – a feature of the cranium which results from anaemia, commonly reflecting iron deficiency in the diet, as dependency on maize would provide.[74]

Skeletal material (from almost 10,000 individuals) from a broad range of mainly agricultural prehistoric sites in the US Southwest gives useful information on the effects of diet on children's health.[75] This confirms a common decline in health with the transition from a foraging to a mainly agricultural economy, but an improvement thereafter. The child mortality rate was high, at 42%, and this figure will not even account for any infants whose bodies did not receive a formal and retrievable burial, or are absent from the archaeological record because of their fragility. While rising with the beginning of agriculture, child mortality rates appear to fall to 35% from around 1300 AD, when the Anasazi (ancestral Puebloans) experienced social upheavals. No trend was noticed in adult height (which would be influenced by childhood diet) but the porotic hyperostosis was confirmed as related to dependence on maize rather than on mixed food sources. Other diseases of childhood appear common after the arrival of agriculture, but we can also consider that farming communities contain larger, denser and far less mobile populations than forager groups, and that infections can spread much more easily.

Later studies in the agricultural Anasazi culture of Black Mesa, Arizona, dated between 900 and 1150 AD, indicated the effects of poor diet and a poor economy on nursing mothers and their infants. Alongside maize and other cultivated plants, wild plant foods were an important but unreliable part of the diet.[76] The skeletal remains of 80 children showed frequent and high impacts of chronic anaemia and infections but with the youngest most affected, suggesting that dietary limitations on the mothers impacted their infants before they were even weaned, and in many cases caused early death.

Poor childhood health was seen in burials at the Arizona site of Grasshopper Pueblo, dated to 1300–1400 AD.[77] This was a substantial community with 500 rooms within which burials took place. The juvenile proportion of recovered burials was very high, at 66% (26% foetuses or infants), which suggests that many adults could have been buried elsewhere. Unlike at the other sites, the prevalence of porotic hyperostosis was not high but the condition was most visible in children aged 12–18 months, suggesting nutritional issues during the weaning phase. Other indicators on the bones indicated the effects of mothers' poor diet during pregnancy.

In the US Woodland cultures of Illinois, the introduction of maize as a major food crop resulted initially in a worsening of health, but in time the pattern improved.[78] At the site of Dickson Mounds in Illinois, changes from a largely foraging economy to an agricultural one dominated by maize cultivation and diet, between 950 and 1350 AD, showed a deterioration of health across this change.[79] Iron deficiency grew fourfold in the population. The children with the worst signs of stress were between 2 and 5 years of age, after the time of weaning, and the effect of these early challenges was to lower the age of death as adults. Control of economic resources implied by the move to a farming economy led to a reduction in health and affected longevity.

In the US state of Georgia, where foraging was replaced by agriculture around 1150 AD, the new maize-based culture resulted in reduced stature and bone strength and increased dental caries and signs of bone stress, with a greater negative impact on females than males. A younger age at death was a marked change between forager and agricultural communities: children under 16 were 26% of burials in the forager group but 38% among the early agriculturalists. Reaching maturity did not change the pattern: 58% of forager burials were of individuals aged under 25 years, compared with 78% for the early agriculturalists (if we assume no selectivity was at play in burial practices).[80] Although a widely attested pattern, this was not universally the situation, with some case studies actually showing improved health of children and improved life expectance with the introduction of agriculture.[81]

In contrast to the image of poor childhood health in much of the region, finds from a village site dated to the 13th century AD (with 20 children out of 30 burials) at Sand Canyon Pueblo in Colorado, USA, showed better health and nutrition – though, as noted in Chapter 8, some had met a violent end.[82] Their health would suggest they and the site may have represented an elite situation.

In prehistoric agricultural communities of the US Midwest – Woodland and Mississippian cultures – despite initial responses to maize introduction, there was no increase over time in juvenile mortality, so that increases in fertility meant increased populations and population pressure.[83] One reason for increasing fertility may lie in the use and availability of a maize-based gruel suitable for early weaning.

A study of nearly 1500 skeletons from pre-Columbian Peru suggested that the main cause of juvenile anaemia was illness rather than diet.[84]

In the Old World, a number of sites have shown evidence of scurvy – caused by a deficiency in ascorbic acid (vitamin C). The incidence of scurvy was estimated to be almost 14% among European Bronze Age infants; the same research identified endocranial lesions in up to 22% of the remains of Bronze Age children, for which meningitis is one possible cause.[85]

Dental studies show us some interesting images from the end of prehistory: in this case, as Iron Age Britain became part of the Roman Empire.[86] Examination of the teeth of children of all ages (from young infants to late adolescents) showed a dramatic change in weaning practices and in the diet given to the young during the weaning process, following the cultural impacts of occupation. Just as with the impact of western colonialism on African and Asian societies, Romanisation seems to have 'educated' local

Britons into new aspects of child rearing, but often with negative results. Dental health improved but the incidence of scurvy and rickets increased, perhaps through a change from a traditional diet to one influenced by the new Romanised economy.

CONCLUSIONS

The further application of newer scientific methodologies to human remains will allow a much fuller picture to emerge of the ages and stages of human weaning: the transition from a diet provided entirely from mother's milk to a mixed diet of prepared food, and then to an adult diet. The introduction of solid food is culturally rather than just biologically determined. The mother who no longer has a child at the breast has a new mobility; the child who is admitted to an adult meal has a new status; and the child who now contributes to the family or group diet is advancing towards adulthood. The food a child is allowed to eat relates to the individual's social position as well as cultural norms in the particular society.

Alongside the biological studies we need to discuss and find more evidence of food preparation for the young. Preservation of a ground or mushed food is rare but informative; identification of the remains of food that had been in a form suitable for weaning is a challenge but not impossible. Signs of pounding and grinding may apply to other than infant foods; while pre-mastication to feed an infant may be invisible, food remains in cooking vessels can be preserved and identified. Only in a body fully preserved – in a bog, in a frozen glacier or in a desiccated condition – can we expect to find food in the digestive system, but such evidence will be invaluable for seeing when and whether a child has moved to an adult food.

Linking maternal health, weaning and childhood diet to childhood health (and lack of health) is a field of growing importance. We can anticipate that further application of isotope studies of excavated skeletal material, and the development of new techniques of analysis, will unfold a fuller picture of the changing diets of the young in a wide range of prehistoric communities, and the impact of changing diets on patterns of infant and child health and mortality through time and place.

NOTES

1   Lancy, *Anthropology* 2ed, pp. 107–108.
2   L.T. Humphrey et al., 'Unlocking evidence of early diet from tooth enamel', *Proceedings of the National Academy of Sciences* 105 (2008): 6834–6839; T. Tsutaya & M. Yoneda, 'Reconstruction of breastfeeding and weaning practices using

stable isotope and trace element analyses: a review', *Yearbook of Physical Anthropology* 156 (2015): 2–21.

3 See for instance P.A. Sandberg et al., 'Intra-tooth stable isotope analysis of dentine: a step toward addressing selective mortality in the reconstruction of life history in the archaeological record', *American Journal of Physical Anthropology* 155 (2014): 281–293.

4 L.M. Reynard & N. Tuross, 'The known, the unknown and the unknowable: weaning times from archaeological bones using nitrogen isotope ratios', *Journal of Archaeological Science* 53 (2015): 618–625.

5 Thoughtfully argued in G.E. Kennedy, 'From the ape's dilemma to the weanling's dilemma: early weaning and its evolutionary context', *Journal of Human Evolution* 48 (2005): 123–145.

6 A. Fletcher, 'Development of infant independence from the mother in wild mountain gorillas' in M. Robbins, P. Sicotte & K.J. Stewart (eds), *Mountain Gorillas: three decades of research at Karisoke*, Cambridge: Cambridge University Press, 2001: 153–182; A.A. Nowell & A.W. Fletcher, 'Development of independence from the mother in *Gorilla gorilla gorilla*', *International Journal of Primatology* 28 (2007): 441–455.

7 M de Lathouwers & L. van Elsacker, 'Comparing infant and juvenile behavior in bonobos (*Pan paniscus*) and chimpanzees (*Pan troglodytes*): a preliminary study', *Primates* 47 (2006): 287–293.

8 The anomaly of alcohol in wild chimpanzee diet was noted in 2015: K.J. Hockings et al., 'Tools to tipple: ethanol ingestion by wild chimpanzees using leaf-sponges', *Royal Society Open Science* 2 (2015): 150150.

9 W.C. McGrew, 'Evolutionary implications of sex differences in chimpanzee predation and tool use' in D.A. Hamburg & E.R. McCown (eds), *The Great Apes*, Menlo Park, CA: Benjamin/Cummings, 1979: 441–463.

10 D.P. Watts, 'Scavenging by chimpanzees at Ngogo and the relevance of chimpanzee scavenging to early hominin behavioral ecology', *Journal of Human Evolution* 54 (2008): 125–133.

11 D.P. Watts et al., 'Diet of chimpanzees (*Pan troglodytes schweinfurthii*) at Ngogo, Kibale National Park, Uganda, 1. Diet composition and diversity', *American Journal of Primatology* 74 (2012): 114–129.

12 T. Nishida, *Chimpanzees of the Lakeside: natural history and culture at Mahale*, Cambridge: Cambridge University Press, 2012, pp. 98–101, 104.

13 J. Goodall, *The Chimpanzees of Gombe: pattern of behavior*, Cambridge, MA: Harvard University Press, 1986, pp. 265–266.

14 A. Ueno, 'Food sharing and referencing behavior in chimpanzee mother and infant' in T. Matsuzawa, M. Tomonaga & M. Tanaka (eds), *Cognitive Development in Chimpanzees*, Tokyo: Springer, 2006: 172–181.

15 Nishida, *Chimpanzees of the Lakeside*, pp. 92–93.

16 Matsuzawa et al. (eds), *Cognitive Development*, pp. 201–213.

17 W.C. McGrew, *Chimpanzee Material Culture: implications for human evolution*, Cambridge: Cambridge University Press, 1992, pp. 106–113.

18 K. Hardy et al., 'The importance of dietary carbohydrate in human evolution', *Quarterly Review of Biology* 90 (2015): 251–268.

19 P. Mellars, *The Neanderthal Legacy: an archaeological perspective from Western Europe*, Princeton, NJ: Princeton University Press, 1996, pp. 220–227.

20 M. Sponheimer et al., 'Isotopic evidence of early hominin diets', *Proceedings*

of the National Academy of Sciences 110 (2013): 10513–10518; M. Sponheimer, 'Some ruminations on Australopith diets' in K. Reed, J.E Fleagle & R.E.Leakey (eds), *The Paleobiology of Australopithecus*, Dordrecht: Springer, 2013: 225–233.

21 L.M. Martínez et al., 'Testing dietary hypotheses of East African hominines using buccal dental microwear data', *PLoS ONE* 11 (2016): e0165447; phys.org/news/2016-11-tooth-patterns-paranthropus-early-hominins.html#jCp

22 M. Ben-Dor, A. Gopher & R. Barkai, 'Neandertals' large lower thorax may represent adaptation to high protein diet', *American Journal of Physical Anthropology* 160 (2016): 367–378.

23 M.O. Richards & E. Trinkaus, 'Isotopic evidence for the diets of European Neanderthals and early modern humans', *Proceedings of the National Academy of Sciences* 106 (2009): 16034–16039.

24 B. Hockett, 'The consequences of Middle Paleolithic diets on pregnant Neanderthal women', *Quaternary International* 264 (2012): 78–82.

25 S.E. Churchill, *Thin on the Ground: Neandertal biology, archeology and ecology*, Hoboken, NJ: Wiley Blackwell, 2014, pp. 94–97, 344.

26 A, Estalrrich, S. El Zataari & A. Rosas, 'Dietary reconstruction of the El Sidrón Neandertal familial group (Spain) in the context of other Neandertal and modern hunter-gatherer groups. A molar microwear texture analysis', *Journal of Human Evolution* 104 (2017): 13–22; A. Radini et al., 'Neanderthals, trees and dental calculus: new evidence from El Sidrón', *Antiquity* 90 (2016): 290–301.

27 See for instance G.H.J. Langejans et al., 'Middle Stone Age shellfish exploitation: potential indications for mass collecting and resource intensification at Blombos Cave and Klasies River, South Africa', *Quaternary International* 270 (2012): 80–94.

28 C.W. Marean et al., 'Early human use of marine resources and pigment in South Africa during the Middle Pleistocene', *Nature* 449, no. 7164 (2007): 905–908.

29 A special issue of the *Journal of Human Evolution*, vol. 77 (2014), addressed many aspects of this question. See especially C.W. Marean, 'The origins and significance of coastal resource use in Africa and Western Eurasia', pp. 17–40. The significance of a transition to an aquatic diet has, though, been challenged by nutritionists: J.H. Langdon, 'Has an aquatic diet been necessary for hominin brain evolution and functional development?', *British Journal of Nutrition* 96 (2006): 7–17.

30 K. Kyriacou et al., 'Marine and terrestrial foods as a source of brain-selective nutrients for early modern humans in the southwestern Cape, South Africa', *Journal of Human Evolution*, 97 (2016): 86–96.

31 Kyriacou et al., 'Marine and terrestrial foods', p. 94.

32 S.L.R. Mason, J.G. Hather & G.C. Hillman, 'Preliminary investigation of the plant macro-remains from Dolní Věstonice II, and its implications for the role of plant foods in Palaeolithic and Mesolithic Europe', *Antiquity* 68 (1994): 48–57, pp. 53–54.

33 G.C. Hillman, 'Late Palaeolithic plant foods from Wadi Kubbaniya in Upper Egypt: dietary diversity, infant weaning, and seasonality in a riverine environment' in D.R. Harris & G.C. Hillman (eds), *Foraging and Farming: the evolution of plant exploitation*, London: Unwin & Hyman, 1989: 207–239.

34 G.C. Hillman, S.M. Colledge & D.R. Harris, 'Plant-food economy during the Epipalaeolithic period at Tell Abu Hureyra, Syria: dietary diversity, seasonality, and modes of exploitation' in Harris & Hillman (eds), *Foraging and Farming*: 240–268.

35 T. Molleson & K. Jones, 'Dental evidence for dietary change at Abu Hureyra', *Journal of Archaeological Science* 18 (1991): 525–539, p. 532.
36 R.J. Schulting & M.P. Richards. 'Dating women and becoming farmers: new palaeodietary and AMS dating evidence from the Breton Mesolithic cemeteries of Téviec and Hoëdic', *Journal of Anthropological Archaeology* 20 (2001): 314–344; M.C. Lillie, 'Suffer the children: "visualising" children in the archaeological record' in *BRIPP*: 33–43, p. 35.
37 F. Clayton, J. Sealy & S. Pfeiffer, 'Weaning age among foragers at Matjes River Rock Shelter, South Africa, from stable nitrogen and carbon isotope analyses', *American Journal of Physical Anthropology* 129 (2006): 311–317.
38 K.L. Endicott, 'Gender relations in hunter-gatherer societies' in R.B. Lee & R.H. Daly (eds), *The Cambridge Encyclopedia of Hunters and Gatherers*, Cambridge: Cambridge University Press, 1999: 411–418.
39 R.L. Kelly, *The Foraging Spectrum: diversity in hunter-gatherer lifeways*, Washington, DC: Smithsonian Institution Press, 1995, pp. 262–266; R.B. Lee, 'What hunters do for a living' in R.B. Lee & I. DeVore (eds), *Man the Hunter*, Chicago, IL: Aldine, 1968: 30–48, p. 43.
40 Endicott, 'Gender relations', p. 413.
41 M. Shostak, 'A !Kung woman's memories of childhood' in R.B. Lee & I. DeVore (eds), *Kalahari Hunter-Gatherers: studies of the !Kung San and their neighbors*, Cambridge, MA: Harvard University Press, 1976: 246–278.
42 Kelly, *The Foraging Spectrum*, pp. 246–249; M. Konner, 'Hunter-gatherer infancy and childhood: the !Kung and others' in *HGC*: 19–64, p. 58.
43 Konner, 'Hunter-gatherer infancy and childhood', pp. 35–36.
44 Kelly, *The Foraging Spectrum*, pp. 268–269.
45 A.C. Zeller, 'A role for children in hominid evolution', *Man* 22 (1987): 528–557, pp. 541–548.
46 D.W. Bird & R. Bliege Bird, 'Martu children's hunting strategies in the Western Desert, Australia' in *HGC*: 129–146, pp. 135–136.
47 Zeller, 'A role for children', p. 553.
48 P. Draper, 'Social and economic constraints on child life among the !Kung' in Lee & DeVore (eds), *Kalahari Hunter-Gatherers*: 201–217, p. 201.
49 Draper, 'Social and economic constraints', p. 213; N. Blurton-Jones, K. Hawkes & P. Draper, 'Difference between Hadza and !Kung children's work: original affluence of practical reason?' in E.S. Burch & L.J. Ellanna (eds), *Key Issues in Hunter-Gather Research*, Oxford: Berg, 1994: 189–215.
50 L.S. Sugiyama & R. Chacon, 'Juvenile responses to household ecology among the Yora of Peruvian Amazonia' in *HGC*: 237–261.
51 Blurton-Jones et al., 'Difference between Hadza and !Kung children's work', pp. 194–195.
52 D.F. Lancy, 'Children as a reserve labor force', *Current Anthropology* 56 (2015): 545–568: pp. 546–547.
53 Zeller, 'A role for children', p. 543.
54 Lancy, *Anthropology* 2ed, pp. 267–269.
55 Lancy, *Anthropology* 2ed, pp. 105–108.
56 D.W. Sellen & D.B. Smay, 'Relationship between subsistence and age at weaning in "preindustrial" societies', *Human Nature* 12 (2001): 47–87.
57 M.R. Schurr, 'Stable nitrogen isotopes as evidence for the age of weaning at the Angel site: a comparison of isotopic and demographic measures of weaning

age', *Journal of Archaeological Science* 24 (1997): 919–927; L.E. Wright & H.P. Schwarcz, 'Stable carbon and oxygen isotopes in human tooth enamel: identifying breastfeeding and weaning in prehistory', *American Journal of Physical Anthropology* 106 (1998): 1–18; M. Jay, 'Breastfeeding and weaning behaviour in archaeological populations: evidence from the isotopic analysis of skeletal materials', *CitP* 2 (2009): 163–178; F. Fulminante, 'Infant feeding practices in Europe and the Mediterranean from Prehistory to the Middle Ages: a comparison between the historical and bioarchaeology', *CitP* 8 (2015): 24–47; S.Mays et al., 'Child bioarchaeology: perspectives on the past 10 Years', *CitP* 10 (2017): 38–56, pp. 6–8.

58 J.C. Coltrain, J.C. Janetski & S.W. Carlyle, 'The stable-and radio-isotope chemistry of western Basketmaker burials: implications for early Puebloan diets and origins', *American Antiquity* 72 (2007): 301–321, p. 312.

59 A.M. Greenwald et al., 'Stable isotope evidence of juvenile foraging in prehistoric Central California', *Journal of Archaeological Science: Reports* 7 (2016): 146–154.

60 C.M. Watts, C.D. White & F.J. Longstaffe, 'Childhood diet and Western Basin tradition foodways at the Krieger site, southwestern Ontario, Canada', *American Antiquity* 76 (2011): 446–472.

61 J. Jovanović et al., 'Diet and health status of children at the Mesolithic Neolithic transition in the Danube Gorges', *Archaica* 3 (2015): 64–65 [English summary].

62 J. Jovanović et al., 'Children feeding practices and growth patterns during the Mesolithic–Neolithic transition in the Danube Gorges', paper at the World Archaeological Congress, 2016.

63 Sofija Stefanović, personal communication; S. Stefanović et al., 'New weaning food for prehistoric babies and origin of caries', paper at the 20th Congress of the European Anthropological Association, 2016.

64 J.A. Pearson et al., 'Exploring the relationship between weaning and infant mortality: an isotope case study from Aşıklı Höyük and Çayönü Tepesi', *American Journal of Physical Anthropology* 143 (2010): 448–457.

65 H. Bocherens, C. Polet & M. Toussaint, 'Palaeodiet of Mesolithic and Neolithic populations of Meuse Basin (Belgium): evidence from stable isotopes', *Journal of Archaeological Science* 34 (2007): 10–27, p. 20.

66 P. Bickle & L. Fibiger, 'Ageing, childhood and social identity in the Early Neolithic of Central Europe', *European Journal of Archaeology* 17 (2014): 208–228, pp. 209, 218.

67 M. Jay et al., 'Iron Age breastfeeding practices in Britain: isotopic evidence from Wetwang Slack, East Yorkshire', *American Journal of Physical Anthropology* 136 (2008): 327–337.

68 R. Howcroft, G. Eriksson & K. Lidén, 'Conformity in diversity? Isotopic investigations of infant feeding practices in two Iron Age populations from southern Öland, Sweden', *American Journal of Physical Anthropology* 149 (2012): 217–230.

69 A. Gamal-el-Din Fahmy, 'Plant remains in gut contents of Ancient Egyptian predynastic mummies (3750–3300 BC)', *Online Journal of Biological Sciences* 1 (2001): 772–774.

70 L.M. Robbins, 'A Woodland "mummy" from Salts Cave, Kentucky', *American Antiquity* 36 (1971): 200–206.

71 A.D. Lacaille, 'Infant feeding-bottles in prehistoric times', *Proceedings of the Royal Society of Medicine* 43 (1950): 565–568.

72 J.A. Evans, C.A. Chenery & A.P. Fitzpatrick, 'Bronze Age childhood migration of individuals near Stonehenge, revealed by strontium and oxygen isotope tooth enamel analysis', *Archaeometry* 48 (2006): 309–321.
73 M. Parker Pearson et al., 'Beaker people in Britain: migration, mobility and diet', *Antiquity* 90 (2016): 620–637.
74 A. Palkovich, 'Agriculture, marginal environments, and nutritional stress in the prehistoric Southwest' in Cohen & Armelagos, *Paleopathology*: 425–438, p. 429.
75 K.D. Sobolik, 'Children's health in the prehistoric Southwest' in *CPPS*: 125–151.
76 D.L. Martin, J.L. Thompson & J.J. Crandall, 'Children of the working class: environmental marginality and child health at Black Mesa, Arizona' in *TCBI*: 198–216.
77 S.M. Whittlesey, 'The cradle of death: mortuary practices, bioarchaeology, and the children of Grasshopper Pueblo' in *CPPS*: 152–168.
78 D.C. Cook, 'Subsistence and health in the Lower Illinois Valley: osteological evidence' in Cohen & Armelagos, *Paleopathology*: 235–269, p. 261.
79 A.H. Goodman & G.J. Armelagos, 'Infant and childhood morbidity and mortality risks in archaeological populations', *World Archaeology* 21 (1989): 225–243.
80 C.S. Larsen, 'Health and disease in prehistoric Georgia: the transition to agriculture' in Cohen & Armelagos, *Paleopathology*: 367–392, p. 369.
81 M.N. Cohen & G.J. Armelagos (eds), *Paleopathology at the Origins of Agriculture*, Orlando, FL: Academic Press, 1984, p. 592.
82 C.S. Bradley, 'Thoughts count: ideology and the children of Sand Canyon Pueblo' in *CPPS*: 169–195, pp. 172–183.
83 J.E. Buikstra, L.W. Konigsberg & J. Bullington, 'Fertility and the development of agriculture in the Prehistoric Midwest', *American Antiquity* 51 (1986): 528–546, pp. 536–538.
84 D.E. Blom et al., 'Anemia and childhood mortality: latitudinal patterning along the coast of pre-Columbian Peru', *American Journal of Physical Anthropology* 127 (2005): 152–169.
85 G.J. Armelagos et al., 'Analysis of nutritional disease in prehistory: the search for scurvy in antiquity and today', *International Journal of Paleopathology* 5 (2014): 9–17.
86 R.C. Redfern, A.R. Millard & C. Hamlin, 'A regional investigation of subadult dietary patterns and health in late Iron Age and Roman Dorset, England', *Journal of Archaeological Science* 39 (2012): 1249–1259.

5

WEARING

Clothing, adornment and body shaping

Our clothing and personal adornment reflect both need and want, individuality and the broader society. An adult or adolescent puts on clothing to meet practical needs: protection from cold or heat, wind or rain; protection also from the impacts of the landscape; clothing that suits the daily round, whether hunting or fishing or tending livestock, or working in agricultural lands, or in specialised crafts and economic roles. Clothing and personal adornment may also serve to signal messages about gender, age, group affiliation, social status, sexual status, self-image and much more. Ornamentation can appear as features attached to clothes, as freestanding adornments like jewellery, as tattoos or paint on the skin or piercings on the body; not to mention hairstyle; and even body deformation. Function and signalling may complement each other. They may also be in conflict: a fashion model dressed for an outdoor shoot waiting huddled from the wind in the cameraman's anorak; or the nudists I once accidentally encountered on a breezy Vancouver beach, wearing sweaters on top but asserting their commitment to nudism from the waist down.

The clothing of infants and young children may be the choice of adults and can reflect a family's social status alongside functional needs. Where we most often encounter children's wear in archaeology – in the burials of the young – the selection of clothing and personal adornments tell us about the adult decision on how those children will look as they leave the world of the living. A child buried in clothing and jewellery does not represent a random snapshot of the individual's appearance in life.

This chapter reviews the kind of evidence available to us for children's wear in prehistory, in the broader context of the development of clothing in the deep past.

ORNAMENTATION AND CLOTHES

When Europeans arrived in Australia from the end of the 18th century, what they found astonished them. Despite changes in seasonal climate and significant changes in daily temperatures, they found Aboriginal foragers (men, women and children) in many areas who were commonly completely naked, or in communities where some had partial body covering made from animal skins but others did not, regardless of season or time of day.[1] Rock overhangs and temporary shelters constructed from plant materials served to provide primary protection against the elements. Yet personal decoration, whether painted bodies or wearable adornments, was common. Social signalling was strong; clothing as protection appeared less so. Indeed, without the social signalling of clothing, other items of personal adornment or body decoration come to the fore.

No less remarkable, visitors (including Charles Darwin) encountering the indigenous nomadic foragers of Tierra del Fuego, on the frequently cold southern tip of the Americas, were struck by their nakedness in such an inhospitable climate and lack of more than flimsy shelters to rest in. 'But these Fuegians in the canoe were quite naked, and even one full-grown woman was absolutely so. It was raining heavily, and the fresh water, together with the spray, trickled down her body. In another harbour not far distant a woman, who was suckling a recently-born child, came one day alongside the vessel, and remained there out of mere curiosity, whilst the sleet fell and thawed on her naked bosom, and on the skin of her naked baby.'[2] Yet Fuegians put elaborate painted decoration on their bodies.

Aboriginal Australian mothers or Fuegian mothers were not neglectful of their children's needs and protection. Mothers in all societies care for their young, but even in communities where clothing rules for adults are established, young children may roam naked. We must be cautious in making conclusions about clothing in prehistory based on climate, environment or analogy. Nor can we make assumptions about the clothing of young children based on what we see as adult wear.

By the time outside observers first encountered supposedly isolated smaller-scale societies, these would already commonly possess items of non-traditional clothing and exotic items of personal ornamentation traded from the changing world of modernity. Because clothing and ornamentation are status commodities, they move fast as trade items and are quickly adopted. Objects move more rapidly than people, in the sense that traded goods can travel from community to neighbouring community well ahead of the movement of individuals from distant societies.

In excavations I directed at the Central African Iron Age agricultural site of Kalala Island in the Kafue River of Zambia, equidistant from the continent's western and eastern coasts, we found nearly 1500 glass beads that

Australian Aboriginal family near Sydney, early 19th century

had been traded from across the distant Indian Ocean (some as necklaces on two infant burials) as well as an Indian Ocean *Conus* shell, all dating from centuries before the first European colonial contact.³

Studies of recent forager groups have paid little attention to the question of traditional clothing of the young, and useful information is limited on the clothing of modern hunter-gatherer children before outside influences were encountered. Mid-19th-century photographers seeking to capture the traditional lives of supposedly 'primitive' people commonly had them remove the items of clothing which reflected direct or indirect outside influence, and ask them to put on their 'traditional' wear for the photograph.

For the prehistoric past we need to look for direct archaeological evidence: clothing and ornamentation found on the bodies of the dead. Yet interpretation of this also needs care. The clothing the deceased was dressed in to take into the grave – or into an afterlife – may not be typical of that worn in life. The clothing assigned to children in the grave may or may not be similar to that of their own age cohort in life. Jewellery and personal decoration may be finer than in life, as a tribute to the lost family member. Or it may be less than worn in life, as valuables are retained for further use. And we tend to emphasise the exceptional in grave goods and ornamentation over the more typical and perhaps mundane.

PREHISTORIC FORAGERS' BODY COVERING AND BODY ORNAMENTATION

Increasingly complex society in human development would see increasing complexity in the way the human body was augmented: by arrangement of hair, permanent markings on skin, temporary decoration directly on the body, items of personal ornamentation such as jewellery, items of clothing and what we see most clearly in the archaeological record of prehistoric childhood – clothing itself decorated with non-functional elements. If ethnographic observation suggests that clothing is not a universal biological necessity, there is a stronger argument that body ornamentation is essential in providing social signals.

Direct body painting may be much older than Neanderthals. Substances such as ochres and specularite (a shiny form of haematite) have been found at Middle Stone Age and even earlier sites in Southern Africa: certainly by around 300,000 years ago and possibly as early as 500,000 years.[4] Such materials could readily be used to decorate the body.

We cannot be certain which early prehistoric communities had developed clothing or at what stage in hominin development we might identify this innovation. Visual reconstructions of Australopithecines usually show them with body hair but no artificial covering and even *Homo erectus*, the maker of the most perfectly formed symmetrical handaxes, is conventionally depicted naked, if less hirsute. There is active debate on the date and evolutionary value of losing body hair, with a suggestion that only when species of early *Homo* occupied lower-lying open environments in savannah Africa was the loss of body hair an advantage.[5]

By contrast, European Neanderthals are commonly depicted in museum dioramas with basic clothing of animal skins (or, occasionally, in imaginative artistic rendering, far more elaborate clothing and decoration). Curiously, such reconstructions often serve modesty rather than warmth: men with loincloths braving the Ice Age climate, a concept possibly designed for modern museum visitors rather than based on historical analysis. Although Neanderthal bodies were more suited to cold climates than those of their Upper Palaeolithic successors, they may have met the challenges of European (and Middle Eastern) winters and cold eras with animal skins to cover their bodies, and to protect their young children, but such skins have not been recovered.[6] The increased sophistication of Neanderthal Middle Palaeolithic stone tool technology may have provided some more flexibility in preparing skins for such use, as they allow for scraping and cutting, but with only basic borers, of more limited functionality than the tools used by the Neanderthals' *Homo sapiens* successors.[7]

If skins were to provide only some pre-modern modesty we can imagine Neanderthal children naked. But if the clothing was for warmth, helping the survival of Neanderthal communities in harsh climates, then clothing made for infants and children would be a reasonable supposition. Some argue that as the Neanderthal short and stocky body form was itself adapted for resisting cold, clothing may not have been part of their cultural apparatus, with feet of course well suited to travel without footwear, as with modern hunter-gatherers.[8]

The earliest real (and sometimes dramatic) direct evidence for clothing, and for early objects of personal decoration, comes from burials of anatomically modern humans, *Homo sapiens*, and especially from Upper Palaeolithic finds of the later Ice Ages in Europe, which are described and discussed more fully in Chapter 9. These include the careful burials of children placed in graves and wearing clothes which they may have possessed during their own shortened lives, and some with lavish decorative items which may be specific to their burial. We often rely on the surviving decorative additions to clothing made of hard substances to infer what the clothing was, as it has decayed and disappeared.

Our modern species is physically quite different from Neanderthals: its origins in savannah Africa make successful adaption to cold climates more a question of cultural adaptation (clothing, fire, shelter) than of biological change, although we cannot dismiss the physical differences that emerged in different climatic zones. The technology which *Homo sapiens* brought with them into new areas allowed them to create clothing that met their needs throughout the changing year in these different environments. Their mental apparatus – the modern mind – stimulated the creation of decorative items for adults and children. And the combination of functional clothing and personal decoration gave us a Late Pleistocene origin for fashion. Our museum displays and artistic reconstructions present a modern human physique in a range of clothing and personal ornamentation. Yet as shown by the encounters with Australian Aborigines and Fuegians from South America (and the rare examples of lost children surviving in the wild), the modern human body can adapt to and survive the cold without warm clothing.[9]

There is an unusual source of supporting evidence for the idea that clothing originated only with anatomically modern humans and the emergence of *Homo sapiens* from Africa. The body louse *Pediculus humanus* lives in clothing and geneticists have used molecular dating to suggest its origin only in the era of *Homo sapiens*, with its spread probably linked to anatomically modern humans' spread out of Africa. There is no evidence for other clothing lice that might have been associated with Neanderthals or other earlier hominins.[10]

European Upper Palaeolithic working of stone and organic materials produced a toolkit of specialist items: for processing skins, for boring and sewing, and more, as did the Later Stone Age of Africa and developed industries in Asia.[11] Sophisticated and specialised stone artefacts could also help create bone awls and needles, which allowed detailed handling and adaptation of animal skins.[12] Now clothes could be cut and sewn from skins to make an adult jacket, a baby's swaddling wrap or a strong sling to carry an infant. Leather could be made into footwear, and soft stone, wood or other organic material could be modified for personal decoration. Skills in manufacturing clothing or personal ornaments, and the time involved in this, may have been gained by particular individuals in a forager group, giving them social status. Acquiring and wearing finer items would be a sign of social position too.

In addition to clothing made from skins, we see from the site of Dzudzuana in the Republic of Georgia, dated around 30,000 years ago, evidence that wild flax was used to produce a textile. This could have been more for making cords, which could be used in sewing through skins, than for wearing as cloth.[13] The possibility remains that materials were woven into fabric for clothes in parts of the Upper Palaeolithic. Impressions in baked clay at the Czech sites of Pavlov and Dolní Věstonice show that fabrics were being manufactured from vegetable fibres.

The famous 'Venus' figurines are naked, although they do often have decorative hairstyles, but other small sculptures from Europe's Upper Palaeolithic suggest some of the ways clothing was worn and support the idea of woven cloth.[14]

We have no clear answers as to why so many Upper Palaeolithic figurines of women (and indeed those of some later contexts) have them naked. We certainly do not need to assume that warm climate or social tradition led the community's women operate on this basis. Even less do we need to adopt the suggestion attributed to one now deceased British archaeologist, that without public nudity a male artist would have been unable to create such images.

Generally, the evidence of clothing from the Upper Palaeolithic is indirect: tools, representations, ancillary items rather than the clothing itself. This makes it difficult to distinguish children's clothing from that of adults. But a possible such item appears on a statuette carved from a mammoth tusk found at Buret' (in southern Siberia), dated some 25–20,000 years ago. This close-fitting garment, with a fitted hood, is the kind of item that would best suit and protect a small child against the cold. It would be made of a series of furs sewn together: 'a complete tailored fur suit' is one description.[15]

Other forms of body ornaments and ancillaries to clothing are attested by more direct evidence, often highly dramatic, with lavish (we could suggest loving) treatment of the bodies of the deceased children, buried with items whose creation represented many hours of dedicated and skilled craft.

Decorative items on children's clothing are more common in burials than as separate items of jewellery, but because they survive and attract

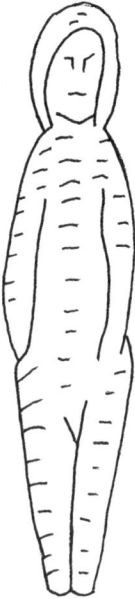

Statuette carved from a mammoth tusk showing a close-fitting garment, from the Upper Palaeolithic of Buret' in Siberia

archaeological comment when skins and cloth do not survive, we may have a biased and selective image of the appearance of prehistoric children as they were laid in their graves.

The burial of a 4- or 5-year-old child lying on her or his back with crossed feet was discovered at Lagar Velho in Portugal, near to a cliff face in a settlement site. Dated to the Upper Palaeolithic, around 25,000–24,000 years ago, it nevertheless had some Neanderthal elements in its ancestry. The body had ochre staining, which probably came from a stained or dyed shroud or cloak. The child had a necklace with a perforated shell pendant, and ochre-stained canine teeth of a red deer suggested decoration on a hat.[16]

The double infant burial from the Gravettian Upper Palaeolithic site of Krems-Wachtberg in Austria had a string of at least 35 drop-shaped beads made from mammoth ivory around the waist of one body: either from a waistband or decoration on an item of clothing.[17] Such adornment for a baby is notable, with personal decoration in death they would be unlikely to have had in life. Another burial of an infant had an ivory pin which probably fastened to a wrap of fur or leather.

Hundreds of perforated shells and canine teeth of deer, which suggest a lavish item of headgear, were found on the burial of an adolescent boy aged about 15 at the Italian site of Arene Candide, a cave site 90 m (300 feet)

Burial of an adolescent ('The Prince') in the Gravettian era, at Arene Candide, Italy, with elaborate shell bead headdress

above sea level. This was also of Gravettian date (around 23,500 years ago), though the cave itself continued to be a place for shelter over a longer stretch of time. A belt may be represented by other items found around his torso: mammoth ivory pendants, perforated cowrie shells and more.[18] As in other Upper Palaeolithic burials of children (but not of adults) at the site, squirrel tails were commonly found on the chest: evidence of a very specific article of clothing. The clothing and decoration for the 15-year-old was so elaborate that he has been nicknamed 'The Prince', and his comparatively

Reconstruction by Libor Balák of a burial of an adolescent ('The Prince') in the Gravettian era, at Arene Candide, Italy

lavish burial is certainly a sign of how seriously the death of this young man was taken by his forager band.

The burial of an Upper Palaeolithic child aged 6 or 7 years in a small pit at Kostenki on Russia's Don River included a headdress made with 150 perforated fox canine teeth.[19] Even more remarkable was the later Upper Palaeolithic infant burial in the rock shelter of La Madeleine in the French Dordogne; the body of a child aged between 2 and 4 years had been decorated with substantial ornamentation, which it is hard to imagine as any child's

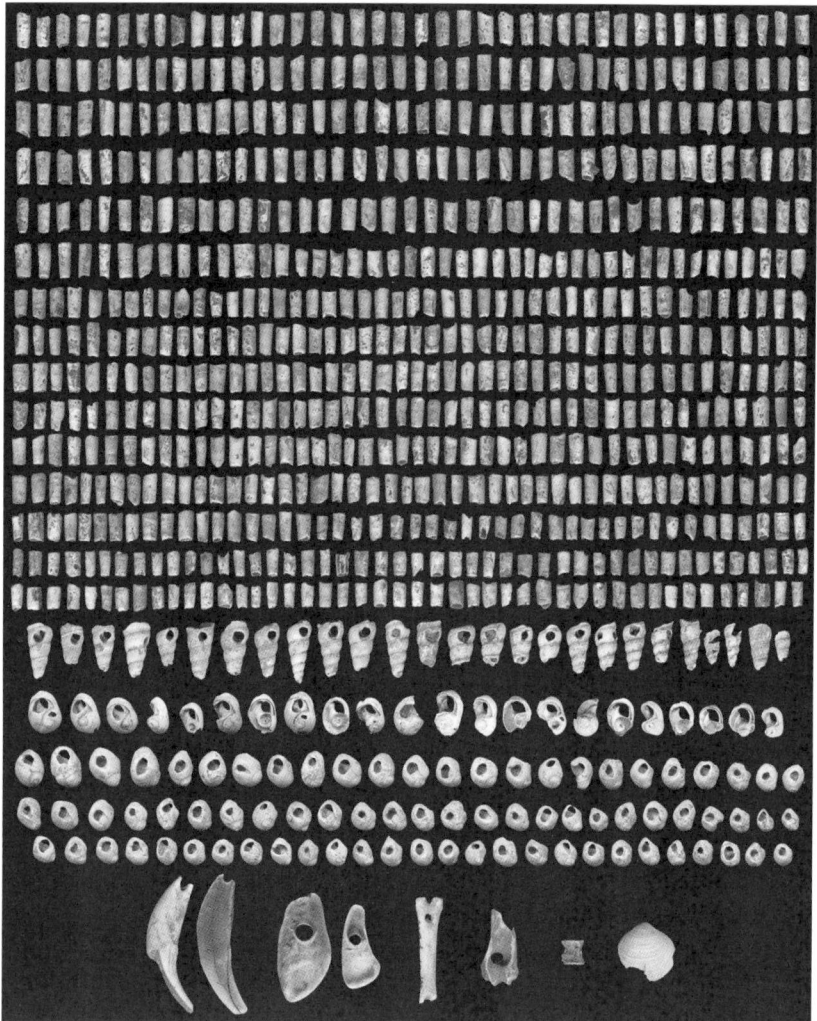

Perforated teeth and beads accompanying the burial of an Upper Palaeolithic child aged between 2 and 4 years, at La Madeleine, France

everyday wear: many perforated teeth and beads made of *Dentalium* and other shells, with over 1000 items in total.[20] It seems the beads, snapped or sawn from the shell, were embroidered on to the child's clothing and indeed needles suitable for such work have been found at the site. Did this child hold some special role in the band, to be buried with such richness? The cave itself was an archaeological site containing high-quality art, both sculptural pieces and on the cave walls.

At Grotta dei Fanciulli in Italy a double child burial had hundreds of pierced shells which seem to have been fastened on to their clothing. They were spread over their loins, so most probably represented a skirt.

Particularly lavish (and early) personal decoration accompanied burials at the Russian site of Sunghir. Sunghir lies on a river some 200 km (125 miles) east of Moscow, and is an open-air site which was occupied seasonally by Upper Palaeolithic hunter-gatherers around 32,000–29,000 years ago.[21] A buried adult man had bracelets, headbands of fox teeth and strings of nearly 3000 mammoth ivory beads from his body clothing.

Nearby were significantly more lavish burials, of a 9- or 10-year-old girl and an 11- or 12-year-old boy buried head to head.[22] A human femur was buried with them. Sixteen spears made of mammoth ivory accompanied the young couple, ranging in length from 2.5 m and 1.2 m down to 27 cm (100 to 11 inches); some were pointed at both ends, some just at one. The body of the boy was buried with his left hand and forearm missing, and there was some ochre staining on his bones. A belt is suggested by the presence of 250 perforated fox canine teeth at his waist. On his body were 4900 ivory beads from a garment. These beads would have involved thousands of hours of work on strips of mammoth ivory: thinned, then drilled from both sides (presumably with stone borer tools) from both sides; the beads on both children were smaller than those found with the adult burial. Three rows of beads on his forehead suggest they were decoration from a hat or headdress. Others were found scattered around the body so may have been decoration on a cloth or skin garment: some positioned to circle the arms, others around leggings, and some in a position like a tail. There were ivory bands on his arms. An ivory pin found near his throat would seem to be a fastening which held a garment. Other figures may have been items of personal decoration: a carved ivory figurine of a four-legged animal. And below his shoulder was a large carving of a mammoth.

The girl's body had more ochre staining than the boy's. She had nearly 5300 ivory beads from a costume, some also suggesting a triple band on headgear: a remarkable concentration that represented a vast commitment of labour. She too had an ivory pin on her throat to hold a cloak or shroud and 13 ivory arm bands. Four carefully carved ivory discs accompanied her burial: round, with a central hole surrounded by a ring of large perforations. Their function is unclear though they may have been associated with the spears. Two deer antlers with decorative lines were also present.

While the associated objects might be those owned in life, it is hard to believe that all of the numerous decorative items of carved ivory represent the normal daily possessions of ordinary young people. It is the exceptional nature of these finds that is so striking, and the burial of these children and the associated ritual imply some special circumstances which we can only surmise. We can see these items as examples of what was possible in

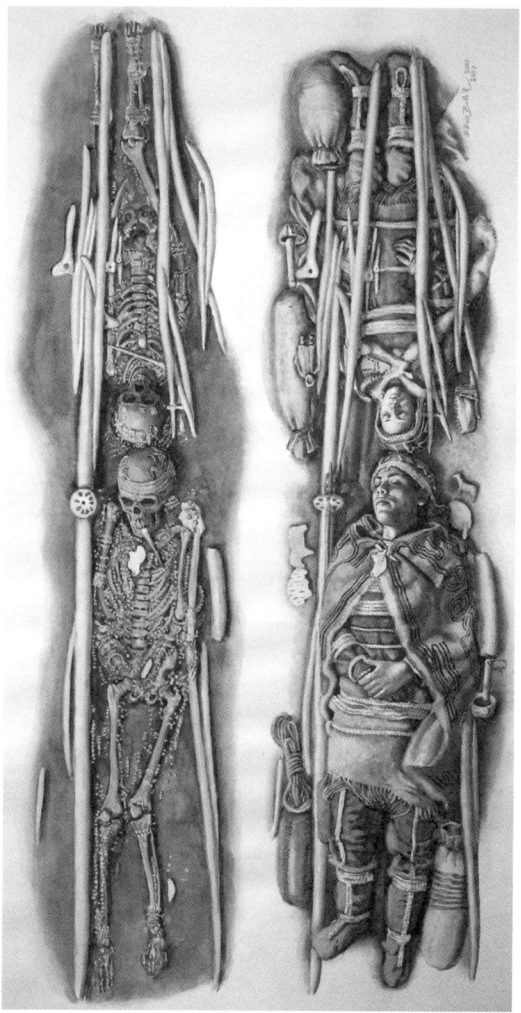

Reconstruction by Libor Balák of two lavishly decorated Upper Palaeolithic child burials at Sunghir, Russia

the clothing and personal adornment of the European Upper Palaeolithic, without suggesting this was other than exceptional.

Fish teeth and beads made from perforated snail shells accompanied burials of infants in the Mesolithic of Danube Gorges at Vlasac in Serbia.[23] These were not newborns but babies who had survived to 2–4 months. One infant aged about 1 year had 701 beads of perforated (but otherwise unmodified) carp teeth buried with it: presumably decoration for a garment or swaddling cloth in which it was buried.

There are examples of personal jewellery found on burials of children without being part of a garment, especially from later forager sites. At Wilczyce in Poland a newborn infant dated around 13,500 BC was buried with a necklace of 80 pieces made from drilled teeth of the arctic fox.[24] And at the Polish Upper Palaeolithic site of Borsuka Cave, six teeth of a child aged 12–18 months were found together with over 100 pendants made from the teeth of wild elk and aurochs. While this may be a child burial, the child's teeth may just be lost teeth used in a different context.[25]

A child buried at the site of Osipovka in the Dnieper basin of Ukraine had a group of 200 carp teeth we can see as personal decoration. In the Middle East, Natufian burials included personal decorative items buried with children, including beads of perforated shells, pendants of bone and, in one case, at the site of El Wad in Israel, an elaborate headdress of gazelle phalanges, such as also found at adult burials.[26]

Looking further afield, in the advanced hunter-gatherer Jomon societies which occupied Japan until the 1st millennium BC, children carried necklaces and bracelets of shell and stone beads, whereas adult burials had more elaborate decorative items on the whole of their bodies.[27] One original and interesting line of thought links the body ornamentation of the child with that of the adult. Shell bracelets found on the wrists of deceased adult women of advanced foragers in the Jomon period in Japan were recorded as too small in diameter to have been put on in adulthood. The interpretation is that they must have been placed over the hands in childhood and not removed as the owner grew.[28] The adult remains tell us of the child's wear; other such examples remain to be identified.

Among New World examples, children in the Argentine forager burials of Chenque 1 were buried with beads made of shell and of stone, over 1000 in one burial, but some of these beads may have been sewn onto a leather container rather than onto clothing or strung as a necklace.[29] One child aged 2–3 years had a necklace of 178 bone beads, 42 copper beads and 3 snails (the remains were also accompanied by a dog and a copper artefact). By contrast, a burial of the Formative period in Argentina, from around 100 BC, contained one child, aged 8–12, buried just with a stone bead and copper pendant; this lay alongside a contemporary grave which mixed together adult and children's bones of some 14 individuals, associated with a copper mask.[30]

Clearer evidence of clothing comes when arid conditions prevent decay, as with finds from Chinchorro foragers and fishing communities of the Chilean Andes dated between the 5th and 2nd millennia BC. Well preserved bodies of infants show loincloths, fringed skirts and headbands similar to those of adults.[31] At a fishing and foraging community in Peru, in the same date range, a buried child had a cord bracelet and a covering of twined textile which could have been either clothing or a carrying wrap. Another infant aged about 2 months was buried with a cut shell disk, an animal skin and fine fabric showing colouring of a red pigment.[32]

How do we make sense of this kind of evidence from small-scale hunter-gatherer societies? In infancy and in the lives of young children, we can assume the kind of maternal care outlined in Chapter 2, where clothes are an inessential part of childhood in warm climates but a basic functional protection in colder climes. The death and burial of children – whether a few months old or much closer to adulthood – could be marked by an excess of personal decoration, such as a necklace or a headdress, items sewn onto clothing or wrapped over the body. Whether we see this as signs of personal grief or community loss, the quality and quantity of such burial items in dressing the child for burial is one of the more striking elements of the prehistoric forager sites discussed here. What we cannot see is how much decoration was painted on the body itself in death and how much was painted on the child's body at important stages of life.

PREHISTORIC AGRICULTURALIST CLOTHING AND ADORNMENT

The emergence of farming transformed settlement patterns, skills, social and personal life, and impacted on the roles children could play in the family's economic life. As reviewed in Chapter 10, burials of children show us aspects of their roles in life as well as their own society's view of their death. Archaeological discoveries of burials (and in many contexts, cremations) now become more common. Decorative items on children's bodies as seen in forager prehistory continue, but items of jewellery are now more frequent in these burials.

Agricultural communities are generally larger than forager groups, and social stratification and status are more marked. A family may demonstrate its social position by what clothing and ornamentation its members wear, and this can apply to older children as well as to adults. In death this status may continue to be marked by the burial clothes and ornamentation that accompany the dead child, and we can see this extended to a deceased infant or young child whose family status is marked in death even though the individual died too young to achieve a personal status. But the archaeological studies often emphasise those buried with marks of higher family or personal status; the unadorned clothing in which other infants and children were buried remains largely unknown.

Clothing and decoration were also major markers of differences between different cultural and language groups. When literate urban societies such as the Romans encountered (and sometimes conquered) 'barbarian' tribes, they would describe the visual appearance of clothing, body paint and body

Decorated pottery from the US Southwest showing the 'butterfly' hair decoration of young women

decoration which distinguished these different groups. Ancient Egyptian iconography presented images of different groups of foreigners standardised by their dress.

Many markers such as face decorations and hair styling are almost always lost to the archaeological record, while we may fail to recognise others. However, as a mark of reaching puberty, a hair decoration (with hair divided on both sides of the head in a 'butterfly' effect) seen in more recent Pueblo and communities of the US Southwest can been identified also in archaeological data from rock paintings and decorated pottery.[33] Such pre-modern representations extend as far back as Basketmaker culture sites in the 7th century AD.

Without bodies to show skin markings or colouring, decorative items sewn onto clothes and jewellery worn on the body remain our main surviving pieces of evidence. Most prehistoric clothing from burials has decayed, but very dry or waterlogged conditions provide valuable exceptions which allow the reconstruction of garments and the techniques involved in creating them.[34] The body of a Chalcolithic 'Iceman', whom the researchers named Ötzi, found frozen on the Italy–Austria border had a cloak of woven grasses and leather shoes.[35] Indirect evidence of fabrics and adult apparel includes clothing on small sculptures, fabric impressions on clay objects and the tools used in sewing and related crafts.

Domestication of animals and cultivation of crops allowed a greater range of materials for clothing: wool as well as fabrics made of cloth to complement leather and skins. The elaboration of the toolkit allowed subtler means of preparing both clothing and items of personal decoration.

A burial of a 1-year-old child in a pit in the Neolithic of Tell Hazna in Mesopotamian Syria was decorated with hundreds of stone, copper and shell beads, which together may have formed a complex necklace.[36] A flax cloth wrapped around an infant buried at Çatalhöyük in Anatolia may be a burial cloth rather than a wrap used in life.[37]

An Early Bronze Age child's burial at Kalavan in Armenia, dated to the early 3rd millennium BC, produced evidence of decorative clothing.[38] Dog molar teeth had been bored to serve as part of a necklace on plant fibre, together with two bored stone beads. The owner was 5–6 years old.

Also in the Bronze Age, from Lake Itkul in Russia, an infant burial had a unique item of clothing: a cap with copper plaques.[39] These small pieces of copper – most less than 1.5 cm wide – had holes in them for fastening with leather straps, traces of which were also recovered. This burial was accompanied by remarkable carved figurines (see p. 241), a bored stone bead, and some leather, on which copper plaques were fastened, and which may have been a piece of child's clothing.

In the Azov-Dnieper Neolithic of Mariupol in Ukraine (6th to 5th millennia BC), a child's burial had shell beads whose positions suggested they were sewn at the base of a wide skirt extending below the knees.[40] A reconstruction indicates what the full garment might have looked like. At Ovnigi, also in Ukraine, a child's long dress seems to have been decorated with fish teeth on a hem near the ankles, while at Vilnjanka fish teeth were sewn on the sleeves of a child's dress. A contrast lay in another contemporary Neolithic culture, the Surskaja, whose children were buried in less elaborately decorated clothing.

In the Early Bronze Age of Greece and the Aegean, children have been found buried with personal decoration: amulets and well as rings made of metal or shell.[41]

An infant buried in the large Chalcolithic (5th millennium BC) burial ground of Varna in Bulgaria had a necklace of stones and shell, as well as shell bracelets.[42] Shell had also been used as decoration for clothing.

In Neolithic Hainburg-Teichhal in Austria, from around 5100 BC, shell beads around the knees of a 2-year-old child also suggest the decorative hem of a garment. There were further beads at the neck, waist and elbows.[43]

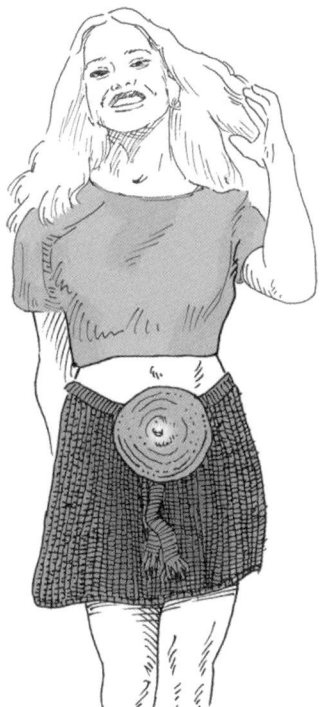

Reconstruction of woollen clothing and a bronze disc found on a Bronze Age girl from Egtved in Denmark

Several hats have been found in the Hallstatt site and culture of the Iron Age of Austria. These are made of sheepskin held together with a leather strap, and one is a size that could only be that for a young child.[44] This, together with small leather boots, were in a salt mine where the young children apparently laboured. The bodies of adult mine workers showed the effects of manual work since an early age, yet their grave goods showed there were material rewards for this.

The jewellery found with a child at the German Hallstatt site of Bettelbühl included fine bronze fibulae and pendants, in a style typical of adults.

Items of personal ornamentation decorated the Early Bronze Age burials of young children at Peñalosa in Spain: beads of jasper and quartzite and rock crystal, silver rings or bracelets for fingers, wrist and arms (see Chapter 10).[45]

A 16–18-year-old girl from the Bronze Age of Egtved in Jutland, Denmark (from the 14th century BC), whose remains were well preserved, wore clothing made of wool which had been obtained via long-distance trade (beyond Denmark), illustrating the importance and complexity associated

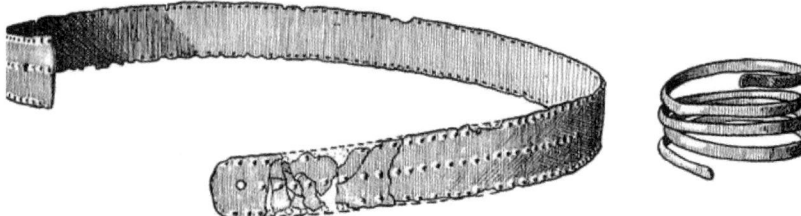

Copper diadem from the grave of an 8-year-old child of the Bronze Age at Abbekås, Sweden

with appropriate clothing.[46] She had a blouse, a corded skirt and belt, and foot wrappers as well as a woollen blanket. A bronze plate on her belt was a disc shape perhaps symbolising the sun.

Finds from late Neolithic or early Bronze Age Abbekås in Sweden include a bronze 'diadem' found on the body of an 8-year-old child. This may have been part of a cloth headdress.[47]

From the Swedish island of Öland in the Iron Age, numerous beads were attached to children's dresses, representing significantly more ornamentation than on adult clothes.[48]

The Iron Age burials of children in central Italy often show evidence of the clothes they had been buried in (a fibula to fasten a cloak or gown being especially common) and it is thought that both boys and girls wore bracelets.[49] Material associated with weaving can be found buried with young as well as adult females. Later Iron Age burials of the Wielbark culture in Eastern Europe are similarly commonly found with fibulae, some of which are quite lavish: manufactured of silver or with silver coating, probably for boys as well as girls.[50] Disc-shaped brooches are also found on bodies, as are bracelets and beads of glass, amber and metal (one such necklace on an older child has nearly 250 elements). Buckles from necklaces are present at children's burials, of bronze and in one case of gold. Pins used to fasten a garment have also been found. It appears that children were buried with their finest garments and personal decoration.

Chapter 10 mentions other scattered examples of decorative items found in Africa with the burials of children: isolated finds which include bronze pendants, stone and glass beads, and bracelets of copper and iron for arms and legs.

The Neolithic cemetery (5th millennium BC) at Dongola Reach in Sudan has children buried with lavish personal decoration, which seems to reflect the relative wealth of their families.[51] Stone beads of amazonite were more common with children than adults; red ochre was a feature of women and children but not adult males; and many carnelian and ostrich eggshell

Bead necklaces on children at burials from the 4th millennium BC, Adaima, Egypt

bead accompanied child burials. A necklace on a 2-year-old had 140 stone beads, as well as iron bracelets and grave goods of more adult use. Another infant was buried with 120 ostrich eggshell beads. The body of a 9-year-old child lay on an animal skin and was decorated with ivory finger rings and a necklace of amazonite and carnelian beads. Another 9-year-old had even more beads, together with ivory bracelets.

Once we are at the dawn of urban literate civilisation, we see the impact of greater wealth and greater social stratification in life and in death. At the very end of Egyptian prehistory and the beginning of the pharaonic era, a large cemetery at Adaima in Upper Egypt included infants and very young children with quite lavish personal items.[52] A study of eight such burials on nets in pits, or within large jars, described jewellery buried on the bodies of the young. One child aged between 18 and 24 months, buried lying on a mat, had two large shell bracelets, a bracelet of 33 carnelian beads, another bracelet of 21 limestone beads and a necklace made up of 37 limestone beads, a carnelian pendant and a large shell pendant. Another child aged 2 years had nine large bone bracelets, a necklace of 60 beads of cornelian and glazed clay (frit), and a complex necklace made of over 1000 ceramic beads. A child of 12–18 months buried in a large jar had bracelets of shell and ostrich eggshell beads and a necklace of 91 frit and 2 bone beads. Another burial of a child of the same age, also in a pot, had three large ivory bracelets, a necklace of over 100 beads of stone and frit, a second necklace of 67 beads of stone, bone and ostrich eggshell, and an amethyst pendant. Other burials of young children had beads, pendants and a bracelet of copper and bone.

This remarkable decoration of the young here repeats ornamentation found on female (but not male) adult burials, and a third of the child burials carried such personal decoration. We think of ancient Egyptian burial as a forerunner to an afterlife, and there were items of use in the graves, but this level of decoration suggests something less utilitarian and more human. There is no need to think of this jewellery as the infants' wear in life (indeed some is too large) but the items could have been possessions received or earmarked by a family for a child's future. In any case, we are now seeing a world in which even the youngest children receive full and formal burial and those families with sufficient wealth are conveying their dead infant into the afterlife with lavish personal decoration.

BODY SHAPING

A process which reshaped rather than decorated the body was a feature of many societies of both Old and New Worlds. Such shaping needs to begin before a child reaches the age of 3 years. It may arise to distinguish a family's status in society, whether by wealth, ethnic or other identity, and of course can be gender specific. Whereas dress and personal decoration for an adult and adolescent are matters of choice (even if constrained by social norms, family and peer pressure) something as dramatic as head shaping can only be imposed by a family and cannot be undone in adulthood. The commonness of the practice demonstrates that it was not normally found to have to intellectual or physiological side-effects.[53]

Head shaping is found from Late Neolithic and Chalcolithic Iran and this transformation of the infant skull reflects a tradition occasionally found elsewhere in the Middle East. Adult skeletons show the signs of cranial deformation: shaping of the skull which could have been undertaken only during infancy, when tight cloth bandaging or a wooden board tied to the back of the still plastic skull ensured that a child grew with a flattened head. This procedure was applied only to a minority of people in Iran of the Chalcolithic period (though to both males and females).[54] At two sites, Ganj Dareh and Choga Sefid, all 20 skulls recovered had undergone this procedure – suggesting that the specific burial place was intended for those who had been chosen for this procedure when born. Small figurine heads at Choga Mish seem to show the same feature, of flattened heads,

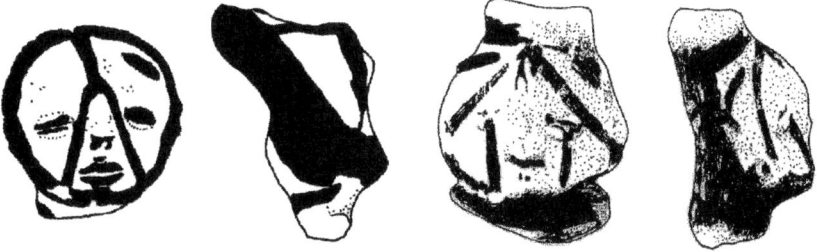

Figurines with artificially flattened heads, from Chalcolithic Choga Mish, Iran

with a black painted band which could represent the binding used in the flattening process. Ethnographic and historical analogy raise the question whether such selective and irreversible deformation was the sign of a socially elite group (as seen in the bound feet of elite women in Chinese tradition) or linked to a religious ritual role. Head shaping from childhood is seen in Neolithic Greece and in Cyprus from the Neolithic through to Early Iron Age times.[55]

Head binding is attested in a broad range of times and places in the prehistory of the Americas. It is found in Chile in both archaic forager groups and early agriculturalists – a spread of up to five millennia.[56] A study of over 400 skulls found that 90% had been deformed in youth, and equally in males and females – with change over time but also in different regional styles which demonstrate that not just the action but the specific details and style were markers of a particular community.[57] In Ecuador a style of flattening the top of the head is found from 2000 BC and patterns of deformation seem to have spread from there into adjacent regions.[58]

In north-west Patagonia, Argentina, deformation was found in burials from the 2nd millennium BC onwards.[59] Although the practice continued, there were significant changes in style by the middle of the 2nd millennium AD.

In parts of the pre-Incan Tiwanika culture of the Andes from the late 1st millennium AD, head binding during childhood was the norm, with 80–85% of all burials at the site of Chen Chen in Peru attesting this. It applied equally to males and females and was already present in the bodies of children who died before the age of 3 years.[60] A slightly different form of head binding in an adjacent Tiwanika region shows the local cultural differences.

Such bindings as markers of ethnic identity or social status were not always beneficial – the mummy of a Peruvian Inca child aged 4–6 months suggested the infant had died from cranial damage and fatal infection that had resulted from head binding.[61]

In Mesoamerica the head-binding tradition has an exceptionally long history, persisting from pre-urban communities through the Olmec and Maya civilisations to Spanish colonial times.[62] Accidental head deformation arising from the use of cradle boards in North America was described in Chapter 3.

CONCLUSIONS

Throughout many cultures of later prehistory, our image is that often when children died, and they were buried with care, items of personal decoration on clothes and bodies, as well as other items reflecting daily life, accompanied them into the grave. As the children left the world of the living, they took with them material goods that also departed the living world for whatever lay thereafter and this included the clothing and personal ornamentation chosen for their burial.

Because so much of our evidence for the clothing and ornamentation of children in prehistory comes from burial sites, it is important to reiterate the special case that death presents. When we look at the clothing in which a child is buried, and the jewellery or other ornamentation that has been preserved, we are not seeing what the infant or child looked like in daily life. The selection of burial clothing and ornamentation is an action that accompanies death, not life. Unless we encounter the survival of an accidental death, as with the Chalcolithic 'Iceman' Ötzi from the European Alps, we are seeing the result of decisions and selections made by adults. A carefully buried child is likely to be dressed in more lavish wear than the individual would have normally worn in life. The survival record limits our perception: an apparently plain burial may have been a body highly decorated by paint for burial or highly decorated by paint or tattoo in life. Nevertheless, archaeology gives us some insights into the clothing of the young in a range of prehistoric societies.

NOTES

1 I. Gilligan, 'Clothing and climate in Aboriginal Australia', *Current Anthropology* 49 (2008): 487–495; V. Attenbrow, *Sydney's Aboriginal Past: investigating the archaeological and historical records*, Sydney: UNSW Press, 2002: 107. The long-term biological basis for Aboriginal tolerance of extreme cold has been confirmed by genetic studies: see A.-S. Malaspinas et al., 'A genomic history of Aboriginal Australia', *Nature* 538 (2016): 207–214.
2 C. Darwin, *Voyage of the Beagle*, London: John Murray, 1905 edition (first published 1839), p. 202.

3 R. Derricourt, *Man on the Kafue: the archaeology and history of the Itezhitezhi area of Zambia*, London: Ethnographica, 1985, pp. 69–71.
4 I. Watts, M. Chazan & J. Wilkins, 'Early evidence for brilliant ritualized display: specularite use in the Northern Cape (South Africa) between ~500 and ~300 Ka', *Current Anthropology* 57 (2016): 287–310.
5 T. Dávid-Barrett & R.I.M. Dunbar, 'Bipedality and hair loss in human evolution revisited: the impact of altitude and activity scheduling', *Journal of Human Evolution* 94 (206): 72–82.
6 The question is discussed in detail in N. Wales, 'Modeling Neanderthal clothing using ethnographic analogues', *Journal of Human Evolution* 63 (2012): 781–795, with arguments that clothing (not just loin cloths!) was an essential precondition of Neanderthal occupation of cold-climate Europe.
7 I. Gilligan, 'Neanderthal extinction and modern human behaviour: the role of climate change and clothing', *World Archaeology* 39 (2007): 499–514, p. 502.
8 Gilligan 'Neanderthal extinction'.
9 I. Gilligan, 'The prehistoric development of clothing: archaeological implications of a thermal model', *Journal of Archaeological Method and Theory* 17 (2010): 15–80, is a very thoughtful and wide-ranging paper.
10 R. Kittler et al., 'Molecular evolution of *Pediculus humanus* and the origin of clothing', *Current Biology* 13 (2003): 1414 – 1417; M.A. Toups et al., 'Origin of clothing lice indicates early clothing use by anatomically modern humans in Africa', *Molecular Biology and Evolution* 28 (2011): 29–32.
11 Gilligan, 'The prehistoric development'.
12 O. Soffer, 'Recovering perishable technologies through use wear on tools: preliminary evidence for Upper Paleolithic weaving and net making', *Current Anthropology* 45 (2004): 407–413.
13 E. Kvavadze et al., '30,000-year-old wild flax fibers', *Science* 325 (2009): 1359–1359.
14 O. Soffer, J.M. Adovasio & D.C. Hyland, 'The "Venus" figurines: textiles, basketry, gender, and status in the Upper Paleolithic', *Current Anthropology* 41 (2000): 511–537; Gilligan 'The prehistoric development', pp. 56–58.
15 J.F. Hoffecker, 'Innovation and technological knowledge in the Upper Paleolithic of northern Eurasia', *Evolutionary Anthropology* 14 (2005): 186–198, p. 188.
16 P. Pettitt, *The Palaeolithic Origins of Human Burial*, London: Routledge, 2011, pp. 168–169; C. Duarte et al., 'The early Upper Paleolithic human skeleton from the Abrigo do Lagar Velho (Portugal) and modern human emergence in Iberia', *Proceedings of the National Academy of Sciences* 96 (1999): 7604–7609.
17 Pettitt, *The Palaeolithic Origins*, pp. 170–173; M. Händel et al., 'New excavations at Krems-Wachtberg – approaching a well-preserved Gravettian settlement site in the middle Danube region', *Quartär* 56 (2009): 187–196; T. Einwögerer et al., 'Upper Palaeolithic infant burials', *Nature* 444 (2006): 285–285; T. Einwögerer et al., 'The Gravettian infant burials from Krems-Wachtberg, Austria' in *BRIPP*: 15–19.
18 Pettitt, *The Palaeolithic Origins*, p. 182 ff.; P.B. Pettitt et al., 'The Gravettian burial known as the Prince ("Il Principe"): new evidence for his age and diet', *Antiquity* 77 (2003): 15–19.
19 Pettitt, *The Palaeolithic Origins*, p. 198.
20 Pettitt, *The Palaeolithic Origins*, pp. 236–239.
21 The uncalibrated C14 dates are 27,000–30,000 BP. See S. Nalawade-Chavan, J.

McCullagh & R. Hedges, 'New hydroxyproline radiocarbon dates from Sungir, Russia, confirm early Mid Upper Palaeolithic burials in Eurasia', *PloS ONE* 9 (2014): e76896.

22 Sunghir 2 and 3. The site is also spelled Sungir. E. Trinkaus et al., *The People of Sunghir: burials, bodies, and behavior in the Earlier Upper Paleolithic*, New York: Oxford University Press, 2014, pp. 18–23; Pettitt, *The Palaeolithic Origins*, pp. 203 ff.

23 D. Borić & S. Stefanović, 'Birth and death: infant burials from Vlasac and Lepenski Vir', *Antiquity* 78 (2004): 526–546, pp. 529–531; E. Cristian & D. Borić, '8500-year-old Late Mesolithic garment embroidery from Vlasac (Serbia): technological, use-wear and residue analyses', *Journal of Archaeological Science* 39 (2012): 3450–3469; D. Borić et al., 'Late Mesolithic lifeways and deathways at Vlasac (Serbia)', *Journal of Field Archaeology* 39 (2014): 4–31.

24 J.D. Irish et al, 'A late Magdalenian perinatal human skeleton from Wilczyce, Poland', *Journal of Human Evolution* 55 (2008): 736–740, p. 737.

25 J. Wilczyński et al., 'A mid Upper Palaeolithic child burial from Borsuka Cave (southern Poland)', *International Journal of Osteoarchaeology* 26 (2016): 151–162.

26 B.F. Byrd & C.M. Monahan, 'Death, mortuary ritual, and Natufian social structure', *Journal of Anthropological Archaeology* 14 (1995): 251–287, p. 270.

27 Y. Yamada, 'Mortuary practices for children in Jomon Japan: an approach to Jomon life history' [in Japanese], *Japanese Archaeology* 4 (1997): 1–39.

28 J. Habu, *Ancient Jomon of Japan*, Cambridge: Cambridge University Press, 2004, p. 139, citing Okamoto (1975).

29 M.A. Berón, C.M. Aranda & L.H. Luna, 'Mortuary behaviour in subadults: children as social actors in the hunter-gatherer societies of Argentine Pampas', *CitP* 5 (2012): 51–69.

30 L.I. Cortés & M.C. Scattolin, 'Ancient metalworking in South America: a 3000-year-old copper mask from the Argentinian Andes', *Antiquity* 91 (2017): 688–700, pp. 689–690.

31 V.G. Standen, B.T. Arriaza & C.M. Santoro, 'Chinchorro mortuary practices on infants: Northern Chile Archaic Period (BP 7000–3600)' in *TCBI*: 58–74, p. 67.

32 J. Quilter, *Life and Death at Paloma: society and mortuary practices in a preceramic Peruvian village*, Iowa City, IA: University of Iowa Press, 1989, pp. 41, 58.

33 K. Hays-Gilpin, 'Wearing a butterfly, coming of age: a 1,500-year-old tradition' in *CPPS*: 196–210.

34 K. Grömer, *The Art of Prehistoric Textile Making*, Vienna: Natural History Museum, 2016, is an appealing and broad-ranging illustrated survey, available on line at www.oapen.org/search?identifier=604250

35 F. Rollo, S. Sassaroli & M. Ubaldi, 'Molecular phylogeny of the fungi of the Iceman's grass clothing', *Current Genetics* 28 (1995): 289–297.

36 K. Bacvarov, 'A long way to the west: earliest jar burials in southeast Europe and the Near East' in *BRIPP*: 61–70, p. 66.

37 Grömer, *The Art of Prehistoric Textile Making*, p. 43.

38 M. Poulmarc'h et al., 'Dog molars as personal ornaments in a Kura-Araxes child burial (Kalavan-1, Armenia)', *Antiquity* 90 (2016): 953–972.

39 A.V. Polyakov & Y.N. Esin, 'Horn figurines from an Okunev burial on Lake Itkul, Khakassia, southern Siberia', *Archaeology, Ethnology and Anthropology of Eurasia* 43 (2015): 43–57, p. 45.

40 N. Kotova, 'Burial clothing in Neolithic cemeteries of the Ukrainian steppe', *Documenta Praehistorica* 37 (2010): 167–177.
41 C. Marangou, 'Social differentiation in the Early Bronze Age: miniature tools and child burials', *Journal of Mediterranean Studies* 1 (1991): 211–225.
42 T. Higham et al., 'New perspectives on the Varna cemetery (Bulgaria) – AMS dates and social implications', *Antiquity* 81 (2007): 640–654, p. 645.
43 Grömer, *The Art of Prehistoric Textile Making*, p. 335–336, citing Krenn & Krumpel.
44 Grömer, *The Art of Prehistoric Textile Making*, p. 415; D. Pany- Kucera, H. Reschreiter & A. Kern, 'Auf den Kopf gestellt? – überlegungen zu kinderarbeit und transport im prähistorischen Salzbergwerk Hallstatt', *Mitteilungen der Anthropologischen Gesellschaft in Wien*, 140 (2010): 39–68.
45 E. Alarcón García, 'Social relations between adulthood and childhood in the Early Bronze Age site of Peñalosa' in *CSI*: 59–74, p. 70.
46 K.M. Frei et al., 'Tracing the dynamic life story of a Bronze Age female', *Scientific Reports* 5 (2015): 10431.
47 S. Bergerbrant, *Bronze Age Identities: costume, contact and conflict in northern Europe 1600–1300 BC*, Stockholm: Bricoleur Press, 2007, p. 112.
48 S. Welinder, 'The cultural construction of childhood in Scandinavia 3500 BC – 1350 AD', *Current Swedish Archaeology* 6 (1998): 185–204, p. 188.
49 K. Hladíková, 'Perception of children in Villanovan period in southern Etruria' in *CCLA* 41–74, pp. 56–57.
50 M. Chmiel, 'Children in the Wielbark culture societies' in *CCLA*: 89–112, p. 100.
51 S. Salvatori & D. Usai (eds), *A Neolithic Cemetery in the Northern Dongola Reach: excavations at site R12*, BAR International Series 1814, Oxford: Archaeopress, 2008.
52 S. Duchesne et al., 'Le rôle des parures dans les cérémonies funéraires au prédynastique: l'exemple des sépultures d'enfants à Adaïma', *Bulletin de l'Institut français d'archéologie orientale* 103 (2003): 133–166.
53 E. Schijman, 'Artificial cranial deformation in newborns in the pre-Columbian Andes', *Child's Nervous System* 21 (2005): 945–950.
54 A. Daems & K. Croucher, 'Artificial cranial modification: evidence from skulls and figurines', *Iranica Antiqua* 42, 2007: 1–22; 'Prehistory of Iran: artificial cranial modifications' in *Encyclopaedia Iranica* online at www.iranicaonline.org/articles/prehistory-of-iran-artificial-cranial-modifications
55 K.O. Lorentz, 'The malleable body: headshaping in Greece and the surrounding regions', *Hesperia Supplements* 43 (2009): 75–98.
56 G. Manríquez et al., 'Deformación intencional del cráneo en poblaciones arqueológicas de Arica, Chile', *Chungará: Revista de Antropología Chilena* 38 (2006): 13–34.
57 P.C. Gerszten, 'An investigation into the practice of cranial deformation among the pre-Columbian peoples of northern Chile', *International Journal of Osteoarchaeology* 3 (1993): 87–98.
58 J.R. Munizaga, 'Intentional cranial deformation in the precolumbian populations of Ecuador', *American Journal of Physical Anthropology* 45 (1976): 687–694.
59 S. Perez et al., 'Deformaciones artificiales del cráneo en cazadores-recolectores del Holoceno medio-tardío del Noroeste de Patagonia', *Magallania* 37 (2009): 77–90.

60 D.E. Blom, 'Embodying borders: human body modification and diversity in Tiwanaku society', *Journal of Anthropological Archaeology* 24 (2005): 1–24.
61 S.M.F. Mendonça de Souza, K.J. Reinhard & A. Lessa, 'Cranial deformation as the cause of death for a child from the Chillon river valley', *Chungará* 40 (2008): 41–53.
62 A comprehensive survey for the region is V. Tiesler, *The Bioarchaeology of Artificial Cranial Modifications: new approaches to head shaping and its meanings in pre-Columbian Mesoamerica and beyond*, New York: Springer, 2014.

6
LEARNING
Knowledge and skills

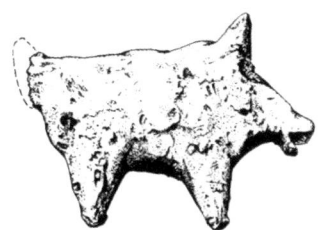

Ethnographic studies of foragers and village farmers alike emphasise that much of the learning in childhood comes from interaction with peers and older children, significantly complementing that from parents, other adults or formal instruction. By analogy, we can extend this back to prehistoric communities and prehistoric childhoods. Studies of other higher primates attest something similar. Chapter 7 emphasises that play is one of the main ways in which children learn and develop the skills required to participate in society and, in due course, to operate as adults.

Archaeological evidence provides further images of the learning process. It can inform, and be informed by, debates about childhood acquisition of skills and knowledge. As examples in this chapter show, examination (or re-examination) of excavated stone artefact assemblages can indicate places and stages of apprenticeship, and of trial and error in tool preparation. Prehistoric art carries the marks of children's participation. Pottery can present evidence of young and learner potters, both in the form and competence of the pots and in fingerprints on the pots themselves. Less easy to locate is specific evidence of other crafts learned in childhood; here we may relay on analogies with recent small scale societies.

A core argument of this book is that children are important to our understanding the human past because childhood is the time when knowledge (social and practical) is transmitted: knowledge that provides the continuities in human culture. How do we see the process of learning in prehistory? We can identify evidence of the acquisition of craftmanship in the archaeological record, but for the most part we have to imagine the acquisition of skills relating to the non-material aspects of society. We can also consider how the acquisition of knowledge by early hominins has differed from that among living higher primates.

Prehistorian Clive Gamble has suggested the evocative word 'childscapes' for the human environment in which culture is transmitted and learned.[1] Such a concept reminds us that children are central to the social worlds of the past. The environment that provides for children is one that provides for the learning process, to ensure the continuity of culture and skills: material culture, economic and social relations with the rest of society, and belief systems too.

The human child is born with an instinctive drive to learn, and a brain patterned to process experience into accumulated knowledge and new behaviours. The human world he or she encounters – mother, family, social group – serves to utilise these brain patterns, bringing the child into a world of social interaction, and developing skills from feeding to moving to language, and in due course to tool making, food acquisition, mate selection, and ethical and spiritual values. Whatever the balance between nature and nurture, between biological and cultural influences, the transformation of the newborn through to the adolescent on the brink of adulthood involves a long and complex learning process.[2]

The highly influential body of work on childhood learning by psychologist Jean Piaget, published between the 1920s and the 1970s, has led thinking about the stages of children's development and learning.[3] His studies were based in advanced western societies and were not actively cross-cultural, though by implication he deemed the results to be applicable across all societies. Anthropologists long continued to debate the applicability of his ideas to the communities they study, noting that the biological age of Piaget's development stages in his western context varies widely in other societies.[4] In Piaget's schema, children develop new styles of cognitive development from age 2 to around 7 years, with symbolic and make-believe play important. From 7 to 11 more analytical and logical approaches to knowledge apply, after which an adolescent stage involves more reasoning and analysis on the path to the adult mind.

Piaget's analyses did lead to applied educational approaches in formal teaching, which contrast with the pattern of acquired learning in traditional small-scale societies.

A key period for acquiring knowledge comes early: the fastest period of human learning is between the ages of 6 and 18 months. Here the primary influence is the mother: the maternal bond, essential for feeding, is also the first source of knowledge, and the mother's voice conveys mood, introduces language and in time imparts knowledge. In his book *The Singing Neanderthals*, Steven Mithen has suggested a sequence of development in hominin societies, in which he seeks to integrate concepts of vocalisation, music, rhythm and language origins.[5] Where a mother is on a foraging trip and may need, even briefly, to put her young baby down, her voice (singing or otherwise) can provide comfort: we can readily envisage such a phenomenon among pre-modern hominins.[6] At the very least, our earlier hominin ancestors may have used some clear vocalisation to indicate to an infant what substances were foods to be eaten and what items were to be avoided: Mithen's 'Yuk' theory.

While much human learning comes from imitation, the evolution of language brought a new dimension to instruction and cultural development. As noted below, scholars are not in agreement on the point at which true language can be said to have existed in prehistory. One difference between humans and other higher primates (apart from gibbons) appears to be the greater role of human fathers, and their contribution to assist socialisation and learning.[7] While the form and degree are, of course, culturally constrained and often culturally determined, the extended monogamous unit which is the norm in the majority of human societies provides a framework to allow and require such interactions. This does not contradict the dominant role of the mother in care and provision of security.

LEARNING AND TOOL USE AMONG THE GREAT APES

Like humans, all primates acquire skills as juveniles through different learning processes: skills of acquiring food, skills of social interaction and skills of survival. Many studies have eroded the distinction of *Homo sapiens* as the only living tool users and even as the only tool-makers. Tools have even been identified and recorded archaeologically from macaque monkeys, while New World monkeys have been found to pound food with stone tools to make it ready to eat.[8]

Actual teaching of skills is rare across all non-human primates, in contrast to those mammals which rely on active hunting to secure food. Acquiring knowledge through 'observational learning' better describes the great ape pattern; in contrast, when the human child imitates an adult it is a more accurate, more complex and more receptive process.[9] Among chimpanzees in the wild many innovations are easily forgotten: this is not a world of reliable cultural transmission.[10]

Though essentially tree dwellers, young orangutans still have to learn climbing techniques from adults. Studies of captive orangutans show that such skills are not instinctive. After an initial reluctance to move away from their mothers, their extreme caution slowly gives way to more adventurous excursions. Orangutan young learn primarily by observation, which means mainly watching their mothers' behaviour, which leads in turn to imitation.[11] Captive orangutans have also learned tool use from observing humans.

Gorillas too acquire skills mainly by observation. In the wild they have limited use of 'tools' – physical objects to assist in achieving goals.[12] Rather more can be observed in the artificial context of captivity.

Chimpanzee mother demonstrating tool use to her young in Bossou, Guinea

The more detailed studies of chimpanzees in the wild suggest they learn skills through repetitive observation of a process undertaken by their mother or another adult. Even when the observed adult is the mother, this is not active teaching and training but passive: it is the juvenile who acts to learn and imitate. Adult tolerance of the inquisitive young appears fundamental to the learning process.[13]

But mothers are active to prevent an infant doing something dangerous: for example, eating a plant which may be toxic, or indeed approaching an adult who may prove hostile. The Japanese primatologist Satoshi Hirata observed a chimpanzee mother pulling her young infant away from investigating too closely a chain which might have caused injury.[14] Biological fathers play no specific role in the raising of the chimpanzee young because they cannot know which are their own offspring. While this is the pattern noted in the eastern chimpanzee groups, an extended study in the Taï Forest of Côte d'Ivoire found that the specialist nut-cracking habit was acquired when the mothers stimulated and facilitated their offspring's learning, but that mothers would interfere with active demonstration when emulation proved inadequate.[15]

Most knowledge about chimpanzees' learning abilities has come from chimpanzees kept (and often born) in captivity, which presents an artificial framework, measuring what skills they *can* acquire rather that how and what learning is experienced in the natural community. Experiments with captive chimpanzees – including some famous examples of those raised within human families – demonstrate the potential of the chimpanzee brain (to learn sign language, vocal responses, manual skills and puzzle solving). They do not tell us what happens in the wild.

Tool use and some basic tool making are now recognised as a feature of chimpanzee groups.[16] Major studies on tool use and learning by chimpanzees have been led by Tetsuro Matsuzawa and his colleagues at the Primate Research Institute of Kyoto University, Japan. Tool use by chimpanzees can involve a range of natural materials and modification of these (tool making), and an innovation may be transmitted to others. The young acquire from an adult skills which we could describe as cultural, as with humans and their hominin ancestors, not biological.[17] Controlled experiments with captive chimpanzees undertaken at the Primate Research Institute by Misato Hayashi and her colleagues show that adults have the ability to use object with object (like a selected hammer stone and a selected anvil stone), for instance to crack a nut.[18] This combination is not achieved by young chimpanzees until their fourth year.

In a chimpanzee group studied at Bossou in Guinea, infants learn by the age of 18 months the different skills involved in nut cracking, but it takes two more years before they are able to put them together in sequence to crack a nut, which requires the use of two appropriate stones together as hammer and anvil.[19] This nut cracking at Bossou is part of a set of skills involving tool use by the young.[20] A 'wand' is used to dip into an ants' nest. A folded leaf is used to obtain drinking water from a hole in a tree. A pestle is used to pound the shoots of a palm tree before eating. A grass stalk is used to scoop algae from a pond before consuming them. Sticks are used to fish for termites, and also to obtain insect larvae, and dip for honey or resin gum. On occasions a chimpanzee may even use a stick to probe a small animal inside a tree hollow or to deactivate a snare. This wide range of tool use, mainly as strategies for food, is not instinctive but learned: as the young grows he or she is more able to apply what skills and use of tools they have observed in adults in their community.

Chimpanzees in Gombe, Tanzania (at the eastern extreme of today's chimpanzee distribution) have become expert at using a stick to obtain termites to eat, a skill learned by imitation.[21] Interestingly, young females learned this skill more than two years earlier than males, and practised it more frequently and more proficiently. Daughters copied their mothers' termite-fishing techniques carefully, sons less conscientiously. Typically, at the termite mound, the young females would observe their mothers carefully while young males would spend more of the time playing.

Experiments with apes in captivity have included attempts to teach the modification of stone to use as tools. The conclusions of archaeologist Nicholas Toth from experiments over many years with the bonobo Kanzi was that bonobos lacked the ability to make a consistent shape: the results were still far from the first human tools found in the archaeological record.[22] But another experiment involving infant chimpanzees copying their mothers in manipulating objects of different shapes showed them to be comparable with human infants at 8–11 months in some but not all applications.[23]

Another experiment with chimpanzees in captivity showed infants of a little less than 2 years of age observing over a period, then successfully repeating, a task of using tools to dip into a container to obtain honey.[24] Different possible tools were made available. In the 'learning' process, when the infants were observing their own mothers and other females, mothers proved somewhat tolerant to infants other than their own, but most tolerant to their own offspring. The infants learned not just the methodology, but two of the three participants followed adults in the selection of the most suitable of the available possible tools. The less passive form of learning observed in the Taï Forest of Côte d'Ivoire, where mothers did teach their infants how to crack a nut, was noted above.

Thus chimpanzees can show some skill as basic tool-makers in the wild, copying adult behaviour, and even more abilities can be taught in captivity. But there is evidence for basic abilities in both humans and other higher primates beyond those learned by imitation. Young children are shown to teach themselves (invent) some of the same skills acquired by great apes.[25]

For comparison, a test of 50 British and German children aged from 2 to 3½ years doing four tasks lasting 1 or 2 minutes each demonstrated their ability to solve problems by inventing new skills of tool use. The tasks were similar to those of the adult great apes (although the reward was not food, but social praise in the form of stickers!). The goal of the test was to see whether children of this age could independently invent a new skill of tool selection and tool use to undertake an unfamiliar task that is seen in chimpanzee or orangutan behaviour in the wild. For 11 of 12 such behaviours the answer was positive, and the success rate was highest for skills seen frequently among apes than for infrequent ones, with the children's success rate improving with age. The experimenters concluded that 'in the tool-use domain humans are not born special'.[26] It would, however, be interesting to see whether similar results are found in different societies, including those which might put less emphasis on early education than in the driven culture of modern urban western European young families.

HOMININ EVOLUTION AND KNOWLEDGE TRANSMISSION

By analogy with higher primates, we can suggest for early hominins a learning pattern involving observation and imitation, with the role of mothers of central importance. In the foraging communities of the Palaeolithic such learning would include female juveniles copying their mothers' contribution to food gathering, including the use of tools associated with this. We conventionally envisage males in Palaeolithic societies as hunters and as the primary makers of stone tools: skills which require careful emulation to become successful members of a social group and attractive as potential mates.

Psychologist Mark Nielsen recently suggested that the continuity of Acheulean handaxe technology – the apparent imitative reproduction of form in the era associated mainly with *Homo erectus* –implies that the life stage of imaginative learning that marks human childhood had not existed in the Lower Palaeolithic.[27] By this interpretation, 'childhood' emerged no earlier than with Neanderthals – the Middle Palaeolithic of Europe and the Middle East from 300,000 years ago until their replacement by *Homo sapiens*. But even if this argument has some validity, the Lower Palaeolithic young had to acquire knowledge of how to make Acheulean handaxes: learning rather than creative innovation.

Arguments and evidence (including that from burials described in Chapter 9) have been increasingly supported the idea that some Neanderthal groups demonstrated ritual and visual expression, and that they undertook 'symbolic' activity. However, the evidence for Neanderthal 'symbolic' behaviour is patchy, and the breadth of the temporal and geographical spread of Neanderthals makes generalisation on Neanderthal cultures and abilities problematic.[28] A construction made from stalagmites dated ca. 175,000 years ago in the French cave of Bruniquel is so far a unique find.[29]

Symbolic activity and the use of language may be related but are not a package, and one is not a direct proxy for the other. There are still differing views on whether Neanderthals had language, as we understand it, and these debates involve palaeoanthropologists, archaeologists, linguists, behavioural scientists and others. Certainly language was part of modern human behaviour, present by the time anatomically modern humans spread out from Africa by around 60,000 years ago; and the vocal chords of *Homo sapiens* may be little changed since their origins in Africa. Language lubricates forward planning and negotiated outcomes as well as the transmission of knowledge.[30] Before the evolution of language, important areas of learning (foraging, hunting techniques, tool making and use of the landscape) must have been acquired by observation and imitation, rather than through detailed verbal instruction, and could not reach the level of imaginative development and originality seen in the modern human species.[31]

Whether Neanderthal communication contained what we would describe as elementary speech (or indeed more advanced language) will remain a topic for debate. There are proponents of an early origin for language – at least as far back as the earliest Neanderthals, with arguments that reflect perceptions on how different genetically and physically Neanderthals were from modern humans.[32] Such views remain at present the minority; the dominant view sees language attributed exclusively to anatomically modern humans.[33] The fact that Neanderthals appear to have had a hyoid bone in the neck similar to that of modern humans does, though, support the idea of Neanderthal speech ability.[34]

When we consider prehistoric *Homo sapiens*, we are aware of their physical similarities to our modern population, and not least the similar brain size. Changes in physique reflect adaptation and selection but we are not dealing with inexplicable mindsets of alien creatures.[35] The difference from earlier hominin ancestors lay in the nature and range of cultural knowledge passed down from elders to the young, who in turn transmitted it to the next generation. With the development of language, such learning was not just in material culture, social practice and food-gathering strategies: it could extend to ideas. The capacity and scope for learning are increased when there is language and social complexity.

LEARNING AND WORK IN RECENT SMALL-SCALE SOCIETIES

Childhood is the period of transition towards biological maturity (marked by the role of generating and maintaining the next generation of children) and the period of transition towards social maturity (marked by mastering and using the social, practical and economic skills needed to operate as an adult). We can augment our understanding of prehistoric learning by considering some more recent communities.

Observation of small-scale societies serves to emphasise the long period of learning in our species, compared with other primates. But the learning process among most such groups includes learning by practice and involvement, helping in the activities of the group. In Chapter 4 the activities of children of some communities in food collection were noted. And as discussed in Chapter 7, in a typical hunter-gatherer group young children will play with older children and learn from them. Games may involve practising the skills of adults – yet may also just be for fun, for exercise, for excitement and to fill the time. Not all play is a social mechanism for the acquisition of skills.

In his review of childhood as understood through the anthropological study of many different societies, David Lancy emphasises as common in traditional small-scale communities the pattern in which children learn but are not taught. They gain knowledge by close observation and imitation of parents or of other members of the group if they are the ones looking after the young.[36] In this framework children are tolerated, and may be warned off harmful activity, but are expected to teach themselves the skills they will need to become valuable members of the family and of the society. Lancy notes that the range of practical skills a child needs to acquire in such societies can be quite limited, although they have far longer to learn life skills than do other primates. While economic participation may begin very young and children become reasonably competent at an early age, more technical craft skills could take much of a lifetime to perfect. But even a formal apprenticeship, acquiring specific skills from a master, may involve observation rather than formal teaching.[37]

In a further argument, Lancy has suggested that children in small-scale societies often represent a 'reserve force' of labour.[38] They acquire practical skills from a young age: skills which may or may not be needed as an essential part of the household life and economy, depending on circumstances. The child's ability may be a useful part of family life, or it may be held in reserve for use if required by illness, disability, economic pressure; or it may be applied minimally – skills and knowledge which the child has stored for future use as he or she grows to play a more adult role in society. A child's learning is closely related to a child's work.

The contribution a child can make to the family, group and society is established by culture as much as biology. A mother who takes her young infant on a foraging trip or with her into the cultivated garden may encourage the child to help: whether as distraction, or training or direct contribution to the household economy. As a boy grows, the father may bring his son into the roles he will pay as a young adult. Children acquire knowledge for their future roles in the family, in society, in the household economy, in household crafts and in more specialised activities. The role of learning is transformed gradually (and sometimes less gradually) into the roles of work.

The potential of young children to learn, contribute and work is given a chilling reality in the historical world of slavery. Thomas Roughley's 1823 volume *The Jamaica Planter's Guide* helps the slave-owner with getting the most work from young slaves (that is, those born into slavery).[39] A danger for such infants is that if they stay with their mothers 'the child becomes accustomed to too much tenderness, unsuitable to its station'.[40] They should be removed from their mother at the age of 1 year and at 3 years joined with others of the same age to learn work by collecting leaves of weeds into a basket. At the age of 5 or 6 they could join a work gang proper, weeding and also scattering dung behind adult planters. When they reached the age of 12, they would join in a work gang to plant and maintain corn or crops until they were ready, at age 18, for the heaviest work.

The idea of children undertaking harsh manual labour comes to us not just from the era of slavery but from images of early industrial Europe and from modern campaigns on child labour in developing counties. But evidence can also occur in prehistory, including mines, where the small bodies of children could reach areas not accessible to adults, but sometimes fell foul of accidents. At the salt mines of Iron Age Hallstatt in Austria, in the mid-1st millennium BC, children seem to have been very much part of the activity, doing heavy labour, as shown by the examination of the musculoskeletal system of 40 children who did not survive.[41]

A collation of data recorded from 14 small-scale societies in the modern era (mainly hunter-gatherers or garden horticulturalists) showed the wide range of tasks in which even very young children were engaged, and the typical age at which they began such roles.[42] Children of 3 to 5 years were already active in some care of young siblings in five of these groups, and in all of them by the age of 10. Carrying firewood was a universal, with 3- to 5-year-olds in six of the groups running errands for their family and 8-year-olds carrying water. In the age group 6–10 years, children in a number of the groups were active in caring for a grandparent, or for livestock in the groups which owned domestic animals. In hunter-gatherer societies young children from an early age familiarise themselves with tools by playing with them; even 4-year-olds use snares or digging sticks. Across the 14 societies, young children (aged 3 to 5 years) were already using knives or other tools in three or four groups, and helping with food collection in two, while older children (up to 10 years) helped in this in the majority of the societies; slightly fewer were involved in food preparation.

A child's learning begins as a small infant, under the mother's guidance, and until the age of 5 most learning is at the hands of mother and father. Observers of African hunter-gatherers have noted how soon mothers engage babies in 'gymnastic behaviour' exercises in jumping and later in sitting and standing, which tend to make them physically more advanced than western urban infants.[43]

In the Aka and Bofi forager communities of Central Africa, from around the age of 5 to age 12, children learn especially from their association with other (and often older) children. By imitating them they gain specific skills and knowledge, while their participation in these groups generates social knowledge.[44] The Aka Pygmies were said to have more involvement of fathers in infant care than any other known society.[45]

Children must learn social skills, acquire technical abilities and gain appropriate spiritual (or non-material) knowledge. But they must also gain the expertise they will require as an adult and a parent, including contributing food to family and group. A child who is not trained in the acquisition of food will be disadvantaged through life, for example if a boy in a hunting society is removed from his community during the key learning years.[46] Preparation for this role may involve practice with weapons from an early age, increasing accuracy with spear or with bow and arrow. It involves practice at tracking prey and setting snares. The Aleut of Alaska teach specific strengthening exercises to help in sea hunting from a kayak.[47] One study from the 1950s comparing multiple societies with subsistence economies suggested a difference in attitude between foraging and agricultural societies: while agriculturalist parents as a priority required children to be compliant in their learning, societies reliant on gathering and especially on hunting or fishing emphasised assertiveness over compliance.[48] Perhaps this is just a feature of *Homo sapiens*: a million years of handaxe makers does not suggest much priority was given to individualism or innovation for *Homo erectus*.

Consistent across forager societies is a gender division of skills, requiring the acquisition of those skills by children in anticipation of their adult roles. But the nature of this division necessarily varies widely between different societies, such as the contribution men may make to food gathering as well as hunting, or women may make to animal kills, and the different patterns of decision making in different societies. Anthropological study of the Akwe-Shavante of the Amazon suggested that while a young girl behaves like a smaller version of a young woman, a boy of the same age is just playing.[49]

Observers noticed the relaxed and casual life of !Kung San children of the arid Botswana–Namibia region: mingling with adults day and night, with few duties or responsibilities. Older children do not even look after their younger siblings. !Kung children are not expected to play any significant role in food production until they are well into their teenage years.[50] Boys may accompany a hunting party from the age of about 12 and the point at which they make their first significant kill is an important one, celebrated by ceremonial skin cuts. Hunting skills make a man a desirable marriage partner.

A typical !Kung community has the widespread forager characteristic: that young men do not learn to hunt by formal training but by observation. In such San societies they are not 'taught' hunting techniques but are expected to observe, learn, practise – and succeed.[51] While the young copy their elders in making snares or bows and arrows, and experimenting with these, young men work with older men in collaborative hunts: these can succeed only if the knowledge and expertise of the older men is applied by the whole hunt, and the young thus learn by participation. Additionally, a large part of men's conversation is accounts of their successful hunts which the young will hear: if not direct instruction, it serves this purpose.

A valuable essay by Nicholas Blurton Jones contrasted the child-rearing practices of the !Kung with the Hadza of the rocky hills of north-west Tanzania.[52] He notes that !Kung parenting keeps children close at hand, under constant care and indulgence, with no responsibilities in the camp and a quick response to any anxieties: '!Kung mothers are among the most indulgent and attentive ever described'. By contrast, in Hadza society children are expected to assist adults in undertaking a wide range of social duties, often out of sight or supervision of adults: 'Hadza mothers are noisy, intimidating, and often not very responsive'. They can ignore crying and smack their offspring. Children in both societies thrive, are sociable and happy. The differences may reflect their different physical and economic environments and the pressures arising from producing many babies while keeping safe the children you already have.

Hunting ability by males is learned throughout life. Some young foragers may be expert hunters and their abilities continue to develop through childhood and with experience through adulthood. Meriam children from the Torres Strait community of garden horticulturalists and fishers are described as better spear fishers than their parents.

As an example of other skills, the Mansi of Siberia combine foraging with reindeer herding and are thus provided with skins. A young girl learns the important skills of sewing and making clothes by making coverings for her dolls, under family supervision.[53]

There is an enigmatic, and controversial, exception to the pattern of the gradual informal induction of children into adult skills. The Ik people on the borders of Uganda and Kenya were described in Colin Turnbull's 1972 monograph *The Mountain People*.[54] In this foraging group, age cohorts of children appeared to raise each other, relatively independent of parents, who gave little support and indeed behaved selfishly and at times cruelly. The Ik had been agriculturalists but had turned to foraging after being moved from their traditional territory. What seemed to observers to be levels of dysfunctionality and lack of family emotion may reflect this circumstance. But the wide range of social patterns found among foragers may remind us that there is no standard model for analogy with prehistoric peoples; in times of social and environmental crisis there were no doubt dysfunctional behaviours and major social changes.

A detailed study of childhood among Aboriginal people of Maningrida in Arnhem Land in 1961–62 dealt with communities already heavily disrupted, modified and controlled by European settlement. Maningrida had been started as a government settlement for Aboriginal people just 10 years earlier. It is problematic to try to distinguish between 'traditional' practices retained in a community like Maningrida and patterns which specifically reflect the new world. The values recorded seemed to represent very different traditions from those of white Australia. Infants received no name until they were 12 months old, and were weaned at about 2 years of age. They received little guidance from elders, learning rather than being taught; even toilet training was absent. The word 'why' was missing from the vocabulary – the world worked as it worked – and moral approbation or punishment seemed minimal or absent.[55]

The image is presented of young who learned primarily from their own peer group more than from adult training; a 'kid mob' of children aged from 9 to 12 was all-important (even more for boys than girls) but in the government settlement the age cohort would, of course, be much larger than in a mobile forager band.

As a climax to the period of gradual learning which marks childhood, many forager societies (like other communities) have a formal rite of initiation which marks the transition from the stage of being a child, if not yet full acknowledgement as an adult. Such initiation may include formal instruction in adult knowledge, distinguished by gender. Australian Aboriginal initiation has a strong element of acquiring new knowledge of the traditions, myths, beliefs and the land itself, and may follow a period of formal induction.[56] At initiation a child may be an adult, yet the learning processes of life continue.

Studies of remote Australian Aboriginal communities stress the relationship between practical learning and ritual learning, as a child becomes an adult.[57] Both may involve observation and copying, but a formal initiation brings the juvenile into the adult world, and many archaeological sites in Australia, especially those with significant rock painting or engraving, are considered places of ritual initiation into adulthood and the secret and sacred knowledge associated with this. Terms such as 'the Dreaming' and 'songlines' only hint at the complexities of this relationship.

Such knowledge may combine the spiritual with the practical: knowledge of the land is also identity with the land, and for nomadic communities of the past in the vast arid areas of mainland Australia, an essential basis for survival. The landscape has possibilities and threats: these are reflected in a combination of practical and abstract knowledge. Yet the ritual aspect is emphasised by the very different inductions of males and females: ritual and practical knowledge are segmented by age and by gender, but they are not necessarily segmented between practical economic material skills and other forms of knowledge.

STONE TOOLS AND APPRENTICESHIP

Evidence for apprenticeship and learning practical skills can be traced in archaeological deposits, once we begin to search for it. The ages and stages of apprenticeship vary significantly. In one society an important technology might be learned from early in childhood, but in another it may be a secret craft accessible only to young adults enrolled in the craft group. In Chapter 1 I mentioned my grandmother who became a school teacher at 15; with increasing emphasis on postgraduate education many people in, say, western European societies do not qualify in their profession until their very late 20s. There are constantly changing patterns of the timing of craft training. I worked as a volunteer on archaeological excavations in each of my teenage years from the age of 12, and one of the most professional digs I have ever encountered, of a Roman palace in southern Britain, was directed by a university student (called Barry Cunliffe).

What can archaeology say about how detailed technical abilities and traditions are learned? In a collection of essays published in 2012 (from a 2005 conference), a number of authors discussed approaches that might fit the availability and limitations of our data.[58] A key question remains how we recognise evidence in the archaeological record for apprenticeship and the stages of acquiring technical craft ability.[59] A poorly made object need not necessarily be a sign of an active learner, while a managed apprentice can produce very competent pieces. A key feature of poor, experimental work is that it may not be preserved in the record – depending on time, place and culture. Metalwork will be reused, poor pots will not be fired and inadequate carvings may be finished off by an expert. In many crafts, the novice or apprentice is not necessarily a child and not all children in a society (even where roles are gender determined) are expected to master all the skills in a pre-industrial small-scale community.[60]

The most visible sign of the skills of prehistory is the vast corpus of stone tools and the waste products of stone tool manufacture. The first stone tool assemblages generally date from at least 2.6 million years ago, although a 2015 find from Lomekwi in Kenya is suggested to date back 3.3 million years.[61] Remote Central Australian communities continued to produce stone tools in the mid-20th century, and stone tool manufacture and use are still to be found within the technologies of other small-scale societies.[62]

Stone tools provide our best (though still limited) evidence of the learning process.[63] Unlike metal-working, in many regions there is plenty of raw stone for apprentices to test and develop their skills in stone tool manufacture, although in those areas with a shortage of suitable materials we may expect to find trial work only in a few zones where there is plenty to waste.[64] Badly made tools will be discarded and their materials rarely reused. The challenge is how we might confidently identify the trial pieces, the inexpert work of a child or adolescent learning to work stone and create tools in the style of their society: a skill which inspired Nyree Finlay's pun 'kid knapping'.[65]

In assemblages from early 'pebble tool' industries it is easy to imagine some unfinished or uneven pieces as the work of the young. But in the subsequent Acheulean Lower Palaeolithic societies of Africa, the Middle East and Europe the ability to make a high-quality handaxe was clearly highly valued and highly important. These are neatly prepared symmetrical tools, often pear shaped, with a pointed end opposing a rounded end linked by parallel trimmed edges. The regularity and frequency of the form suggest it was more than just a convenient tool: it was a symbol too of personal ability, social position and adulthood. The care and detail of handaxe manufacture may well have served to show off a masculine skill and influence mate selection.[66] An enormous number of handaxes have been discovered and their distribution in time and space is vast. The earliest handaxes in Africa may date from before 1.6 million years ago and in Europe from at least 400,000 years ago, possibly significantly longer.[67] They continue to be found in Africa and Europe to around 300,000 to 250,000 years ago: an astonishing continuity of tradition, one associated primarily with *Homo erectus* and archaic *Homo* such as *Homo heidelbergensis* in Europe. Learning to make high-quality handaxes would be a careful and involved process. So where are all the trial pieces produced when children sought to imitate adults, and locations where the young trained and practised to match their elders?[68]

The period of stone technology whose image is dominated by tools in the handaxe shape has sometimes been described as 'a million years of boredom', a phrase which implies a prejudice to the view that change and 'progress' are a requirement of human history, even if other advanced mammals are expected to maintain stable social and 'cultural' patterns. There were of course changes and development over the era of Acheulean handaxe makers, but that is not the issue.

The problem of finding and identifying apprentice stone knapping work from young learners applies through all periods of Stone Age prehistory. The minimal visibility of children's stone working has been discussed by archaeologist (and skilled flint-knapper) John Shea.[69] He suggests that children's (i.e. learners') stone tool making should be indicated both by smaller final tools than from adults and by more 'waste flakes', the discard left from all stone tool making. But many of the occasional suggestions that particular small-scale artefacts represent children's work seem inherently improbable, or at least variable and unprovable.[70] A beginning learner would be more likely to be given a large core and then produce crude large flakes: it takes experience and skill to work stone at a small scale. There have been experimental projects with children as stone knappers, using flint in particular.[71]

Interpretations of small handaxes as 'toys' (i.e. made by adults for children) are imaginative but impossible to test.[72] A Cambridge University exhibition on the archaeology of childhood included a miniature handaxe from Ipswich in England, just 7 cm (3 inches) long, with the suggestion that it may have been intended to teach a child tool use.[73]

Prehistorians once considered every significant variation in a stone tool assemblage as a sign of a different people, with their own distribution in time and place and relationship to other groups. Gradually subtler analyses of variability emerged: a recognition that differences might reflect available raw materials, or the function to which tools were put at a site (manufacturing or butchery, at a long-term home base or temporary camp). A single group undertaking a seasonal migration between very different environments offering very different food resources could leave behind quite different tools. But what is commonly missing – perhaps because too difficult – is categorisation of stone tools as the products of master craftsman, apprentice or children, with a gradation of ability from experienced adult to adolescent learner to child's play. In such an analysis we would expect to see a significant difference between the tool assemblage of a camp of adult hunters and a camp composed mainly of women and children, where the young were testing their skills with trial stone chipping. And if stone tool technology over the last two and a half million years shows an overall development through stages of ability, it may also be reasonable to think of the youngest stone workers initially mastering some of the simpler techniques: a progress of the individual in life, not just of the hominin line through time.

As an example of the conventional approach to stone assemblage variability, in his thorough survey of the European Middle Palaeolithic and Neanderthal world, Paul Mellars presents François Bordes' classic typology of flake tools where the poorest are considered accidental, perhaps geological in origin: none are described as trial or trainee pieces.[74]

Increasingly, though, there are sites where archaeologists do identify the work of learners (usually, by implication, the young) in stone artefact assemblages.[75] These approaches suggest the products of learning can be found in specific parts of a settlement site, identified by unfinished or poor-quality results. In the search for 'apprentice' stone tool manufacture, certain specific techniques have been suggested as typical of beginners.[76]

An example is the intensive programme by Jun Takakura of refitting obsidian flakes to cores from the Upper Palaeolithic of Hokkaido in northern Japan.[77] This complex and lengthy exercise allowed a close examination of the stages of working the raw material to create artefacts. Results suggested that one site (Hattoridae 2) represented a practice site used by an apprentice, while another site (Kamirishirataki 2) suggested a master craftsman working with pupils and guiding them in the techniques of stone tool making. Such exhaustive studies of already excavated materials may well identify such nuances in sites.

Among the Neanderthals of Middle Palaeolithic Europe, different levels of ability were noted in the stone tool assemblage at Arcy-sur-Cure.[78] Neanderthal apprentice work appears to be present at Netherlands sites of Maastricht-Belvédère, Rhenen and Warandebergen.[79]

At a few Upper Palaeolithic sites in Europe archaeologists have suggested that the skill levels required to produce the materials found reflect the learning process and are the products of apprentices.[80] At Solvieux in the French Dordogne, reassembled stone flakes suggest the work of an apprentice knapper, working with good-quality raw material under the supervision of an expert.[81] At the French site of Etiolles, stone artefacts have been considered to be signs of apprentice learning.[82]

At a Magdalenian Upper Palaeolithic campsite in Pincevent, near Paris, France, some 12 millennia old, it was possible to refit flakes to cores and to see in more detail how a crude level of flint knapping operated: possible evidence of training by apprentices beginning to learn the craft, sometimes on inferior raw materials – although poor workmanship should not always be attributed to the young! Skills can also decrease as part of the ageing process.

The excavators at Pincevent felt confident that the different skill levels marked out different adult individuals, from experts whose products might be of sufficient quality for exchange, to cruder work less skilled individuals undertook for themselves.[83] Indeed, we have conventionally thought of the Palaeolithic as a period of generalists, in which everyone made their own stone tools. But given the sophistication of the best tools, especially in the European Upper Palaeolithic, it may be more realistic to acknowledge a culture of excellence in which expert stone knappers with extended periods of training and practice traded their skills in society for other advantages.[84]

After the end of the Pleistocene – the period of the European Ice Age – hunting and foraging groups classified as Mesolithic continued to settle in Europe, gradually replaced by (or transformed into) 'Neolithic' farming economies. These later hunter-gatherers are visible through their more sophisticated (though still flaked) specialised stone tool technology. Some Mesolithic artefacts have been identified as the work of children or apprentices. In Denmark a study suggested that reuse of stone cores with multiple marks of impact, as well as discarded items, represent work by beginners who were unable to match the skills of the adults.[85] The site of Trollesgave in Denmark had separate areas of stone tool manufacture showing different skills, interpreted as the work of an adult expert and a juvenile novice.[86]

Of similar 8th millennium BC Mesolithic date, the lakeside camp at Lough Boora in Ireland had areas of stone tool making (using chert) which showed variable abilities all in the same location. This suggests a learning process by individuals of different ages and skill stages. The scatters were near to hearths, and create an image of people sitting and practising their skills. Another Mesolithic settlement a millennium later, Coulelerach in western Scotland, had a range of ability levels displayed, from carefully prepared blades to crudely battered cores.[87] While traditional prehistorians might exult in the discovery of beautifully formed artistic artefacts, those interested in prehistoric childhood can celebrate the recovery of crude, experimental, unskilled work that demonstrates the humanity and efforts of the young learner.

Stone manufacturing continued as the main tool source for early agriculturalists. At a Neolithic settlement in southern Sweden a flint knapping area was uncovered, with about 400 flakes spread around two large stones.[88] In one part of this area the finds represent a skilled conventional approach to creating a Neolithic axe. In another part, the stone flakes had an unsystematic and unskilled approach, which suggested a beginner imitating a skilled adult.

Elsewhere in this chapter the pattern is noted – common to other primates, recent foragers and others – that knowledge is transmitted by observations and imitation more than formal teaching (and as noted in Chapter 7, much play involves imitation of the adult world). But does this model fit well with the development of tool-making skills? Where accidents are too easy, materials are limited and techniques are complex, then we can suggest a role for formal teaching, with detailed knowledge imparted under the active supervision of a senior skilled guide.[89] The knowledge of how to make a finely designed, highly functional artefact from a selected stone pebble is one of the most complex forms of knowledge in forager prehistory, and forms the basis of cultural continuity.[90]

Examination of stone artefacts from the Archaic hunter-gatherers of the US Great Basin in Nevada suggested the presence of juvenile apprentices creating projectile points from chert nodules.[91] Since raw materials were local and plentiful there was no requirement to rework trial pieces; the process was even described as 'wasteful'. Specific locations of trainees could be identified from the comparative location of skilled and unskilled pieces.

Early hunter-fisher people of the Arctic from before 1000 AD – referred to as Palaeo-Eskimos – have also provided archaeological evidence of the learning process in stone tool manufacture.[92] The abundance of flint in the interior of Baffin Island, Canada, made this a suitable area for trial work, and evidence of apprentice-level work has been found. By contrast, coastal Palaeo-Eskimo sites on the island, where raw materials were at a premium, lacked the poor-quality products. This supports the image of teaching and learning stone tool technology as a summer seasonal activity associated with the time of inland occupation.

It is commonly assumed that in most prehistoric communities learning to make stone tools was a necessary and universal step to (male) adulthood. But in some societies the pattern may have been different. In Irian Jaya (the western part of New Guinea, now part of Indonesia) stone working of adzes appears to have been a specialist craft mastered only by certain families. Apprenticeships began about the age of 12–13 years and it could take up to 10 years to master the craft.[93]

That relatively few 'apprentice' sites have been identified among the enormous number of sites with stone artefacts suggests that most archaeologists have not considered their material in the light of the variable of quality and competence. As the exact positions of finds are recorded and refitting studies take place on waste materials, it is likely that more locations within prehistoric campsites will be identified as the places where the young learned and practised stone tool-making skills.

CHILDREN'S INVOLVEMENT IN ROCK ART

How much were children involved in the creation of rock art, and more specifically in some of the painted marks in the European caves utilised in the Upper Palaeolithic?[94] We noted in Chapter 3 the stencilled hands and footprints which suggested children were present in the caves when adults were painting or engraving works of art on the cave walls.

The finger marks ('flutings' impressed into the limestone or similar soft walls of caves) may be the result of children drawing in the soft clay.[95] The size of the marks indicates the size of the fingers used to create them and therefore the approximate age of the artists. The site of Rouffignac in the French Dordogne has adult and child flutings over an area of 500 m². As well as a couple of older juveniles, the suggested age of the young artists ranged from 2 to 5 years, probably both boys and girls, and adults would need to have held them on their shoulders to allow them to reach the marked surfaces. One child seemed to draw with two hands together.[96] The images are patterns, not attempts at any naturalistic representation.

A similar phenomenon was noted in the Cosquer Cave near Marseilles, whose now underwater entrance was discovered in 1985. Animal figures and hand stencils decorate the cave's walls. Evidence of lighting was found: a shell which held a burning ember and a flat plaque worked for use as a simple lamp. Handprints of a child's size have been found about 2.4 m (8 feet) above ground level: easy to reach only when sitting on an adult's shoulders.[97]

In a cave at El Castillo in Spain, flutings made by a child's hand are also at a height where the child would need to have been held up by an adult. A child's footprints were found on the floor of the cave.[98] The nearby site of Las Chimeneas was easier to access by young artists, who seem to have included three children and an adolescent. An animal figure drawn in finger marks was the size of an adult finger. Gargas in France shows flutings by different small hands: one of about 2–3 years, one of 4–5.

There are many caves and rock shelters in Australia with finger flutings, as well as ochre painted lines. Chronologically similar to the European Upper Palaeolithic, the site of Koonalda in the Nullarbor Plain is a cave

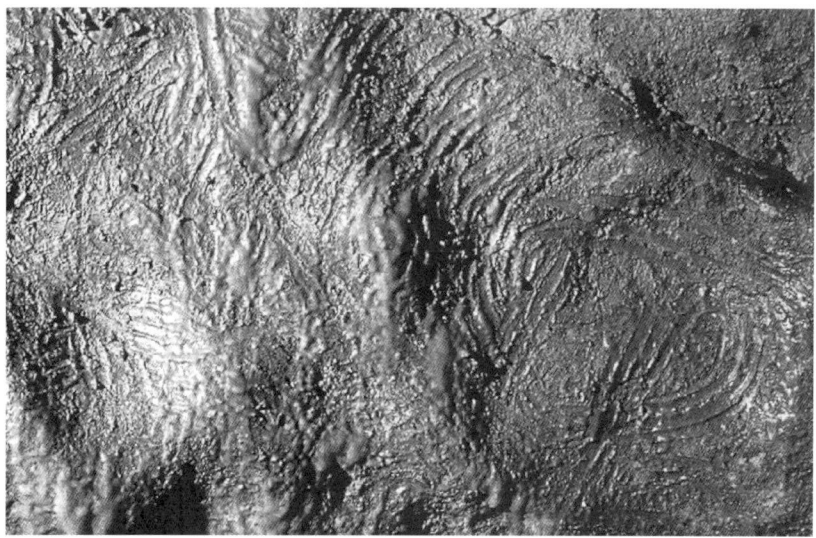

Children's finger fluting on the cave walls of Upper Palaeolithic Gargas, France

with multiple decorations of finger fluting marks.[99] Entry to the cave requires ladders or their equivalent (presumably, in the past, hanging ropes of fibre were used) followed by a climb up a rock face to reach the area of art. In addition to adults, at least three children seem to have been involved in creating these marks, and their finger widths suggest they were less than 5 years old.

The significance of finger fluting is open to debate. The adult markings may well have been designs to record information about place. But given the difficulty of access we can envisage a whole family or small band entering the cave together and allowing their small children to imitate their parents with what we would today describe as finger painting.

The linkage to shamanism of many detailed images and scenes of humans and animals in Southern Africa's Later Stone Age rock art has been widely discussed. Some note that where geometrical patterns are found they are not so different from those produced by modern children, and have raised the untestable question of whether children may have been responsible for creating some of these.[100]

The evidence noted here is of signs which have survived. The artistic output of prehistoric children in intangible materials, their temporary work on temporary locations, is lost to us.

In a different kind of art, at the Upper Palaeolithic Enlène cave (close to Tuc d'Audoubert in the Pyrenees) rather crude engravings on bone have been suggested as the work of apprentices, and the site has even been claimed as a training workshop: ideas which it would be hard to prove or disprove.[101] The quality of artwork does not need to reflect the age of the artist.

A different type of artwork is the carvings of footprints found in open-air sandstone sites in the US Midwest, attributed to prehistoric agriculturalists. Careful and detailed engravings seem to include the feet of young children.[102]

POTTERY AND CRAFTS IN PREHISTORIC FARMING COMMUNITIES

The new technologies developed in prehistoric agricultural groups required new kinds of learning and apprenticeships. But it is a challenge to find evidence of trial work by the young. Pottery made experimentally by children may end up unfired and dissolving back into earth, although there are plenty of examples of badly made pots that could be the work of learners.[103] Metal pieces would be melted down for reuse, items made of organic material may not be recovered in the archaeological record and even trial stone tools may be reworked by an expert.

Working with textiles and fabrics is one of the key crafts in any farming community. Early Bronze Age burials at Mokrin in Serbia, where over 300 graves were excavated, had sewing equipment in child and adult female graves, and bone needles were most common with children (presumed to be girls) aged 6 to 13.[104] By contrast, knives, found with adult males, were not buried with any juveniles.

In Iron Age graves in central Italy, equipment associated with weaving like spindle whorls accompanied burials attributed to girls.[105] Spindles are common in the burials of the later Iron Age of the Wielbark culture of Eastern Europe.[106]

Among a small-scale indigenous group studied in Mexico, mothers were typically teaching their daughters weaving from the age of 9. Styles of teaching could vary – when children were allowed to proceed by trial and error there was greater innovation in the pattern used. The implication here is that societies where learning is by direct instruction may maintain greater stylistic conformity than contexts where the apprentices are encouraged to learn by their own initiative.[107] Innovation may best arise with the young.

A comparison of 100 traditional pottery-making communities reported that in almost half of these, children learned the skill only by observation and imitation, while in a quarter of the societies they received instruction from family members and in another quarter potters were trained in formal apprenticeships.[108]

While pottery making may be a female activity in traditional African societies, not all women make pots. Those who do make them have been

Reconstruction by Libor Balák of children involved in craft in a Neolithic village of the Danube valley

trained over a long period, and may start the process while very young children, although others can become apprentice potters as adults or near-adults.[109] Among the Luo of Kenya, most women who become potters start their training as married adults, not as children.[110] They may have their daughters help them by collecting clay and mixing it. Potters are a small minority among the Luo: it is now a specialised craft, although not in itself enough to provide a high income. We must consider, however, that a study such as this, made only 30 years ago, was in a context where many modern manufactured alternatives to traditional pottery were available. Earlier Luo societies where ceramics provided the only vessels may have operated in quite a different model.

In modern Dowayo communities of Cameroon pottery making is a specialised skill of women in specific families.[111] Girls learn from their mothers with training that continues until the eve of marriage, when they are considered fully trained. Girls start with an assisting role around the age of 6. After a couple of years more they are allowed to experiment with making small pots. Thereafter they can make full-size pots, though these are not yet decorated, and at the final stage they are allowed to decorate their pots. Recognition that they are fully trained potters is marked by a ceremony when they receive a set of tools to use in their craft, set at a time when typically they are also betrothed. Craft learning is thus very much a symbol of social status rather than just technical facility. Curiously, in one village (Boulko), newly married girls were subjected by their mothers-in-law to a new apprenticeship and required to make only small pots again. By this analogy, miniature pots found in the archaeological record may not always be those of young trainees.

Studies from the Americas of prehistoric and more recent children's learning and involvement in pottery production have contributed to discussion about skill acquisition. In the context of continuity between prehistoric and modern Puebloan peoples of the US Southwest, it is interesting to note the very broad range of labour contributions made by children in recent groups, with allocations of tasks by gender the norm.[112] Most of these activities that contribute to the economic and social welfare of the family and group would be invisible in the archaeological record. Where we see direct evidence of children's crafts, as in pottery making, this marks an investment of time for a future contribution.

A proportion of pots from the prehistoric US Southwest showing poor workmanship are likely to have been children's trial pieces.[113] While they do not show fingerprints, the size or the quality of form or of decoration implies a learner: while effort and time have been put into decoration the results are not those of the society's standards. Ethnographic accounts of Native American people in the same area noted that girls began to learn pottery making around the age of 5 and were expected to be competent by 15.[114]

At Pecos Pueblo in New Mexico, USA, miniature and badly made pots have mainly been seen as prehistoric children's trial pieces.[115] Some of the small pots, however, were skilled items – whether made by adults as children's toy items or for undefined 'ritual' purposes.

Pots also show signs of combining adult and children's skills. One study of the pots from this area found many examples in which badly made pots had been finished off by skilled decoration, and of well made pots on which unskilled (and presumably learner) potters applied the decorative elements, or at least to the interior while the able potter completed the outside.[116] This is a reminder of the difficulty of identifying the young learner in the archaeological record. If pots could be finished off by an expert, learners' stone tools could be reflaked while apprentice metalwork would certainly be melted down and reused.

Ceramic items from the Sinagua culture of northern Arizona, USA, dated around 1100–1250 AD, included both small vessels and figurines of animals that appear to have been made by children.[117] The size of fingerprints on the clay supports this view. Since the animal figures were presumably made as toys, the pots may also have been designed as toy items, even if modelling both served as training for future adult pottery production. The fingerprints of older children on some full-size and well formed pots show that these early exercises could have good results.

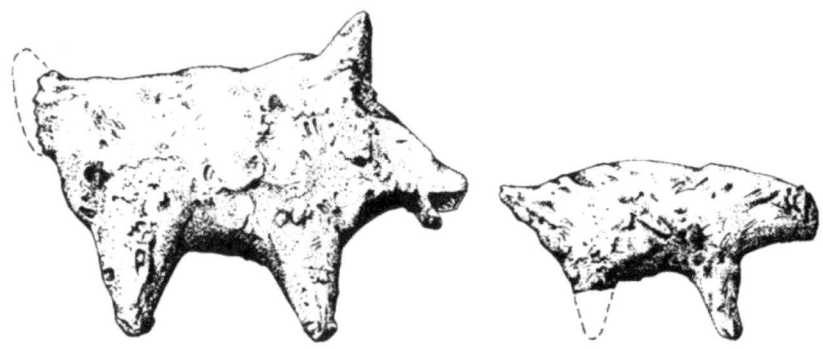

Figurines from the Sinagua culture of Lizard Man village, Arizona, USA

After the mid-13th century AD, the same community the Sinagua moved from dispersed homesteads to fortified settlements.[118] In this period of upheaval and threat, the children's small vessels and clay figurines almost disappeared. Pots of course remained, but as adult production and perhaps with adult apprenticeship. A concentrated population would benefit specialist rather than household production.

From the Iroquoian Huron people of southern Ontario, Canada (dated ca. 1450–1600 AD), small vessels have been seen as the production of children.[119] These pots are generally small and have some unevenness in their form and poor spacing in the decoration. Interestingly, these pots suggest innovation and difference from the dominant styles, whereas most assumptions about craft learning prioritise the idea of close imitation. Some of the decorations on children's pots reflect slightly older traditions ('the influence of grandmothers') while some herald styles which were to become more common in the near future.

In the prehistory of the Old World, interesting evidence of children's involvement in pottery making comes from the study by Natalia Berseneva of Bronze Age Trans-Urals in Russia.[120] Children are common in the burials associated with Sintashta settlements of the early 2nd millennium BC. Small pots have been found in these children's burials bearing fingerprints of a size that only children aged 5–8 years could have made. Children, of course, do not choose their own burial goods. Either these were playthings the individual child had made, or they were made by other children specifically to bury with their age mates, as part of the burial ritual.

Miniature pots and metal tools were found in burials of children in the Early Bronze Age of the Aegean.[121] These may be symbolic of items used in life, or (as suggested in Chapter 7) possibly toys, but do not appear to be the production of children themselves.

Pottery vessel with fingerprints of the child who made it, from the Bronze Age of Kamennyi Ambar-5, in the Trans-Urals, Russia (scale in cm)

The miniature pots found in burials of the Chalcolithic period of Spain (spanning Neolithic to Bronze Age) can be understood in different ways.[122] Some of these small pots, scaled down versions of normal ware, are finely crafted by expert potters while others show the crudity of an early-stage apprentice. Yet both kinds of miniature pot can be found in adult graves, indicating that the important factor is not the recipient but the identity of the maker, depositing their work in the burial of an adult. Later in Spain, at the Iron Age site of Las Cogotas, children's finger marks are seen in pottery clays and these would be of young (would-be) potters ranging between 6 and 16 years of age.[123]

CONCLUSIONS

Direct evidence from archaeology suggests some of the stages of learning and skills in the transition from child to adult. We need to use analogy from other sources to fill out a fuller picture.

We can see childhood as important to the story of human culture because it is the period when human culture is acquired, learned and transmitted. Necessarily we use analogy to amplify the picture: from great apes when we consider the beginnings of culture in the hominin line; and from ethnographic accounts when creating an image of prehistoric hunter-gatherers or farmers. This moves us well away from the modern urban western image that learning is a process systematically and purposefully managed by adults. Adults may indeed teach but, primarily, children *learn*.

The archaeology of prehistory is about continuity and change, and change as well as continuity form part of the long learning process. Continuity reflects the learning process: a child isolated from society will not learn and will not maintain the cultural elements we observe and interpret in archaeology. But it is largely the young to whom we look for innovation – those at the neurochemically defined risk-taking stage of adolescence, cited in Chapter 1. The extended phase before adulthood that is unique to the human species is a basis for complex cultural continuity but also potential cultural innovation.

The kinds of direct evidence cited above help to fill out this picture: children's signs in rock art; stone artefact assemblages showing stages of learning the craft; trial pieces of pottery; and craft tools buried with children.

Relatively little is known from prehistory compared with our knowledge of learning and apprenticeship in the archaeology of urban societies, when specialisation of production was the norm. The need now is to extend our enquiry further into past and future excavations. We can expect to see more stages of learning if we look not just at the best-quality stone tools, pots or craft items, but at those which reflect the necessary gradual stages of acquiring skill. What archaeologists have long dismissed as the worst examples of a craft may well be invaluable as our best physical examples of childhood and the learning process.

NOTES

1 C. Gamble, *Origins and Revolutions: human identity in earliest prehistory*, Cambridge: Cambridge University Press, 2007, pp. 207, 228ff.
2 Steven Mithen considered some of these questions in the framework of prehistory in *The Prehistory of the Mind: a search for the origins of art, religion and science*, London: Thames & Hudson, 1996.
3 From J. Piaget, *The Language and Thought of the Child*, London: Routledge & Kegan Paul, 1926 (French edition 1923), to J. Piaget, *The Development of Thought: equilibration of cognitive structures*, Oxford: Blackwell, 1978 (French edition 1975).
4 G. Saxe, 'Piaget and anthropology', *American Anthropology* 85 (1983): 136–143.
5 S. Mithen, *The Singing Neanderthals: the origins of music, language, mind and*

body, London: Weidenfeld & Nicolson, 2005; Cambridge, MA: Harvard University Press, 2006.
6   Mithen, *The Singing Neanderthals*, p. 202.
7   M.W. Yogman, 'Male parental behavior in humans and nonhuman primates' in N.A. Krasnegor & R.D. Bridges (eds), *Mammalian Parenting: biochemical, neurological, and behavioral determinants*, New York: Oxford University Press, 1990: 461–481. This study argues that modern observations of western society can be applied far more broadly.
8   M. Haslam et al., 'Archaeological excavation of wild macaque stone tools', *Journal of Human Evolution* 96 (2016): 134–138; M. Haslam et al., 'Pre-Columbian monkey tools', *Current Biology* 26 (2016): R521–R522.
9   L.M. Hopper, S. Marshall-Pescini & A. Whiten, 'Social learning and culture in child and chimpanzee' in F.B.M. de Waal & P.F. Ferrari (eds), *The Primate Mind: built to connect with other minds*, Cambridge, MA: Harvard University Press, 2012: 99–118.
10 T. Nishida, *Chimpanzees of the Lakeside: natural history and culture at Mahale*, Cambridge: Cambridge University Press, 2012, p. 280.
11 G. Kaplan & L.J. Rogers, *The Orang-Utans*, Sydney: Allen & Unwin, 1999, ch. 5.
12 E.V. Lonsdorf, S.R. Ross, S.A. Linick, M.S. Milstein & T.N. Melber, 'An experimental, comparative investigation of tool use in chimpanzees and gorillas', *Animal Behaviour* 77 (2009): 1119–1126.
13 T. Matsuzawa et al., 'Emergence of culture in wild chimpanzees: education by master-apprenticeship' in T. Matsuzawa (ed.), *Primate Origins of Human Recognition and Behavior*, Tokyo: Springer, 2001: 557–574; S. Hirata & M.L. Celli, 'Role of mothers in the acquisition of tool-use behaviours by captive infant chimpanzees', *Animal Cognition* 6 (2003): 235–244. A classic field study of chimpanzees is that of Jane Goodall, *The Chimpanzees of Gombe: pattern of behavior*, Cambridge, MA: Harvard University Press, 1986, with discussion of chimpanzee learning patterns on pp. 20–21 and pp. 568–571.
14 S. Hirata, 'Chimpanzee social intelligence: selfishness, altruism, and the mother–infant bond', *Primates* 50 (2009): 3–11 (see figure 3).
15 C. Boesch & H. Boesch-Achermann, *The Chimpanzees of Taï Forest: behavioural ecology and evolution*, Oxford: Oxford University Press, 2000, pp. 214–216.
16 R.H. Tuttle, *Apes and Human Evolution*, Cambridge, MA: Harvard University Press, 2014, p. 337.
17 W.C. McGrew, *Chimpanzee Material Culture: implications for human evolution*, Cambridge: Cambridge University Press, 1992, especially pp. 79–87.
18 M. Hayashi, Y. Mizunu & T. Matsuzawa, 'How does stone-tool use emerge? Introduction of stones and nuts to naïve chimpanzees in captivity', *Primates* 46 (2005): 91–102.
19 D. Biro, C. Sousa & T. Matsuzawa, 'Ontogeny and cultural propagation of tool use by wild chimpanzees' in Matsuzawa et al. (eds), *Cognitive Development*: 476–508, p. 491; M. Hayashi, 'Juvenile learning of stone-tool use in wild chimpanzees of Bossou, Guinea, West Africa', paper at World Archaeological Congress, Kyoto, 2016.
20 G. Ohashi, 'Behavioral repertoire of tool use in the wild chimpanzees at Bossou' in Matsuzawa et al. (eds), *Cognitive Development*: 139–451.
21 E.V. Lonsdorf, L.E. Eberly & A.E. Pusey, 'Sex differences in learning in chimpanzees', *Nature* 428 (2004): 715–716.

22 But also see I. Roffman et al., 'Stone tool production and utilization by bonobo-chimpanzees (*Pan paniscus*)', *Proceedings of the National Academy of Sciences* 109 (2012): 14500–14503.
23 M. Hayashi & T. Matsuzawa, 'Cognitive development in object manipulation by infant chimpanzees', *Animal Cognition* 6 (2003): 225–233.
24 Hirata & Celli, 'Role of mothers'; S. Hirata, 'Chimpanzee learning and transmission of tool use to fish for honey' in T. Matsuzawa, M. Tomonaga & M. Tanaka (eds), *Cognitive Development in Chimpanzees*, Tokyo: Springer, 2006: 201–213.
25 E. Reindl et al. 'Young children spontaneously invent wild great apes' tool-use behaviours', *Proceedings of the Royal Society B* 283 (2016): 20152402.
26 Reindl et al., 'Young children', p. 6.
27 M. Nielsen, 'Imitation, pretend play, and childhood: essential elements in the evolution of human culture?', *Journal of Comparative Psychology* 126 (2012): 170–181.
28 C. Finlayson et al., 'Birds of a feather: Neanderthal exploitation of raptors and corvids', *PLoS ONE* 7 (2012): e45927; M. Romandini et al., 'Convergent evidence of eagle talons used by late Neanderthals in Europe: a further assessment on symbolism', *PloS ONE* 9 (2014): e101278.
29 J. Jaubert et al., 'Early Neanderthal constructions deep in Bruniquel Cave in southwestern France', *Nature* 534 (2016): 111–114.
30 C. Gamble, *The Palaeolithic Societies of Europe*, Cambridge: Cambridge University Press 1999, p. 265–266.
31 J. Hawcroft & R. Dennell, 'Neanderthal cognitive life history and its implications for material culture' in *CMC*: 89–99.
32 D. Dediu & S.C. Levinson. 'On the antiquity of language: the reinterpretation of Neandertal linguistic capacities and its consequences', *Frontiers in Psychology* 4 (2013): 397.
33 R.C. Berwick, M. Hauser & I. Tattersall, 'Neanderthal language? Just-so stories take center stage', *Frontiers in Psychology* 4 (2013): 671; J.L. Bolhuis et al., 'How could language have evolved?', *PLoS Biol* 12 (2014): e1001934.
34 R. D'Anastasio et al., 'Micro-biomechanics of the Kebara 2 hyoid and its implications for speech in Neanderthals', *PLoS ONE* 8 (2013): e82261.
35 An intriguing paper suggests cranial changes in *Homo sapiens* over time imply changes in androgen reactivity and circulating testosterone, leading to 'enhanced social tolerance': R.L. Cieri et al., 'Craniofacial feminization, social tolerance, and the origins of behavioral modernity', *Current Anthropology* 55 (2014): 419–443. This argument is unnervingly (and unwittingly) reminiscent of 19th-century ideas of the physiognomy of the criminal and degenerate physical type.
36 Lancy, *Anthropology* 1ed, pp. 116, 234ff.; 2ed, pp. 124, 254ff.
37 Lancy, *Anthropology* 1ed, pp. 6, 249, 257; 2ed, pp. 7, 256.
38 D.F. Lancy, 'Children as a reserve labor force', *Current Anthropology* 56 (2015): 545–568.
39 T. Roughley, *The Jamaica Planter's Guide; or, a system for planting and managing a sugar estate, or other plantations in that island, and throughout the British West Indies in general*, London: Longman, 1823, pp. 102–113, 118–127; cited by M. Bundock, *The Fortunes of Francis Barber*, New Haven, CT: Yale University Press, 2015, pp. 21–22.

40 Roughley, *The Jamaica Planter's Guide*, p. 121.
41 H. Reschreiter, D. Pany-Kucera & D. Gröbner, 'Kinderarbeit in 100m Tiefe? Neue Lebensbilder zum prähistorischen Hallstätter Salzbergbau. Interpretierte Eisenzeiten, Fallstudien, Methoden, Theorie. Tagungsbeiträge der 5. Linzer Gespräche zur interpretativen Eisenzeitarchäologie,*Studien zur Kulturgeschichte von Oberösterreich* (Linz) 37 (2013): 25–38.
42 A.C. Zeller, 'A role for children in hominid evolution', *Man* 22 (1987): 528–557, pp. 541–548.
43 A. Takada, 'Mother–infant interactions among the !Xun' in *HGC*: 289–308.
44 B.S. Hewlett et al., 'Social learning among Congo Basin hunter-gatherers', *Philosophical Transactions of the Royal Society B: Biological Sciences* 366 (2011): 1168–1178.
45 H. Montgomery, *An Introduction to Childhood: anthropological perspectives on children's lives*, Chichester: Wiley-Blackwell, 2009, p. 107; B.S. Hewlett, *Intimate Fathers: the nature and context of Aka Pygmy paternal infant care*, Ann Arbor, MI: University of Michigan Press, 1991.
46 W.S. Laughlin, 'Hunting: an integrated biobehavior system and its evolutionary importance' in R.B. Lee & I. DeVore (eds), *Man the Hunter*, Chicago, IL: Aldine, 1968: 304–320, pp. 305–307.
47 Laughlin, 'Hunting', pp. 306–307.
48 H. Barry et al., 'Relation of child training to subsistence economy', *American Anthropologist* 61 (1959): 51–63.
49 Montgomery, *An Introduction to Childhood*, p. 53, citing D. Maybury-Lewis.
50 R.B. Lee, *The !Kung San: men, women and work in a foraging society*, Cambridge: Cambridge University Press, 1979, pp. 236–238.
51 M. Rockman, 'Apprentice to the environment: hunter-gatherers and landscape learning' in *AAA*: 99–118; M. Lombard, 'Hunting and hunting technologies as proxy for teaching and learning during the Stone Age of Southern Africa', *Cambridge Archaeological Journal* 25 (2015): 877–887.
52 N. Blurton Jones, 'The lives of hunter-gatherer children: effects of parental behavior and parental reproductive strategy' in M.E. Pereira & L.A. Fairbanks (eds), *Juvenile Primates: life history, development and behavior*, New York: Oxford University Press, 1993: 309–326.
53 E.G. Federova, 'Women's role in Mansi society' in P.P. Schweitzer, M. Biesele & R.K. Hitchcock (eds), *Hunters and Gatherers in the Modern World: conflict, resistance and self-determination*, New York: Berghahn, 2000: 391–398, p. 396.
54 C. Turnbull, *The Mountain People*, London: Cape, and New York: Simon & Schuster, 1972.
55 A. Hamilton, *Nature and Nurture: child rearing in North-Central Arnhem Land*, Canberra: Australian Institute of Aboriginal Studies, 1981, pp. 15, 37, 68, 80, 111.
56 See for instance F.G.G. Rose, 'Australian marriage, land-owning groups, and initiations' in Lee & DeVore (eds), *Man the Hunter*: 200–208, pp. 207–208; W.E.H. Stanner, *On Aboriginal Religion*, Sydney: Oceania Monographs, 1966.
57 S. Holdaway & H. Allen, 'Placing ideas in the land: practical and ritual training among the Australian Aborigines' in *AAA*: 79–98.
58 Chapters in *AAA*. Papers on the learning of stone toolmaking from an earlier (2002) conference were published under the title 'Skillful Stones: Approaches to Knowledge and Practice in Lithic Technology' in *Journal of Archaeological Method and Theory* 15:1 (2008).

59 W. Wendrich, 'Recognizing knowledge transfer in the archaeological record' in *AAA*: 255–262.
60 J.R. Ferguson, 'The when, where, and how of novices in craft production', *Journal of Archaeological Method and Theory* 15 (2008): 51–67.
61 Announced at a conference; see E. Callaway, 'Oldest stone tools raise questions about their creators', *Nature* 520 (2015): 421.
62 K.J. Weedman, 'An ethnoarchaeological study of hafting and stone tool diversity among the Gamo of Ethiopia', *Journal of Archaeological Method and Theory* 13 (2006): 188–237; M.J. Shott & K. J. Weedman, 'Measuring reduction in stone tools: an ethnoarchaeological study of Gamo hidescrapers from Ethiopia', *Journal of Archaeological Science* 34 (2007): 1016–1035.
63 D.F. Lancy, '*Homo faber juvenalis*: a multidisciplinary survey of children as tool makers/users', *CitP* 10 (2017): 72–90, discusses a range of examples past and present within a broader discussion of the topic.
64 S.B. Milne, 'Lithic raw material availability and Palaeo-Eskimo novice flint-knapping' in *AAA*: 119–144.
65 N. Finlay, 'Kid knapping: the missing children in lithic analysis' in *IPP*: 203–212; N. Finlay, 'Kid-knapped knowledge: changing perspectives on the child in lithic studies', *CitP* 8(2) (2015): 104–112.
66 M. Kohn & S. Mithen, 'Handaxes: products of sexual selection?', *Antiquity* 73 (1999): 518–526.
67 J.M. Jiménez-Arenas et al., 'The oldest handaxes in Europe: fact or artefact?', *Journal of Archaeological Science* 38 (2011): 3340–3349.
68 T. Wynn, 'Handaxe enigmas', *World Archaeology* 27 (1995): 10–24; C. Shipton, 'Imitation and shared intentionality in the Acheulean', *Cambridge Archaeological Journal* 20 (2010): 197–210.
69 J.J. Shea, 'Child's play: reflections on the invisibility of children in the Paleolithic record', *Evolutionary Anthropology* 15 (2006): 212–216.
70 Wileman, *Hide and Seek*, p. 59.
71 A rather inconclusive Polish project let children attempt flint knapping. They were given a brief exercise to produce a flake and then a scraper: K. Orzyłowska & B. Karolak, 'Paleolithic children knapping: the identification of children's flint knapping product – experimental case study' in *CCLA*: 29–40.
72 P. Spikins et al., 'The cradle of thought: growth, learning, play and attachment in Neanderthal children', *Oxford Journal of Archaeology* 33 (2014): 111–134, pp. 126–127.
73 J. Joy et al., *Hide and Seek: looking for children in the past*, Cambridge: Museum of Archaeology and Anthropology, 2016, p. 8.
74 P. Mellars, *The Neanderthal Legacy: an archaeological perspective from Western Europe*, Princeton, NJ: Princeton University Press, 1996, p. 170.
75 Baxter, *Archaeology*, pp. 53–54.
76 Milne, 'Lithic raw material'.
77 J. Takakura, 'Using lithic refitting to investigate the skill learning process: lessons from Upper Paleolithic assemblages at the Shirataki sites in Hokkaido, northern Japan' in T. Akazawa, Y. Nishiaki & K. Aoki (eds), *Dynamics of Learning in Neanderthals and Modern Humans, Vol. 1*, Tokyo: Springer Japan, 2013: 151–171.
78 Spikins et al., 'The cradle of thought', p. 126, citing Bodu.
79 D. Stapert, 'Neanderthal children and their flints', *PalArch's Journal of Archaeology of Northwest Europe* 1 (2007): 16–39.

80 Stapert, 'Neanderthal children'; Spikins et al., 'The cradle of thought', p. 126.
81 L. Grimm, 'Apprentice flintknapping: relating material culture and social practice in the Upper Palaeolithic' in *CMC*: 53–71.
82 B. Roveland, 'Footprints in the clay: Upper Palaeolithic children in ritual and secular contexts' in *CMC*: 29–38, pp. 34–35, citing N. Pigeot.
83 P. Bodu, 'Les chasseurs magdaleniens de Pincevent; quelques aspects de leurs comportements', *Lithic Technology* 21 (1996): 48–70.
84 A. Sinclair, 'All in a day's work: early conflicts in expertise, life history and time management' in F. Coward et al. (eds), *Settlement, Society and Cognition in Human Evolution: landscapes in mind*, Cambridge: Cambridge University Press, 2015: 94–116.
85 F. Sternke and M. Sørensen, 'The identification of children's flint knapping products in Mesolithic Scandinavia' in S. McCartan et al. (eds) *Mesolithic Horizons: papers presented at the Seventh International Conference on the Mesolithic in Europe, Vol. 1*, Oxford: Oxbow Books, 2005: 720–726.
86 Finlay, 'Kid knapping', p. 207, citing Fischer.
87 Finlay, 'Kid knapping', pp. 108, 202.
88 A. Högberg, 'Playing with flint: tracing a child's imitation of adult work in a lithic assemblage', *Journal of Archaeological Method and Theory* 15 (2008): 112–131.
89 A. Högberg & P. Gärdenfors, 'Children, teaching and the evolution of humankind', *CitP* 8:2 (2015): 113–121.
90 A. Högberg & L. Larsson, 'Lithic technology and behavioural modernity: new results from the Still Bay site, Hollow Rock Shelter, Western Cape Province, South Africa', *Journal of Human Evolution* 61 (2011): 133–155, pp. 148–153.
91 G.E. Cunnar, 'Discovering latent children in the archaeological record of the Great Basin' in *TCIN*: 133–148.
92 Milne, 'Lithic raw material'.
93 D. Stout, 'The social and cultural context of stone-knapping skill acquisition' in V. Roux & B. Bril (eds), *Stone Knapping: the necessary conditions for a uniquely hominin behaviour*, Cambridge: McDonald Institute, 2005: 331–340.
94 R.G. Bednarik, 'Children as Pleistocene artists', *Rock Art Research* 25 (2008): 173–182; L. Van Gelder, 'Counting the children: the role of children in the production of finger flutings in four Upper Palaeolithic caves', *Oxford Journal of Archaeology* 34 (2015): 119–138.
95 K. Sharpe & L. Van Gelder, 'Children and Paleolithic "art": indications from Rouffignac Cave, France', *International Newsletter on Rock Art* 38 (2004): 9–17; K. Sharpe & L. Van Gelder, 'Evidence for cave marking by Palaeolithic children', *Antiquity* 80 (2006): 937–947; L. Van Gelder & K. Sharpe, 'Women and girls as Upper Palaeolithic cave "artists": deciphering the sexes of finger fluters in Rouffignac Cave', *Oxford Journal of Archaeology* 28 (2009): 323–333.
96 Van Gelder, 'Counting the children', p. 132.
97 J. Clottes et al., 'Prehistoric images and medicines under the sea', *International Newsletter on Rock Art*, 42 (2005): 1–8.
98 Van Gelder, 'Counting the children', p. 123.
99 L. van Gelder, 'The role of children in the creation of finger flutings in Koonalda Cave, South Australia', *CitP* 8:2 (2015): 149–160.
100 See the discussions and responses to J.D. Lewis-Williams & T.A. Dowson, 'The signs of all times: entoptic phenomena in Upper Palaeolithic art', *Current Anthropology* 29 (1988): 201–245.

101 Mithen, *The Prehistory of the Mind*, p. 254; R. Bégouën & J.Clottes, 'Portable and wall art in the Volp caves, Montesquieu-Avantès (Ariège)', *Proceedings of the Prehistoric Society* 57 (1991): 65–79.
102 B.W. Merwin, 'Rock carvings in southern Illinois', *American Antiquity* 3 (1937): 179–182.
103 Joy, *Hide and Seek*, pp. 32–36, discusses badly made pots from Bronze Age and Iron Age Britain.
104 E. Rega, 'Age, gender and biological reality in the Early Bronze Age cemetery at Mokrin' in *IPP*: 229–247, p. 234. Infants aged under 1 year were missing from the cemetery.
105 K. Hladíková, 'Perception of children in Villanovan period in southern Etruria' in *CCLA*: 41–74, p. 55.
106 M. Chmiel, 'Children in the Wielbark culture societies' in *CCLA*: 89–112, p. 102.
107 P. Greenfield, 'Children, material culture and weaving' in *CMC*: 72–86.
108 P.L. Crown, 'Learning and teaching in the prehispanic American Southwest' in *CPPS*: 108–124, p. 109.
109 M. Calvo Trias et al., 'Playing with mud? An ethnoarchaeological approach to children's learning in Kusasi ceramic production' in *CSI*: 88–104.
110 I. Herbich, 'Learning patterns, potter interaction and ceramic style among the Luo of Kenya', *African Archaeological Review* 5 (1987): 193–204.
111 H. Wallaert, 'Apprenticeship and the confirmation of social boundaries' in *AAA*: 1–19.
112 K.A. Kamp, 'Working for a living: childhood in the prehistoric Southwestern Pueblos' in *CPPS*: 71–89.
113 P.L. Crown, 'Learning to make pottery in the prehispanic American Southwest', *Journal of Anthropological Research* 57 (2001): 451–469.
114 Crown, 'Learning and teaching'.
115 E. Bagwell, 'Ceramic form and skill: attempting to identify child producers at Pecos Pueblo, New Mexico' in *CPPS*: 90–107.
116 Crown, 'Learning and teaching'; P.L. Crown, 'Life histories of pots and potters: situating the individual in archaeology', *American Antiquity* 72 (2007): 677–690.
117 K.A. Kamp et al., 'Discovering childhood: using fingerprints to find children in the archaeological record', *American Antiquity* 64 (1999): 309–315; K.A. Kamp, 'Prehistoric children working and playing: a Southwestern case study in learning ceramics', *Journal of Anthropological Research* 57 (2001): 427–450.
118 K.A. Kamp, 'Children in an increasingly violent social landscape: a case study from the American Southwest', *CitP* 2 (2009): 71–85.
119 P.E. Smith, 'Children and ceramic innovation: a study in the archaeology of children' *CIA*: 65–76.
120 Natalia Berseneva, personal communication; N.A. Berseneva, E.V. Kupriyanova & A.G. Bersenev, 'Traces of childhood: search for children in the archaeological record and study of ceramic artefacts (Bronze Age of the South Trans-Urals)', *Novosibirsk State Pedagogical University Bulletin, Archaeology and Ethnography* 13 (2014): 88–100 [in Russian].
121 C. Marangou, 'Social differentiation in the early Bronze Age: miniature tools and child burials', *Journal of Mediterranean Studies* 1 (1991): 211–225.

122 R. Garrido-Pena & A.M. Herrero-Corral, 'Children as potters: apprenticeship patterns from Bell Beaker pottery of Copper Age Inner Iberia (Spain)' in *CSI*: 40–58, pp. 46–49.
123 J.J. Padilla Fernández & L. Chapon, 'Gender and childhood in the II Iron Age' in *CSI*: 75–87, p. 82.

7

PLAYING

Fun, games, toys and culture

Play is central to the lives of all children: it gives pleasure, it helps in social adaptation and it is a basic source for acquiring skills. Play is one of the most important means of cultural transmission in human societies.[1] Through play children develop skills, as noted in Chapter 6, they learn social interaction and they gain specific knowledge from peers and older children: the 'culture of children' feeds into the culture of all society.

There are many theorists of play, who study it from the perspectives of psychology or education or sociology or anthropology, and data from such studies reveal the breadth of differences in different cultures and contexts.[2] The pattern of mothers' play with their children beyond their infant years, as we see in modern western societies, appears an anomaly in human culture (and therefore, we can surmise, in prehistory), with father–child play even less frequent; in most other societies play after infancy is largely between the young.[3] While play is the great social integrator, it can also be interrupted when adults expect the young to contribute to the household economy.

David Lancy has emphasised the contrast between 'traditional' societies and the contemporary urban western style of parenting, in which much play is controlled and planned. In considering play in prehistory we can learn from the anthropology of foraging and village farming communities. We can also consider the role of play in higher primates for clues (and limited analogy) on its role in the development of our earliest hominin ancestors.[4]

Finding evidence of play in the archaeological record is challenging. Much play is interaction between individuals: whether young infants with adults and siblings, or children with their peers and with older children. Visual representations of such play are hard to find before historic eras. Much of children's play is 'make-believe' (or fantasy play), imitating aspects of the adult world, or creating imaginary worlds that go beyond the everyday.

This can involve only words and actions, or objects and assemblages created to last only for the duration of the game.

Nevertheless, some play, in groups or individually, may involve material objects: toys or pieces of games – which may be found in the archaeological record and identified as such. Where we find crudely made objects we may propose that these are the creations of children themselves. But many playthings, especially those made by children for their own amusement, would have been made of very temporary materials and would not survive in the archaeological record. Other items would have been made for children by adults and designed for longer use, but their identification as toys or games or dolls may be open to challenge. It remains difficult to pin down details of children's play before later prehistory, and challenging even then.

PRIMATES AT PLAY

In considering our early hominin ancestors and the first prehistoric forager groups, studies and interpretations of play among juvenile great apes can contribute to our ideas.

Many fascinating hours can be spent watching the play of young primates in the artificial setting of zoos, while scientists have been privileged to observe over long periods the young playing in the wild. Primate play combines creativity and the transmission of behavioural norms: the young learn to interact, gain skills and social knowledge but also establish, maintain or learn about relationships in their society.[5] Play allows the young to learn about others and anticipate their responses, skills which will ensure survival in a group context.

Among gorillas studied in captivity, play with the mother is the norm, followed by solitary play until playing with other young takes over.[6] Observers have been surprised that solitary play is so important. It chiefly seems to involve seeing what the body can do. This precedes social play, which begins at five months and involves chasing and rough-and-tumble with mock fighting and mock biting, while the mothers maintain a watch over the youngest participants from nearby.

Another study of captive gorillas noted that male infants play significantly more than female infants, and females prefer to play with males, a pattern interpreted as part of the males learning their potential future leadership role, while females are unlikely to form significant social bonds with other females when adults.[7]

With chimpanzees, play is initially between a mother and her infant, but after three to five months the mother may allow 'play-dates' with other young.[8] Play of this social nature was observed to increase until about the age of four, but then decrease over the next year until the juvenile is fully weaned, perhaps reflecting its resistance to that process. Where age mates are not available to play, the young chimpanzee may continue to engage in play behaviour with its mother. Until about 8 years of age, the young gradually devote more time to their play with others. At Gombe, Jane Goodall noted that young males were more willing to play in groups than were young females, despite males' earlier adolescence. Until the age of 8 years, though, the males still stay within reach of their mothers, and the young females may stay closer to their mother for two more years, and remain more committed to the social group than the male thereafter.[9]

With adolescents (9 years old and upwards) play again decreases. Indeed, adolescent males can hold a rather peripheral position in a chimpanzee group, while female adolescents fare better, maintaining a longer relationship with their mothers.[10] Patterns of play seen between young chimpanzees are extended into adulthood, when adults (males with either males or females) engage in play with each other, or adults with young.

For the youngest chimpanzees at play in the Mahale Mountains National Park in Tanzania, play serves as a tool to establish relationships with others: play appears to serve 'friendship', rather than friendship generating play. Play comes therefore to be about society, not just self. To the older adolescent chimpanzees, like adults who engaged in occasional play, devoting time to play had become less important.[11]

In an analysis of such play, some 91 different activities were listed, from leaping and tumbling and pirouetting and using or throwing objects, to water play, wrestling and chasing.[12] Play-fighting young seem to know when to stop, before it turned into aggression, and this was usually in pairs rather than group play, the same as seen among bonobos.[13]

But another interesting form of play exists: notable in itself but also as a form of gender differentiation. Young female chimpanzees have been seen 'play-mothering', nursing sticks and handling them the way mothers carry their babies.[14]

In the early part of the 20th century Russian scientist Nadezhda Ladygina-Kohts undertook a detailed comparison of her own baby with a captive infant chimpanzee.[15] More than some recent experimenters, she concluded by emphasising the limitations and inadequacies of the young chimpanzee. But there were a lot of similarities in the two infants' play and experimentation with learning movement, testing ability and action, and interacting with objects; both expressed love and anxiety and curiosity and anger. The chimpanzee was reported to be more stoic in the face of pain than the child, although one wonders if the experimenter responded to each differently. Both showed similar habits in eating; both would imitate sounds and adult human actions. But there were also, of course, substantial differences, even before the human child made the first efforts at speech.

The chimpanzee was good at climbing trees and using all four limbs to climb stairs, the child at climbing stairs in upright stance. The chimpanzee would roar in anxiety, the child produced tears. In play the chimpanzee was naturally far more energetic and agile. The child showed affection for inanimate objects, and in play with live animals the child was more empathetic, the chimpanzee more cruel.

In terms of practical abilities, the chimpanzee (agility, resistance to pain and dispassion at animal suffering) may be closer to our hunter-forager hominin ancestors than to ourselves today. Play is a prerequisite to the serious aspects of life and to living in a society, but it is an invisible aspect of the fossil record of early hominins, and in the earliest archaeological evidence for human society.

FORAGERS AND FARMERS, ANCIENT AND MODERN

If childhood is dominated by play and play is a major means by which children acquire their culture and social training, then the faster maturity of pre-modern hominins would mean less time to acquire a complex cultural apparatus before becoming fully adult members of society. This argument has been applied specifically to suggest that Neanderthals, who matured faster and earlier than *Homo sapiens*, lacked an extended stage at which play, and in particular make-believe or fantasy play, could serve the creative role seen in later societies.[16] There is thus a link between physical maturity rates, the role of play in an extended period of childhood dependency, and the complexity of the adult world's culture and knowledge.

Toys and the material evidence of games are hard to identify in the archaeological record of the Palaeolithic. We might interpret some Upper Palaeolithic sculptures in Europe as dolls rather than as ritual objects. Although there are many interpretations of the European Upper Palaeolithic female figures, the concept of them as fertility symbols is challenged by the fact that they rarely show signs of pregnancy, childbirth or indeed the developed breasts of lactation.

We might consider some small stone artefacts as scaled down versions of tools and weapons; but we cannot confidently document a set of children's toys or artefacts from games. Manufactured flutes are claimed from quite early in the Palaeolithic, with a sequence of holes in appropriate bones such as the femora of cave bears. However, an alternative interpretation is that these bones carry the tooth marks of hyenas, not the drill marks of musical humans.[17] Even if these were used as musical instruments, music is an adult entertainment as much as a child's. Where children manufacture their own play objects, they are more likely to be made from soft and pliable materials, which have small chance of survival in the archaeological record of early prehistory. We therefore look to more recent forager groups to stimulate our ideas of what child's play might have been in the distant past.

There have been a number of studies of childhood and play in recent and contemporary societies with hunting and food-gathering economies.[18] These emphasise the role of play in social interaction and in acquiring socially (and economically) useful skills, though inevitably with some contrasts between different kinds of societies. In small-scale hunter-gatherer communities, children closely observe all aspects of adult life and their play can include much mimicking of adult behaviours and activities, but it is not limited to this.[19] Foraging, as with the Mikea of Madagascar, may be entirely for fun and not needed as a contribution to economic life.[20]

Play starts with the mother, but the play relation of an infant with the mother changes when a new sibling is born. Before long, play with other children takes over. Studies of modern forager groups serve as a reminder that age mates may be few in number. If a typical forager group is about 25 people, of whom fewer than half are children, then any individual child is unlikely to have many others of their own age in the group. They will therefore be playing with children who are older or younger than they are.[21] The younger will learn from the older without adult involvement. This age mix has another impact on play: with such a range, truly competitive games for children unmatched in age and strength and ability are unfeasible. They may need to wait until occasions when forager groups meet up in larger associations. In games of skill, each player is competing with themselves, not with older or younger children.

The relaxed !Kung world of the Kalahari does not mean, however, that mothers are unaware of their children, and while younger children generally stay within reach of the camp, their mothers would raise concern if their whereabouts are uncertain. Play groups among the !Kung cut across both age and gender. Among the Bofi foragers in Central Africa, children tend to play with others of their own gender after the age of 3 years, though not as much as in a related farming group.[22] Another forager group, the Aka Pygmies of the western Congo basin, play in multi-age groups segmented by gender: segregation which becomes even more fixed as the girls approach adolescence.[23] In Chapter 3 an unusual aspect of the Aka Pygmy foragers was noted, where fathers spend more time with their infant children than seen in any other small-scale society. One observation was that, in this context, fathers' play with their children is not the rough-and-tumble we might expect – it is closer to the continuous interaction between mothers and their infants.[24]

In Brazil's Parakana Indian society, physical exercise play takes the largest proportion of playtime (slightly more with boys than girls), including rough-and tumble games. Make-believe play is important, as is undertaking imitations of adult life, including building a play-house. In this group boys from age seven through to adolescence play more than girls (including practice with a bow and arrow) as girls of this age are involved in family activities such as the protection of younger children. Beyond this, there is play with toys and games and objects which might be expected to have their equivalent in the archaeological record.

Detailed observations in the 1990s of the Baka Pygmy foragers, a Cameroon group in close contact with the outside world, showed the very broad range of children's play.[25] Eighty-five different play activities were distinguished. Once they were aged 4 or 5 years, they played with groups of older children. Some of the play related to mimicking adult behaviour, including foraging itself (such as making a trap). Also imitative was 'playing house': children's play versions of adult activities, including making clothes or household items. There was gender differentiation in much of the play, especially when imitating aspects of adult life.

Other play involved imaginary or created toy objects such as a car or a radio. Music was another form of play: songs, dances, making or playing instruments (music is a strong feature of Baka life). Physical games were important: kicking a ball, wrestling, tag, chasing and so on.

Only a minority of such children's play activity involves material items that would survive in the archaeological record. Temporary playthings made of twigs and wood or gourds or fruit, or of unfired clay, would rapidly decay. But if items from child's play were encountered in archaeological work, they might equally well have been ignored or misinterpreted, as archaeologists have focused on the organised rational world of adults rather than the apparently more random world of children's activities.

Accounts of children's play can be found in a number of ethnographic descriptions of small-scale traditional farming societies. Children's games are universal: both those which involve just personal interaction (like hide and seek) and those which involve toys and objects (like ball games).[26] As with forager groups, in agricultural societies older children may look after smaller children so that children of different ages play together; but the larger the community, the more likely it is that children can play in groups of their own age.

When we interpret the vast corpus of archaeological evidence from prehistoric agricultural societies in the Old World, we are inevitably influenced by our knowledge of historic and modern communities. What we see as resembling familiar playthings in such societies – toys, games and children's items – we can readily interpret as evidence of children in the past. Other prehistoric children's items may seem less familiar. And of course, unknown to us is what does not survive in the archaeological record because of its fragility or temporary nature. We may also misinterpret finds. There is an old joke among archaeologists, that items of unknown function are routinely described as 'ritual objects'. What might seem to be a votive cult item might have been just a child's toy – or the reverse. It is not easy to identify toys confidently.[27]

However, we cannot doubt the universality of play, of the process by which children interact and acquire social and personal and practical skills through play, and pleasure too.

Much play between children is in imitating the adult world with role-play, including building miniature houses, and imitating the economic activities of adults.[28] Since children in traditional agricultural communities typically start early to assist in practical aspects of the household economy, such play is highly functional, as play transforms into work.

GAMES, TOYS AND MINIATURE ITEMS

Playing games is a social mechanism: commonly with other children including older children, rarely with mother and even less with fathers, it establishes or reaffirms relations.[29] It requires and increases skills which may serve other social needs, including those useful for adolescent and adult life.

When we find the burials of children we have to imagine them playing games with their peers; when we find the habitation rooms of a village house we have to reconstruct the play life led outside that house. We can reaffirm our knowledge that play is universal and that games form a universal part of child's play, but can rarely point to details of play in the prehistoric record.

Discs of bone or ivory suggest a spinning or similar game. Knuckle bones (or astragali) of sheep and goat lend themselves to use as dice or for other tossing games seen throughout history.[30] This use may date as far back as Neolithic Europe.[31] Knuckle bones found in a child's grave at Devnja in Bulgaria can readily be seen as gaming pieces.[32]

Gaming pieces, as identified at very late Irish Iron Age and Scandinavian Iron Age sites, are as likely to be from adult activity or the leisure activities of adolescents as from children's games, but are perhaps more commonly assumed to be adult by archaeologists.[33] The Irish finds were in the grave of an adult described by the excavator as 'a gambler', and possibly decapitated: an interesting juxtaposition and an image rather far from our sense of children's recreational games.[34] If we find a group of similar-sized pebbles in the courtyard of a prehistoric settlement they may suggest young people playing a game. But most games would leave nothing behind.

By contrast with games, toys are, by definition, artefacts, material culture, and archaeology deals in artefacts. In play, toys are one means to facilitate interactions between adults and children. Although children make their own toys, those created by adults help children to imitate adult action, though without real-world impact: 'toys reinforce cultural messages'.[35]

Children generally make their own toys from materials which do not survive in the archaeological record.[36] Adults make toys for children, though some of these will be for short-term use, knowing they will be damaged and destroyed. But objects we can identify or interpret as children's toys do occasionally survive in the record of prehistory.

They are of course are well attested in the record of advanced and literate societies. There, archaeological discoveries, textual references and artistic images complement each other to give a far fuller image than we can gain for the prehistoric world.[37] Some dramatic development of children's toys can be found when we encounter early urban societies. A study of items from the Indus Valley Harappan civilisation of the 3rd millennium BC described elaborate model carts and other constructions which showed the active role of children in the cultural life of the city.[38]

But we are also influenced by the over-determination of such evidence. If we see an Egyptian tomb painting with figures playing the board game *senet*, or a Greek carved relief of a ball game, then we confidently identify as recreational finds of artefacts similar to those depicted. Without the representational clue we may fail to identify game pieces and toys from a prehistoric site: a pierced clay disc appears as just that, and we are often not sure whether it is a functional piece or part of a game or toy.

Small crude arrowheads probably for use by children are mentioned in Chapter 6, which discusses other examples of miniature craft which could be toys, or could be experimental products of apprentices. Miniaturised objects have often been interpreted as 'ritual objects' and there are numerous Old and New World contexts that demonstrate this in archaeology and ethnography.[39] Any specific attribution or identification as a child's toy is hard to determine: the context and associations are our best guidelines.

Miniature shields and cauldrons from the British Iron Age of Salisbury were made with such care and attention to detail it is hard to see them as no more than a child's plaything. Similarly carefully made miniature axes come from Iron Age Germany and Switzerland.[40] Many other miniatures of military hardware are found in later Roman imperial contexts.

In the Plains area of Alberta, Canada, poorly made and non-functional (but presumed to be adult-made) arrowheads from the site Head-Smashed-In Buffalo Jump would appear to be toys, and similar items have been covered from other North American sites.[41] This reflects the frequent ethnographic observations of boys copying their fathers with practice (often harmless) bows and arrows: the overlap of play and learning.

The survival record privileges toys made from baked clay, such as the small pots made probably by or for children that were found in the Hallstatt Iron Age in the Czech Republic.[42] In the later prehistory of the region around Croatia, ceramic toys include small pots which preserve the finger

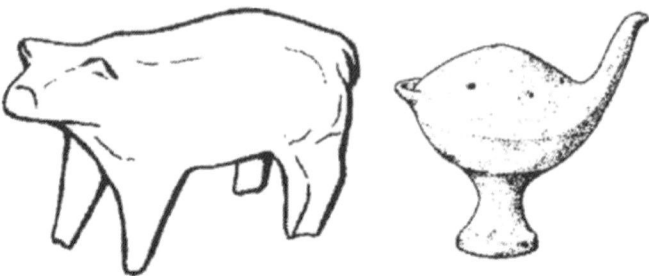

Possible children's items in clay from the Czech Republic: Bronze Age animal from Prague Vinoř (left) and Iron Age rattle from Prague-Střešovice

marks of their young modellers.[43] More unusual are finds of model tables and chairs of fired clay.

Small vessels – sometimes called 'pygmy cups' – are found in Dutch Bronze Age burials. These could be interpreted as miniature food vessels to accompany the young into the afterlife – but they may also have been associated with the buried children during their lives.[44] In Bronze Age Irish sites, though, such miniature vessels were buried with adults too.

Both miniature vessels and, less frequently, miniature tools (like axes and chisels) have been found buried with children in the Early Bronze Age of the Aegean.[45] It is tempting to think of these miniatures as toys created for children to play with in life, when imitating the work of their elders, and buried with them after an untimely death. It is adults who decide what will be buried with a child, what will be retained for others to use and what will be discarded after a child dies.

Occasional finds of model animals made of fired clay could also be considered children's possessions. Such finds are known from the Bronze Age of the Czech Republic and Grootebroek in Netherlands.[46]

In a find near Stovepipe Wells in California, undated but probably from Anasazi (Ancestral Puebloan) agriculturalists, a group of miniature objects included unfired clay vessels and figurines.[47] The form of the vessels suggested imitation of baskets of differing kinds. Use as children's toys seemed a possible explanation.

Clay was also used in many contexts for infants' rattles. Music, from simple rattles to handmade flutes to more complex instruments, can be categorised as toys when in the hands of children. A rattle from the Czech Republic and dated to the later Bronze Age is in the form of a bird, and another, which is essentially a narrow-necked pot, came from Iron Age Hallstatt in Austria.[48]

What are we to make of the remarkable carved-horn figures found on the chest of the burial of an infant under 1 year of age at the Russian site on Lake Itkul (see p. 241)?[49] This burial dates from the Bronze Age, in the late 3rd millennium BC. The baby was buried with a pot and in clothing which includes a copper and leather cap. The figurines – eight in all – were made from the horns of deer. The carved and painted decoration was in the form of animals (elk, boar, birds) and represents a significant amount of careful craftwork. The figurines seem designed to be held on a leather strap. If suspended together on a child's cradle, they could be hit together to make a rattle sound. While it is possible to think of this deposit as linked to some complex ritual and belief system, our instinct is to compare them to a hanging chain over a modern baby's crib, a mobile. Whatever their nature, they were buried with the child, presumably by the parents.

Also from the Bronze Age of the Vengerevo 2 site in Russian Siberia is a child's rattle of clay in the form of a bear's head.[50] Inside the rattle are sealed stones to make the rattling sound. A stamped impression on the outside of the rattle was interpreted by the excavators as the craftsperson's signature. Found abandoned in a domestic setting, the assumption that it was a child's toy, or a toy to entertain a child, seems secure.

The playthings of children in the area now occupied by Inuit communities in Arctic northern Canada and Greenland provide an interesting case study. Ethnographic accounts of modern Inuit emphasise the importance of play and games in Inuit childhoods, in a framework of relative freedom, with imitation of adult activities commonly observed.

Signs of games such as bull roarers, spinning tops and balls have been found in archaeological contexts of the Thule culture, advanced fishers and hunters seen as ancestral to the Inuit and dating back a millennium.[51] In Thule archaeology there is a high incidence of miniature items (4–5% of all items), likely to represent the playthings of children imitating their elders. These include hunting and fishing items such as harpoons, fish spears, knives and bows and arrows. Some are in a form that could actually have been used, although others were wooden imitations. There are miniature sleds, kayaks and boat paddles. Miniature cooking pots and lamps have been found, and of course dolls. Unlike some of the examples cited elsewhere in this chapter, these finds came from winter residential areas rather than graves. The quality of production of these items suggests they were usually made by adults for children, not the product of children themselves.

CHILDREN'S DOLLS AND ADULT FIGURES

If toys and games often allow children to imitate the life of the adults they will become, dolls provide a specific form of such imitation: for example, as a girl imitates her mother and becomes a surrogate mother of a miniature human; or as they are used in make-believe family scenes involving both

Clay doll found in 2017 at the Kori burial mound site of the Yayoi period, Japan, dated between around 300 BC and 300 AD

sexes, as recorded by anthropologists in widely different societies.[52] Human figures are part of the archaeological record of very many diverse communities: the difficult question to consider is which are children's playthings and which have some other, adult function. Is a model figure a ritual or cultic object, associated with some complex belief system, symbolic of a life force? Is it a figure of an ancestor, retained in the home (or buried beneath the house) to remember the dead and bring their support to the living? Does it have a sexual significance? Or is it the plaything of a child, the forerunner of the billions of dolls of the modern era?[53] Such small figures found in children's burials may be children's dolls or may sometimes be representations of those children.

Doll's house or cultic objects? Miniature ceramic items from Neolithic Ovčarovo, Bulgaria

When we understand the belief system of a society – as we do for Christian Europe or the Classical world – we can often tell whether a small human figure is that of a deity or a religious icon, and decide when to assign a small sculpture readily to the category of toy. With prehistoric societies, in the study of which children and childhood were so long ignored, it was easier to suppose a ritual or cultic significance to what may often have been a child's doll. Each object needs to be considered in its broader framework, though some scholars prefer simply to describe, without interpreting function.[54]

Julie Wileman's survey book *Hide and Seek* reviews a number of early figures.[55] Finds from the Neolithic settlement at Ovčarovo in Bulgaria resembled what might be found in a modern doll's house (though archaeological convention would describe it as a 'cult scene'). Here, in an otherwise unremarkable building within the settlement, were four human figures with decorative clothing, a small table, miniature pots and querns.[56] There are not enough parallels to this unusual find to define it as either cult or play, but why something resembling the contents of a child's doll's house should have religious function is not resolved. It is a remarkable 'miniaturisation' of a familiar world, but the context of its creation and social use cannot be determined.

A model house was found beneath the floor of a house at Platia Magoula Zarkou, a mound of remains from seasonal (probably winter) Neolithic occupation in Greek Thessaly.[57] The model includes eight human figures: a male, a female and some ill-defined smaller people, possibly children, and with some linear decoration on the bodies or clothing, and on a clay object

Model house from Neolithic Platia Magoula Zarkou, Greece

in the scene. Again, interpretations could be that this is a symbolic foundation offering – a small house within a large house – though it reminds us today of something that would bring delight to a child. Elsewhere in Neolithic Europe, children were themselves buried under the floor of their parents' house: it is not too unrealistic to think of something relating to a dead child also being buried under the floor.

The different interpretations of small human figures from the European Neolithic, especially those of Eastern and Southern Europe, were reviewed by Douglass Bailey in *Prehistoric Figurines*.[58] The frequency of human figurines of clay in the Neolithic of the Balkans (6500–3500 BC), including presence in adult burials, suggests we cannot simply classify them as children's dolls.

Bailey notes that dolls themselves can serve different purposes: stimulating the imagination, helping in education, establishing understanding of social hierarchies and more. He describes such figures as 'tools for thinking', which leaves open the way in which specific people and societies may have thought about their own creation and use of figurines.[59]

The presence or absence of sexual organs or other details of the body cannot in itself be considered proof that a specific context was present or absent. Where sexual organs are featured and women's breasts or rounded bellies are emphasised (as is also found in the Upper Palaeolithic) we might see these as consciously sexualised representations rather than necessarily some representation of fertility as such.[60] The European 'Mother Goddess' image so beloved of some 20th-century writers is hard to sustain without greater evidence of ritual than offered by clay figurines. So when a small pig carved out of chalk was found with the bones of an Iron Age infant (within a pot) in a pit near Stonehenge, something that any modern young child might have, an archaeological description suggested it 'may have had a ritual significance or may have been a toy'.[61]

Carved figurines were a feature of burials of children of late Iroquois society in Pennsylvania, New York and Ontario.[62] They were made from bone or ivory, usually representing adult women (although examples of men and a small child were also found), and typically 10 cm (4 inches) tall. The position in which they were found, and a suspension hole, suggest that they could have been used as pendants.

Human figures (typically of clay) found in the agricultural prehistory of Africa can be considered to include children's dolls as readily as having an alternative role in initiation and other rituals.[63]

One of the most interesting determinations of archaeological finds as dolls comes from Sanga in the Upemba region of south-east Democratic Republic of Congo, in the Iron Age of the 10th to 13th centuries AD.[64] Finds of leg bones from antelope or goat buried with children (lying alongside them, or even in a 'cradled position') were interpreted by Pierre de Maret as the basic bodies of dolls: a copper bracelet on one being an echo of personal decoration. Comparable uses have been found elsewhere: a bone as the body of a doll which could then be dressed in clothing or ornamentation from perishable materials.

Ethnographic parallels have been seen among modern communities, such as the bones used by Hopi children in the US Southwest, where the calf bone of a sheep represents a family member in children's games. A stick with clothing wrapped around it can play the same role.[65]

This leads to the idea that other animal bones found with prehistoric burials of children outside of Africa (such as Neolithic Europe and Bronze Age Middle East) might have been the 'core' of dolls whose decoration has not survived. However, as these bones have been found with newborn babies and infants, we cannot claim that these were the valued possessions of the buried individuals. It remains possible that these representations of human figures, if that is what they were, had a broader use than just playthings. Some of these bones were found in the graves of adult women, perhaps emphasising their linkage to fertility or the birth and rearing of children. The meanings of dolls may include roles they played both for children and for mothers.

Grave of a newborn from Iron Age Sanga, Democratic Republic of the Congo, with long bones probably used as dolls

'Fertility doll' from Guinea Bissau: an ethnographic parallel to the Sanga find

One argument against well made figures of human or animal form being children's dolls is their scarcity in prehistoric children's burials. These burials may well have included favourite items made from temporary materials that have decayed without trace (a child's straw doll, an unfired clay animal). But whereas we find clothing and jewellery, pots and tools, it is much less common to find a figurine in a burial context, as a favourite doll to accompany the dead child.

Where a figure is crudely made, and perhaps of unfired clay, this might tip the balance of probabilities towards it being a doll made by a child for their own use; but even then, there are examples of adults quickly creating badly made figures for ritual deposit. A finer product leaves us open to wider discussion. Evidence for children as artisans was discussed in the last chapter.

CONCLUSIONS

One reason why so few signs of children's play have been found in two centuries of archaeological work may be that so few people have looked for them. With a research focus that was, at different times, on elites, on the male world and on adult society, unexpected objects and unexpected positions of objects may have been ignored, or assigned to a supposed grand purpose of ritual or belief or other social process. This thought brings us to the brief but significant observation by archaeologist Norman Hammond on the impact of his 15-month-old son on artefacts, who created, by fairly random actions, a play pile which could have left archaeologists puzzling about its significance.[66] Anyone clearing up after the play activities of a small child is aware of the gap between the adult's (and therefore the archaeologist's) sense of order and the distribution of objects that represents the child's play and the child's world. We carefully measure, record and document the position of each artefact we find in an archaeological excavation, distinguishing groupings and interpreting location on the basis of adult rationality. At times we may do better to consider that a find or a group of finds represents the lively activity of a child or group of children at play.

Whether apparently random or clearly deliberate, the grouping and positioning of finds in a carefully excavated settlement or industrial site may give us the direct material reflection of child's play. There will still be subjectivity in whether we identify an object as being from an adult game, a child's game or neither; whether a miniature is a toy or a votive object; and whether a figurine is a child's doll, part of a religious ritual or something else. The answers may be complex but will not come if we do not ask the questions in as broad a context as possible. We should remember that if we time-travelled into a prehistoric community, the first sounds we would encounter would not be from stone tool making, potting, hunting or harvesting, but the sounds of children playing.

NOTES

1. Lancy, *Anthropology* 2ed, p. 213.
2. H.B. Schwartzman, *Transformations: the anthropology of children's play* (New York: Plenum, 1978) is a broad-ranging review of the topic and of its treatment by anthropologists applied to small-scale societies.
3. H. Montgomery, *An Introduction to Childhood: anthropological perspectives on children's lives*, Chichester: Wiley-Blackwell, 2009, p. 143.
4. Lancy, *Anthropology* 2ed, pp. 230–232, 244–245, 251–253.
5. R. Gage, 'Primate juveniles and primate plays' in M.E. Pereira & L.A. Fairbanks (eds), *Juvenile Primates: life history, development and behavior*, New York: Oxford University Press, 1993, pp. 182–196, especially p. 194.
6. M.P. Hoff, R.D. Nadler & T.L. Maple, 'The development of infant play in a captive group of lowland gorillas (*Gorilla gorilla gorilla*)', *American Journal of Primatology* 1 (1981): 65–72, which cites the pioneering work of Dian Fossey.
7. D. Maestripieri & S.R. Ross, 'Sex differences in play among western lowland gorilla (*Gorilla gorilla gorilla*) infants: implications for adult behavior and social structure', *American Journal of Physical Anthropology* 123 (2004): 52–61. They cite a similar pattern among orangutans.
8. J. Goodall, *The Chimpanzees of Gombe: pattern of behavior*, Cambridge, MA: Harvard University Press, 1986, pp. 369–372.
9. Goodall, *The Chimpanzees of Gombe*, pp. 166–168.
10. T. Nishida, *Chimpanzees of the Lakeside: natural history and culture at Mahale*, Cambridge: Cambridge University Press, 2012, p. 112.
11. M. Shimada & C. Sueur, 'The importance of social play network for infant or juvenile wild chimpanzees at Mahale Mountains National Park, Tanzania', *American Journal of Primatology* 76 (2014): 1025–1036.
12. T. Nishida et al., *Chimpanzee Behavior in the Wild: an audio-visual encyclopedia*, Tokyo: Springer, 2010, cited in M. Shimada, 'Dynamics of the temporal structures of playing structures and cliques among wild chimpanzees in Mahale Mountains National Park', *Primates* 54 (2013): 245–257.
13. H. Hayaki, 'Social play of juvenile and adolescent chimpanzees in the Mahale Mountains National Park, Tanzania', *Primates* 26 (1985): 343–360; Nishida, *Chimpanzees of the Lakeside*, pp. 125–156; Shimada, 'Dynamics of the temporal structures'; A.E. Pusey, 'Behavioural changes at adolescence of chimpanzees', *Behaviour* 115 (1990): 203–246.
14. S.M. Kahlenberg & R.W. Wrangham, 'Sex differences in chimpanzees' use of sticks as play objects resemble those of children', *Current Biology* 20 (2010): R1067–R1068.
15. N.N. Ladygina-Kohts, *Infant Chimpanzee and Human Child: a classic 1935 comparative study of ape emotions and intelligence*, Oxford: Oxford University Press, 2002.

16 A. Nowell, 'Childhood, play and the evolution of cultural capacity in Neanderthals and modern humans' in M.N. Haidle et al. (eds), *The Nature of Culture*, Dordrecht: Springer Netherlands, 2016: 87–97.

17 F. d'Errico et al., 'A Middle Palaeolithic origin of music? Using cave-bear bone accumulations to assess the Divje Babe I bone "flute"', *Antiquity* 72 (1998): 65–79; C.G. Diedrich, '"Neanderthal bone flutes": simply products of Ice Age spotted hyena scavenging activities on cave bear cubs in European cave bear dens', *Royal Society Open Science* 2 (2015): 140022.

18 Y. Gosso et al., 'Play in hunter-gatherer societies' in A.D. Pellegrini & P.K. Smith (eds), *The Nature of Play: great apes and humans*, New York: Guilford Press, 2005: 213–253.

19 P. Gray, 'Play as a foundation for hunter-gatherer social existence', *American Journal of Play* 1 (2009): 476–522, pp. 510–512.

20 Montgomery, *An Introduction to Childhood*, p. 150; B. Tucker & A.G. Young, 'Growing up Mikea' in *HGC*: 147–172.

21 M.J. Konner, 'Maternal care, infant behavior and development among the !Kung' in R.B. Lee & I. DeVore (eds), *Kalahari Hunter-Gatherers: studies of the !Kung San and their neighbors*, Cambridge, MA: Harvard University Press, 1976: 218–245, p. 220; P. Draper, 'Social and economic constraints on child life among the !Kung' in Lee & DeVore (eds), *Kalahari Hunter-Gatherers*: 201–217, which gives a valuable observer account of the relaxed world of !Kung San children, and their games.

22 H.N. Fouts, R.A. Hallam & S. Purandare, 'Gender segregation in early-childhood social play among the Bofi foragers and Bofi farmers in Central Africa', *American Journal of Play* 5 (2013): 333–356.

23 M. Konner, 'Hunter-gatherer infancy and childhood: the !Kung and others' in *HGC*: 51.

24 B.S. Hewlett, *Intimate Fathers: the nature and context of Aka Pygmy paternal infant care*, Ann Arbor, MI: University of Michigan Press, 1991, p. 168.

25 N. Kamei, 'Play among Baka children in Cameroon' in *HGC*: 343–359.

26 Lancy, *Anthropology* 2ed, pp. 213–253.

27 Emphasised by S. Crawford, 'The archaeology of playthings: theorising a toy stage in the "biography" of objects', *CitP* 2 (2009): 55–70. She suggests that archaeologists struggle to identify any toys in the hundreds of early Anglo-Saxon settlement sites in England; the problem lies not with their absence but with their identification. From a museum perspective the issue is discussed in the Foreword to J. Joy et al., *Hide and Seek: looking for children in the past*, Cambridge: Museum of Archaeology and Anthropology, 2016.

28 C.R. Ember & C.M. Cunnar, 'Children's play and work: the relevance of cross-cultural ethnographic research for archaeologists' in *TCIN*: 87–103, pp. 93–97.

29 Lancy, *Anthropology* 2ed, p. 246.

30 R. Holmgren, '"Money on the hoof": the astragalus bone – religion, gaming and primitive money' in B. Santillo (ed.), *PECUS: man and animal in antiquity*, Rome: Swedish Institute in Rome, 2002, online at www.isvroma.it

31 F. McCormick, 'Faunal Remains from Prehistoric Irish Burials', *Journal of Irish Archaeology* 3 (1985): 37–48, p. 37.

32 C. Marangou, 'Social differentiation in the early Bronze Age: miniature tools and child burials', *Journal of Mediterranean Studies* 1 (1991): 211–225, p. 212.

33 O. Spjuth, *In Quest for the Lost Gamers: an investigation of board gaming in*

Scania, during the Iron and Middle Ages, Lund University thesis, online at lu.academia.edu/OskarSpjuth

34 G. Eogan, 'Report on the excavations of some passage graves, unprotected inhumation burials and a settlement site at Knowth, Co. Meath', *Proceedings of the Royal Irish Academy, Section C*, 74 (1974): 11–112, pp. 73–77.

35 Baxter, *Archaeology*, pp. 41–42.

36 Ember & Cunnar, 'Children's play and work', pp. 99–100.

37 For example essays on medieval European toys in *CCLA*.

38 E. Rogersdotter, *The Forgotten: an approach on Harappan toy artefacts*, Umeå: Department of Archaeology and Sami Studies, University of Umeå, 2006.

39 For instance S.J. O'Connor, 'Ritual deposit boxes in Southeast Asian sanctuaries', *Artibus Asiae* 28 (1966): 53–60; J.-M. Luce, 'From miniature objects to giant ones: the process of defunctionalisation in sanctuaries and graves in Iron Age Greece', *Pallas* 86 (2011): 53–73; see also the discussion in P. Kiernan, 'Miniature objects as representations of realia', *World Archaeology* 47 (2015): 45–59.

40 Kiernan, 'Miniature objects', pp. 47–48, 55–56.

41 B. Dawe, 'Tiny arrowheads: toys in the toolkit', *Plains Anthropologist* 42 (1997): 303–318.

42 J. Turek, 'Being a Beaker child: the position of children in Late Eneolithic society', *Memoriam Jan Rulf, Památky archeologické – Supplementum* 13 (2000): 422–436.

43 D. Balen-Letunić, 'An overview of prehistoric toys', *Etnološka istraživanja* 18–19 (2014): 11–17, online at www.emz.hr/Istraživanja/Etnološka_istraživanja

44 B. Ó Donnabháin & A.L. Brindley, 'The status of children in a sample of Bronze Age burials containing pygmy cups', *Journal of Irish Archaeology* 5 (1989): 19–24.

45 Marangou, 'Social differentiation'.

46 Turek, 'Being a Beaker child'; J.-F. Altena, G.F.I. Van Regteren & P.J.A. Van Mensch, *Bronze Age Clay Animals from Grootebroek*, Amsterdam: Staatsuitgeverij, 1977.

47 W.J. Wallace, 'A cache of unfired clay objects from Death Valley, California', *American Antiquity* 30 (1965): 434–441.

48 Wileman, *Hide and Seek*, p. 30; Turek, 'Being a Beaker child'. The Hallstatt find is audible online at www.aeiou.at/aeiou.music.1.1

49 A.V. Polyakov & Y.N. Esin, 'Horn figurines from an Okunev burial on Lake Itkul, Khakassia, southern Siberia', *Archaeology, Ethnology and Anthropology of Eurasia* 43 (2015): 43–57.

50 www.natureworldnews.com/articles/30652/20161026/childs-4000-year-old-rattle-unearthed-in-siberia.htm; also siberiantimes.com/science/others/news/n0780-4000-year-old-childrens-rattle-beautifully-crafted-as-bear-cubs-head-and-it-still-rattles

51 R.W. Park, 'Size counts: the miniature archaeology of childhood in Inuit societies', *Antiquity* 72 (1998): 269–281; R.W. Park, 'Growing up North: exploring the archaeology of childhood in the Thule and Dorset cultures of Arctic Canada' *CIA*: 53–64.

52 Lancy, *Anthropology* 2ed, pp. 230–234.

53 A classic article by archaeologist Peter Ucko considered how one might distinguish these: P.J. Ucko, 'The interpretation of prehistoric anthropomorphic figurines', *Journal of the Royal Anthropological Institute* 92 (1962): 38–54. See also P.G. Bahn, 'Children of the Ice Age' in *AOC*: 167–188, p. 181; S.K. Moses, 'From playthings to sacred objects?' in *AOC*: 205–216.

54 S.R. Hutson, 'Method and theory for an archaeology of age' in *AOC*: 53–72, p. 58.
55 Wileman, *Hide and Seek*, pp. 27–43.
56 Turek, 'Being a Beaker child'; A. Whittle, *Europe in the Neolithic*, Cambridge: Cambridge University Press, 1996, p. 94; D. Bailey, *Prehistoric Figurines: representation and corporeality in the Neolithic*, Abingdon: Routledge, 2005, pp. 26–26, 43–44, citing the work of H. Todorova et al., *Ovcharovo (Razkopki i Prouchvaniya 9)*, Sofia: BAN, 1983.
57 Whittle, *Europe in the Neolithic*, pp. 87–88; S. Nanoglou, 'Subjectivity and material culture in Thessaly, Greece: the case of Neolithic anthropomorphic imagery', *Cambridge Archaeological Journal* 15 (2005): 141–156.
58 Bailey, *Prehistoric Figurines*, pp. 66ff.
59 Bailey, *Prehistoric Figurines*, p. 196.
60 Bailey, *Prehistoric Figurines*, pp. 164–166.
61 https://news.nationalgeographic.com/news/2008/10/081021-stonehenge-toy.html
62 E. Carpenter, 'Iroquoian figurines', *American Antiquity* 8 (1942): 105–113.
63 J.-M. Dederen, 'Women's power, 1000 AD: figurine art and gender politics in prehistoric Southern Africa', *Nordic Journal of African Studies* 19 (2010): 23–42; E. Matenga, *Archaeological Figurines from Zimbabwe*, Uppsala: Societas Archaeologica Upsaliensis, 1993.
64 P. de Maret, 'Tea party toys? Classical Kisalian grave goods from the Upemba (D.R. Congo)', *Journal of African Archaeology* 14 (2016): 19–32; P. de Maret, 'Bones, sex, and dolls: solving a mystery in Central Africa and beyond', *Journal of Field Archaeology*, 41 (2016): 500–509.
65 Schwartzman, *Transformations*, p. 158.
66 G. Hammond & N. Hammond, 'Child's play: a distorting factor in archaeological distribution', *American Antiquity* 46 (1981): 634–636.

8
FIGHTING
Conflict and violence

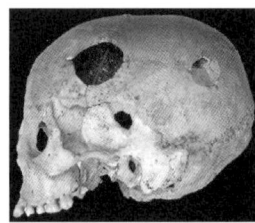

We have a broad range of evidence of war and violence in the lives of prehistoric children: both as victims, and also learning to be active participants in war and defence, acquiring the skills of fighting as aggressors or defenders. In the archaeology of prehistory we can see the direct signs of children's injuries and death at the hands of those making war and from other incidents of violence.

War and conflict affect the combatants with death, physical injury and mental trauma. Capture of a combatant in war can lead to their death, torture, forced labour, permanent enslavement, extended imprisonment or ransom: a range from cannibal consumption to prisoner exchange and ultimate freedom.

Violent conflict affects what today we would call 'civilian' populations both indirectly, for example from forced migration and starvation, and directly, when, at the extreme, non-combatant men, women and children are slaughtered. War in most cultures and at most times means civilian as well as military casualties, as in the biblical instruction to the conquering Israelites: 'But as for the towns of these peoples that the Lord your God is giving you as an inheritance, you must not let anything that breathes remain alive. You shall annihilate them...'.[1]

Violent deaths may come from inter-group conflict: raids for possessions or revenge, or wars for the control of territory. But they may also arise from intra-group conflict: homicide, or the result of conflict between individuals, shown in historical and ethnographic evidence of high rates of violent death in many smaller-scale societies.[2]

Narratives of world history often appear to be dominated by accounts of armed conflict: between nation states and alliances, between political entities and groups asserting a religious or ethnic affiliation or a territorial

A 13-year-old soldier from Vietnam, 1968

claim, between neighbouring communities and within ruling families. The role of conflict in human society has engaged huge numbers of behavioural and social scientists, philosophers and theologians, writers and artists. Citizens have often prayed for peace while engaging energetically in war, peace sometimes being a synonym for victory. Throughout recorded history, it is fair to suggest that most people might expect their society to encounter war or conflict in their lives and we can consider whether the same expectations extended back through different periods of prehistory.

In his broad-ranging study of war, Israeli historian Azar Gat concluded that hostility to war in general was a relatively recent phenomenon: 'Only with modernity, as the liberal outlook that emerged during the Enlightenment gradually grew to dominate the developed world, did war begin to be regarded as something utterly repugnant and futile, indeed incomprehensible to the point of absurdity'.[3] Gat argues that conflict between human groups was the natural order extending back deep into prehistory. He also suggests that a reduction in intra-group violence over time reflects the growth of violence (or at least power) by the state.[4] A powerful state elite can use its resources to guarantee personal safety by the suppression of violent crime while having the authority to recruit its young male citizens to fight its wars.

The early 21st century has seen campaigns against the use of 'child soldiers' – young people who have been forced into taking up arms. But there are numerous traditions of people in what we now call childhood being fully fledged fighters in wars and conflicts. A century ago, teenagers from many nations volunteered to fight in the Great War of 1914–18, often lying about their age to do so, an act which has gained them modern admiration. Recent neurological research has demonstrated the neurochemical basis for risk-taking during adolescence, a willingness to engage in behaviours which older adults would avoid.[5] A military leader or organiser of a terrorist group has good reason to use younger personnel.

Archaeologist Laurence Keeley has argued from our knowledge of both prehistory and the ethnographic record that 'warfare in prestate societies was both frequent and important'.[6] Warfare in small-scale societies might be a token conflict to avenge an injury or slight; it may be a conflict between the young men of two societies; but equally it may be a raid in which armed men seek to destroy the whole of a rival community, killing women and children, old and young. In such a case, there may not even be survivors to give the dead the kind of formal burial which will readily be retrievable by archaeologists.

ARCHAEOLOGICAL EVIDENCE OF CONFLICT

Archaeology and the study of excavated human remains present clear evidence of violent conflict in prehistory.[7] Signs of violent death common to a group of burials are taken to suggest the results of inter-group conflict: in other words, war. The injuries caused by weapons are clear; sometimes the weapons themselves (a spear or arrow point) may be found embedded in the skeleton, including those of children.

Overall, war will produce evidence of death (from trauma) of a particular pattern: men more than women, adults more than children and young adults (or older adolescents) more than old men. Of course, serious and even fatal injuries to isolated adolescents and young men need not reflect intercommunal conflict; these are life stages when interpersonal conflict may anyway be violent, when risk taking is at its highest and when injuries arising from everyday work activities are perhaps more likely.

Individual burials of children showing a healed blow to the body, or a fatal blow to the skull, are found in prehistoric forager and farming societies throughout the world. Where they demonstrate injury leading to death this may reflect wars between neighbouring societies, conflict within a community, domestic violence or ritual killing – or just an accident.[8]

Alongside the effects of war and violent attack, more detailed specialised study of skeletal material (and context) is required to assess whether a child may have died as a deliberate sacrifice by their own community. While the sacrifice of children is well attested in the historical record of both Old and New Worlds (and many such bodies have been recovered from Aztec, Inca and Maya sites), the interpretation of a prehistoric burial as that of a sacrificial cult is often hard to test and confirm.[9]

While evidence of prehistoric brutality continues to accumulate, there remain those who argue that it is modernity, or 'civilisation', or even settled agricultural life, that has stimulated conflict. Ideas that 'primitive' people were naturally peaceable have surfaced among writers and philosophers through the centuries.

One theme in the alternative interpretations from within feminist writings of the later 20th century was the idea that prehistoric societies were matriarchal and peaceful, in contrast to the warlike patriarchal societies of the last five millennia of civilisation.[10] Unfortunately, the evidence from excavated finds does not support the image of a peaceful past, although the levels of conflict were very varied across the broad range of prehistoric societies.

If aggression is considered an innate characteristic of the human species, then it could be expected to present first among the young. Children's play (as noted in Chapter 7) involves much wrestling and mock fighting, and develops into more skilled fighting techniques. Some theories draw analogies with our higher primate relatives. Young chimpanzees in the wild need to learn to fight: mothers must defend their infants, males will fight to establish rank and territory, and both sexes may be proactively aggressive. The males may also use physical aggression to secure sexual domination of a female as well as dispel rivals when a female is sexually receptive.[11] At the same time, chimpanzees may learn to limit aggression, by submissive gestures and the like, or discourage physical attack by displays of aggression.

But chimpanzee violence can extend to greater levels, and there is much debate about the nature and basis of such violence. Males in a chimpanzee group (unlike the norm among bonobos) can attack the males of a rival group, with the aim of killing them, and sometimes succeed in doing so, especially when the 'enemy' is outnumbered.[12] It has been suggested that males in adjacent chimpanzee troops maintain hostile and potentially violent relations, yet mothers with children have been seen to break down these hostile barriers.[13] Since an infant can be so easily killed in an intergroup conflict, a mother's protection of her offspring may override other group loyalties.

CONFLICT AND VIOLENCE AMONG PREHISTORIC FORAGERS

A feature observed among many recent and modern hunter-gatherer groups is the frequency of interpersonal violence: within a community, between similar communities, as well as conflicts with non-forager groups.[14] A recent collection of essays considers examples of conflict and violence in hunter-gatherer societies both ancient and more recent.[15] From different disciplinary backgrounds and regional interests they consider the presence of conflict, though contributors also suggest that it is not an inevitable and permanent feature of traditional forager groups.

The stone and wooden artefacts of Palaeolithic and Mesolithic prehistory which we associate with hunting game animals for food and skins could also serve to hunt down and kill or injure humans. Human physical remains can show direct evidence of violence, but even the evidence of cannibalism is not sufficient to confirm it was associated with inter-group conflict, as cannibalism is also be a form of treatment of the dead within a society. Children as well as adults appear to have been cannibalised in widely different prehistoric and historic contexts.[16]

Famously (or perhaps infamously) palaeontologist Raymond Dart identified the fragments associated with Australopithecines at Makapansgat in South Africa as evidence of interpersonal violence. Dart considered the distribution of Australopithecine bones and evidence from the bones themselves showed a society with an instinct for violence and weapons developed for this purpose, followed by cannibalism.[17] This theme was taken up for a popular audience by writer Robert Ardrey, but subsequent re-evaluation of the Makapansgat finds have eroded these early claims.[18]

The Middle Palaeolithic finds at Atapuerca in Spain, discussed in Chapter 9, included the burial of a young man who died from blows to the head with a club or similar weapon.[19] The position of the blows suggests face-to-face combat – not the death of someone fleeing.

An overall survey of Middle Palaeolithic bodies showing signs of violent trauma has mainly adult bodies, and those on adults (only) from Krapina in Croatia have been interpreted as the kind of injuries natural to hunter-gatherer life.[20]

Excavations at the Upper Palaeolithic site of Předmostí in the Czech Republic's Moravia region have produced numerous human remains, including those of infants and children, although the finds are no longer available for study.[21] There are some multiple burials, with adults and children together. The presence of individuals buried together has been interpreted by some as evidence for a simultaneous and therefore presumably violent death.

A similar argument for a common and violent cause of death was applied to Upper Palaeolithic finds at Maszycka cave in Poland. Here a burial of at least 16 people may reflect a common cause of death: the group comprised five adults, three older children and eight infants, dated about 16,000 BC.[22] The possible evidence of cannibalism gives additional support to the theory of a violent death: the bones had signs of cutting, breaking and smashing.[23]

A flint point penetrates the backbone of one of the two children buried together at the Upper Palaeolithic site of Grotta dei Fanciulli (Grotte des Enfants) in Grimaldi, Italy.[24] A single such death shows violence but not necessarily inter-group conflict.

In the Natufian culture of Israel, a depressed fracture on the skull of a child from Hayonim showed an injury from which the individual had recovered.[25]

From the Nile Valley site of Jebel Sahaba near Wadi Halfa, on the east of the River Nile in Sudan, came evidence of a fight and massacre, with victims including women and children, killed by projectiles.[26] Fifty-eight bodies were recovered, dated to the Epipalaeolithic around 12,000–10,000 BC. The burials had been careful and deliberate, so presumably not undertaken by the killers: flexed, facing east and covered with sandstone slabs. Almost half showed the signs of a violent death. The wounds that had caused death were clear: over 100 artefacts (spear points and other projectiles) were embedded in the skeletons or associated with them and cut marks were also visible on some of the bones, with multiple wounds on a single body common. There was no visible significant distinction between the violence on men, women or children: it was thus a massacre, not the result of a fight between men followed by the slaughter of their dependants.[27] Here was an attack in which children suffered the impact of defeat of a community by a rival group. Careful comparison of the bones suggested their physical resemblance to modern sub-Saharan African groups.

A dramatic prehistoric find in the West Turkana region of Kenya, announced in 2016, demonstrated inter-group violence and its impact on children.[28] At the site of Nataruk were the bones of 27 people: not deliberately buried but abandoned where they lay. These people appear to have been killed at the edge of a lagoon, into which some of them had fallen, at a date around 8000 BC. This hunter-gatherer community fell victim to an attacking group who, from the evidence of their obsidian weapons, came from some distance away. Of 12 skeletons examined in detail, 10 showed signs of violent attack. Most of the 27 were adults (males and females, young and old) but six were children, all but one (a young teenager) being aged under 6 years and killed alongside their parents (or other adults in their kin group). Their bodies were often close to those of the adult females, suggesting a final scenario of unsuccessful attempts at protection. Additionally, the remains of an unborn foetus were found within one woman's skeleton. In the massacre of this community, the bones showed blows to head and neck, legs, hand and ribs, some being arrow wounds, emphasised by the presence of stone points in a skull and in body cavities. Further, two of the skeletons were in a position that suggested they had been bound before being killed. The children's bones were too fragmentary to judge the specific causes of their individual deaths.

In the late Mesolithic site of Grosser Ofnet in Germany's Bavaria (a site discovered in 1908), dated around 6500 BC, two pits contained remains of 34 or more people with decapitated skulls, the majority being children and 16 of them infants (under 6 years of age).[29] They had been buried together soon after death and the decapitation may have been part of a mortuary ritual, as was the scattering of red ochre over the bodies. A violent cause of death was noted in some of the dead: impressions of a heavy blow from a club or mace, and slash marks on both adults and children, the majority on the back of the head. Two adult males showed wounds in other parts of their bodies, suggesting that they fought actively, while the children and adults were killed as they fled.

Nevertheless, this was not just hasty disposal of bodies after a massacre, as grave goods accompanied bodies. Pierced teeth of red deer were placed with the bodies of children and adults, and over 4000 ornaments made of different shells accompanied old and young: jewellery presumably placed to accompany the dead in their collective graves, though associated especially with the adult females.

The burial of man, woman and child together at the late Mesolithic settlement of Vedbaek in Denmark has been seen as evidence of a violent simultaneous death.[30] At the nearby site of Gøngehusvej a 5-year-old child was buried with a 40-year-old woman who had suffered an earlier and apparently non-fatal blow from a blunt instrument.[31] At Dyrholmen in Denmark cut marks on the cranium of a 10-year-old child suggest scalping – but whether this was an act of violence or a ritual part of a burial process we cannot know.[32]

In the Later Stone Age of Southern Africa, a number of juvenile burials have been discovered with evidence of violent death.[33] At the mouth of the Modder River in the Western Cape, from about 800 BC, skeletons of three young people (one aged 11–12, one 6–7, one around 1 year) buried together show evidence of perforated skulls: injuries which could have been created by a stone club – possibly a familiar form of a digging stick with a stone weight.[34] This was clearly a burial following a violent multiple murder.

At the location of Quoin Point on the southern Cape coast of South Africa an infant was buried with a woman who had projectile points in her spine.[35] And at the site of Melkbosstrand, 35 km (22 miles) north of Cape Town, an adult and a young person (aged 13–16 years) had gashes on the skull which were presumed to be the cause of death. There are no cultural traditions of sacrifice in the descendants of Later Stone Age groups, and conflict between groups or families (or even within a family) remains the most likely context for these violent deaths.

There is widespread evidence from the New World of violence and conflict in prehistoric societies, of both foragers and farmers, well before the emergence of pre-Columbian civilisations or European contact.

In Argentina, the young at the late hunter-gatherer site of Chenque I were found in multiple burials and showed clear signs of violent injury.[36] Arrow points were embedded in the bodies of several children, adolescents and adults. In one burial at least 17 individuals were interred together, suggesting the result of a battle or raid. Another burial was of a man aged 17–19 years with two arrow points embedded from the front: he was buried with copper and bead ornamentation. All of this suggests not a child victim of violence but an active young warrior who fell in conflict.

Among a Chinchorro forager group in Chile, dated around 2000 BC, there was plenty of evidence of violence in the adult skeletons, but not among the young: a quartz projectile in the spine of an adolescent of 16–17 years was an unusual exception and cause of death.[37]

A site in Santa Barbara, California, was notable for the cranial fractures of adolescents, but not of children. This is echoed in other sites, such as Norris Farms 36 in Illinois where 43 of 264 burials showed signs of violent deaths and the later Larson Village site in South Dakota.[38] While a raid on a settlement may kill or injure the elderly and the children, men and women, direct conflict between armed members of two groups is most likely to bring to the fore the actions of, and resulting injury or death of, young (but not very young) men.

Many other sites through the prehistory of California attest to violent conflict and the taking of skulls as trophies after a raid or battle, which, overall, appeared to affect men more than women, and adults (including young adults) rather than children.[39] This would be consistent with a pattern of children being taken alive into the raiding community rather than killed.

At Saunaktuk in the Canadian Arctic, in an area where Inuit and Native American groups clashed, bodies of adults and an even larger number of children (24 of a total of 35 bodies) showed signs of violent and fatal attack, followed by defleshing and cannibalism, dated around the 14th century AD.[40] Wounds were from slashing, stabbing and cutting by sharp instruments. Long bones were split, an activity which implies cannibalism (indeed, all the long bones were split except those of of one infant), as does the gouging of the ends of the long bones and some of the cuts seen on the skeleton. Such gouging, seen on both children and adults, can also be the result of a torture practice known later in the area.

CONFLICT AND VIOLENCE AMONG PREHISTORIC FARMERS

By definition, most agricultural societies are less mobile than most foragers, and cannot readily flee threats with a quick and simple shift of location. Agriculturalists' livelihood depends on their cultivated crops and therefore their settlement near their land is central to their existence. So alongside occasional direct signs of conflict in prehistoric agricultural communities we can also see signs of defence, and especially defensive structures. A protective ditch and bank complemented by a circle of post-holes can suggest an era of intercommunal conflict – though we need to distinguish a large-scale defensive structure from a simple containing fence to keep stock animals in and wild animals out.

The millennia of agricultural societies of Neolithic Europe present evidence of conflict in many different areas.[41] This includes fortified settlements as well as mass burials, including children alongside adult males and females, and sometimes with stone artefacts embedded in the bodies of both adults and children.

We also have evidence of other forms of violence against children, not caused by war and external forces. As elsewhere, children were the unwitting victims of conflict and violence.[42]

At Talheim in south-west Germany, 50 km (31 miles) from Stuttgart, a mass burial in a 'death pit' was found from the early Neolithic Linearbandkeramik (LBK) period, dated about 5000 BC. The pit had been dug 1.5 m (5 feet) deep and the bodies had been placed in it without grave goods. It contained 34 bodies: 18 of young adult men or women (the age averaged 23 years) and 16 of children. Genetic analysis showed they were from at least four different families. These bodies carried signs of death from axe or adze blows to the head, often at the back right of the skull, showing that they had been hit from behind with one or more sharp blows.[43] The shape of the injuries suggested that clubs or stone axeheads had been used, but there were also injuries inflicted by stone arrowheads. This was clearly a massacre of a significant part of a community that was at the earliest stage of agriculture in Central Europe, and not the result of a battle between equally armed combatants.

Absent from this burial are infants. This suggests two possibilities. The infants may have been captured and taken away rather than killed. Or when the survivors (or a neighbouring group) came to bury the dead, the bodies of infants may have been treated as too young to require or merit inclusion in the mass grave.[44]

Remains of 215 children from 32 different sites in Neolithic Germany included 13 with signs of head injury: three aged 4–8 years, seven between 8 and 12 years and three over 12.[45] Most wounds show that these children received blows from above, as from taller adults, and were possibly also attacked while fallen. The wound on one body from Otzing may have been from a slingshot rather than a blow with a hand-held weapon.

Other massacre sites from the period have been recovered. At Neolithic Asparn Schletz in Austria, also dated around 5000 BC, a trench built (unsuccessfully) to act as a defence had been used to bury bodies, some of which had been left exposed for a time before burial. The 67 corpses included adults and children: 38% of those killed were infants or juveniles, but young females were absent, presumably having been taken away as captives.[46] Here, too, the skulls suggested heavy fatal blows from clubs and from axes applied from behind as victims were fleeing. As well as the injuries, the skeletons showed signs of carnivore gnawing, which indicated the bodies had been exposed for a period before being collected for burial.

At Menneville in Aisne, France, 11 children were buried at the bottom of a ditch of LBK Neolithic date, possibly the victims of a violent attack, and in Jungfernhöhle Cavern in Germany the remains of 41 people from the LBK were mainly women and children.[47] The simplest explanation is that they were victims of an attack and their bodies were thrown into this space. But studies of bodies from other LBK sites noted cranial wounds in children aged between 8 and 12 years, raising the idea that these might have been caused by initiation rites, or perhaps military training.[48]

Further east, the site of Ostrovul Corbului in Romania had a burial of four people, perhaps a family including two children, with signs of body injuries. One of the children had been wounded in the chest.[49]

At the Late Neolithic (mid-3rd millennium BC) settlement of Eulau in Germany four multiple graves contained the careful burial of individuals killed in a violent attack: a deliberate and attentively arranged burial in contrast to the mass deposit of bodies found elsewhere.[50] Two males, three females and eight juveniles were identified. A 4- or 5-year-old child had a wound from a blow to the head which might have been from an earlier accident. An 8- or 9-year-old had a major wound at the back of the head and adults showed injuries from both arrows and blows with blunt instruments. Studies of the ancient DNA indicated that this was a family group; the children were related to the adults, and the adult females had married into the group.[51]

Signs of trauma on excavated skeletons in Neolithic Britain provide evidence of conflict, but interpreting the nature of such events is challenging.[52] The injuries are primarily on adults (an exception is a child at Belas Knap with a head wound from a blunt instrument), which suggests conflict between individuals rather than a raid and massacre of a community.

Despite these examples, signs of war and conflict are not universal across early stages of European farming communities; for instance, Balkan agricultural and early metalworking communities seem to have little evidence

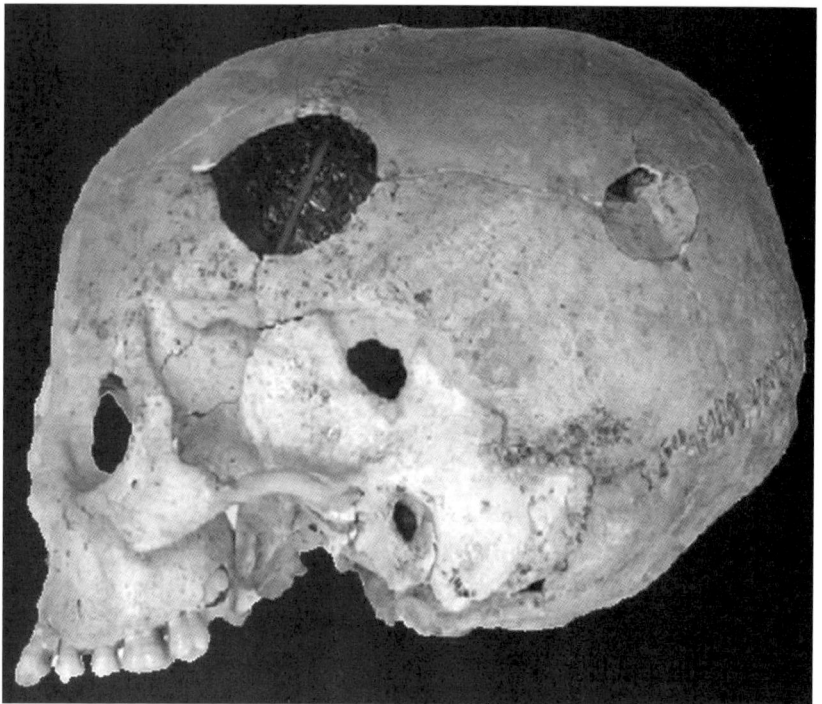

Skull of a 13- or 14-year-old with fatal wound from a macehead blow, from Chalcolithic Shiqmim, Israel

of such conflict.[53] Movements of populations into and through the region occurred but signs of conflict and conquest are few.

Finds at the Chalcolithic (Copper Age) site of Shiqmim in Israel, dated to the 6th and 5th millennia BC, include the body of a male adolescent victim of conflict, probably aged only 13 or 14 years.[54] His skeleton shows fractures on his skull, from three heavy blows to the back of his head. The shape of these suggest the weapon used was of rounded form, such as a mace head, and mace heads have been recovered from archaeological sites of the period.

Children's skeletal material at the early Neolithic site of Çayönü Tepesi in Turkish Anatolia carry cut marks, and these have been interpreted as evidence of child sacrifice but might equally be from a burial practice of separating the bones for burial after death.[55]

Excavations of a mass grave of the Early Bronze Age at Titriş Höyük also in Turkish Anatolia revealed victims of a massacre, with two children and an infant buried together with at least 16 adults.[56] Wounds on the adult skeletons showed the impacts of sharp blows sufficient to have killed them.

At the Bronze Age site of Velim in the Czech Republic, numerous human bodies were buried in a series of large pits.[57] There were complete bodies but also separated skulls and limbs, with infants, older children and adults spread through the remains. The cut marks on many bones suggest that these were the victims of violent attack.

The German Bronze Age finds in the Tollense Valley suggest evidence of inter-group conflict. Most finds are of adults but include one adolescent girl (12–15 years old) with a wound from a blow to the head.[58] In Bronze Age Spain, fractures to the limb bones of three young children (aged 4, 6–7 and 7–8) at Castellón Alto seem to be the result of accident rather than violence.[59]

The British Iron Age site of Kemerton Camp in Worcestershire also presents the marks of conflict, with cut marks and injuries from blows.[60] The bodies were found at the gateway of a defensive hill fort and, while mainly adults, included some adolescents and younger children. Other British Iron Age sites reaffirm the frequency of conflict, with young men the predominant victims showing bodily wounds.[61]

Violent conflict runs through the prehistory of both complex and smaller-scale societies in North and South America, with some dramatic examples.[62] Skeletal remains show evidence of massacres of children alongside adults: for example, the bodies of a 12-year-old and two 15–18-years-olds alongside eight adults, all buried under a pit-house floor (early 1st millennium AD) in Largo-Gallina in the US state of New Mexico.[63]

At an Ancestral Pueblo (Anasazi) site at Arroyo Hondo in New Mexico, burials of three children aged 3–5 years carrying serious wounds were discovered together among a total of 54 children aged under 5 years among 120 burials (no infants were found).[64] Not only did their skulls show the impact of several fatal blows but their ribs indicated they had been beaten and one also had wounds to the teeth. This level of violence suggests some kind of ritualised killing, an action on children selected for ceremonial despatch.

At a small agricultural Anasazi settlement of Chaco Canyon in New Mexico, USA, skeletal remains dated around 900 AD had signs of cannibalism, and included one child, three adolescents over 12 and two adults.[65] Their bones had been broken, cut, burned and boiled. Such a pattern is seen at later south-western Anasazi sites and applied to both adults and the young: one survey identified 295 cannibalised bodies at 32 sites, a phenomenon scholars attributed to Mexican influence.[66]

A group of children and adolescents at Sand Canyon Pueblo in Colorado from the 13th century AD appear to have been victims of violence.[67] Severe wounds to the skull suggest the impact of blunt instruments and this was probably the result of a single incident, at a period near the end of the settlement. Some wounds on younger children had healed (and so had been inflicted before death), indicating the violence (presumably a conflict with a neighbouring group) was extended beyond a single raid.

Also in Colorado, at the Anasazi site of Sleeping Ute Mountain (occupied in the late 11th to the 13th centuries AD), skull injuries had affected 20 of the 53 skeletons examined – men, women and children.[68] These were bone fractures (the result of blows from blunt instruments like a stone axe) rather than arrow wounds; some of the victims had survived and recovered from these attacks, at least for a period. Bones from two of the children, aged about 7 and 11, showed signs of possible mutilation followed by cannibalism. This material implies a society in which violence was common – not just a single incident.

One of the most dramatic sites of massacre anywhere in the archaeological record is Crow Creek in South Dakota, USA, dated about 1325 AD, where almost 500 bodies, including those of men, women and a minimum of 144 children, attest to a massacre which featured mutilation, including scalping of 90% of the bodies.[69] Notably, the scalping of the young (assumed to be a warrior's memento of a victory) was of a smaller cranial area than that of adults.[70] The ratios of males to females were similar until the age of about 15: young females thereafter were fewer than males, suggesting they may have been taken as captives rather than killed.

Three unusual juvenile skeletons from the 1st millennium AD at an agricultural settlement in the US state of Illinois show signs of underdeveloped skulls arising from prematurely closed cranial sutures.[71] Such an occurrence is likely to have reduced the children's intellectual and behavioural development. Numerous injuries to one of these, a girl aged between 12 and 15 years, from the Hopewell site of Pete Klunk, buried together with an adult male, led to an interpretation of physical abuse. Another child, aged 6 or 7 years, from Koster Mound, had a serious but healed wound to the jaw. An adolescent boy had a healed wound to the leg. Were these victimised disabled children? Other examples of children's skeletons found with injuries from blows to the head were at Grasshopper Pueblo in Arizona, McDuffee in Arkansas and Moundville in Alabama.[72] Skeletons recovered from the Chickamauga area in Tennessee, in the Late Mississippian period, showed the results of inter-group violence interpreted as group battles rather than individual conflict.[73] Most injuries were to younger adults: one injury from a blunt instrument at Ocoee was to a child aged 9–11.

We have reviewed here evidence of violence causing injury as well as the contexts in which injury was more probably the result of accidents. But there is another source of apparent damage to the skull: the medical intervention known as trephination – trepanning or cutting a hole in the skull for curative purposes.

In the Neolithic site of Makotřasy in the Czech Republic, a trephination had initially proved successful and the skull had healed before the child died at the age of 4 or 5 years.[74] A second child aged about 4 may have had an unsuccessful trephination.

Another possible trephination of a child was found at the Kazibaba 5 site in northern Uzbekistan, dated to the 4th to 3rd centuries BC.[75] If that was indeed the cause of the hole in the skull it did not heal; the child died at the age of 3 years. And later, from pre-Columbian Peru, where the practice of adult trephination is also known, a child at Ancon had signs of a probable trephination that had healed before the child died aged 4 or 5 years, as did another at Kuelap, where the child lived to the age of 7.[76]

SACRIFICE

A different form of violence against the young is child sacrifice, a theme invoked in a number of interpretations of skeletal finds, and a phenomenon of later European prehistory attested by Classical writers.

Sacrifice of children became a feature of many complex urbanised societies of both the Old World and the New World. Children, especially those captured in raids, could be chosen for a ritual killing and body display.[77]

In excavations of a Late Neolithic site of Lindängelund in Sweden, the body of a 5- or 6-year-old was found in one of 30 prehistoric wells at the location. The position of the limbs suggests the child may have been deliberately lowered in and drowned.[78] Two stones were near the body. A Late Neolithic long house was some 50 m (165 feet) away.

Many prehistoric bodies of adults as well as children have been found preserved by the damp of European bogs, and a proportion of these show signs of forced and violent deaths, for which the concept of deliberate sacrifice remains one explanation.[79] An example is a child's body at the German Iron Age site of Kayhausen, wrapped in fabric and a cloak of calf skin, which showed signs of being stabbed in the neck, tied up and deposited in a bog.[80] The child appears to have been lame in life (with deformities of the right tibia which can arise from malnutrition or disease): a double victim.

In a bog in the Rogaland county of Norway, skulls of four children from the 1st century AD found together show signs of neither injury nor illness. Children's skeletons of the Iron Age come from Danish and Finnish bogs, but again without signs of violence.

The interpretation that prehistoric bog bodies were deliberate sacrifices has been influenced by the narratives of ancient Roman authors and later records of European practices. An alternative explanation for at least some of the bog bodies is that they were executed as criminals, but the presence of children and the very young indicates this could not apply in all cases. Others may be the result of accidents or murders.[81] The only common feature of bog bodies is the location of the corpse: bodies not placed in a conventional burial site on land.

Infanticide undertaken for other reasons other than sacrifice, as discussed in Chapters 9 and 10, remains an explanation for some of the finds of bodies of infants; and the disposal of bodies of children who died naturally might be linked to the 'offering' of the child's body rather than a deliberate killing. Children who have not established themselves in this life may have had their bodies 'returned' to another world.[82]

TOY AND REAL WEAPONS

If an adult needs to possess the skills of fighting – whether for defence or for attack and smaller acts of aggression – then the earlier they begin to acquire these the more confident they will be in their skills. An ability to use the weapons of war will discourage attackers and help to defend a family or community in times of conflict. Alongside the frequent training of children (normally male children) in the use of such weapons is, of course, the ideology of fighting.

Chapter 7 noted how mock fighting is a core part of children's play, a near universal across societies of different scales and types. The pattern of young chimpanzees' play fighting and play biting re-emphasises the view that such behaviour probably traces back to our earliest hominin ancestors.

Weapons of aggression are essential in societies whose economy relies significantly on hunting for meat, but hunting remains part of the activity and economy of most agricultural societies too. The skills used in hunting animals with spear, sling, club or bow and arrow are applicable no less in fighting people. The main difference is defence. A shot bird or antelope resists by escape; a wounded carnivore or elephant may resist by attack; but only humans resist an assault by using the same implements and skills as their human attackers.

Thus, the training of the young in creating stone weapons – as discussed in Chapter 6 – relates not only to the role of hunting but also to the role of fighter in human conflicts. While we can see in the archaeological record some evidence of the apprentice maker of tools and weapons, we cannot easily see the training of the prehistoric young in the use of these weapons, any more than we can witness training in hand-to-hand fighting. But if we assume that prehistoric hunters, Neolithic farmers and metalworking villagers commonly carried a weapon with them, we can surmise that such a practice would begin during (male) childhood. Moving from toy imitation weapons to the right to carry a working weapon is one major stage in the transition to full adulthood; and the nature of these arms would mark family social status within a community.

This is indicated in some of the grave goods of children. Miniature axes can be found with burials of children as young as 2 years in the Neolithic

Linearbandkeramik of Europe.[83] In the earlier Iron Age of central Italy, weapons can be found with burials of quite young boys: spears as well as knives.[84] But weapons can be designed for hunting animals as much as defending the person against human aggressors.

Weapons were not exclusively buried with men but in some contexts with women, and not only with boys but at times with girls. For example, in Ak Alakha 1 from the Iron Age of western Siberia, a 15-year-old girl was buried with a battle axe, a bow and arrows and a dagger, although also dressed in male attire.[85]

Miniature versions of weapons suggest toys, and some small-scale tools were mentioned in Chapter 6. We can interpret such playthings as the tools of children's games, see them as the first stage in the training of the young in artefacts of hunting, or take this role further, to the training of the young as potential fighters with similarly armed men, in defence or attack. Modern western societies have witnessed moves to discourage children from playing with toy guns, swords, and bows and arrows; proponents of such approaches look with dismay at communities in which youngsters may be trained in real firearm use from an early age, while addicted to television dramas and movies with exceptional violence. But this withdrawal from the idea of weapons as toys would appear to be a recent phenomenon. I spent much of my pre-teen years in the garden with bow and arrow, toy sword and then happily roaming Birmingham playgrounds and parks with friends firing refillable cap guns, without later thinking of buying such for my children or grandchildren.

Miniature battle axes and a miniature mace head were found buried with young children at Bronze Age sites in Wales and Scotland: not effective weapons, but symbols of the role they would have played if they had reached adulthood.[86] One such axe head, in the Scottish site of Doune, was with a child aged only 6 or 7 years.

In a Middle Bronze Age settlement at Isleham near Cambridge in England, a bow only 45 cm (18 inches) long was found in a pit.[87] It was made from the antler of a red deer, and was dated to 1750–1600 BC. The small and impractical size suggests that it was a miniature for a child to carry and play with, as practice for future archery.

As a further example, some crudely made tiny arrowheads at a Canadian site in Alberta were considered non-functional for hunting and so likely toys for children in learning the use of a bow and arrow.[88]

Other weapons or possible weapons buried with the young are mentioned in Chapters 9 and 10. We need to remember that miniature weapons may not always be for children. A votive offering can present scaled down versions of the real thing: items which symbolise the utilitarian object, reflect its form, but serve as offerings instead, as shown in the substantial finds of miniature weapons from Roman Mouzon in the

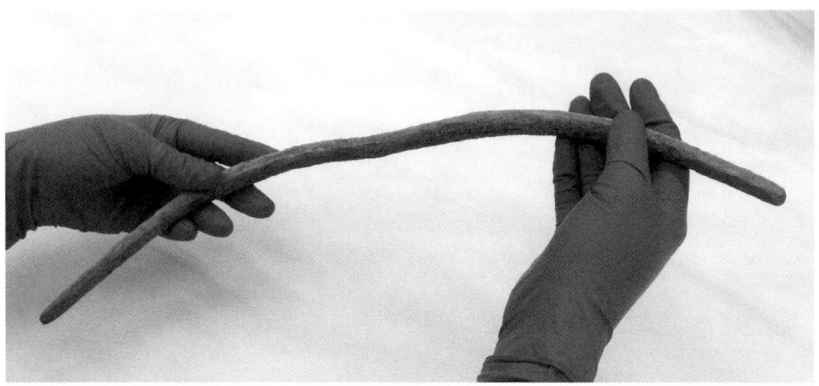

Miniature bow made from deer antler, and presumed to be for a child, from the Middle Bronze Age of Isleham, England

Ardennes region of France.[89] The context of a find is all-important. The challenge is to find evidence which convincingly represents that fundamental stage of childhood when a child learns how to use the implements which will protect the family in adult years.

CONCLUSIONS

If war and conflict are the lot of humankind, our evidence from prehistory suggests a long tradition of interpersonal violence well before urban civilisation. In such a context it is not surprising that the young learn to use weapons, both for defence and for attack. The miniature weapons we find in the archaeological record are only part of the story. As seen in the remains of the massacred young, childhood in prehistory was not only a time to learn the use of weapons but also frequently a time when death and injury were direct threats: an attack from another community, an act of violence within a community, or sometimes the sacrifice of a child as part of a community's ritual and beliefs.

Prehistoric and historic archaeology, history and anthropology all demonstrate the frequency of inter-group and intra-group violence before the modern era. This serves to remind us that while a child may always have been valued by the family, the expectation of safety of a child in our modern, urban, western context may be culturally specific. Injury and early death were often possibilities from intra-group conflict; and as shown in the next two chapters, the early death of a child from other causes was a high risk across prehistoric communities, forager or farmer.

NOTES

1. Deuteronomy 20: 16–17 (New Revised Standard Version, Anglicised).
2. S. Mays, 'The bioarchaeology of the homicide of infants and children' in *TCBI*: 99–122, p. 104.
3. A. Gat, *War in Human Civilization*, Oxford: Oxford University Press, 2006, p. 662.
4. Gat, *War*, p. 665.
5. S. Greenfield, *A Day in the Life of the Brain*, London: Penguin, 2016, pp. 135–138.
6. L.H. Keeley, *War Before Civilization*, New York: Oxford University Press, 1996, p. 39.
7. I.J.N. Thorpe, 'Anthropology, archaeology, and the origin of warfare', *World Archaeology* 35 (2003): 145–165, is a good overview of the issues. A broad range of examples is included in C. Knüsel & M. Smith (eds), *The Routledge Handbook of the Bioarchaeology of Human Conflict*, Abington: Routledge, 2013.
8. M.E. Lewis, 'Sticks and stones: exploring the nature and significance of child trauma in the past' in Knüsel & Smith (eds), *The Routledge Handbook*: 39–63, presents a useful catalogue of examples and discussion of childhood trauma.
9. Mays, 'The bioarchaeology', p. 106.
10. C. Eller, *The Myth of Matriarchal Prehistory: why an invented past won't give women a future*, Boston, MA: Beacon Press, 2000, p. 113.
11. J. Goodall, *The Chimpanzees of Gombe: pattern of behavior*, Cambridge, MA: Harvard University Press, 1986, pp. 355–356.
12. M.L. Wilson et al., 'Lethal aggression in *Pan* is better explained by adaptive strategies than human impacts', *Nature* 513 (2014): 414–417.
13. C. Boesch et al., 'Intergroup conflicts among chimpanzees in Taï National Park: lethal violence and the female perspective', *American Journal of Primatology* 70 (2008): 519–532.
14. V. Cummings, P. Jordan & M. Zvelebil (eds), *The Oxford Handbook of the Archaeology and Anthropology of Hunter-Gatherers*, Oxford: Oxford University Press, 2014; R.B. Lee & R.H. Daly (eds), *The Cambridge Encyclopedia of Hunters and Gatherers*, Cambridge: Cambridge University Press, 1999, p. 5; Gat, *War*, pp. 11–25.
15. M.W. Allen & T.L. Jones (eds), *Violence and Warfare Among Hunter-Gatherers*, Walnut Creek, CA: Left Coast Press, 2014.
16. M.A. Perry, 'Redefining childhood through bioarchaeology: toward an archaeological and biological understanding of children in antiquity' *CIA*: 89–111, p. 95.
17. R. Derricourt, 'The enigma of Raymond Dart', *International Journal of African Historical Studies* 42 (2009): 257–282, pp. 263–264; R. Derricourt, *Inventing Africa: history, archaeology and ideas*, London: Pluto, 2011, pp. 53–54.
18. R. Ardrey, *African Genesis: a personal investigation into the animal origins and nature of man*, London: Fontana; New York: Atheneum, 1961.
19. N. Sala et al., 'Lethal interpersonal violence in the Middle Pleistocene', *PLoS ONE* 10 (2015): e0126589.
20. V.H. Estabrook, 'Violence and warfare in the European Mesolithic and Paleolithic' in Allen & Jones (eds), *Violence and Warfare*: 49–69; V.H. Estabrook & D.W. Frayer, 'Trauma in the Krapina Neandertals: violence in the Middle Palaeolithic?' in Knüsel & Smith (eds), *The Routledge Handbook*: 67–89.

21 J.A. Svoboda, 'The Upper Paleolithic burial area at Předmostí: ritual and taphonomy', *Journal of Human Evolution* 54 (2008): 15–33.
22 P. Pettitt, *The Palaeolithic Origins of Human Burial*, London: Routledge, 2011, pp. 215–216.
23 J. Orschiedt, 'Cave burials in prehistoric Central Europe' in K.A. Bergsvig & R.E. Skeates (eds), *Caves in Context: the cultural significance of caves and rockshelters in Europe*, Oxford: Oxbow, 2012: 212–224, p. 214.
24 Pettitt, *The Palaeolithic Origins*, pp. 243–244.
25 V. Eshed et al., 'Paleopathology and the origin of agriculture in the Levant', *American Journal of Physical Anthropology* 143 (2010): 121–133, p. 126.
26 Thorpe, 'Anthropology', p. 152; F. Wendorf, *The Prehistory of Nubia, Vol. 2*, Dallas, TX: Southern Methodist University Press, 1986, pp. 954–995; T.W. Holliday, 'Population affinities of the Jebel Sahaba skeletal sample: limb proportion evidence', *International Journal of Osteoarchaeology* 25 (2013): 466–476.
27 Wendorf, *The Prehistory*, pp. 992–993.
28 M.M. Lahr et al., 'Inter-group violence among early Holocene hunter-gatherers of West Turkana, Kenya', *Nature* 529 (2016): 394–410.
29 J. Orschiedt, 'The head burials from Ofnet cave: an example of warlike conflict in the Mesolithic' in M. Parker Pearson & I.J.N. Thorpe (eds), *Warfare, Violence and Slavery in Prehistory*, British Archaeological Reports International Series 1374, Oxford: Archaeopress, 2005: 67–74; Thorpe, 'Anthropology', p. 157.
30 Thorpe, 'Anthropology', p. 155, citing Albrethsen & Brinch Petersen (1976).
31 Thorpe, 'Anthropology', p. 156, citing Brinch Petersen et al. (1993).
32 Thorpe, 'Anthropology', p. 157, citing Anger & Dieck (1978).
33 A.G. Morris, 'Trauma and violence in the later Stone Age of Southern Africa', *South African Medical Journal* 102 (2012): 568–570.
34 S. Pfeiffer & N.J. van der Merwe, 'Cranial injuries to Later Stone Age children from the Modder River Mouth, Western Cape Province, South Africa', *South African Archaeological Bulletin* 59 (2004): 59–65; uncalibrated radiocarbon date 2600 BP.
35 Morris, 'Trauma and violence', p. 568.
36 M.A. Berón, C.M. Aranda & L.H. Luna, 'Mortuary behaviour in subadults: children as social actors in the hunter-gatherer societies of Argentine Pampas', *CitP* 5 (2012): 51–69, pp. 60–62.
37 V.G. Standen & B.T. Arriaza, 'Trauma in the preceramic coastal populations of northern Chile: violence or occupational hazards?', *American Journal of Physical Anthropology* 112 (2000): 239–249, p. 241.
38 G.R. Milner, 'Warfare in prehistoric and early historic eastern North America', *Journal of Archaeological Research* 7 (1999): 105–151, pp. 114–115; M.A. Perry, 'Redefining childhood through bioarchaeology: toward an archaeological and biological understanding of children in antiquity' *CIA*: 89–111, p. 95.
39 E.J. Bartelink et al., 'Violence and warfare in the prehistoric San Francisco Bay area, California: regional and temporal variations in conflict' in Knüsel & Smith (eds), *The Routledge Handbook*: 285–307.
40 J. Melbye & S.I. Fairgrieve, 'A massacre and possible cannibalism in the Canadian Arctic: new evidence from the Saunaktuk site (NgTn-1)', *Arctic Anthropology* 31 (1994): 57–77.
41 S. Vencl, 'Stone age warfare' in J. Carman & A. Harding (eds), *Ancient Warfare: archaeological perspectives*, Stroud: Sutton Publishing, 1999: 57–72; C. Meyer

et al., 'The Eulau eulogy: bioarchaeological interpretation of lethal violence in Corded Ware multiple burials from Saxony-Anhalt, Germany', *Journal of Anthropological Archaeology* 28 (2009): 412–423.
42 L. Fibiger, 'Misplaced childhood? Interpersonal violence and children in Neolithic Europe' in Knüsel & Smith (eds), *The Routledge Handbook*: 127–145.
43 T.D. Price, J. Wahl & R.A. Bentley, 'Isotopic evidence for mobility and group organization among Neolithic farmers at Talheim, Germany, 5000 BC', *European Journal of Archaeology* 9 (2006): 259–284; Thorpe, 'Anthropology', p. 149, citing J. Wahl, H.G. Konig & J. Biel, 'Anthropologisch-traumatologische Untersuchung der menschlichen Skelettreste aus dem bandkeramischen Massengrab bei Talheim, Kreis Heilbronn', *Fundberichte aus Baden-Württemberg* 12 (1987): 65–193; Vencl, 'Stone age warfare', pp. 60–61.
44 E. Scott, *The Archaeology of Infancy and Infant Death*, British Archaeological Reports International Series 819, Oxford: Archaeopress, 1999, p. 102.
45 Fibiger, 'Misplaced childhood?'
46 M. Teschler-Nicola et al., 'Evidence of genocide 7000 BP – Neolithic paradigm and geo-climatic reality', *Collegium Antropologicum* 23 (1999): 437–450; Price et al., 'Isotopic evidence for mobility', p. 267, citing H. Windl.
47 Vencl, 'Stone age warfare', pp. 63–64.
48 P. Bickle & L. Fibiger, 'Ageing, childhood and social identity in the Early Neolithic of Central Europe', *European Journal of Archaeology* 17 (2014): 208–228, pp. 219–220.
49 J. Chapman, 'The origins of warfare in the prehistory of Central and Eastern Europe' in Carman & Harding (eds), *Ancient Warfare*: 101–142, p. 106.
50 Meyer et al., 'The Eulau eulogy'.
51 W. Haak et al., 'Ancient DNA, strontium isotopes, and osteological analyses shed light on social and kinship organization of the Later Stone Age', *Proceedings of the National Academy of Sciences* 105 (2008): 18226–18231.
52 M.J. Smith, 'The war to begin all wars? Contextualising violence in Neolithic Britain' in Knüsel & Smith (eds), *The Routledge Handbook*: 109–116.
53 Chapman, 'The origins of warfare', p. 140.
54 L. Dawson, T.E. Levy & P. Smith, 'Evidence of interpersonal violence at the Chalcolithic village of Shiqmim (Israel)', *International Journal of Osteoarchaeology* 13 (2003): 115–119.
55 B. Glencross & B. Boz, 'Representing violence in Anatolia and the Near East during the transition to agriculture' in Knüsel & Smith (eds), *The Routledge Handbook*: 90–108, p. 98.
56 Ö.D. Erdal, 'A possible massacre at Early Bronze Age Titriş Höyük, Anatolia', *International Journal of Osteoarchaeology* 22 (2012): 1–21.
57 A. Harding, 'Warfare: a defining characteristic of Bronze Age Europe?' in Carman & Harding (eds), *Ancient Warfare*: 157–174, p. 158.
58 U. Brinker et al., 'Human remains from a Bronze Age site in the Tollense valley' in Knüsel & Smith (eds), *The Routledge Handbook*: 146–160.
59 S.A. Jiménez-Brobeil, I. Al Oumaoui & P. du Souich, 'Childhood trauma in several populations from the Iberian Peninsula', *International Journal of Osteoarchaeology* 17 (2007): 189–198.
60 A.G. Western & J.D. Hurst, '"Soft heads": evidence for sexualised warfare during the later Iron Age from Kemerton camp, Bredon Hill' in Knüsel & Smith (eds), *The Routledge Handbook*: 161–184.

61 S.S. King, 'Socialised violence: contextualizing violence through mortuary behaviour in Iron Age Britain' in Knüsel & Smith (eds), *The Routledge Handbook*: 185–200.
62 Milner, 'Warfare in prehistoric'.
63 J. Haas, 'The origins of war and ethnic violence' in Carman & Harding (eds), *Ancient Warfare*: 11–24, p. 20.
64 A.M. Palkovich, 'Surviving childhood: health, identity and personhood in the prehistoric American Southwest' in *TCBI*: 219–227.
65 C.G. Turner, 'Cannibalism in Chaco Canyon: the charnel pit excavated in 1926 at Small House ruin by Frank H.H. Roberts, Jr', *American Journal of Physical Anthropology* 91 (1993): 421–439.
66 C.G. Turner & J.A. Turner, 'Cannibalism in the prehistoric American Southwest: occurrence, taphonomy, explanation, and suggestions for standardized world definition', *Anthropological Science* 103 (1995): 1–22.
67 C.S. Bradley, 'Thoughts count: ideology and the children of Sand Canyon Pueblo' in *CPPS*: 169–195, pp. 185–189.
68 P.M. Lambert, 'Violent injury and death in a prehistoric farming community of Southwestern Colorado' in Knüsel & Smith (eds), *The Routledge Handbook*: 308–332.
69 Haas, 'The origins', p. 24; P. Willey & T.E. Emerson, 'The osteology and archaeology of the Crow Creek massacre', *Plains Anthropologist* 38 (1993): 227–269.
70 Willey & Emerson, 'The osteology', p. 253.
71 D.C. Cook, A.R. Thompson & A.A. Rollins, 'Death and the special child: three examples from the ancient Midwest' in *TCBI*: 17–35.
72 Lewis, 'Sticks and stones', p. 49.
73 M.O. Smith, 'Beyond palisades: the nature and frequency of late prehistoric deliberate violent trauma in the Chickamauga Reservoir of East Tennessee', *American Journal of Physical Anthropology* 121 (2003): 303–318.
74 A. Shbat & V. Smrčka, 'Children's cranial lesions from Neolithic', *Prague Medical Report* 110 (2009): 114–119.
75 S. Blau, 'An unusual aperture in a child's calvaria from western Central Asia: differential diagnoses', *International Journal of Osteoarchaeology* 15 (2005): 291–297.
76 K. Kato et al., 'A possible case of prophylactic supra-inion trepanation in a child cranium with an auditory deformity (pre-Columbian Ancon site, Peru)', *Anthropological Science* 115 (2007): 227–232; K.C. Nystrom, 'Trepanation in the Chachapoya region of northern Perú', *International Journal of Osteoarchaeology* 17 (2007): 39–51.
77 T.A. Tung & K.J. Knudson, 'Childhood lost: abductions, sacrifice, and trophy heads of children in the Wari empire of the ancient Andes', *Latin American Antiquity* 21 (2010): 44–66.
78 A. Carlie et al., 'Archaeology, forensics and the death of a child in Late Neolithic Sweden', *Antiquity* 88 (2014): 1148–1163; A. Carlie, 'Archaeology and ritual: a case study on traces of ritualisation in archaeological remains from Lindängelund, southern Sweden', *Folklore: Electronic Journal of Folklore* 55 (2013): 49–68.
79 G. Lillehammer, 'The children in the bog' in *RLA*: 47–62; P. Bennike et al., 'The bog find from Sigersdal: human sacrifice in the Early Neolithic', *Journal of Danish Archaeology* 5 (1986): 85–115; P.V. Glob, *The Bog People: Iron Age man preserved*, London: Faber, 1998.

80 Mays, 'Bioarchaeology', p. 106, citing H. Hayen; see also F. Both & M. Fansa (eds), *Der Junge von Kayhausen und die Haut aus dem Bareler Moor*, Oldenburg: Isensee, 2010: 87–90.
81 M. Giles, 'Iron Age bog bodies of north-western Europe: representing the dead', *Archaeological Dialogues* 16 (2009): 75–101.
82 Lillehammer, 'The children in the bog, p. 57.
83 Bickle & Fibiger, 'Ageing, childhood and social identity', p. 213.
84 K. Hladíková, 'Perception of children in Villanovan period in southern Etruria' in *CCLA*: 41–74, pp. 57–58.
85 N.A. Berseneva, 'Sargat burial sites in the Middle Irtysh area: a gender analysis', *Archaeology, Ethnology and Anthropology of Eurasia* 38 (2010): 72–81, p. 78.
86 P. Garwood, 'Vital resources, ideal images and virtual lives: children in Early Bronze Age funerary ritual' in *CCS*: 63–82, p. 64; J.R.C. Hamilton, 'Food vessel cist at Doune, Perthshire', *Proceedings of the Society of Antiquaries of Scotland* 90 (1957): 231–234.
87 K. Gdaniec, 'A miniature antler bow from a Middle Bronze Age site at Isleham (Cambridgeshire), England', *Antiquity* 70 (1996): 652–657.
88 B. Dawe, 'Tiny arrowheads: toys in the toolkit', *Plains Anthropologist* 42 (1997): 303–318.
89 P. Kiernan, 'Miniature objects as representations of realia', *World Archaeology* 47 (2015): 45–59, pp. 51–53.

9
DYING 1
Death and burial in forager societies

The contribution and excitement of archaeology lie in the reconstruction of life, yet all those we study are dead. A major source of our evidence for past lives comes from the burials of the dead, and the constructions, social practices and objects associated with their burial, cremation or disposal.

This is especially true for children in the prehistoric past. We can interpret occasional finds in settlement sites as the activities of the young, but the best direct information on prehistoric children is from the remains of those who did not survive to adulthood. Through most of time and most of the world, only a proportion of a family's children could be expected to reach adulthood. But the predictability of children's death did not make the event any less of a loss, as attested by the burial practices we see in the broad range of prehistoric and historic societies. Through the prism of the grave and the visibility of the dead we can see something of the lives of children, their position and value in a family and in a society, and the role they played.

So for the scope of this book, much of our knowledge of the lives of children in prehistory is reconstructed from evidence that surrounds their death: the form and ritual of their burials, the material culture associated with their graves and the study of their bones to understand their health and patterns of life. The study of children's remains is a growing part of the applications of biological anthropologists to the prehistory of humankind.[1] This chapter and the next review the range of finds and sites across time and space in different areas, with a focus on examples from the Old World. These show the development and variability in practices of disposing of the bodies of the young.

Burials and the disposal of the dead provide information about living children and their place in society. The misfortune of children's deaths

Kindertod (*Death of a Child*), woodcut by Ernst Barlach, 1919

has provided a boon to the archaeological study of prehistoric childhood. Our knowledge of children in the deep past relies heavily on the remains (and any associated material culture) of those who died young: from bodies abandoned where they lay or scavenged by carnivores, to children buried in natural hollows and fissures, infants and young children buried within the boundaries of the household itself, through to graves dug to provide them with a burial place, sometimes accompanied by grave goods which reflected their possessions and clothing in life, or a special ritual associated with their burial or with more complex beliefs about death and after. Studies of the skeletal remains of children can tell us about their lives, their ancestry, their diet, their illnesses and their context in wider society, though there any many challenges, both practical and theoretical, in such studies.[2]

THE DEATH OF CHILDREN

In many countries of the developing world today, the death of children remains an expected part of life. But it is not just a statistic of underdevelopment. The death of children was not only frequent in the past of our 'developed' societies but was the norm. Parents would not expect all their children to survive to adulthood. Only in recent generations have improvements in diet and in medical care reduced infant and child mortality. But despite this progress, modern wars and major civil conflicts have continued to maintain a world in which older adults bury younger adults and parents bury their children. A 1996 report from UNICEF suggested that in the previous decade armed conflict had resulted in the death of 2 million children, and more than double that number had been disabled.[3] In the subsequent 20 years the numbers of child victims of wars appears to have well exceeded those figures.

In an attempt to quantify changes from 1820 to the present day, a report by the Organisation for Economic Co-operation and Development (OECD) identified certain long-term trends, which emphasise how recent is the expectation that a child, once born alive, will become an adult.[4] Life expectancy in western Europe has moved from 33.4 years in the 1830s to 79.7 years in the 2000s (this excludes the incidence of miscarriage and stillbirth). In Southeast and East Asia life expectancy moved from 24.6 years in the 1880s to 65.9 years in the 2000s, and in sub-Saharan Africa to a recent figure of just 52.1 years. In each case, figures close to 20% for infant mortality (defined as death before the first birthday) were common at the beginning of these periods. Infant mortality figures for France moved from 182 per 1000 live births in 1820 to 8.4 per 1000 by 1980; for Sweden from 173.9 per 1000 live births in 1830 to 6.5 per 1000 in 1980.[5]

A statement repeated by different English-language newspapers in 1854–85 suggested the average human lifespan in the world was 33 years, with one-quarter of humanity dying before they reached 7 years of age and one-half before they reached 17.[6] While these figures were guesswork they present the perceptions of the era and the quote was repeated to the end of the century.

Figures for England suggest 27% of children in the 16th century died in their first year.[7] Records for London before 1800 – one of the greatest cities of the age – recorded 30% of all deaths as those of children below the age of 2 years, and half the deaths were of people below the age of 20.[8] In 10th-century England, some samples of burials suggest 50% of all those born alive died before their 18th birthday.[9]

We are reminded that historical civilisation had death rates more in common with recent 'third world' societies than with our modern urban life. Mary Beard has no qualms in suggesting that in ancient Rome half the children born would have died before the age of 10, although those who survived childhood might have the expectation of surviving into late adulthood.[10]

If all deceased children were given the same formal burial in similar places to adults we might expect them to be a significant proportion – 30% or at least 20% – of the bodies we discover in archaeological work, but this is not always so.[11] If children are under-represented in parts of the archaeological burial record, young infants are even less often directly visible. This does not imply that the infant death rate was low. In some societies, an infant was not considered to have become yet a full member of society, and the handling of the remains reflected that – disposed of in a less formal manner and outside of community burial locations, or beneath the floors of living spaces, or even less formally.

If birth does not yet establish an infant as part of the community, that both allows and explains the common practice of infanticide. We see the death of an infant as tragic, but historical and ethnographic evidence suggests that selective infanticide has been an extremely common human practice: to adjust sex ratios, limit population size, euthanise the disabled, expel those born out of social convention, fulfil ritual obligations and more. Archaeological and historical evidence of infanticide is not hard to find and reflects what is found in the ethnographic record of some forager societies, as discussed below.[12]

There are other challenges in retrieving and interpreting infant skeletal material. Bones identified as 'newborn' may be those of a stillborn child, or a child who failed to survive the first few days; they may be from a victim of illness or malnutrition, or of infanticide. The small fragile bones of a stillborn child or infant may not be recovered in the archaeological process, especially in older styles of excavation. Where the incidence of infant bones does exceed their expected proportion of burials, this might be interpreted as evidence for infanticide, or it may be a feature of different practices, for example where an infant who dies is buried inside the walls or floor of the domestic home, while burials of older children are outside the settlement. It is challenging for the bioarchaeologist to make reliable demographic interpretations from infant remains when the remains of stillborn babies and young infants may be difficult to find and difficult to distinguish.[13] The emergence of bacterial bioerosion studies may help distinguish stillbirths from live births in skeletal remains: a stillborn foetus that has never accessed maternal milk will lack evidence of gut bacteria, which will show up as differences in the internal bone microstructure. Such a research approach is new and experimental, so requires caution.[14]

For the earliest periods of prehistory, we rely mainly on palaeoanthropology, the sister discipline of archaeology, while considering also what we can learn from study of living great apes. Our Australopithecine ancestors and the first members of the genus *Homo* are encountered only as fossilised bones, sometimes scattered and showing signs of attrition by carnivores. By contrast, when we encounter the Neanderthals we can see the first signs of the impact the death of a child had on a community, with some deliberate burials, and even (as at Teshik-Tash in Uzbekistan) including animal bones as a grave marker.

Fossil finds have been interpreted as male or female on the basis of size difference, and as adult or juvenile on the basis of both size and the stage

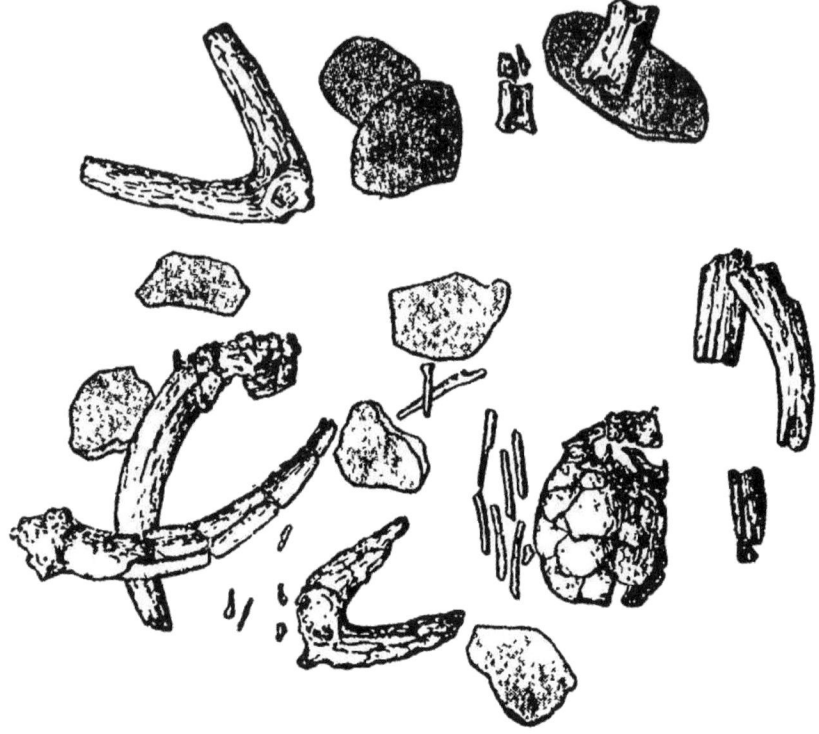

Ibex horns surrounding a Neanderthal child's body at Teshik-Tash, Uzbekistan

of tooth development, by comparison with modern humans. This can give only estimated ages, as fossil hominins are thought to have matured faster than our species. Fossil hominin teeth may have erupted earlier than in modern humans, with maturity in perhaps two-thirds of the time. Within these specimens are a small number of remains of the young, but rarely of the smallest infants, whose remains would have been too frail to survive the process of deposition, fossilisation and recovery. Infancy, too, may have been shorter than in modern humans, as indicated by the teeth and smaller brain size.[15]

Some finds of juvenile fossil and skeletal materials have been ascribed both an age and a sex. It should be noted that many and perhaps most forensic anthropologists, specialists in the modern identification of human remains, consider that the sex of a skeleton is impossible to determine before the age of puberty.[16] There have been attempts to assess the sex of a child from the teeth or other skeletal parts, but these are limited and considered by many specialists to be unreliable.[17] DNA analysis is emerging to provide a better option for specifying sex.[18]

GREAT APES

Juvenile death among our early hominin ancestors can be contrasted with that among our own species, but also compared with the pattern seen among the other great apes.

As longer-term studies of primate communities in the wild came to supplement studies in zoos and laboratories, they often revealed a pattern of high infant mortality, including infanticide and even cannibalism of infants.

Orangutans are an exception, not providing significant evidence of infanticide.[19] But in gorilla groups, infanticide (though without the cannibalism of chimpanzees) is not uncommon in the eastern groups, where an infant lacks the protection of an adult male:[20] other males attack and kill them.[21] The male infants are at even higher risk than the female infants, which suggests that males are disposing of potential future competitors when these are at their weakest and most exposed. Infanticide, observers note, is always to be anticipated where a mountain gorilla female moves away from or loses her protector male, though this is not the experience among eastern lowland gorillas.[22] By contrast, infanticide was not observed in the extended research project in the Taï Forest of Côte d'Ivoire in West Africa, although early death from other causes was common.[23] Overall, maybe half of gorilla young in the wild will die before they reach the age of 5 years.

The killing of infants is common among chimpanzees. Although regularly called infanticide, this slaughter does not match the human practice in history of selective killing of unwanted offspring or to control surplus population in crises of resources.

Disease (as well as accidents) can also take their toll on young chimpanzees. With the reliance of young chimpanzees on their mothers, as noted in Chapter 2, the death of a mother will commonly result in the death of an unweaned child.

Different groups show different patterns of infant death. In a chimpanzee group in Mahale Mountains National Park in Tanzania 50% of chimpanzees (or even more) died before they were weaned, with aggression by males in the group the primary cause, and the majority of victims less than 1 year old.[24] By contrast, chimpanzees seem only rarely to be the victims of death from carnivore attack. Observation of chimpanzee mothers carrying the corpses of their dead offspring (for as long as three months) suggests that the regularity of infant deaths need not destroy chimpanzees' maternal attachment.

Aggression by adult males against young males, even cannibalism, suggests that aggressive competition underlies this.[25] At Gombe, Jane Goodall's group recorded the death (usually followed by cannibalism) of six infants: three by males attacking the offspring of female outsiders to the group, and three by what humans would consider psychopathic behaviour, by an adult female and her adolescent daughter.[26] Cannibalism among chimpanzees has now been observed at several locations in the wild, with these victims all aged 3 years or younger.[27]

By contrast, infanticide is not a norm in communities of bonobos (pygmy chimpanzees), perhaps because females work together to provide protection.

Why is infanticide so common among primates? Reported rates of infanticide among primate infants include 18% for a lemur species, up to 16% for various species of monkeys, 13% for western gorillas and 10% for the Mahale chimpanzees.[28] Killing by females is known, but killing by males is the norm, reflecting the role of males in different primate societies. A specialist study of the issue concluded that infanticide is part of the natural means to reinforce sexual selection, a strategy in which the social side of reproduction takes precedence over the biological. 'The relative rate of male replacement is a major first predictor of infanticide rates.'[29] Mothers may have the means to reduce the risk of infanticide of their offspring but here too there are social limits. The longer the period of infant dependency on the mother, the greater is the risk of death by male aggression.

This raises the questions of whether infanticide was a feature in our early hominin ancestors, and of whether the relationship between males and females was closer to that of later *Homo*. Only limited evidence can address these issues. Because infant remains can be so readily scattered and lost to the archaeological record, we cannot say whether our early ancestors practised infanticide as do our chimpanzee relatives; and we must be cautious in considering their life stages of growth and development.

AUSTRALOPITHECINES

The very first Australopithecine find, which confirmed our African ancestry, was in fact that of a child. The Taung fossil from South Africa was found during limestone quarrying north of Kimberley in 1924 and passed into the hands of the Australian anatomist Raymond Dart at the Medical School in Johannesburg. He was quick to describe this as a new species, 'the Man-Ape of South Africa',[30] describing it as 'a new race of apes intermediate between living anthropoids and man ... a pre-human stock' and evidence in support of Darwin's suggestion that Africa was the cradle of humankind. Until then the consensus was that Asia had been the setting for the evolution of the hominin line, or Eurasia, since the Piltdown forgery, 'found' in Britain 12 years earlier, was at the time considered an authentic ancestral hominin fossil, *Eoanthropus dawsoni*. Dart named the new species *Australopithecus africanus*. The size of the Taung child and more importantly the teeth

Reconstruction at the University of Padua of the Taung Australopithecine child

pattern suggested to Dart this was a youngster of about 6 years of age; more recent research suggests this individual was a year or two younger.[31] Like later hominins, the brain was large compared with the body, although the actual shape of the brain was more ape-like, and is now thought to date from about 2.7 million years ago. From the puncture marks on the skull, it has been suggested that the child's death was caused by an eagle or other large raptor.[32]

Among the many fossilised skeletal remains of the different Australopithecine species found since Taung, in Southern and Eastern Africa (and also in Chad), a proportion have been considered juvenile, either because of their size or from the growth pattern of teeth. Relative size and teeth can also allow a suggestion (but no certainty) of the sex of well preserved finds.

A young *Australopithecus boisei* from southern Ethiopia, aged somewhere between 8 and 12 years and dated 2.1 million years old,[33] had a round hole perforating its skull: an injury thought to be the bite of a large carnivore. The cranium also showed signs interpreted as osteoporosis, such as arises from malnutrition in modern humans. Other signs of bone disease have been found in juvenile Australopithecines. Prepubertal periodontitis – the early onset of a disease of the tissues around the teeth – was seen in the cranium of a 6-year-old *Australopithecus africanus* from Sterkfontein in South Africa's 'cradle of humankind' 50 km (31 miles) from Johannesburg, dated to approximately 3 million years.[34] This individual would have suffered pain for two or more years before death, and eventually experienced serious difficulty in eating. The survival of the child despite the difficulties this individual would have faced suggests continuing social support, or at the very least extended maternal nurturing.

While most fossil hominin remains are of individuals, a group of finds from a site in the Afar region of Ethiopia (officially AL-333 and nicknamed the 'First Family') appear to represent a group of hominins who died together, with a flash flood as a possible cause of their collective demise. Their context in the Dene Dora level of the Hadar Formation is dated at 3.2 million years ago (older than the species from Taung). The excavators eventually identified some 260 specimens of *Australopithecus afarensis* from at least 17 individuals, most concentrated in an area just 7 m (23 feet) across.[35] The First Family could be sample of a mobile band of foragers.

Following death there may have been some scavenging of their remains by carnivores. An alternative suggestion is that the bodies were not buried where they died, but represent a deliberately placement by other members of the same species, which would imply considerably more 'advanced' behaviour than commonly attributed to the period.[36] Of the original 13 individuals identified, nine were adult and four were children, the youngest thought to be about 2 years old. With subsequent finds, it was suggested that the group could be nine adults, three adolescents and five younger children.[37] This is close to the balance of half adults, half juvenile in a population, especially given that the remains of any small infants might have been unrecoverable if carnivore predation took place. This snapshot of a mobile group of at least 17 individuals – adult males, adult females and young – gives us our earliest image of social composition, slightly smaller than some chimpanzee groups and some modern hunter-gatherer groups.[38] The Laetoli footprints in Tanzania, discussed in Chapter 3, give us another image of early hominins on the move.

A later Australopithecine family was found together at Malapa, another site in the 'cradle of humankind'. The excavators suggested this represented an accident in which a mobile group were swept to their death in a crevice (also in a flash flood) at a date just under 2 million years ago.[39] The fossil bones of the group represented an adult male, an adult female, a juvenile male (with teeth development equivalent to a 12–13-year-old of modern humans) and an infant. The finds were assigned to a new species, *Australopithecus sediba*, on the basis of the juvenile skeletal remains; a further analysis of the juvenile's remains suggested the individual had greater similarities to *Australopithecus africanus* than to species in the *Homo* genus.[40]

A very well preserved fossil of a 3-year-old *Australopithecus afarensis* was recovered in 2000 at Dikika in Ethiopia, not far from the site of the First Family, with a date of 3.3 million years. On the basis of permanent tooth crowns it was assumed to be female, though not all bioanthropologists would be confident in such an identification. Fortunately this body had not been dispersed by animal scavengers but had been protected by geological processes. 'She' was nicknamed Selam (and officially DIK-1/1). Artists' reconstruction from the skull gave Selam a very ape-like face and plenty of hair. The discoverers considered the body showed abilities both for bipedal movement and for tree climbing, already present at this young age: abilities which would give her advantages throughout life in access to ground and tree food resources but also the safety of trees – similar to chimpanzee life patterns.[41] Unlike the great apes, she did not have the kind of thumb and hand that would allow her to cling on to her mother. In fact, the completeness of the remains allowed an assertion that bipedal movement had been fully established in the hominin line this early.[42]

A study of a sample of juvenile Australopithecines has suggested a peak of deaths between 2½ and 3½ years of age: perhaps a response to the independence that followed weaning. An earlier study suggested that many Australopithecine adults died young, not long after what for modern humans would be late teens or early 20s.[43]

A more recent study has compared the age at death of adults in four groups: Australopithecines, early members of the *Homo* genus, Neanderthals and Upper Palaeolithic people (who were biologically modern humans).[44] This compared older adults – those over 30 years – with 'young' adults – estimated (from the eruption of their third molars) to be between 15 and 30 years, that is, old enough to be parents but not yet grandparents. Of the Australopithecines, 316 of the total of 353 adults (90%) died as young adults. This compares with 166 of 208 (80%) of early *Homo*, 96 of 113 Neanderthals (85%) but only 24 of 74 (32%) Upper Palaeolithic people. The last figure is not very different from the death pattern in modern populations which face a high risk of mortality.[45] These classifications and calculations have some problems (the ageing done on the basis of tooth wear and the age of molars is uncertain) and the calculations exclude children under 15, but the basic principle seems proven: that few Australopithecine adults reached old age, and that as human evolution continued so the life expectancy of adults improved.

EARLY *HOMO*

The first stone tools in the archaeological record appear alongside the first fossil hominins to be classified as part of our genus: *Homo habilis*. This species was first identified at Olduvai Gorge in Tanzania, and the type specimen (the basis for defining the species) was a juvenile discovered in 1960, OH7, nicknamed Jonny's Child, and perhaps a young teenager.[46]

The spread of humans outside of savannah Africa is associated with *Homo erectus*, marked by the development from a pebble tool industry into one with carefully shaped 'Acheulean' bifacial handaxes found in Africa, the Middle East and Europe, and with adaptation of settlement to suit a much broader range of environments.[47]

The finest specimen in this family of our ancestors is Nariokotome Boy (officially KNM-WT 15000), a near-complete skeleton found without archaeological associations in 1984 near Lake Turkana in Kenya, which had provided an open savannah environment for his community.[48] This find, some 1.5 million years old, allows the reconstruction of a child originally considered to be aged around 10–12 years, but already about 1.60 m (5 foot 3 inches) tall. Subsequent studies of his strong and healthy teeth led to suggestions he was only 8 years old, which, if correct, would makes his height notable, and which might support the interpretation of the fossil as male.[49] We do not know why a strong young person met such an early death.[50]

A late descendant of *Homo erectus* is *Homo floresiensis* – the small hominin found on the Indonesian island of Flores and nicknamed 'the Hobbit'. These hominins survived to live alongside *Homo sapiens* in the late Pleistocene. Finds at the Flores site of Mata Menge included jawbone and teeth of an adult and deciduous teeth lost by two children, dated around 700,000 years ago, in an open savannah landscape, and associated with stone tools and bones of food animals.[51]

There is a modest range of sites producing fossil remains of the archaic *Homo* who developed from *Homo erectus* in different regions. These species include *Homo antecessor*, *Homo rhodesiensis* and *Homo heidelbergensis*. DNA analysis of a child's finger bone from Denisova cave in Siberia, dated about 41,000 years ago, suggested another branch of *Homo* contemporary with Neanderthals and modern humans, called Denisovans, after the find site.

Finds of *Homo antecessor* at Atapuerca in Spain, dated around 780,000 years ago, show cut marks on the bones which have been claimed as evidence of butchery and cannibalism on the young.[52] The initial study identified six individuals, later extended to 11: four infants of 0–4 years, two children aged 5–9, two aged 10–14 and three adults aged 15–20. The cut marks are similar to those on animal bones at the site. The excavators argued that the animal remains showed there were no desperate circumstances of hunger forcing cannibalism for consumption. Yet by contrast a nearby site of similar age has yielded the remains of a child deformed and disabled from birth (aged somewhere between 5 and 12 years) but clearly supported by the community.[53] The site gives early evidence of the deliberate disposal of the dead, even earlier than Neanderthal Europe.[54] A further find of a young adult showed evidence of a violent death arising from blows to the skull from a blunt instrument.[55] After death, the body had been moved and placed in the location where it was discovered. The Happisburgh footprints of a family of adults and children (discussed in Chapter 3) are of similar date.

Identified as another species of hominin, from the Rising Star Cave in South Africa, *Homo naledi* has been dated to shortly before the emergence of modern *Homo*, at 335,000–236,000 years old.[56] In the Lesedi chamber, skeletal material came from at least two adults and one juvenile of indeterminate age, while the first find site, in the Dinaledi chamber, had at least 15 individuals, including three infants, three young children, one older child, one sub-adult, four young adults and one older adult.[57] With no stone tools present this was clearly not a living site, which leaves the possibility of the deposit being a deliberate disposal of the dead.

But it is only with the much later emergence of the Neanderthals in Europe (and adjacent areas of the Middle East) that we begin more confidently to see some human remains buried by their community, rather than discarded corpses; and these burials reveal to us the lives and deaths of children in the Neanderthal community.

NEANDERTHALS AND THE MIDDLE PALAEOLITHIC

Numerous remains of Neanderthals have been located in Europe and in the Middle East, associated with stone tool industries of Middle Palaeolithic style.[58] There are differing interpretations of the demographic and the cultural significance of these finds.

The age at death of Neanderthal adults shows an improved life expectancy compared with their predecessor hominins, but still a typically younger demise than anatomically modern humans of the Upper Palaeolithic. Neanderthal remains that have been found include fewer infants and fewer older people than might be expected, but a significant proportion of young adults. The young deaths suggest the stresses and dangers of Neanderthal life.[59]

The lack of infants is likely to reflect the locations of death, burial practices and poor survival of remains. Higher child mortality rates than in later populations would imply higher fertility rates to have maintained a viable population over such a long stretch of successful occupation of Europe and the Middle East.[60]

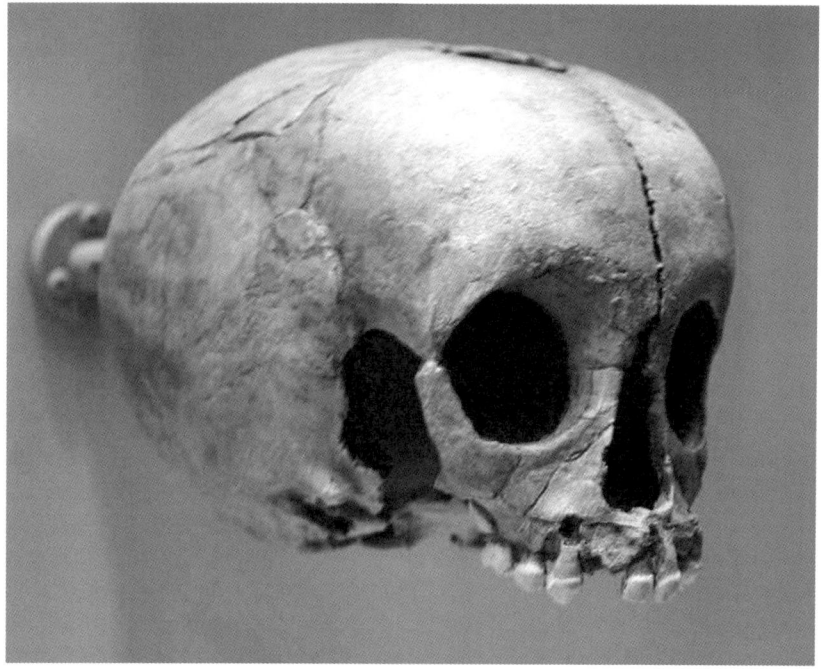

Cranium of a Neanderthal child

One implication of the lack of older adults is that few members of Neanderthal society lived beyond their reproductive years: the era of grandparenting (non-reproductive adults to help care for children) was still to come.[61]

The Neanderthals were the first hominins with evidence that has been interpreted (though not universally accepted) as deliberate care in disposal of the dead: they often 'cached' their bodies in natural fissures or in existing hollows within sites such as rock shelters, which were also used for occupation, rather than purposefully excavating a grave.[62]

A striking feature of Neanderthals is that, where burials are found, children and even some newborn infants seem to have received the same treatment and care as adults.[63] More than a third of Neanderthal burials discovered have been of children under 4 years of age, which would seem to reflect a commitment by at least some Neanderthals to undertake a proper burial for their deceased babies and young children.[64] The high frequency of children's burials may be because children died and were buried near the home base cave or shelter, while adults may have been killed and buried far away, when hunting or otherwise on the move. Where individual Neanderthal bodies were deliberately buried in isolation elsewhere, there is little chance of them surviving, being discovered and entering the archaeological record. Being represented in only a portion of the skeletal material uncovered, we can assume that deliberate burial was not a universal practice in Middle Palaeolithic and Neanderthal society. But the examples we have are dramatic and those which show the care of burying children are important parts of our narrative of the prehistory of childhood.

The site of Teshik-Tash in Uzbekistan revealed the partial skeleton of a Neanderthal child associated with Mousterian (Middle Palaeolithic) artefacts, considered to be about a boy 8–10 years old (though, as noted above, establishing sex from skeletal remains at this age is very unreliable).[65] Ibex (or wild goat) horns were found in a circle around the body, where the excavators considered they were deliberately placed. If a sign of ritual and of respect for the deceased, this was all the more notable for being at a child's burial.

An equally dramatic claim was made for finds at Shanidar, in Iraqi Kurdistan, where a Mousterian site dated to 70,000–80,000 years ago has a significant quantity of skeletal material, which may be Neanderthal. The original excavator, Ralph Solecki, believed the site represented deliberate burial of the dead, which included an infant, and supported this view by observing evidence of flowers placed by the adult dead, which stimulated him (or his publisher) to subtitle his popular 1971 book 'the first flower people'.[66] This association has been challenged, with the suggestion that the flowers may have been brought into the cave in antiquity by a rodent, the Persian jird.[67] Since 2015 the site has been undergoing re-excavation and re-interpretation.

Dated around 30,000 years later, but still Middle Palaeolithic, at the Israeli cave site in Wadi Amud, articulated bones of an infant of around 8–10 months (Amud 7) were found with bones of a red deer. Some consider this a deliberate burial and the deer bones a deliberate association, grave goods to accompany the child in death, while others see this association as accidental, or even question whether the child was deliberately buried.[68]

At Dederiyeh cave in Syria, finds dated within a few millennia of 50,000 years ago included two children aged about 2 years: one buried on its back, with a stone 'plaque' beneath its head like a pillow; the other a partial skeleton buried in a pit with animal bone and tortoise shell.[69]

Important finds from two sites in Israel, Jebel Qafzeh and Skhul, show the development of funerary practice in the Middle Palaeolithic.[70] At a cave in Jebel Qafzeh, excavations uncovered skeletal material (including nine juveniles) associated with the Middle Palaeolithic of around 100,000 years ago, but of individuals closer in appearance to modern humans than to Neanderthals. Only a third of the burials were of adults. Among the remains of about 14 or 15 individuals, an adolescent aged about 13 years had been buried with the skull as well as antlers of a large fallow deer. The body of a 6-year-old child lay across the feet of another adolescent, and this young child's skeleton showed signs of a benign tumour and a non-fatal skull injury.

The caves of Skhul contained burials of male and female adults and three children of the Middle Palaeolithic, also now dated around 100,000 years ago, and also more modern in skeletal form than Neanderthals. A boar jaw bone accompanied one of the adults. A 3-year-old child was buried just outside a cave, with the body flexed and squatting.

In Europe, the site of Le Moustier in the Dordogne region of France was the type site for the stone tool industry of the Mousterian. The cave produced skeletal material of a Neanderthal adolescent and an infant less than 4 months in age, found in 1908 and 1914. These have been interpreted as deliberate burials, either in natural hollows or in pits dug for the purpose. More dramatic were the finds at La Ferrassie in the same region.[71] As well as apparently deliberate adult burials in a flexed position, here were found bones of the young, including a child of about 10 years, a newborn and a foetus. Subsequent finds included a 3-year-old whose head was buried at some distance from its body. All these finds stimulated the suggestion that they represented some form of ritual burial by the Neanderthal population, inspiring some to suggest infanticide for ritual purposes. It is uncertain whether an infant skeleton at the Dordogne site of Roc de Marsal was a deliberate burial or not.[72]

At Sima de las Palomas in Spain a Neanderthal child was buried with burnt horse bones and stone artefacts next to an adult female.[73] The group of Neanderthals from El Sidrón cave in Spain, mentioned in Chapter 3, included adults, adolescents and children, all presumed to have met accidental deaths. The site of Cova Negra in Spain[74] had skeletal material of late Neanderthals who were almost all children, found in a cave site which had had periodic short-term occupation.

At Grotta delle Fate in Italy's Liguria, the burials included five young among 13 individuals.[75] A Neanderthal burial at Krapina in Croatia had five infants and five juveniles alongside 14 adults, with cut marks interpreted as defleshing before burial, mainly on the juveniles, although an alternative approach sees just natural adult injury.[76] Remains of young Neanderthals found elsewhere give us a fuller portrait of the life and death of the young in the Neanderthal world.[77]

The debate continues over whether or not these were deliberate burials and, if so, whether features such as animal bones found near them were deliberately positioned or not.[78] In his broad survey of Palaeolithic burial practices, Paul Pettitt argues that where Neanderthals buried their dead, this was limited to 'caching' in available hollows or fissures, not in dug graves; and he does not accept that grave goods were deliberately buried in this era.[79] Most Neanderthal burials, he notes, are from the later period of their existence. By this argument, excavated burials and deposition of the dead with their clothing and with personal possessions were not seen until after the arrival in Europe of *Homo sapiens*, in the middle part of the Upper Palaeolithic.[80]

As noted in Chapter 2, Neanderthal society had major achievements in technology, environmental adaption and economic strategy, and clear evidence has emerged from genetics that our species had mated successfully with Neanderthals, with the latter thereby contributing 1–3% of the genome of modern Europeans.[81] The idea that Neanderthals would always just abandon their dead children to the elements and animal scavengers does not fit comfortably with such a model, but the evidence is insufficient to define a Neanderthal 'norm' of careful deposition of deceased children.

We see wide variability across the extended space and time of Neanderthal settlement. Alongside the image of Neanderthal communities who treated their own dead with a measured process of burial, we now also have evidence of Neanderthal cannibalism in Europe: on the bodies of adolescents from the Troisième cave at Goyet in Belgium. The cannibalism seems to have extended to a younger child and even a newborn.[82] The bodies appeared to have been butchered for food consumption, and the bones used in retouching stone tools.

HOMO SAPIENS AND THE UPPER PALAEOLITHIC

Skeletal remains of anatomically modern humans dating from the Middle and Upper Palaeolithic include relatively few older adults.[83] A more modern physique did not inevitably bring with it a longer life. What proportion of children in the Upper Palaeolithic survived to adulthood? One early estimate by suggested only slightly more than half, similar to a pattern seen among recent hunter-gatherers.[84] Once adulthood had been reached, however, mortality rates significantly slowed.[85]

The first anatomically modern humans who emerged in Africa have not yet provided us with a large sample of remains. At the time of writing, the earliest dated material, from Jebel Irhoud in Morocco, includes the mandible of a juvenile.[86] The cranium of a 6- or 7-year-old child found at Herto in Ethiopia, dated around 160,000 years, is considered *Homo sapiens* by many specialists. It shows cut marks and scoring, and these have been interpreted as indicating that the flesh was deliberately removed from the bone before burial, but not as signs of cannibalism; there is also evidence of polishing.[87]

One later find is at a chert mining site at Nazlet Khater in Upper Egypt, dating from about 38,000 years ago. Here an adult female was buried with what may be a late miscarried foetus or a stillborn infant; the miscarriage or delivery resulted in the death of the mother.[88]

After our species expanded beyond the African continent we have much more evidence for burial and broader cultural patterns, especially in the many excavated sites of Upper Palaeolithic Europe.[89] But while there is greater evidence for burial practices by *Homo sapiens* than for Neanderthals, it is still inevitable that most such disposals of the dead will not show up in the archaeological record, which is focused on sites of occupation or intensive activity. A burial within an occupied cave or rock shelter is much more likely to be recovered than a hole dug in the open landscape.[90]

Deliberate burials (and often multiple burials) are clearly attested in the Upper Palaeolithic of Europe and often with 'grave goods', possessions associated with life and perhaps intended for an afterlife. Here we see evidence for complex practices around burial, as both adults and children were sometimes buried with clothing, with decoration and with stone tools or animal bones.

This does not mean that such formal burials were universally practised. In the early part of the period they seem less frequent among *Homo sapiens* than among the Neanderthal populations of Europe.[91] The earlier stages of the Upper Palaeolithic, which reflect the arrival of *Homo sapiens*, continues to see the use of natural hollows for caching the dead rather than specially dug graves.

From 35,000 years ago onwards, purposely constructed burial pits, containing bodies and other items, are more common. Ritual associated with burial begins in the mid Upper Palaeolithic, alongside new cultural developments such as the Gravettian. Sites excavated in Eastern and Western Europe contribute plentiful evidence for burial practices often involving multiple, even mass, graves of adults and children, with grave goods. The latest Upper Palaeolithic of Europe – from around 21,000 years ago to the end of the Pleistocene, around 12,000 years ago – has more sophisticated stone tool industries and further evidence of burial practices.

Almost 30% of the burials from the latest stages of the Upper Palaeolithic of France are of children.[92] But over the fuller extent of the Upper Palaeolithic, children represent about 10% of the bodies: a statistic which may suggest that more adults than before were brought back from wherever they died to formal places of burial; and that younger children at least were not given the same burial rites as adults. The Upper Palaeolithic burials of older children, as at Sunghir or Dolní Věstonice, may signify the death of adolescents in the process of 'becoming adults'.[93]

The Russian site of Kostenki on the Don River included important evidence of child burial, within a long sequence of local human occupation right through the Upper Palaeolithic: one of the longest sequences of burials and settlement of modern humans in Europe.[94] From the period around 26,000–21,000 years ago, the site included a child of 6 or 7 years buried in a small pit, covered with fragments of mammoth scapula. Within the grave, clay had been used to build a seat on which the body was placed. The burial also contained stone artefacts and a bone awl. Over 150 perforated fox teeth appear to have come from a headdress in which the child had been buried. A newborn buried on her or his back was also found at Kostenki with radiocarbon dates between 29,000 and 23,000 years.

Even more notable is the Russian site of Sunghir (Sungir),[95] of roughly similar date, discussed in detail in Chapter 5. The remains were interpreted as those of a girl aged 9–10 and a boy aged 11–12: the sex assigned from a study of the hip bone shape and later endorsed by DNA studies.[96] They were buried within a settlement head to head, covered with ochre, apparently clothed with thousands of ivory beads sewn onto cloth, a headdress of fox teeth, together with pendants, animal figurines (a mammoth and a possible horse) and ivory discs and items resembling spears of mammoth ivory, as well as (strangely) a femur from another human. Both showed signs of some deformity – the congenital bowing of the long bones. Some see this double burial and its lavish clothing and grave goods as signs of a sacrifice.

The Upper Palaeolithic Polish site of Maszycka cave, with a burial of five adults, three children and eight infants, mentioned in Chapter 8, suggested violent death followed by cannibalism.[97] The infant teeth at another Polish site, Borsuka cave, were deciduous and not part of a burial.[98] A newborn or foetus was found buried with a necklace of fox teeth at Wilczyce in Poland.[99]

At Předmostí in the Czech Republic a mass grave was discovered in the 19th century: eight adults and 12 children buried near a living site now dated around 29,000 years BC.[100] At Dolní Věstonice in the Czech Republic a grave contained three adolescents buried together: two healthy males and one female who appeared to be disabled by a misshapen spine and deformed femur. They were accompanied by necklaces of pierced teeth of arctic fox and wolf as well as pendants of mammoth ivory, and red ochre had been placed over the heads. Detailed analysis suggested that they were genetically related: in other words, siblings or cousins.[101]

Moving further west, at Krems-Wachtberg in Austria a burial of two newborn infants was discovered dated from the Gravettian era, about 27,000 years ago. The bodies were embedded in red ochre, one with more than 30 ivory beads around the pelvis.[102] The burial was covered by a mammoth tusk and a mammoth shoulder blade, which showed signs of burning and flaking. It is tempting to see these as twins who did not survive, although perhaps the historically attested practice of deliberate killing of twins was represented here.

Another infant aged less than 3 months was buried in a flexed position nearby with ochre and an ivory pin, perhaps fastening a wrap.[103] Here is evidence of the honour with which an Upper Palaeolithic family treated a baby who did not live. The whole site is one of major human activity, including painting, with thousands of items from stone tool manufacture, as well as from the processing of bone and mammoth ivory.

One of the most remarkable burials from the era is that of an adolescent male, nicknamed 'Il Principe', from Arene Candide in Liguria, Italy. He was buried on a bed of ochre in a grave marked by a large stone block.[104] Buried with him were mammoth ivory pendants, perforated cowrie shells and deer teeth, 'batons' of elk antler and a long flint blade. The clothing is mentioned briefly in Chapter 5.

At Ostuni in south-east Italy an adult female (with personal ornament of beads and pendants) was buried with a newborn or foetus – another possible example of death in childbirth.

In the Romito cave in Calabria, Italy, a burial dated a little over 13,000 years ago has an adolescent (perhaps 17 years old) showing signs of dwarfism, lying in the arms of an older female.[105]

From the site of Grotta dei Fanciulli (the 'Cave of the Children' on the Italian border near France)[106] a double child burial with shells from clothing and a flint point embedded in a vertebra suggests a violent death, discussed in Chapter 8. The bones also showed that in life they had suffered the effect of the inflammatory condition of periostitis.

The child found in a rock shelter in at Lagar Velho in central Portugal was mentioned in Chapter 5.[107] Here, with a date around 25,000–24,000 years, was a grave dug into the soil with a piece of Scots pine timber added, containing a child of 4 to 5 years as well as ochre, which suggests the body was dressed in an ochre-stained shroud. Deer teeth were probably from a hat; there was a shell pendant, the body of a young rabbit lay on the child's legs, and two red deer pelvises were at the child's shoulders.

At Cromagnon (Les Eyzies, Dordogne region of France) a collective grave dated around 28,000 years ago held an adult male, an adult female and a newborn buried together.[108]

At La Madeleine from the final Upper Palaeolithic of France a child aged 2–4 years was found in an ochre-stained grave lined with three stones at the head, and decorated with many perforated teeth and beads made of shells.[109] The richness of these decorations may mark a high-status family: the length of time involved in preparing the shells would have been substantial.

A different approach to death, a complex and lengthy ritual process, was uncovered at the British site of Gough's cave, Cheddar, dating from the very end of the Upper Palaeolithic, at about 12,750 BC. Here, human remains included those of a child (of about 3 years) and two adolescent youths. The skulls were cleaned, broken and shaped in a form that suggests their use as a drinking (or libation) vessel: the brains may even have been consumed. Such 'skull-cups' are known in later times and other places. Other adult bones were defleshed, disarticulated, crushed and chewed on, and split to remove marrow.

The late Ice Age occupants of Europe, anatomically modern humans with the advanced blade tool technology of the Upper Palaeolithic, have thus provided broad evidence of responses to the death of newborn infants, children and adolescents as well as adults. Their burials, often with precious ornamentation, gives us an image of a complex (even sophisticated) set of attitudes and beliefs held by our forebears and a range of different social rituals associated with death and burial.

ADVANCED FORAGERS OF THE PREHISTORIC WORLD

The Upper Palaeolithic record of the later Ice Age of Europe, as outlined above, presents a dramatic image of the new kinds of society in which *Homo sapiens*, equipped with new technologies and new complexities of social organisation, created art, social practices and rituals for the dead which contrast with those of Neanderthal groups. Following the end of the Pleistocene era in much of the Old World, forager societies developed new forms of stone tool technology and new strategies for intensive exploitation of natural resources, until the emergence of agricultural practices at widely different dates. Meanwhile, in the Late Pleistocene, hunter-gatherers crossed the land bridge from Northeast Asia and began populating the Americas.

Children in the advanced hunter-gatherer-fisher economies of Mesolithic and Epipalaeolithic Europe and the Middle East are known from numerous burials, often following the pattern associated with adults. This supports an image that children were commonly considered full members of society, playing an active role in the household and in food provision.

Burials in the semi-sedentary Natufian cultures dating around 12,500 to 9500 BC included group graves with adults, children and infants, perhaps as a family burial place. Grave goods associated with both adults and children at Ain Mallaha and Hayonim in Israel and at other Natufian sites included shell beads. At Hayonim 31% of the burials were those of children.[110] The children's burials were accompanied by bone pendants, perforated fox teeth and a headdress of 32 gazelle bones. Some infants were buried below house floors.

Infant burials were found in the Serbian site of Vlasac, where the majority of the excavated graves appear to belong to the Mesolithic era.[111] The burials include foetuses (one within a deceased mother) and newborns, buried on their own or with an adult. Several infants were buried with a decorative item of a set of fish teeth, and one with 50 perforated beads of snail shells together with fish teeth. Red ochre is present in a number of burials, including those where infant and adult are buried together.

Lepenski Vir in Serbia was another early Mesolithic village succeeded by early agricultural Neolithic people. It was a permanent or semi-permanent settlement with structures of floors plastered with limestone. Stone framed hearths were constructed in each building. Burials of newborn infants were found underneath floors. From the position of the skeleton it is possible that some of these infants were placed in a bag before burial. An older child, of around 2 years, was buried under a stone block with two sculptural pieces. It is striking that the bodies of infants who died at or soon after childbirth were not discarded but buried within the building itself: assuming these were domestic dwellings, a presence under the domestic floor maintained them as part of the household in which they had spent so little time when alive.

The Dnieper basin of Ukraine held many settlements spanning Mesolithic and late Neolithic, and provided samples of adult and juvenile burials, with no major difference in the way children or adults were buried.[112] Grave goods with children included a string of beads and deer tooth pendants. A cemetery of 67 burials at Osipovka from the 7th millennium BC included a child interred alongside an adult, and another child associated with some 200 carp teeth.[113]

Burials of children in Mesolithic Greece, in the period 8500–6500 BC, had elements similar to adult burials: a semi-contracted position, sometimes buried with shells and coloured with ochre.[114]

At the other side of the European continent, children's graves in the Mesolithic cemetery of Vedbaek, Denmark, also had red ochre as well as animal bones, including one burial under a swan's wing.[115] This child lay next to a woman, buried resting on what appears to be a cushion decorated with shells and deer teeth.[116]

The late Mesolithic site of Tågerup in Sweden was a forager settlement with some solid residential structures. Burials at the site included one of a child (perhaps 9 or 10 years old) with a stone arrowhead embedded in the pelvic region – a violent death reflecting the inter-group violence in other adult remains of the region.[117]

Burials at the winter-season fishing, hunting and foraging camp of Skateholm in southern Sweden suggested different patterns according to the age of death.[118] After the age of 14, burials were indistinguishable from those of older adults: the bodies were interred with flint and bone artefacts as well as animal jaws or teeth. Younger children were generally buried without such grave goods, other than an occasional arrowhead or other stone or bone tool, while infants appear to have been buried together with other bodies, not in individual graves. Ochre, however, was a feature of the children's graves but not the adults. And interestingly, domestic dogs were also buried at Skateholm.

In Africa, groups reliant largely on a hunter-gatherer economy continued in parts of the continent through to modern times, including ancestors of the San (or Bushmen) of Southern Africa. In a prehistoric archaeology context they are often classified as Later Stone Age (LSA), and the recovered skeletal remains present a sample of adult and juvenile burials.[119] Such burials include occasional evidence of violence upon adults and children, outlined in Chapter 8.

At the site of Byneskranskop in South Africa, dated around 3600 BC, a baby aged between 3½ and 5 months was seen to have severe rickets.[120] This was despite the mother's mixed and adequate diet, which included marine and land foods. The baby had been kept alive through family care and was given formal burial in line with normal LSA practice.

A newborn LSA baby was found buried in a cave on the Atlantic coast of South Africa.[121] It had been buried with care and there was no obvious cause of death; analysis of the bones showed that the mother had had a marine food diet.

One slightly unusual burial, some 2100 years old, was a double burial of children aged 3 years and 6 or 7 years on the Lorraine farm in the Western Cape. The two children were laid out on a large piece of leather, incised with decorative lines, which had been placed on a bed of grass within a hollow excavated for the double grave.[122]

Studies of childhood in prehistoric Japan are at an early stage, with relatively little detailed work to date, and there is substantial potential for more studies, although acidic soils limit the survival of the most fragile bones. In the Jomon era, from ca. 14,000 BC to the late 1st millennium BC, Japan was populated by foragers who developed pottery and at least seasonal sedentism. Above the age of 2 years a deceased child had much of the same treatment as for adults, being buried singly or within multiple burials and in the same posture as adults, with burials in dug pits the customary pattern.[123] In the later Jomon era, some of the child burials had very rich grave goods, indicating the growth of family wealth and inequalities. A study of late-Jomon skeletal material showed how trauma and stress in childhood could reduce life expectancy.[124]

Jar burials were frequent for Jomon infants (and also foetuses), a pattern seen in Korea too, although infants are also found buried with women. At the site of Sannai Maruyama some 800 jars were described as the burials of infants, while a sample of 36 burials had 12 foetuses, 17 infants aged under 1 year, six infants aged between 1 and 6 years, and only one older child.[125]

A contrast was the discovery of the remains of two young children (aged 3–4 and 5–6 years) beneath rocks in the Tochibora rock shelter in Nagano Prefecture. The excavators assumed they had been crushed by an accidental rockfall; with the bodies were a snail shell and shell ornaments.[126]

The frequency of early death is noticed at many New World sites of forager communities. An early study of burials at the site of Indian Knoll (3rd millennium BC) in the US state of Kentucky noted that 165 of the burials (about 30%) were of infants or young children (under 5 years), with environmental factors as well as genetic factors suggested as the cause for depressed bodily growth rates.[127]

The burials of children in an Archaic hunter site (2nd millennium BC) in Newfoundland, Canada, had child burials which were as well equipped with grave goods as those of the adults, or even better, including adult tools and weapons.[128]

The community of advanced fishers, hunters and food gatherers at Paloma in Peru (occupied ca. 5000–2500 BC) had an unusual pattern of burials.[129] Children and particularly infants received special attention in their burial, and the young had the greatest number of grave goods in a sample of 200 burials studied. One infant was buried within a large gourd, but the largest group of infants was beneath a house. Despite this, it is possible that infanticide, especially of females, was practised, so perhaps the rich grave goods implied a ritual rather than natural death.

In the Argentine site of Chenque 1, dated to the first half of the 2nd millennium AD, almost half of the 216 burials were of children or adolescents, including some who met violent deaths, as mentioned in Chapter 8.[130] They were buried with grave goods including shell and stone bead necklaces, and items of leather; there was ochre both on their bodies and on ornaments.

A distinctive pattern was found among Chinchorro foragers and fishers of the Chilean Andes from the 5th to the 2nd millennia BC.[131] Bodies of infants and children were, like those of adults, 'mummified' with clay and fibre coverings, and the clay was at times modelled into human form. Bodies were often processed by defleshing and evisceration. Even infants had items of fishing equipment buried with them (though not hunting items). One implication may be that they accompanied their mothers on fishing trips.

The diversity of burial treatments of the young in different advanced hunter-gatherer societies reflects changing cultures and changing social patterns. But within most individual prehistoric cultures there is a difference between the treatments in death of children of different ages. Infants may be treated differently from older children, and children's burial differentiated from that of adults. However, the stage at which a child is regarded in death as meriting an adult style of burial is specific to the social group, and perhaps even to the family. In questioning and interpreting the pattern of the latest prehistoric forager groups, we can also consider and compare aspects of more recent hunter-gatherer societies.

MODERN HUNTER-GATHERERS

The demography of forager groups in the modern era has been substantially modified by their contact with outside groups. Such contact may bring pressure on resources but add opportunities for trade and innovation; it commonly introduces new disease but in time also provides the possibility of new treatments for health. One estimate claims that in some African communities and across the Pacific region, the arrival of new sexually transmitted diseases was a major cause of the reduction of fertility, with up to 40% of women in some communities bearing no children and others bearing only one or two children.[132] In Chapter 2 considered patterns of childbirth in recent hunter-gatherer communities. Some of the same studies have considered patterns of juvenile death.

A review of data on different kinds of small-scale society compared death rates (and therefore the rates of survival) in a number of separate communities, categorised as hunter-gatherers, acculturated hunter-gatherers and forager-horticulturalists, and for comparison historical data from mid-18th-century Sweden. All groups had a high death rate in the first year and this rate remained somewhat high between the ages of 5 and 10, after which it evened off. Overall, 43% of hunter-gatherers died before the age of 15, compared with 36% of acculturated hunter-gatherers and 33% of forager-horticulturalists.[133] The figure was 40% for 18th-century Swedes. Once adulthood had been reached in these small-scale societies, there was a reasonable chance of avoiding death until around the age of 40, after which death rates started to increase again, and 72 was suggested as the modal age of a full lifespan for adults. This is a warning about concepts of 'average' lifespan of prehistoric societies: infant and childhood deaths were significant, but once adulthood had been safely reached, longevity might ensure a majority of people in later prehistoric forager groups became grandparents, a role which in itself is important in both social organisation and the transmission of cultural knowledge.

Another comparative analysis of foragers shows a wide range of childhood mortality rates in societies for which data are available between the 1970s and the 1990s.[134] Death rates in the first year of life ranged from 8% in a !Kung group to 33% in an Mbuti (Pygmy) community and 34% in a Philippine Agta group. Death rates before the age of 15 were just 12% of the !Kung group, 56% of the Mbuti group and 49% of the Agta. Higher levels of female than male death were noted in several societies. Infectious and parasitic diseases were a major cause of fatalities. Since these were far from isolated forager groups, the impact of contact with other groups should be considered a contributing factor. Across all the groups studied, illness was the cause of death in 65% of cases for the under-15s, with a very variable number of victims of violence, at a rate higher than for adults. Death from accidents (averaging 8% of cases) was a lesser cause of death for children than for adults. Violent death can be observed in recent forager societies (as in prehistoric societies, as noted above). In the Ache people of Paraguay, if a woman remarried, her children's lives were said to be at risk from her new husband if he wished to favour his own new family.[135]

A different study of the !Kung San of the Kalahari from the 1960s and 1970s suggested a 40% death rate of the young – not far different from the historic pattern with which we began this chapter. By this analysis, 'one would expect 23% to die within the first year of life, 40% to be dead before reaching the age of 15, 60% before the age of 45, while 15% can be expected to live to 60 and beyond'.[136] Given the average number of children for a child-bearing woman was five, this implies no more than three living to reproductive age themselves, and allowing for those women who do not bear children, only a modest growth rate (if any) in overall population.

In the 1940s an Australian Aboriginal group in the northern island of Groote Eylandt had an infant mortality rate of about 60% and a continuing high mortality rate of young children, in a period shortly before antibiotics and modern medical care were introduced.[137]

In neither prehistoric communities nor forager societies encountered in the modern world can we assume or assign constant growth in population or in population density. Although women in hunter-gatherer societies typically may have had five or six live births, the death of girls from illness and accident before reaching reproductive age means population density can remain relatively stable.

But there is one additional factor. A dramatic influence on the pattern of children in traditional forager societies is the complex issue of *infanticide*.[138] It was noted earlier that in our primate relatives infanticide may be the action of adult males acting against offspring who are not their own. But in the ethnographic record we find forager communities where infanticide is the action of the mothers themselves: to limit family size, achieve spacing between infants, or to manage the sex balance of the society, as well as a response to deformity or the birth of twins. !Kung women, for whom infanticide was rare, cited deformity, twins and 'when one birth follows another too closely, and the baby would drink the milk of this older brother or sister ... or when the woman feels she is too old to produce milk for another baby'.[139] One of the influences of the intrusion of the industrialised world on these communities is the suppression or cessation of such traditional practices (and also, perhaps, its denial to the ethnographic observer).

In the absence of reliable means of contraception and safe means of abortion, infanticide was recorded as a means of population control in a range of traditional forager societies, spacing children to be raised. But it was often gender biased. Selectivity to favour male babies meant more future hunters, rather than simply more young mouths to feed; and it also meant fewer future mothers. Evidence suggests that it was not necessarily a male decision that infanticide should take place.

Rates of infanticide observed in forager societies of the recent past varies.[140] If it was only 1% for a !Kung group in Botswana, and 5–11% among the Northern Australian Anbarra, the Netsilik of the Canadian Arctic in the early 20th century had reported infanticide rates of 67% for female babies. Such a pattern, in a region of extreme climate and a male-led food procurement, cannot be assumed to be typical of any prehistoric society.

The Yanomami foragers and garden horticulturalists of the northern edge of the Amazon basin were the subject of studies starting in the 1960s, by when modern influences were already present. One effect of these had been to reduce the incidence of infanticide, which, it was suggested by the leaders of the 1960s study, had applied to some 15–20% of births, as a response of deformity, sex selection (in favour of males) or the wish to space children. Such infanticide would take place immediately after birth.[141] Including deaths from natural causes and accidents as well as infanticide, infant and childhood mortality was estimated to be about 50%. Other groups in the Amazon basin adopted infanticide to manage both the proportions of the sexes and the overall population numbers.[142]

Anthropologist Joseph Birdsell advanced an argument that prehistoric infanticide needed to have been practised at levels from 15% to 50% of births if prehistoric foragers were to maintain viable and relatively stable population levels. Such a claim needs to be weighed against the limitation of our direct evidence and the limitations of analogy.[143] Our perception of the incidence of infanticide, and all our interpretation of treatment of infant and childhood death in prehistory, need to be influenced primarily by archaeological finds, with only cautious inference from widely differing recent communities.

CONCLUSIONS

The wide range of patterns observed in recent forager societies means there is no 'norm', no average pattern of mortality which can be transferred to our understanding of prehistoric societies. The indicative figures for forager groups noted above show what can happen in communities; it does not tell us what did happen in the prehistoric past.

In using the ethnographic record there are dangers in citing an 'average' lifespan.[144] There are also limits to the construction of an image of average fertility. Not all women marry and bear children; and miscarriages were rarely measured by external observers. Infanticide of newborns may have limited visibility in the ethnographic record (if informants are not open or accurate) and such tiny skeletons may be retrieved only rarely in the archaeological record, especially if they are not given the burial afforded to older individuals. The dangers of the first year of life bias figures for life expectancy, and there are continuing high death rates throughout early childhood. However, if a child survives to adulthood there is a reasonable expectation of a full adult life for the majority: long enough to be a parent, and very often long enough to be a grandparent too.

The archaeological examples described in this chapter and the next show the range of direct and indirect information that can be gained from the disposal of children's bodies. The variability in Neanderthal communities does include some examples which appear deliberate burial, and the subsequent cultures of advanced prehistoric foragers show practices which differ not just by region and period, but also by age of the deceased child. Children do not bury themselves: the position and nature of their burial, its associations with other burials, the objects placed on and with the child, all tell us of the adult world and in particular the social context and outlook of the parent, as well as the position of the child in the family and society.

Future studies of burials of children from archaeological sites can be expected to take research in new directions: genetic linkages at the regional and family level; dietary patterns; studies of physical condition and illness, alongside demographic and cultural interpretations. This is a rich area for expanding research.

NOTES

1 Lewis, *Bioarchaeology*, is a good survey of what is and is not possible in such studies.
2 S.E. Halcrow & N. Tayles, 'The bioarchaeological investigation of children and childhood' in S.C. Agarwal & B.A. Glencross (eds), *Social Bioarchaeology*, Malden, MA: Wiley-Blackwell, 2011: 333–360.
3 www.unicef.org/sowc96/1cinwar.htm
4 OECD, *How Was Life? Global well-being since 1820*, Paris: OECD Publishing, 2014.
5 'Infant mortality' from www.clio-infra.eu
6 For instance the *Sydney Morning Herald*, 12 May 1854, p. 3, citing *English Quarterly*; *Illinois State Chronicle*, 18 October 1855; repeated in S.G. Goodrich, *Peter Parley's Thousand and One Stories of Fact and Fancy, Wit and Humor, Rhyme, Reason, and Romance*, New York: Derby & Jackson, 1857.
7 Lewis, *Bioarchaeology*, pp. 82–83, citing N. Orme, *Medieval Children*, New Haven, CT: Yale University Press, 2001; though in a sample of villages, infant death rates of about 13% were recorded: R. Schofield & E. Wrigley, 'Infant and child mortality in England in the late Tudor and early Stuart period' in C. Webster (ed.), *Health, Medicine and Mortality in the Sixteenth Century*, Cambridge: Cambridge University Press, 1979: 61–95.
8 Wileman, *Hide and Seek*, p. 142.
9 R. Fleming, *Britain After Rome: the fall and rise 400–1070*, London: Penguin, 2010, pp. 352, 365.
10 M. Beard, *SPQR: a history of ancient Rome*, London: Profile, 2015, p. 316.
11 E. Scott, *The Archaeology of Infancy and Infant Death*, British Archaeological Reports International Series 819, Oxford: Archaeopress, 1999, p. 90.

12. S. Mays, 'The archaeology and history of infanticide, and its occurrence in earlier British populations' in *CMC*: 180–190.
13. S.R. Saunders & L. Barrans, 'What can be done about the infant category in skeletal samples?' in R.D. Hoppa & C.M. Fitzgerald (eds), *Human Growth in the Past: studies from bones and teeth*, Cambridge: Cambridge University Press, 1999: 183–209.
14. T.J. Booth, 'An investigation into the relationship between funerary treatment and bacterial bioerosion in European archaeological human bone', *Archaeometry* 58 (2016): 484–499.
15. A.T. Chamberlain, *Demography in Archaeology*, Cambridge: Cambridge University Press, 2006, pp. 138–139; C. Gamble, *Timewalkers: the prehistory of global colonization*, Cambridge, MA: Harvard University Press; London: Penguin, 1994, p. 110.
16. M. Lewis, 'The osteology of infancy and childhood: misconceptions and potential' in *RLA*: 1–13.
17. Lewis, *Bioarchaeology*, pp. 47–54.
18. K.A. Brown, 'Placing children in society: using ancient DNA to identify sex and kinship of child skeletal remains, and implications for gender and social organisation' in *AOC*: 129–148.
19. L.H. Beaudrot, S.M. Kahlenberg & A.J. Marshall, 'Why male orangutans do not kill infants', *Behavioral Ecology and Sociobiology* 63 (2009): 1549–1562.
20. pin.primate.wisc.edu/factsheets/entry/gorilla/behav
21. J. Yamagiwa & J. Kahekwa, 'Dispersal patterns, group structure, and reproductive parameters of Eastern lowland gorillas at Kahuzi in the absence of infanticide' in M Robbins, P. Sicotte & K.J. Stewart (eds), *Mountain Gorillas: three decades of research at Karisoke*, Cambridge: Cambridge University Press, 2001: 89–122; A.H. Harcourt & K.J. Stewart, *Gorilla Society: conflict, compromise and cooperation between the sexes*, Chicago, IL: University of Chicago Press, 2007, pp. 202ff.; D. Fossey, 'Development of the mountain gorilla (*Gorilla gorilla berengei*): the first thirty-six months' in D.A. Hamburg & E.R. McCown (eds), *The Great Apes*, Menlo Park, CA: Benjamin/Cummings, 1979, pp. 155–156.
22. Yamigawa & Kahekwa, 'Dispersal patterns', p. 101.
23. C. Boesch & H. Boesch-Achermann, *The Chimpanzees of Taï Forest: behavioural ecology and evolution*, Oxford: Oxford University Press, 2000, pp. 33–34, 151–153.
24. T. Nishida et al., 'Demography, female life history, and reproductive profiles among the chimpanzees of Mahale', *American Journal of Primatology* 59 (2003): 99–121. Nishida later raised this to 60% not surviving beyond the weaning stage: T. Nishida, *Chimpanzees of the Lakeside: natural history and culture at Mahale*, Cambridge: Cambridge University Press, 2012, p. 123.
25. See for instance M. Hamai et al., 'New records of within-group infanticide and cannibalism in wild chimpanzees', *Primates* 33 (1992): 151–162.
26. J. Goodall, *The Chimpanzees of Gombe: pattern of behavior*, Cambridge, MA: Harvard University Press, 1986, pp. 283–285.
27. R.H. Tuttle, *Apes and Human Evolution*, Cambridge, MA: Harvard University Press, 2014, pp. 317–319.
28. C.H. Janson & C.P. van Schaik, 'The behavioral ecology of infanticide by males' in C.H. Janson & C.P. van Schaik (eds), *Infanticide by Males and Its Implications*, Cambridge: Cambridge University Press, 2000: 469–494, pp. 476–477, table 19.1.

29 Janson & Schaik, 'The behavioral ecology', pp. 469, 471, 490.
30 R.A. Dart, 'Australopithecus africanus: the Man-Ape of South Africa', *Nature* 115 (1925): 195–199.
31 J.H. Schwarz & I. Tattersall, *The Human Fossil Record, Vol. 4: Craniodental morphology of early hominids (genera, Australopithecus, Paranthropus, Orrorin), and overview*, Hoboken, NJ: Wiley, 2005, pp. 439–447; C.M. Dean & V.S. Lucas, 'Dental and skeletal growth in early fossil hominins', *Annals of Human Biology* 36 (2009): 545–561.
32 L.R. Berger & W.S. McGraw, 'Further evidence for eagle predation of, and feeding damage on, the Taung child', *South African Journal of Science* 103 (2007): 496–498.
33 Y. Rak & F.C. Howell, 'Cranium of a juvenile *Australopithecus boisei* from the lower Omo Basin, Ethiopia', *American Journal of Physical Anthropology* 48 (1978): 345–365.
34 U. Ripamonti, 'Paleopathology in *Australopithecus africanus*: a suggested case of a 3-million-year-old prepubertal periodontitis', *American Journal of Physical Anthropology* 76 (1988): 197–210.
35 D.C. Johanson, M. Taieb & Y. Coppens, 'Pliocene hominids from the Hadar Formation, Ethiopia (1973–1977): stratigraphic, chronological and paleoenvironmental contexts, with notes on hominid morphology and systematics', *American Journal of Physical Anthropology* 57 (1982): 373–402; A.K. Behresmeyer, 'Paleoenvironmental context of the Pliocene A.L. 333 "First Family" hominin locality, Hadar Formation, Ethiopia' in J. Quade & J.G. Wynn (eds), *The Geology of Early Humans in the Horn of Africa*, Special Paper 446, Boulder, CO: Geological Society of America, 2008, ch. 9; D. Johanson, 'Lucy, thirty years later: an expanded view of *Australopithecus afarensis*', *Journal of Anthropological Research* 60 (2004): 465–486.
36 P. Pettitt, *The Palaeolithic Origins of Human Burial*, London: Routledge, 2011, p. 45.
37 D.C. Johanson & B. Edgar, *From Lucy to Language*, New York: Simon & Schuster, 2006, p. 135.
38 Though there is scientific disagreement on the sex and number of the individuals: see J.M. Plavcan et al., 'Sexual dimorphism in *Australopithecus afarensis* revisited: how strong is the case for a human-like pattern of dimorphism?', *Journal of Human Evolution* 48 (2005): 313–320; P.L. Reno et al., 'Sexual dimorphism in *Australopithecus afarensis* was similar to that of modern humans', *Proceedings of the National Academy of Sciences* 100 (2003): 9404–9409.
39 D.J. de Ruiter, S.E. Churchill & L.R. Berger, '*Australopithecus sediba* from Malapa, South Africa' in K.E. Reed, J.G. Fleagle & R.E. Leakey (eds), *The Paleobiology of Australopithecus*, Dordrecht: Springer, 2013: 147–160 (the volume is an edited collection papers presented at a 2007 symposium); L.R. Berger et al., '*Australopithecus sediba*: a new species of *Homo*-like Australopith from South Africa', *Science* 328 (2010): 195–204.
40 W.H. Kimbel & Y. Rak, '*Australopithecus sediba* and the emergence of *Homo*: questionable evidence from the cranium of the juvenile holotype MH 1', *Journal of Human Evolution* 107 (2017): 94–106.
41 Z. Alemseged et al., 'A juvenile early hominin skeleton from Dikika, Ethiopia', *Nature* 443 (2006): 296–301.
42 C.V. Ward et al., 'Thoracic vertebral count and thoracolumbar transition in

Australopithecus afarensis', *Proceedings of the National Academy of Sciences* 114 (2017): 6000–6004.
43 N.M. Tanner, *On Becoming Human*, Cambridge: Cambridge University Press, 1981, p. 210, citing work from the 1970s by A.E. Mann.
44 R. Caspari and S-H.Lee, 'Older age becomes common late in human evolution', *Proceedings of the National Academy of Sciences* 101 (2004): 10895–10900.
45 Chamberlain, *Demography in Archaeology*, p. 140.
46 L.S.B. Leakey, P.V. Tobias & J.R. Napier, 'A new species of the genus *Homo* from Olduvai Gorge', *Nature* 202 (1964): 7–9.
47 Including *Homo ergaster* in this broad classification.
48 A. Walker & P. Shipman, *The Wisdom of the Bones: in search of human origins*, London: Weidenfeld & Nicholson, 1996.
49 C. Dean et al., 'Growth processes in teeth distinguish modern humans from *Homo erectus* and earlier hominins', *Nature* 414 (2001): 628–631; R.R. Graves et al., 'Just how strapping was KNM-WT 15000?', *Journal of Human Evolution* 59 (2010): 542–554; R. Schiess & M. Haeusler, 'No skeletal dysplasia in the Nariokotome boy KNM-WT 15000 (*Homo erectus*) – a reassessment of congenital pathologies of the vertebral column', *American Journal of Physical Anthropology* 150 (2013): 365–374.
50 Other juvenile probable *Homo erectus* has been found in South Africa at Cave of Hearths and in Indonesia at Kedungbrubus and Ngandong (Solo).
51 G.D. van den Bergh et al., '*Homo floresiensis*-like fossils from the early Middle Pleistocene of Flores', *Nature* 534 (2016): 245–248; A. Brumm et al., 'Age and context of the oldest known hominin fossils from Flores', *Nature* 534 (2016): 249–253.
52 Y. Fernández-Jalvo et al., 'Human cannibalism in the Early Pleistocene of Europe (Gran Dolina, Sierra de Atapuerca, Burgos, Spain)', *Journal of Human Evolution* 37 (1999): 591–622.
53 A. Gracia et al., 'Craniosynostosis in the Middle Pleistocene human cranium 14 from the Sima de los Huesos, Atapuerca, Spain', *Proceedings of the National Academy of Sciences* 106 (2009): 6573–6578; E. Carbonell et al., 'Cultural cannibalism as a paleoeconomic system in the European Lower Pleistocene', *Current Anthropology* 51 (2010): 539–549; restudied in J.L. Arsuega et al., 'Neandertal roots: cranial and chronological evidence from Sima de los Huesos', *Science* 344 (2014): 1358–1363.
54 Pettitt, *The Palaeolithic Origins*, pp. 49–50.
55 N. Sala et al., 'Lethal interpersonal violence in the Middle Pleistocene', *PLoS ONE* 10 (2015): e0126589.
56 P.H.G.M. Dirks et al., 'The age of *Homo naledi* and associated sediments in the Rising Star Cave, South Africa', *eLife* 6 (2017): 10.7554/eLife.24231.
57 J. Hawks et al., 'New fossil remains of *Homo naledi* from the Lesedi chamber, South Africa', *eLife* 6 (2017): 10.7554/eLife.24232.
58 J.H. Schwarz & I. Tattersall, *The Human Fossil Record, Vol. 1: Terminology and craniodental morphology of genus Homo (Europe)*, New York: Wiley, 2002; *Vol. 2: Craniodental morphology of genus Homo (Africa and Asia)*, New York: Wiley, 2003.
59 E. Trinkaus, 'Neanderthal mortality patterns', *Journal of Archaeological Science* 22 (1995): 121–142.
60 S.E. Churchill, *Thin on the Ground: Neandertal biology, archeology and ecology*, Hoboken, NJ: Wiley Blackwell, 2014, pp. 347–349.

61 Trinkaus, 'Neanderthal mortality patterns'; M. Cartmill & F.H. Smith, *The Human Lineage*, Hoboken, NJ: Wiley, 2009, p. 384, citing Trinkaus & Tompkins (1990).
62 Pettitt, *The Palaeolithic Origins*, p. 4; older discussions are R.H. Gargett, 'Grave shortcomings: the evidence for Neandertal burial', *Current Anthropology* 30 (1989): 157–190; F.B. Harrold, 'A comparative analysis of Eurasian Palaeolithic burials', *World Archaeology* 12 (1980): 195–211 (which considered just 132 individuals from the Middle and Upper Palaeolithic, of which juveniles were 45% and 37% respectively).
63 Pettitt, *The Palaeolithic Origins*, p. 105.
64 P. Spikins et al., 'The cradle of thought: growth, learning, play and attachment in Neanderthal children', *Oxford Journal of Archaeology* 33 (2014): 111–134, p. 117.
65 Schwarz & Tattersall, *The Human Fossil Record, Vol. 2*, p. 394; Gargett, 'Grave shortcomings', pp. 168–169. Inevitably, some doubt on the Neanderthal identity has been raised: M. Glantz, S. Athreya & T. Ritzman, 'Is Central Asia the eastern outpost of the Neandertal range? A reassessment of the Teshik-Tash child', *American Journal of Physical Anthropology* 138 (2009): 45–61.
66 Ralph S. Solecki, *Shanidar: the first flower people*, New York: Knopf, 1971.
67 J.D. Sommer, 'The Shanidar IV "flower burial": a re-evaluation of Neanderthal burial ritual', *Cambridge Archaeological Journal* 9 (1999): 127–129.
68 R.H. Gargett, 'Middle Palaeolithic burial is not a dead issue: the view from Qafzeh, Saint-Césaire, Kebara, Amud, and Dederiyeh', *Journal of Human Evolution* 37 (1999): 27–90; E. Hovers et al., 'The Amud 7 skeleton – still a burial: response to Gargett', *Journal of Human Evolution* 39 (2000): 253–260.
69 Pettitt, *The Palaeolithic Origins*, pp. 105–110.
70 A.-M. Tillier, 'Early deliberate child burials: bioarchaeological insights from the Near Eastern Mediterranean' in *BRIPP*: 3–14; C. Stringer & C. Gamble, *In Search of the Neanderthals*, London: Thames & Hudson, 1993, pp. 97–98.
71 Rediscovered material from the site was analysed in A. Gómez-Olivencia, I. Crevecoeur & A. Balzeau, 'La Ferrassie 8 Neandertal child reloaded: new remains and re-assessment of the original collection', *Journal of Human Evolution* 82 (2015): 107–126.
72 D.M. Sandgathe et al., 'The Roc de Marsal Neandertal child: a reassessment of its status as a deliberate burial', *Journal of Human Evolution* 61 (2011): 243–253.
73 M.J. Walker et al., 'The excavation of buried articulated Neanderthal skeletons at Sima de las Palomas (Murcia, SE Spain)', *Quaternary International* 259 (2012): 7–21; Spikins et al., 'The cradle of thought', p. 120.
74 J.L. Arsuaga et al., 'New Neandertal remains from Cova Negra (Valencia, Spain)', *Journal of Human Evolution* 52 (2007): 31–58.
75 Pettitt, *The Palaeolithic Origins*, p. 93.
76 Pettitt, *The Palaeolithic Origins*, pp. 95–96; V.H. Estabrook & D.W. Frayer, 'Trauma in the Krapina Neandertals: violence in the Middle Palaeolithic?' in C. Knüsel & M. Smith (eds), *The Routledge Handbook of the Bioarchaeology of Human Conflict*, Abington: Routledge, 2013: 67–89.
77 These include a child aged between 3 and 5 years at Devil's Tower in Gibraltar, whose teeth and skull suggest it grew up faster than a modern human: Stringer, *In Search of the Neanderthals*, pp. 85–86; M. Dean, C. Stringer, & T. Bromage, 'Age at death of the Neanderthal child from Devil's Tower, Gibraltar and the implications for studies of general growth and development in Neanderthals',

American Journal of Physical Anthropology 70 (1986): 301–309, pp. 307–308. At the site of l'Hortus were at least 20 individuals, including many children, whose remains were found in a fissure. Mezmaiskaya cave in the Caucasus has a burial of an infant under 2 months old. Other infant and juvenile Neanderthal finds have come from Archi, Derediyeh, Engis Cave, Kebara, La Quina, Sipka, Spy, Subaluk, Zaskalnaya and Saint-Césaire (discovered among boxed faunal remains from the site) and from Jebel Irhoud a juvenile archaic *Homo* of Middle Palaeolithic date: Schwarz & Tattersall, *The Human Fossil Record*, *Vol. 1* and *Vol. 2*; Spikins et al., 'The cradle of thought'.

78 Stringer & Gamble, *In Search of the Neanderthals*, pp. 158–160, and Gargett, 'Grave shortcomings', argue against deliberate burial. A defence of Neanderthal ability and activity is Spikins, 'The cradle of thought'.

79 Pettitt, *The Palaeolithic Origins*.

80 There is some ambiguity over the date and context of finds in Border Cave, on the Swaziland–South Africa borders. An infant of Middle Stone Age date, probably about 76,000 years old, was buried with a *Conus* shell and ochre staining in a cut grave: Pettitt, *The Palaeolithic Origins*, pp. 72–73.

81 S. Sankararaman et al., 'The genomic landscape of Neanderthal ancestry in present-day humans', *Nature* 507 (2014): 354–357; B. Vernot & J.M. Akey, 'Resurrecting surviving Neandertal lineages from modern human genomes', *Science* 343 (2014): 1017–1021.

82 H. Rougier et al., 'Neandertal cannibalism and Neandertal bones used as tools in Northern Europe', *Scientific Reports* 6 (2016): 29005.

83 E. Trinkaus, 'Late Pleistocene adult mortality patterns and modern human establishment', *Proceedings of the National Academy of Sciences* 108 (2011): 1267–1271.

84 K.M. Weiss, *Demographic Models for Anthropology*, Memoir Series no. 27, Washington, DC: Society for American Archaeology, 1973; F.A. Hassan, 'The growth and regulation of human population in prehistoric times' in M.N. Cohen, R.S. Malpass & H.G. Klein (eds), *Biosocial Mechanisms of Population Regulation*, New Haven, CT: Yale University Press, 1980: 305–319, pp. 307–308.

85 M. Gurven & H. Kaplan, 'Longevity among hunter-gatherers: a cross-cultural examination,' *Population and Development Review* 33 (2007): 321–365.

86 J.-J. Hublin et al., 'New fossils from Jebel Irhoud, Morocco and the pan-African origin of *Homo sapiens*', *Nature* 546 (2017): 289–292.

87 J.D. Clark et al., 'Stratigraphic, chronological and behavioural contexts of Pleistocene *Homo sapiens* from Middle Awash, Ethiopia', *Nature* 423 (2003): 747–752; T.D. White et al., 'Pleistocene *Homo sapiens* from Middle Awash, Ethiopia', *Nature* 423 (2003): 742–747.

88 Pettitt, *The Palaeolithic Origins*, p. 147.

89 V. Formicola, 'From the Sunghir children to the Romito dwarf: aspects of the Upper Paleolithic funerary landscape', *Current Anthropology* 48 (2007): 446–453.

90 F.B. Harrold, 'A comparative analysis of Eurasian Palaeolithic burials', *World Archaeology* 12 (1980): 195–211.

91 See Pettitt, *The Palaeolithic Origins*, for detailed discussion of Upper Palaeolithic burials; also C. Gamble, *The Palaeolithic Societies of Europe*, Cambridge: Cambridge University Press, 1999, pp. 404–405; Schwartz & Tattersall, *Human Fossil Record*, *Vol. 1* and *Vol. 2*; G.P. Rightmire, 'Middle and later Pleistocene hominins in Africa and Southwest Asia', *Proceedings of the National Academy of Sciences* 106 (2009): 16046–16050. Other sites include an adolescent at Svitavka.

92 C. Gamble, *Origins and Revolutions: human identity in earliest prehistory*, Cambridge: Cambridge University Press, 2007, p. 150.
93 V. Cummings, *The Anthropology of Hunter-Gatherers: key themes for archaeologists*, London: Bloomsbury, 2013: 66–67.
94 Pettitt, *The Palaeolithic Origins*, p. 198.
95 Pettitt, *The Palaeolithic Origins*, pp. 203ff.; V. Formicola & A.P. Buzhilova, 'Double child burial from Sunghir (Russia): pathology and inferences for Upper Paleolithic funerary practices', *American Journal of Physical Anthropology* 124 (2004): 189–198.
96 Formicola & Buzhilova, 'Double child burial', pp. 191–192.
97 Pettitt, *The Palaeolithic Origins*, pp. 215–216; J. Orschiedt, 'Cave burials in prehistoric Central Europe' in K.A. Bergsvig & R.E. Skeates (eds), *Caves in Context: the cultural significance of caves and rockshelters in Europe*, Oxford: Oxbow, 2012: 212–224, p. 214.
98 J. Wilczyński et al., 'A mid Upper Palaeolithic child burial from Borsuka Cave (southern Poland)', *International Journal of Osteoarchaeology* 26 (2016): 151–162.
99 J.D. Irish et al., 'A late Magdalenian perinatal human skeleton from Wilczyce, Poland', *Journal of Human Evolution* 55 (2008): 736–740.
100 J.A. Svoboda, 'The Upper Paleolithic burial area at Předmostí: ritual and taphonomy', *Journal of Human Evolution* 54 (2008): 15–33.
101 B. Klima, 'A triple burial from the Upper Paleolithic of Dolní Věstonice, Czechoslovakia', *Journal of Human Evolution* 16 (1987): 831–835; K.W. Alt et al., 'Twenty-five thousand-year-old triple burial from Dolní Věstonice: an ice-age family', *American Journal of Physical Anthropology* 102 (1997): 123–131.
102 T. Einwögerer et al., 'Upper Palaeolithic infant burials', *Nature* 444 (2006): 285; T. Einwögerer et al., 'The Gravettian infant burials from Krems-Wachtberg, Austria' in *BRIPP*: 15–19; Pettitt, *The Palaeolithic Origins*, pp. 170–173.
103 Pettitt, *The Palaeolithic Origins*, pp. 170–173.
104 Pettitt, *The Palaeolithic Origins*, p. 182 ff.; P.B. Pettitt et al., 'The Gravettian burial known as the Prince ("Il Principe"): new evidence for his age and diet', *Antiquity* 77 (2003): 15–19.
105 Formicola, 'From the Sunghir children'.
106 Pettitt, *The Palaeolithic Origins*, pp. 243–244.
107 Pettitt, *The Palaeolithic Origins*, pp. 168–169; C. Duarte et al., 'The early Upper Paleolithic human skeleton from the Abrigo do Lagar Velho (Portugal) and modern human emergence in Iberia', *Proceedings of the National Academy of Sciences* 96 (1999): 7604–7609.
108 Pettitt, *The Palaeolithic Origins*, p. 152.
109 Pettitt, *The Palaeolithic Origins*, p. 236–239; M. Vanhaeren & F. d'Errico, 'La parure de l'enfant de la Madeleine (fouilles Peyrony): un nouveau regard sur l'enfance au Paléolithique supérieur', *Paléo* 13 (2001): 201–240.
110 B.F Byrd & C.M. Monahan, 'Death, mortuary ritual, and Natufian social structure', *Journal of Anthropological Archaeology* 14 (1995): 251–287, p. 270; A. Belfer-Cohen, 'The Natufian graveyard in Hayonim cave', *Paléorient* 14 (1988): 297–308.
111 B. Dušan & S. Stefanović, 'Birth and death: infant burials from Vlasac and Lepenski Vir', *Antiquity* 78 (2004): 526–546; E. Cristian & D. Borić, '8500-year-old Late Mesolithic garment embroidery from Vlasac (Serbia): technological,

use-wear and residue analyses', *Journal of Archaeological Science* 39 (2012): 3450–3469.
112 M.C. Lillie, 'Women and children in prehistory: resource sharing and social stratification at the Mesolithic–Neolithic transition in Ukraine' in *IPP*: 213–228.
113 M.C. Lillie, 'Suffer the children: "visualising" children in the archaeological record' in *BRIPP*: 33–43, p. 39.
114 M. Georgiadis, 'Child burials in Mesolithic and Neolithic southern Greece: a synthesis', *CitP* 4 (2011): 31–45.
115 Lewis, *Bioarchaeology*, p. 31; Scott, *The Archaeology of Infancy*, p. 96.
116 Wileman, *Hide and Seek*, p. 71.
117 P. Karsten & B. Knarrström, 'Tågerup – fifteen hundred years of Mesolithic occupation in western Scania, Sweden: a preliminary view', *European Journal of Archaeology* 4 (2001): 165–174, p. 171.
118 F. Fahlander, 'Mesolithic childhoods: changing life-courses of young hunter-fishers in the Stone Age of southern Scandinavia', *CitP* 5 (2012): 20–34; A. Whittle, *Europe in the Neolithic*, Cambridge: Cambridge University Press, 1996, pp. 154–155.
119 L. Harrington & S. Pfeiffer, 'Juvenile mortality in Southern African archaeological contexts', *South African Archaeological Bulletin* 63 (2008): 95–101.
120 S. Pfeiffer & C. Crowder, 'An ill child among mid-Holocene foragers of Southern Africa', *American Journal of Physical Anthropology* 123 (2004): 23–29.
121 A. Jerardino, J. Sealy & S. Pfeiffer, 'An infant burial from Steenbokfontein cave, west coast, South Africa: its archaeological, nutritional and anatomical context', *South African Archaeological Bulletin* 55 (2000): 44–48.
122 J. Sealy et al., 'Hunter-gatherer child burials from the Pakhuis Mountains, Western Cape: growth, diet and burial practices in the Late Holocene', *South African Archaeological Bulletin* 55 (2000): 32–43.
123 Y. Yamada, 'Mortuary practices for children in Jomon Japan: an approach to Jomon life history' (in Japanese), *Japanese Archaeology* 4 (1997): 1–39; J. Habu, *Ancient Jomon of Japan*, Cambridge: Cambridge University Press, 2004, pp. 159, 177–178, citing Nakamura (2000).
124 D.H. Temple, 'Plasticity and constraint in response to early-life stressors among late/final Jomon period foragers from Japan', *American Journal of Physical Anthropology* 155 (2014): 537–545.
125 Habu, *Ancient Jomon*, pp. 166–169, citing Okada (1995) and Kikuchi (1983).
126 Y. Kohara et al., 'Human infant remains of the Jomon period, suffering death by a falling rock', *Journal of the Anthropological Society of Nippon* 79 (1971): 55–60.
127 F.E. Johnston, 'Growth of the long bones of infants and young children at Indian Knoll', *American Journal of Physical Anthropology* 20 (1962): 249–254.
128 J.A. Tuck, 'An Archaic cemetery at Port au Choix, Newfoundland', *American Antiquity* 36 (1971): 343–358.
129 J. Quilter, *Life and Death at Paloma: society and mortuary practices in a pre-ceramic Peruvian village*, Iowa City, IA: University of Iowa Press, 1989, pp. 41, 48, 58, 62, 66.
130 M.A. Berón, C.M. Aranda & L.H. Luna, 'Mortuary behaviour in subadults: children as social actors in the hunter-gatherer societies of Argentine Pampas', *CitP* 5 (2012): 51–69.

131 V.G. Standen, B.T. Arriaza & C.M. Santoro, 'Chinchorro mortuary practices on infants: northern Chile Archaic period (BP 7000–3600)' in *TCBI*: 58–74.
132 R. Pennington, 'Hunter-gather demography' in C. Panter-Brick, R.H. Layton & P. Rowly-Conwy (eds), *Hunter-Gatherers: an interdisciplinary perspective*, Cambridge: Cambridge University Press, 2001: 170–204, p. 181.
133 Gurven & Kaplan, 'Longevity among hunter-gatherers', p. 326; this paper complements these figures with a valuable broad discussion.
134 R.L. Kelly, *The Foraging Spectrum: diversity in hunter-gatherer lifeways*, Washington, DC: Smithsonian Institution Press, 1995, pp. 251–254. See also Pennington, 'Hunter-gather demography'.
135 Kelly, *The Foraging Spectrum*, p. 243, citing Hill & Kaplan (1998).
136 N. Howell, 'Toward a uniformitarian theory of human paleodemography', *Journal of Human Evolution* 5 (1976): 25–40, p. 35. Broadly similar figures were noted by H. Harpending, 'Regional variation in !Kung populations' in R.B. Lee & I. DeVore (eds), *Kalahari Hunter-Gatherers: studies of the !Kung San and their neighbors*, Cambridge, MA: Harvard University Press, 1976: 152–165.
137 F.G.G. Rose, 'Australian marriage, land-owning groups, and initiations' in R.B. Lee & I. DeVore (eds), *Man the Hunter*, Chicago, IL: Aldine, 1968: 200–208, p. 203.
138 Kelly, *The Foraging Spectrum*, pp. 233–244, 358–360. See pp. 206–208 for differential gender ratios which may reflect migration and other factors as well as infant deaths.
139 N. Howell, 'The population of the Dobe area !Kung' in Lee & DeVore (eds), *Kalahari Hunter-Gatherers*: 137–151.
140 Kelly, *The Foraging Spectrum*, p. 233.
141 J.V. Neel & K.M. Weiss, 'The genetic structure of a tribal population, the Yanomama Indians. XII. Biodemographic studies', *American Journal of Physical Anthropology* 42 (1975): 25–51; J.D. Early & J.F. Peters, *The Xilixana Yanomami of the Amazon: history, social structure, and population dynamics*, Tampa, FL: University of Florida Press, 2000, p. 205.
142 H. Montgomery, *An Introduction to Childhood: anthropological perspectives on children's lives*, Chichester: Wiley-Blackwell, 2009, p. 64.
143 J.B. Birdsell, 'Some predictions for the Pleistocene based on equilibrium systems among recent hunter-gatherers' in Lee & DeVore (eds), *Man the Hunter*: 229–240, p. 239.
144 Weiss, *Demographic Models*, gives 16.5 years as an average life expectancy at birth based on seven hunter-gatherer groups. This is less than suggested for prehistoric foragers, perhaps because of differential survival of infant skeletal material.

10

DYING 2

Death and burial in Old World farming societies

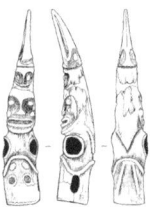

The transitions of human societies from a hunting and food-gathering economy to settled agricultural life did not necessarily bring improvements in infant survival, life expectancy or changes in family size. We know that the transformations were often gradual, with domestication of plants and animals developed separately in widely different parts of the world. The spread of agriculture involved both the movement of populations and the adoption of a new economy and technology by existing forager groups. Crop and vegetable farming involves a settled lifestyle which provides its own opportunities and social constraints.

We have plentiful information about small-scale 'traditional' farming communities of recent times from anthropological and other accounts. We know that infant and child mortality was commonly high in such modern communities, just as in prehistory. A study of change through time in Scandinavia emphasises the commonness of infants' and young children's death, from prehistory to pre-modern times.[1] The inevitability that a proportion of a family's children will not survive into adulthood need not diminish their sense of loss from the death of a child, and for prehistory our record of this loss is shown in burials. We can use the burials of these children to understand aspects of their social, personal and material lives, and also to examine aspects of their medical history, through the analysis of their bones.

We can assume that infant and child mortality rates in most prehistoric agricultural societies were not significantly lower than the high rates seen in more recent small-scale farming groups. Where less than 20–30% of the remains are non-adult in a burial ground from a prehistoric agricultural society, we can assume that actual deaths of the young at the site are under-represented. The wide variation in the proportion of juveniles found in formal burial sites demonstrates different cultural traditions.[2] Children may have been buried elsewhere, the bones of infants may not have survived or may have been dispersed, while perinatal, stillborn or foetal infants may have been disposed of without any formal burial. The presence and frequency of child burials are influenced by social traditions, individual family circumstances, biological factors and the nature of the preservation and recovery of the evidence.

Formal burials may reflect the point at which children were considered to have become established members of society. Infants may be few or absent from a society's burial ground, their early death keeping them outside society. In many societies of later prehistory we can see a marked difference between the responses to the death of infants and to the death of older children. The newborns may have died (or been the victim of infanticide) soon after birth. Infants under 1 year were highly susceptible to illness or injury and had not yet established themselves as part of family or society. Both practically and emotionally, if there is a high risk that an infant will not survive, the child's life and death may have been considered in a different way from those of a healthy older child.

But once a child had passed infancy, and especially once the child began to acquire some skills and start to participate in the household economy, premature death could be marked by burial practices, including grave goods, which emulated at least in part those of adult members of the group. According to the society's traditions, older children might be buried in an area where adults were buried or elsewhere; in an empty grave, or with other children or an adult. They could be accompanied by no grave goods, or by grave goods appropriate to their age (including food offerings), or by grave goods relating to a fully adult role they had not yet reached (such as weapons and specialised tools). These items as well as personal decoration and clothing can not only indicate age and life stage but also emphasise the difference between rich and poor, elites and others, in societies which were often distinctly hierarchical.

This chapter surveys the range of child burial practices within prehistorical agricultural communities, primarily of Europe, for which our information is particularly rich, as well as from the Middle East, before the dawn of civilisation, but with selective reference to other regions.

NEOLITHIC OF THE MIDDLE EAST AND EUROPE

In the first agricultural communities of Europe, the Middle East and much of Asia – the Neolithic – a new technology of stone tools, the introduction of pottery and concentrated settlement near cultivable land all marked significant changes to prehistoric society. The increasing attention given to child burials in many Neolithic cultures does, however, vary widely. Cemeteries associated with, but separate from, human settlement are common in much of Europe.

By contrast, some burials within settlements, and beneath house floors, are to be found in Middle Eastern sites.

Children were buried in an adult cemetery or on their own. The grave goods buried with children can indicate something of the funeral ritual, and those graves containing dramatic and lavish items of ornamentation as well as material possessions can indicate differences in family wealth and status.

When a mother died in advanced pregnancy or in childbirth, the remains of her unborn or stillborn child may be found with her: a pattern found in both prehistoric and historic sites.[3] In some cases the position of the foetus can suggest the cause of death of the mother.

In the Middle East, the large proto-urban site of Çatalhöyük in Turkish Anatolia held many burials below the floors of mudbrick dwellings, and about 60% of these were of children. The location of these burials seems to depend on the age of the child.[4] Bodies of newborn infants have been found near the hearth or in the south of the dwelling and some were built into house walls. The location of a deceased child within the home is open to a range of interpretations, but given that we know there are high levels of infant mortality in small-scale agricultural societies there seems no need to assume that such deaths were deliberately caused as part of a ritual or sacrifice, although this remains a possibility. Older children had grave goods deposited with them.

Çatalhöyük is also the site of a medically strange sculpture, resembling conjoined twins. This was originally described as 'double goddess' but an alternative is to see it as an image of a congenital abnormality from which children would not survive.[5] The body decoration throws doubt on the latter interpretation.

At the Pre-Pottery Neolithic site of Khirokitia in northern Cyprus, dated 7th to 6th millennia BC, infants and young children were buried, like adults, beneath house floors.[6] These houses were built from several round-walled rooms, and the burials seem to have taken place while the houses were still occupied. In a sample of 240 burials, 99 were of newborn or stillborn infants and 10 others were of children under 1 year, with only 25 children older than 1 year or adolescent, while 106 were adults. Most bodies were buried in a contracted position. The small number of buried older children compared with infants is surprising, and the large proportion of infants has raised the question of whether infanticide was practised. Yet burial in the house, with the same care given to adults, would challenge such a suggestion, and the rate of young death may reflect poor diet or infectious disease. Stone bowls, as buried with some adults and older children, can be found with some of the infants, as can an occasional animal bone. A deer scapula lay on the head of one of the infants and a goat or sheep horn next to another.

Children are scarce at many Neolithic burial locations in Greece.[7] There are burials of newborn infants at the early site of Nea Nikomedia, and multiple burials typically make no clear difference in their treatment by age or by sex. At Neolithic Souphli Magoula in mainland Greece, only adults and an adolescent had grave goods of meat or food vessels. Six newborns buried at Knossos in Crete were interpreted by archaeologists as a deliberate 'foundation deposit' in a dwelling area, but this remains a hypothesis, alongside an alternative view that a family may wish to keep its short-lived children close at hand. At Franchthi Cave (which has both Mesolithic and Neolithic child and adult burials) the Middle Neolithic remains included those of 16 young children, and one newborn was buried with a miniature stone bowl.

At Lerna in the Greek Peloponnese, burials of the Middle Neolithic were placed outside but close to houses. Infants, children and adults were all buried in shallow pits, and the association of the adults with the children may be deliberate. The site of Aria in the eastern Peloponnese has a stone circle marking a pit grave of a 4-year-old child buried with pots, which presumably held food offerings. One of the largest burial sites is at Alepotrypa, where half of the 161 bodies were of juveniles.[8]

More children's burials are found in the later Neolithic, from the mid-6th to the mid-4th millennia BC. Again, children may be buried, reinterred (or at times cremated) in similar fashion to adults, and sometimes together with adults. An exception in the southern Aegean region was the deposition of the body of newborns and young infants inside a pottery vessel which was then interred.[9] One newborn at Alepochori cave was placed inside a fine-quality ceramic vase, which was then sealed in another ceramic jar. At Kephala on the Greek island of Keos, two infants were buried together in a large jar.

Spanning the late Neolithic and the subsequent Chalcolithic ('Copper Age') are large cemeteries in the lower Danube valley and near the Black Sea, where children were buried like adults with significant grave goods, items which might be useful in an afterlife.[10]

Children's burials are common in the cemeteries of the Balkan Neolithic, with grave goods often similar to those of adults, though not so rich.[11] In Serbia, the Neolithic site of Gomolava revealed burials of 19 adult males and six child burials (which were interpreted as male, despite the widespread perception that determinations of sex from young skeletons are unreliable). While there were no grave goods with three newborn bodies, pots as well as some decorative items accompanied the burial of older children; copper and bone beads were found with two 1-year-olds. This suggests a clear distinction between those infants who had established themselves in the community and those who, through perinatal death, had not.[12]

In Romanian sites of the Neolithic, as well as the subsequent Chalcolithic sites, children were frequently buried like adults.[13] This again suggests that they were now regarded as members of the social group. Only a proportion of adult and a third of child burials have grave goods, though at one site, Cernavoda, animal bones appear only in adult graves.

Burials of infants and young children inside pottery jars as featured in several European Neolithic traditions continued in some areas into the Early Bronze Age, and are also found in the later Neolithic, Chalcolithic and Early Bronze Age of the Middle East.[14] At Kovačevo in Bulgaria, such burials were in between houses, with the bodies either crouched or positioned as semi-seated, and wrapped in a fabric or leather covering. A jar at Rakitovo under a house floor contained a flint blade and red ochre with a newborn while at Ezero another newborn was buried with a shell and flint blade. Most such burials unsurprisingly do not have space for grave goods.

The burials of children within a vessel and in the residential area of an agricultural community clearly represent a common social tradition. Some have suggested it reflects not just a wish to retain the lost child within the community, but a more complex system of belief in the child as a foundation symbol for a house. Others have seen the burials as support for prehistoric infanticide, even ritual sacrifice. But to be confident of infanticide as the cause of these deaths, there would need to be signs of trauma and where the bodies are sufficient to examine the details, trauma cannot normally be found. Death caused by damage to the soft tissue (such as strangulation) would not present us with evidence. Infanticide represents unwanted, unvalued births; careful burial suggests a different emotion. In contexts where both adult and child burials are within pots, for example those found at a Chalcolithic cemetery at Byblos in Lebanon, the extreme interpretations invite little support.

More unusual for the Neolithic period are burials within caves. These include burials of adults (mainly female) and children in Jungfernhöhle in German Bavaria, and a child buried in a cave at Felsställe near Ulm.[15]

In the Central European Neolithic societies of the 6th to 5th millennia BC, conventionally called the Linearbandkeramic (LBK), children's remains are rare in formal cemeteries but can be found buried within settlements.[16] Such 'domestic' burial includes pits between houses in the settlement or in ditches nearby. One child at Zauschwitz near Leipzig in Germany was buried face down in a pit with the remains of a house (daub and charcoal and ash from wood) over the body. This child showed medical evidence of long-term emaciation, suggesting poor diet and poor health. Such an approach to burial implies those children remained part of society by their posthumous presence in the settlement itself while not acknowledged as full members of society requiring burial in the community cemetery. But most of these LBK burials are of children older than 1 year; infants were generally not part of this burial practice. The largest group of child burials appears to be those between 8 and 12 years.[17]

By contrast, in some later Neolithic European settlements the care taken to bury children matched that for adults.[18] This supports a view that burial was not tied to a ritual designed to help honour ancestors.[19] Some graves were collective burials of adults and children. Grave goods included stone tools and pottery, and cattle killed for the burial rite.

Late Neolithic Portuguese burial sites indicate that children were treated much like adults, and the proportion of children (averaging around 30%) is close to what we would expect from children's deaths, although infant burials are rarely found.[20]

In a group of burials at the Ertebølle culture site of Strøby Egede in the Netherlands, infants and children were buried with adults, and one buried infant was described as being cradled by a male adult.[21] Red ochre was sprinkled on the bodies, with the greatest amount placed on the children.

Neolithic chambered tombs at Bury in northern France show changes in burial patterns. In the earliest phase, from later 4th millennium BC, infants under 1 year are missing, presumably because they were buried or disposed of elsewhere. Children were buried in the same places as adults and there were significant numbers of children in the estimated age range of 5–9 years. Skulls of adults (but not those of children) were removed after the bodies had decomposed. In the early 3rd millennium settlement of the area, young children are missing from the main burial sites.[22]

New work on the British site of Stonehenge has reanalysed the Neolithic cremations there, dated 3000–2500 BC. Most were of adults rather than children: a minimum of 22 adults and five children from Aubrey Hole 7, supporting the interpretation that this was a place of particular ritual significance rather than the routine burial ground of a community.[23]

The body of a child drowned – and perhaps deliberately drowned – in a well at the Swedish site of Lindängelund was discussed in Chapter 8. It serves as a reminder of the complexity and range of approaches to death of children in the long and varied Neolithic of Europe and the Middle East.

COPPER AND BRONZE AGES OF THE MIDDLE EAST AND EUROPE

The spread of metalworking for tools and weapons was a gradual one. Initially items were manufactured from copper without deliberate alloys, and groups with this technology are described as as Copper Age, or Chalcolithic, or Aeneolithic. Copper use can be found in parts of the Middle East and the Balkans through the 5th millennium BC, and spread west into many parts of Europe. The use of alloys to create a stronger material, bronze, emerged in the Middle East early in the 4th millennium BC, giving the name to Bronze Age cultures, and in parts of Western Europe the Bronze Age can be seen as the direct successor to the Neolithic. It was marked not just by new technologies but by new social patterns. The Bronze Age of Europe and the Middle East is represented by a wide range of societies until the gradual transformations of the Iron Age in the late 2nd millennium to mid-1st millennium BC. Within this period we see a diversity of approaches to death, and specifically to the death of children.

In the Middle East and east Mediterranean the emergence of urban civilisations with specialised crafts, large concentrated population settlements, kingships and written records were the most dramatic changes in the Bronze Age, creating societies whose practices are outside of the scope of this study of the prehistoric world.

Burials of children within pots, first seen in the Neolithic, continued in the Middle East and are found at sites spread through Iran, Iraq and Syria, into the first half of the 4th millennium BC. Most pot burials of infants in Southwest Asia lack associated grave goods. An unusual find was the burial of a 1-year-old child at Tell Hazna in Mesopotamian Syria, where the body was accompanied by a clay cup, stone vessel and decorative beads.[24] But otherwise infants were commonly buried without possessions or decoration, and within the domestic area. Such a pattern for infant burials, most commonly under floors, continued through into historic periods.[25]

Pot burials of Chalcolithic and Early Bronze Age date at Kenan Tepe in Turkey contained young children, and these were associated with grave goods, which suggests provisioning for an afterlife.[26] One infant aged less than 1 year was buried under a house floor with stone and shell beads and a grinding stone. The Anatolian Early Bronze Age site of Titriş Höyük, mentioned in Chapter 8, gives a contrasting image of children's death as part of a massacre.

Finds at the site of Peqi'in in Israel are very different from the burial pattern of infants near settlements.[27] Here, in a cave, was the Chalcolithic reburial of over 450 individuals: adults, older children, but no children under 5 years. The bodies of these individuals had initially been preserved elsewhere, and the infants of the community seem therefore to have remained in an original location, probably in the domestic homestead.

As the advanced Chalcolithic and early Bronze Age societies of Mesopotamia approached the cusp of transformation to literate civilisation, their burial practices showed substantial complexity and sophistication.[28] In the 'Ubaid period (roughly 5500–4000 BC) the village scale reflected control of cultivable land through irrigation. Communal graveyards for adults lay outside the settlement areas, but children and infants can be found buried within the domestic areas. At Tell Abu Husaini in northern Iraq, 23 graves of infants and children were found under walls and floors – all except one with the body placed inside a pottery vessel.[29] The vessels were of different types and it seems that appropriate domestic ceramics were used rather than pots specially designed for burial purposes. Another pot could be used as a covering of the first. Since every excavated house had a burial, we can suggest that it was the norm for those who did not survive their early years to be buried in their own family's homestead. A similar pattern was noted at other 'Ubaid period sites: at Tell Abada (with 125 infant burials from the excavation of the settlement site) one burial had beads and another was accompanied by a 'figurine' of a female human, assigned a ritual function by archaeologists – though in other contexts it might have been classified as a doll.[30]

At Tepe Gawra in north-west Iraq were some 217 pottery burials, mainly of children, and grave goods with these were less common: they include bead necklaces, a clay pipe or whistle and additional pots.[31] Over time, more elaborate burials developed, including the use of cists and stone construction and some very lavish items are found with child burials of the late 5th to early 4th millennia BC.[32]

Where we see richer burials of children, or burials in the richest areas of a settlement, we assume they reflect increasing social hierarchies. An alternative interpretation would see the deposition of valuable items with the bodies of the young inside the domestic homestead as a ritual intended to ensure future wealth. Such links between the mortuary rites of infants and the economic imperatives of a society are hard to prove. With no suggestion of infanticide, the model in which family loss was turned into anticipated gain invites further debate.

Overall, unlike the Middle East, the Caucasus region to the north did not see the burial of children in pots in the Chalcolithic.[33] In Godedzor in Armenia, a child aged about 5 years was buried in a pit and covered in broken potsherds. Also in Armenia, the Early Bronze Age site of Kalavan contained a child burial with a necklace, described in Chapter 5.[34]

Barrows in the River Manych area of Russia, east of the Black Sea, have provided a large sample of burials from Middle Bronze Age society of the late 3rd millennium BC.[35] Children are under-represented, and young infants are even rarer, but the sites still provided a sample of 100 burials of children and adolescents. Infants and younger children were generally not buried on their own but were found within a barrow of an adult burial, with pottery vessels and incense cups. A minority of adult and child remains were in collective burials which archaeologists consider simultaneous burials from simultaneous deaths. If correct, this would support the possibility that children were sacrificed to accompany an adult in death.

In an unusual Bronze Age burial near Lake Itkul in Russia, an infant lay in a birch bark cradle with small figurines and a cap with copper plaques.[36] A pot was placed to the side of the child.

Bronze Age infant from Lake Itkul, Russia, buried with figurines and a cap with copper decoration

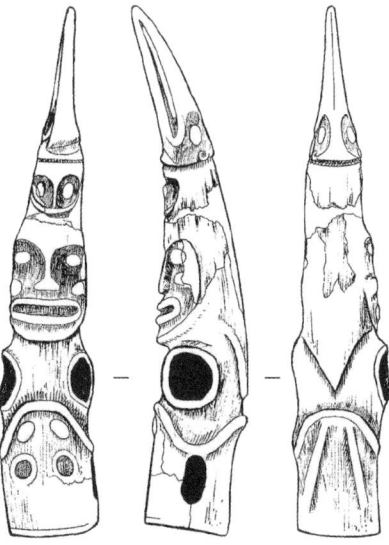

Figurines with the Bronze Age infant from Lake Itkul

At the Bulgarian Chalcolithic site of Varna on the Black Sea, a cemetery of the 5th millennium BC had almost 300 burials of adults, in simple rectangular pits, and the grave goods here implied a heavily stratified society with an elite group of adults.[37] An infant burial included a decorative necklace and bracelets and clay pots.

The Bulgarian site of Durankulak had many Chalcolithic burials, and grave goods accompanied those of children as well as adults.[38] A cattle skull was buried with one child at the site. The main deposits, though, were flint artefacts buried with the newborns and infants: almost half the infant burials had grave goods, ranging from decorative items and food containers to stone artefacts (present with older children but not with the youngest).

In the Early Bronze Age of Bulgaria, infant burials are found with settlements, both in jars beneath house floors and in pits.[39] The pots are not of designs specific to burials: domestic style pots were chosen according to size.

At Mokrin in Serbia, near the border with Romania, an Early Bronze Age cemetery, burials of children included items associated more with adult life.[40]

The Aegean was, of course, one of the areas with early civilisation emerging from prehistory in the local Bronze Age: the Minoan of Crete and the Mycenaean of the mainland. Children's burials in the Early Bronze Age of the Aegean can contain grave goods, including personal ornamentation and occasional miniature items.[41] Some of the burials are indeed quite rich in their contents, suggesting the importance of family status and wealth in society, while others are buried with few items or none.

As the Bronze Age developed in the Aegean region, signs of high infant mortality appear.[42] Infant deaths could be marked by burial in cloth or baskets or wooden boxes, or in pots; and in dug pits or stone cists or even a brick enclosure. More than one infant might be buried together. These infant burials were typically within the domestic space, not in an external adult cemetery. Despite not reaching the social status assigned to older children, after their early death they remained physically close to the family that had lost them.

In Hungary, at the Copper Age site of Tiszapolgár-Basatanya, a child of 5 or 6 years (presumed to be a girl) was buried in the community burial ground in a fashion similar to that for adult women.[43] A group of pottery vessels – which may have contained food offerings – accompanied her. Elaborate clothing and decoration included copper arm bangles, a necklace of limestone beads and strings of beads around her hips and from her waist: perhaps items that had been fastened on to her clothes.

At the same site, boys were buried after the fashion of adult males (men were flexed on their right side, women on their left), and had grave goods similar in type (though not in quantity) to those of adults.[44] But generally children, and especially infants, are under-represented in the site.

A large cemetery at Branč in Slovakia lacked newborn burials but did include many older infants and young children.[45] Miniature pots were buried with the young, and the distribution of grave goods showed the variation in family wealth and status.

In the Bronze Age of central Italy, children have been found buried in the same caves used for burying adults, and include a child at the feet of two adults under a rock cairn.[46] Bones were typically disarticulated: in other words, the skeletons had been reburied after removal from an initial site of conservation, evidence for a ritual approach to the dead. By the Later Bronze Age, cremation was common, with the burnt remains deposited in an urn. In both burials and cremations, children were sometimes accompanied by grave goods: pottery vessels – some of these of small size – and a bronze fibula (or brooch pin) suggesting a fastening for clothing. At Le Caprine in Italy an infant younger than 2 years was buried with a miniature knife, glass beads, combs of ivory and bone, weaving equipment, small pots and two stylised birds in a small urn.[47] Here, as in the subsequent Early Iron Age, items buried with young children reflect domestic activities they could not yet be involved with. But the decorative element with these Iron Age graves – fibulae, rings, bracelets, pendants and necklaces – reflect a care for a child in a technologically advanced social setting.

In a group of 32 Early Bronze Age burials at Peñalosa in south-east Spain, a third of the bodies were of children of 6 years or less.[48] Graves were created from stone slabs. Items buried with the young included pots and the items of personal decoration mentioned in Chapter 5.

Further to the west in Spain, in the Jarama and Henares valleys, there is enough evidence to show change through time in the burial of infants in the Chalcolithic and Bronze Ages.[49] Initially, young infants were absent from the main burials (in earth barrows and also in caves), but children over 1 year old had the same burial practices as adults, sharing in collective burial spaces. Subsequent patterns show children over six months (though not the youngest) buried with adults as a common feature of the collective burials. Then in the Bronze Age even the youngest infants received burials similar to those of older children, including grave goods. One notable feature is the burial of some of the children with dogs; at the site of Caserio de Perales two children aged 5 and 9 were buried together with a dog at their feet, while at Camino de las Yeseras a 2-year-old child had both a dog and a raven in the grave.[50] This anticipates the feature of dogs found in later European child burials.

An unusual find from a Bronze Age site in south-east Spain, at the site of El Cerro de las Viñas de Coy, was a woman who died in childbirth, with the foetus in position.[51] The attitude of the foetal bones shows that the foetus was in a transverse position with an arm extended, thus preventing its birth.

While it has been suggested that collective burial represents the mausoleum of a single family, this need not necessarily be so. Examination of the genetic make-up of skeletons of five children and three adults in a Bronze Age cave site near the Pyrenees suggested they were not closely related.[52]

Bronze Age burials in Scandinavia and Northern Europe show a detailed pattern of differentiation by family status, sex and age.[53] Burial treatment of young people aged 14–15 (such as those in mounds in Scania, Sweden) suggests they may already have been considered adults by this age.[54] Oak coffins were provided for children's burials as they were for adults, surrounded by packed stones; in other cases there was simple burial of a body, typically in crouched position, or a body was buried in a leather bag. The bronze grave goods found in both children's and adult graves reflect family wealth rather than age at death. Burials of infants are rarely found in the region; indeed, burial practices imply that children in the Middle Bronze Age were not regarded as established members of society until about the age of 5 years.[55]

A remarkably well preserved body of a girl of 16–18 in an oak coffin at Egtved in Denmark, from the Bronze Age of the 14th century BC, was buried with woollen clothing and blanket and a belt with a large bronze disc (see p. 113).[56] The cremated remains of a girl of 5 or 6 years, together with a bronze awl and hair net, were placed in a box at her head. Isotopic studies showed that she had travelled widely during her short life.

In the Bronze Age of Britain, identified burials of children are scarce, at least compared with the adult burials attested by frequent earth barrow mounds.[57] Although children's bodies were positioned like those of adults, the grave goods which accompanied them were very limited: pots were smaller or of poorer quality than those buried with adults.

There were changes to customs over time.[58] Initially, British Bronze Age burials of infants or very young children were not far from the burials of adults: almost as if the deceased child was presented as part of the funeral offering accompanying an adult (which is not to suggest they had other than a natural death). But the few bodies found of children over the age of about four were separate burials, laid out much as adult graves.

The Early Bronze Age ring ditches at Milton Keynes in England contained the interred bodies of women and infants, rather than of older children and adult males, and burials of males separate from women or children have been noted elsewhere in the Bronze Age.[59]

In the British Middle Bronze Age of Dorset, two-thirds of a sample of excavated barrows included remains of children (including many newborn infants) and these made up nearly 40% of all bodies. Associated with these burials were diverse grave goods: pottery vessels containing food and drink (even for the youngest infants, which suggests a symbolic role beyond that of providing food for an afterlife). Rarer were tools of flint or bronze, which were found with older children: perhaps by the age of 12 or 13 they were already considered adults. By the final Bronze Age of the region, child burials are again rare and infants rarer still.

A study of 93 Bronze Age children's burials in south-east England, often within barrows and associated with adult burials, showed both inhumation and cremation practices for older children.[60] Newborn and infants were not cremated. The main grave goods associated with children in this sample were pots. At Hove, a child aged between 4 and 6 years was buried with a deer antler, and an infant at Alfriston was buried with snail and limpet shells. Pebbles found in graves may have been amulets and flint tools occasionally accompanied the burials.

An exceptional Bronze Age find was the burial of a young child (under 9 years of age) at Doune in Perthshire, Scotland: the grave goods included both a miniature battle axe and a small pottery vessel, while a miniature mace head came from another grave at the same site. Small adult items are found in other child burials, while more pacific 'toys' are not.

IRON AGE EUROPE

When the civilisations of the Mediterranean impacted on the farming communities of Central, Southern and Western Europe, as traders or invaders, they were dealing with Iron Age societies: communities whose material culture had changed with the spread of a new technology from the Middle East after 1200 BC. Social and political structures had developed and changed too, when expanding Roman imperial ambitions encountered 'barbarian' chiefdoms they described with names whose familiarity continues today. To the north, beyond the reach of the Roman Empire, the prehistoric Iron Age can be said to have continued into the 1st millennium AD. But whereas children are buried with adults in parts of the European Bronze Age, some subsequent Iron Age community cemeteries have relatively few children's graves, suggesting they were buried elsewhere. European Iron Age infant burials have been found associated with foundations of buildings, a practice seen at later Roman sites.[61] With a wide variety of cultural and social patterns in the Iron Age, very different patterns can be found in the treatment of deceased children.

In the Mediterranean region, Iron Age societies reflected contact with advanced trade and urban networks. In the Villanovan cemeteries of central Italy, which preceded the emergence of the Etruscans, children's graves can be found within the settlement areas as well as in the large communal burial fields. A common pattern was cremation and deposition of the remains in an urn covered by another pot, together with grave goods.[62] Children followed this adult pattern but infants aged under 1 year are rare or absent. Children and adults have also been found buried in stone or wooden sarcophagi, and in grave pits, though children were sometimes buried with others of similar age. The differences in grave goods appears to be not between young and old, or men and women, but between rich and poor. After the emergence of Etruscan urban life, there were separate cemetery areas for the newborn and probably also for young children.[63]

One unusual skeleton was at Tarquinia-Pian di Civita in Italy, dated to the end of the 9th century BC.[64] A child aged 7 or 8 years (described as male) lay with a bronze pin on his chest and with a bronze pendant. Analysis of his remains indicated that he suffered from epilepsy and encephalopathy, perhaps even albinism, which suggests that he may have been marked out as symbolically important in his society.

Other child burials and remains of young infants have been found under settlement walls and have been interpreted as sacrifices, a judgement which may be valid but which is hard to prove. Classical sources drew attention to the Carthaginian sacrifice of infants, a practice for which archaeological work has yet to produce confirmation.[65]

In the Iron Age of Central Europe, infants are rare in cemeteries but can be found buried within the settlement areas themselves.[66] A group of skeletons of newborn babies from the Austrian Iron Age site of Ramsautal was found within and alongside dwellings, which were constructed of wooden beams and clay floors. The burial locations were not just random disposals, but at boundary positions: at the wall edge or in a ditch separating a building from the outside. Such a pattern is widespread across Iron Age Europe: infants buried specifically in a boundary location. This could imply a deliberate and symbolic parallel between physical boundaries of earth and the boundary between life and death.[67] But it could also be interpreted as a wish to keep dead children within the family in which they had failed to establish themselves; or just a convenient and emotionally acceptable means to deal with a body which did not merit the full ceremonial of a social funeral.

The Bettelbühl burial site in the Hallstatt Iron Age of southern Germany held an impressive deposit of a richly decorated adult female burial and an infant aged between 2 and 4 years, with similar rich jewellery.[68] Like other Hallstatt child burials, these elite items did not appear to be designed specifically for a child, but symbolised the wealth and status of the family.

A much later Iron Age (so-called despite the paucity of iron) was the Wielbark culture of Eastern Europe, dated the 1st to 4th centuries AD. Burial traditions here included both inhumation and cremation in urns or pits.[69] In a cemetery of 5000 burials at Kowalewko in Poland some 22% were of children. In one case the remains of a cremated child were placed with the inhumation of an adult, suggesting a family association. Grave goods

Bronze fibulae and pendants from an Iron Age child's burial at Bettelbühl, Germany

were common with children: Wielbark child burials include lavish items of clothing and personal decoration (as mentioned in Chapter 5), combs, pots, spindles and other items, and even in two cases caskets buried with what were assumed to be girls.

A site at Bredsätra in Swedish Öland had a cairn with numerous children buried together, while mass graves for infants have also been found at Gotland in west Sweden.[70] If some children had individual graves and others were in mass graves, was this a question of social status (and parental wealth) in definitively hierarchical societies?

Infant burials in the British Iron Age involved both specially dug graves or pits and ditches dug for other purposes.[71] At Poundbury, infants were buried together away from the graves of other members of the community and generally in a crouched position. Deposits with the infant burials were rare, a newborn calf being one such find. A Later Iron Age burial next to an adult and under a limestone slab found in Bath, England, was that of a 2-year-old showing signs of inflammatory illness.[72]

With the end of the indigenous Iron Age, under late Roman occupation British infants and very young children could be found in the same cemeteries as adults. But once the Romans had withdrawn from Britain in the 5th century AD, and the pattern of urban life supported by the trade of agricultural surpluses ended, infants disappeared from common burial grounds, perhaps returning to the marginal role they had played in pre-Roman society.[73]

Different treatments of the dead raise questions about other Iron Age practices. The Iron Age site of Wandlebury near Cambridge, England, contained a pit in which a 6-year-old child had been buried in a sack after the child's legs had been removed at the time of death.[74] At the site of Hornish Point in Scotland's South Uist, the butchered body of a 12-year-old was buried with sheep and calves.[75] Were these the victims of sacrifice, reflecting Classical authors' descriptions and denunciations of barbarian practices often deemed propagandist exaggerations? An alternative explanation could be a practice of the exposure of the dead before selective deposition.

AFRICAN FARMERS

The largest sample of archaeological work on Old World prehistoric farming communities, and therefore our best evidence for the range of practices in the treatment of childhood deaths, is that from Europe and the Middle East. But the ever-growing corpus of knowledge from work on the agriculturalist prehistory of Africa, Asia and the Pacific region is providing new data and new opportunities for study of prehistoric children and childhood.

A large Neolithic cemetery excavation of about 200 bodies at site R12 in the Upper Dongola Reach of Sudan, dated to the early 5th millennium BC, included an unusually high proportion of burials of the young: children and adolescents more than infants, who comprised only five of 47 identified juveniles.[76] The excavators suggested this implied the strong health of infants, but it seems more likely that some infant deaths were not marked by inclusion in the general cemetery.

The formal nature of such burials indicates the value of the children, but the value of the items buried with some of the children serves to demonstrate the relative status of their families within the community. Thus their family's wealth trumped their relative age when grave goods were assigned. Adult males, adult females and children were present in similar numbers and no area had been set aside specifically for the young. In addition to plentiful beaded jewellery (mentioned in Chapter 5), the more lavish burials included items more symbolic of adult wealth than juvenile practicality: tools and weapons. The burial of a 2-year-old child (grave 142) contained stone axes, a pumice macehead, granite and ceramic pots, parts of six cattle skulls, and decoration with stone beads and iron bracelets.

In the Sudanese Neolithic site of Kadero, also from the 5th millennium BC, a small number of adults and children were found buried together.[77] Children were adorned with carnelian bead necklaces and nose studs and had pottery grave goods. The variation in the quality of the materials with the dead at this site seemed to reflect not age but family wealth and status.

The predynastic Egyptian communities before the rise of literate Pharaonic civilisation typically buried their dead unmummified in burial grounds beyond the cultivable land. Remains of stillborn babies have been found within settlements and sometimes older children are found buried inside large pots in the settlement areas. The proportions of children in cemeteries vary; 51 children and 198 adults were identified at Gerza, where a grouping of infants and small children was in the middle of the cemetery.[78]

Although many excavations of predynastic cemeteries took place before the development of modern scientific method, new discoveries allow new approaches. At Adaima in Upper Egypt there were undisturbed burials of children, many within pots (burials of 388 children were recovered) and some had quite lavish personal decoration (see p. 115), as well as pots and other grave goods.[79] Examination of a child aged 4 or 5 years from Adaima, dated round 3200 BC, at the start of urban settlement, showed clear signs of tuberculosis, but with no sign of malnutrition.[80] The Egyptian tradition of burial in pots is one that would continue alongside mummification throughout the period of pharaonic Egypt, for both children and adults.[81]

The remains of prehistoric animal herders in the Sahara are dispersed or in small groups, as one would expect from nomadic communities.[82] One rock shelter, Takarkori in Libya, held only bodies of women and children, who appear from the close similarity of the strontium isotope analysis of their remains to be a close kinship group. Elsewhere there seems to be no distinction between the burial treatment of adults, children and even infants, and grave goods are scarce.

In Africa outside of the Nile Valley, despite the substantial growth of archaeological research, there is still relatively little detailed analysis of burials in prehistoric agricultural societies.[83] Sometimes (but not always) this reflects the sensitivity of local communities to the unearthing of any deceased whom they may consider ancestors.

Children may be found buried in the same cemetery areas as adults. At Namoratunga in north-west Kenya, children and women were both present but under-represented in an area of burials (without grave goods) marked by tall stone slabs outside and inside the graves, and by the presence of rock engravings.[84] These remains appear to be from a group of herders of the late 1st millennium BC.

In sites in north-eastern Nigeria, infant burials were found at Daima (one with iron decorative rings and a quartz bead), and a pot burial of an infant at Gilgil had bronze pendants and carnelian beads: all surprising accompaniments for such young children.[85]

The burial of a child around 7 years old was found in the Cameroon Early Iron Age (early 1st millennium AD) site of Mouanko-Lobethal. The child had been buried with iron rings, which appeared to be decorations for arm, leg and neck.[86]

Interesting information on children comes from work by Pierre de Maret, on the Iron Age of the Upemba Depression in south-east Democratic Republic of Congo. Children were buried with the leg bones of antelope or domestic goats, interpreted as the body parts of dolls, or at least 'figurines' (see p. 170).[87] Over half the burials excavated in the region are of children, whose graves are broadly similar to those of adults. Grave goods included miniature pots: some such miniatures were in adult graves, but generally the younger the children, the greater was the proportion of pots that were miniatures. A miniature iron axe and miniature spearheads were found with an infant.

Further south, older children can also be found in the same burial locations as adults, commonly in unlined pits. In the late 1st millennium AD at settlements of the Limpopo valley, children's burials were accompanied by grave goods: pots, copper bracelets, cowrie shells and beads, even stone artefacts and in one case animal bones, though not the valuable items associated with some elite adults.[88]

Within the agricultural societies of Central and Southern Africa (the 'Iron Age' of the last two millennia) burials of deceased or stillborn infants within pots resemble a similar process noted above from Europe and the Middle East.[89] Such burials may be in or near the domestic homestead or close to a river. Older children are found buried in the ground accompanied by domestic pottery as grave goods. The practice of infant pot burials continued into recent times, with strict rules on the treatment of infant death. Some modern communities show a tradition in which the naming of children is delayed for some time after birth, by when they have shown they have the strength to survive. There are records which show that deformed babies, breech-born infants and twins could be the subject of infanticide, sometimes by drowning in a vessel. Use of a pot to bury a deceased infant was seen in recent communities as essential to restoring the role and fertility of the mother, perhaps reflecting a symbolic link between the vessel and the uterus. However, we should not assume that all prehistoric pot burials in other parts of the world imply such an interpretation.

OTHER REGIONS

While Southwest Asia was a source of urban literate civilisations of the Bronze Age, regions of Central, Southern, Southeast and East Asia maintained their own trajectories, whether influenced by trade that linked them to Southwest Asia, developing their own civilisations, or retaining an extended period of farming economies that fall within the cultural definition of prehistory. The archaeology of these diverse groups provides further examples of the treatment of children in death.

In the Bronze Age of the Trans-Urals of Asiatic Russia, children were buried in the same cemeteries as adults but young children, and especially infants, were also buried within villages.[90] The settlement burials were at the entrance of houses, in one case near a well within a dwelling and even inside a well (which suggests a drowning rather than a deliberate disposal). The houses continued in use after the burial of the lost child. Older children, typically interred in the communal burial mounds, had grave goods dominated by pottery.[91] Also present even with young children were tools and weapons: an 8-year-old had a set of arrowheads. Items of personal decoration were common and knuckle bones (astragali) probably represented gaming pieces.

Some remarkable burials in the Andronovo Bronze Age of Siberia include adult couples buried together – holding each other in death as if in life – and children buried with adults.[92] These are not sequential burials in a common site, but simultaneous burials in a carefully crafted grave pit. Was one killed to accompany the other into an afterlife, or both sacrificed in a common ritual? Metal and other grave goods accompany the burials, which suggests they were not sacrificed 'outsiders'.

The 'Scythian' Iron Age groups of Siberia were semi-nomadic herders with a sophisticated craft technology. Burials were typically in large earth mounds (kurgans) on high river terraces, each containing a number of bodies, and high-status families could fashion high-status burials marked by rich and lavish grave goods, with jewellery, ceramics and weapons rather than tools.[93] Children were buried with adults, within wooden coffins and with their own grave goods. At Strizhevo a child aged 6 or 7 years was buried within a boat, itself placed in a pit covered by a wooden roof.[94] The child's grave goods included a bronze mirror, a gold earring, beads of stone and glass, and a spindle whorl. Grave goods in other children's graves were not so lavish, and young children's burials lacked items associated with adult life. For children younger than 4 or 5 years, burials are simpler, but are still found within the kurgans.

At a site called Log House II.8 in south Siberia, from the 3rd to 2nd centuries BC, a child of 6 or 7 years was buried with a leather bag whose contents included three gold plates, gold earrings, a knife, an awl and a mirror of bronze, an iron pin and vessels of wood and clay.[95] By now we are dealing with a community on the margins of a world of civilised states.

Mehrgarh in Pakistan is the location of a Chalcolithic community of the 5th to 4th millennia.[96] In a sample of 99 burials from the site, 26 were of juveniles, most of whom (like adult males but unlike adult females) were buried without grave goods. Only eight burials were of infants and children under 5 years, which indicates a socially determined selection for the burial practice. Such separation by age continued: a burial area dated 1000 years later was specifically for infants and the very young.[97] There is room for far more study of prehistoric South Asian burial practices and the information that can be derived from skeletal materials.[98]

Evidence comes from Southeast Asia for children in early agricultural societies being treated in death as full members of society. The majority of children of all ages at the Vietnamese late Neolithic site of Man Bac had grave goods, most commonly pots but occasionally stone or bone tools and rarely shells or beads.[99] Children, including young infants, represented more than half the burials, suggesting both a high juvenile and very high infant death rate, with a broadly uniform treatment of the dead. The poor health of the children showed up in an examination of the skeletons. Serious caries affected the teeth of three of six children of 3 years of age or less at Man Bac and five of 22 children of that age at three other sites.[100] Bony lesions to the skull (cribra orbitalia) were common, affecting half the children at Man Bac, and similarly large proportions at other Vietnamese sites. Such a frequency can indicate poor diet, leading to anaemia, scurvy or other health issues.[101]

A high level of stillbirths and infant deaths is apparent at some other Southeast Asian prehistoric sites.[102] This could reflect medical or dietary issues; an alternative explanation might be infanticide, but this seems unlikely given the burial ritual associated with the deaths. The concentration of such burials indicates a different pattern from that applied to older children and adults; moreover, it is unusual for stillborn babies to be given the same treatment as very young infants who died.

At Khok Phanom Di in Thailand, two burials of newborns with women suggest deaths during childbirth. Burial traditions in later prehistoric Thailand include infant burial in pottery jars, while older children's burials can have lavish grave goods like those of elite adults.[103]

In Iron Age Myanmar, infants under 2 years of age were buried in pottery jars, sometimes associated with additional jars.[104] An alternative form of burial used for infants and some children was a wooden coffin in which the body was placed, wrapped in a mat. Grave goods for children included pots, shells, animal bones and beads of stone, glass or bone, but not tools or weapons as found in adult graves. Elsewhere in Southeast Asia such items can be found: in Vietnam a baby had a bronze dagger and a 4-year-old had a bronze axe and small sword.[105]

A burial ground from the Iron Age site of Phum Snay in Cambodia contained bodies of men, women and children.[106] An infant had ivory bangles on the arms, bronze anklets on the legs, glass beads and broken pots: grave goods in the same range as those found with adults.

An unusual find from Taiwan was announced in the media in April 2016.[107] This came from the earliest period of Taiwan's prehistory, that of agriculturalists who had crossed from mainland Asia. The find in the Taichung area, dated to 4800 BC, was a grave containing the burial of a woman who had the body of a child (50 cm or 20 inches tall) cradled in her arms.

The prehistoric societies in Japan show different a pattern of differential burial according to age at death.[108] In Chapter 9 the patterns of jar burials and other types of disposal of the dead in the Jomon period of Japan were noted. In the subsequent Yayoi era of metal working rice farmers (ca. 5th century BC to 3rd century AD), burials involved a range of practices and regional variations: in pits, wooden coffins, stone cists, pottery jars, stone-lined chambers, earth mounds and raised tombstones.[109] At the site of Itazuke probable infants and very young children were buried between settlement ditches away from the adult cemetery, and at Yoshitake Takagi pot burials were near adult burials. Otherwise, where they are found, they are mixed with the adults, as seen at the formal cemetery of Nagaoka, where many pot burials of infants and children were inserted into recent graves of adults, and made up half the excavated bodies.[110] Sometimes four or five infants were found with one adult. Such an approach implies a collective rather than just family engagement with burials of the young. In the Middle Yayoi period at Kuriyama, infants were no longer inserted into adult graves and were a minority of burials.

A change during the Yayoi was noted: the initial pattern of burials of young children among the adults was changed in the Middle Yayoi, where they were placed elsewhere. In Kanenokuma, 54% of 145 burials were loosely classified as 'sub-adult', of whom children aged between 2 and 6 years seem to have been the largest group.[111]

In the islands of the Pacific, archaeological and bioanthropological work is beginning to add new data to the story of childhood, in a region that was the last to be settled by humans, one of the last we can class as prehistoric, in the sense of traditional non-literate societies. In Tonga, a study was made of the remains of young children from 'Atele dating from the era preceding first European contact (1500–1800 AD). The children's ages ranged from 6 months to 3 years. Infection and poor nutrition had affected the dentition.[112] Lesions on the crania and limbs suggest a similar combination of infant infection and either poor early childhood nutrition or infection causing poor food absorption, leading to scurvy, alongside possibly toxic levels of vitamin A.

The thematic chapters earlier in this book have drawn data from the rich record of prehistoric agricultural societies of the Americas, before these evolved into advanced urban civilisations or encountered the impact of European colonialism. Many of the same themes noted in Old World prehistory can be found in the New World: the differences between infant, child and adult burials, and the wide variety of burial practices and associated grave goods in different cultures.[113] The pattern of stillborn baby and infant burials beneath the floors of still occupied rooms and older children buried with beads, necklaces and pendants under abandoned dwellings, as seen in the European Neolithic, has its echoes millennia later in the Puebloan cultures of Arizona, where burials in mounds away from the living area were specifically for adults.[114]

Specific examples can be found in numerous field studies, while pioneering work has sought to link the distant and the more recent past in the US Southwest.[115] A detailed survey of prehistoric agriculturalists' burial practices across the Americas – North, Central and South – remains to be done. Such a survey would draw not just from recent work in archaeology and bioanthropology, but reflect and incorporate the continuities between prehistory and the present, also using oral history and written history, and the studies and perceptions of cultural anthropology.

CONCLUSIONS

The above survey indicates the broad range of burial practices in prehistoric agricultural societies of the Old World. Amid the diversity there are some themes and trends which recur in a number of different times and places. Although unusual burials and dramatic grave goods attract our attention, the majority of deaths of children would have been marked by modest rituals of deposition.

We can outline a simplified (if over-generalised) image or model of death and burial in prehistoric Old World agricultural societies. There would be a strong possibility that you would not survive into adulthood – and if you did, a near certainty that one of your siblings did not. A first requirement was surviving to a live birth: if you were stillborn your body could be discarded, unless it were deposited in a pot and buried within or near your family home. If (as was quite possible) your mother also died during childbirth, your stillborn remains might be buried with her in your community's burial ground outside of the settlement. Otherwise you had to survive the first year or so of infancy, a time of greatest risk from disease (or even malnutrition). If you died as an infant, before you established yourself as a full member of the family, then you might be buried in a pot under the floor or walls of the home or in the area of the immediate homestead.

But if you showed yourself physically strong enough to survive infancy, subsequent death as a child would be recognised more formally, as you had developed your contribution to the household and even to the family economy. Now an early death would be marked by formal burial: perhaps in a grave shared with other adults who had died; perhaps in a general community burial ground; or perhaps in a special burial area where children were all of the dead, or the majority.

At some stage in your teens – depending on your sex but also on social customs – you would be considered an adult, not yet ready to marry and raise a family (if male at least) but old enough to play a full role in the community's economic life. A death at this age would be treated much like that of an adult, though for males in their late teens or early 20s the risk of death from accident (or violence) was higher than later in life. However, if you survived your youth then you could expect a high probability of surviving to old age.

And to be buried not just in a formal burial ground but with lavish ornamentation, clothing and grave goods? Your best chance of this probably lay in being in a society that was wealthy and prosperous, and in being part of the elite of this society. If your group was of the most developed and complex type, a prehistoric community on the edge of urban civilisation with its specialised crafts and extremes of hierarchy, then being part of the wealthiest elite would help you achieve the finest of burials. Yet, despite the reconstruction of all these social trends, one underlying factor in the treatment of the death of children remains: the care and affection of the family for the member they have lost.

NOTES

1 S. Welinder, 'The cultural construction of childhood in Scandinavia 3500 BC – 1350 AD', *Current Swedish Archaeology* 6 (1998): 185–204.
2 E. Scott, *The Archaeology of Infancy and Infant Death*, British Archaeological Reports International Series 819, Oxford: Archaeopress, 1999, pp. 90 ff.
3 Lewis, *Bioarchaeology*, pp. 34–37.
4 S. Moses, 'Çatalhöyük's foundation burials: ritual child sacrifice or convenient death?' in *BRIPP*: 45–52; S. Moses, 'The children of Neolithic Çatalhöyük: burial symbolism and social metaphor', www.catalhoyuk.com:8080/archive_reports/2004/ar04_34.html
5 M. Yurdakök, ' Neonatal medicine in ancient art', *Turkish Journal of Pediatrics* 52 (2010): 218–226, p. 222; M. Yurdakok, 'Neonatal medicine in prehistoric times in Anatolia', *Journal of Clinical Neonatology* 4 (2015): 153–157.
6 F. le Mort, 'Infant burials in pre-pottery Neolithic Cyprus: evidence from Khirokitia' in *BRIPP*: 23–32.
7 M. Pomadère, 'Des morts peu faibles: les sépultures néolithiques d'immatures en Grèce' in *BRIPP*: 53–60; M. Georgiadis, 'Child burials in Mesolithic and Neolithic Southern Greece: a synthesis', *CitP* 4 (2011): 31–45.

8 Georgiadis, 'Child burials', p. 38, citing Papathanasiou.
9 Pomadère, 'Des morts peu faibles', p. 57.
10 A. Whittle, *Europe in the Neolithic*, Cambridge: Cambridge University Press, 1996, p. 96.
11 D. Bailey, *Prehistoric Figurines: representation and corporeality in the Neolithic*, Abingdon: Routledge, 2005, p. 7.
12 S. Stefanović, 'Late Neolithic boys at the Gomolova cemetery (Serbia)' in *BRIPP*: 95–99.
13 R. Kogălniceanu, 'Child burials in intramural and extramural contexts from the Neolithic and Chalcolithic of Romania' in *BRIPP*: 101–111.
14 K. Bacvarov, 'A long way to the west: earliest jar burials in Southeast Europe and the Near East' in *BRIPP*: 61–70; G. Artin, 'The jar burials of the Chalcolithic "necropolis" at Byblos' in *BRIPP*: 79–85. Some extreme interpretations are offered by E. Orrelle, 'Infant jar burials – a ritual associated with early agriculture?' in *BRIPP*: 71–78.
15 J. Orschiedt, 'Cave burials in prehistoric Central Europe' in K.A. Bergsvig & R.E. Skeates (eds), *Caves in Context: the cultural significance of caves and rockshelters in Europe*', Oxford: Oxbow, 2012: 212–224.
16 U. Veit, 'Burials within settlements of the Linienbandkeramik and Stichbandkeramik cultures of Central Europe', *Journal of European Archaeology* 1 (1993): 107–140; Whittle, *Europe in the Neolithic*, pp. 167–169; Scott, *The Archaeology of Infancy*, p. 98; P. Bickle & L. Fibiger, 'Ageing, childhood and social identity in the Early Neolithic of Central Europe', *European Journal of Archaeology* 17 (2014): 208–228.
17 Bickle & Fibiger, 'Ageing', p. 216.
18 Whittle, *Europe in the Neolithic*, p. 211, including child burials in Italian sites at Grotta Pacelli, Unang, Grotta Continenza and Remedella Di Sotto.
19 A.J. Waterman & J.T. Thomas, 'When the bough breaks: childhood mortality and burial practice in Late Neolithic Atlantic Europe', *Oxford Journal of Archaeology* 30 (2011): 165–183, pp. 166–167.
20 Waterman & Thomas, 'When the bough breaks', pp. 168ff.
21 Lewis, *Bioarchaeology*, p. 31; Whittle, *Europe in the Neolithic*, pp. 197–198.
22 L. Salanova et al., 'From one ritual to another: the long-term sequence of the Bury gallery grave (northern France, fourth–second millennia BC)', *Antiquity* 91 (2017): 57–73, pp. 61–64.
23 C. Willis et al., 'The dead of Stonehenge', *Antiquity* 90 (2016): 337–356.
24 Bacvarov, 'A long way', p. 66.
25 P.J.P. McGeorge, 'Intramural infant burials in the Aegean Bronze age', *2èmes Rencontres d'archéologie de l'IFEA: Le Mort dans la ville Pratiques, contextes et impacts des inhumations intra-muros en Anatolie, du début de l'Age du Bronze à l'époque romaine*, Istanbul: IFEA-Ege yayınları, 2011: 1–20, pp. 6ff.
26 D.E. Hopwood, 'The changing relationship between the living and the dead: child burial at the site of Kenan Tepe, Turkey' in *BRIPP*: 113–121.
27 Y. Nagar & E. Vered, 'Where are the children? Age-dependent burial practices in Peqi'in', *Israel Exploration Journal* 51 (2001): 27–35.
28 G. Brereton, 'Cultures of infancy and capital accumulation in pre-urban Mesopotamia', *World Archaeology* 45 (2013): 232–251.
29 L. Chiocchetti, 'The children's burials of the Ubaid period: Tell Abu Husaini, the Hamrin area and beyond', *Mesopotamia* 42 (2007): 117–142.

30 Chiocchetti, 'The children's burials', p. 126, citing Jasim.
31 Chiocchetti, 'The children's burials', pp. 133 ff.
32 Brereton, 'Cultures of infancy', p. 244.
33 M. Poulmarc'h & F. Le Mort, 'Diversification of the funerary practices in the southern Caucasus from the Neolithic to the Chalcolithic', *Quaternary International* 395 (2016): 184–193.
34 M. Poulmarc'h et al., 'Dog molars as personal ornaments in a Kura-Araxes child burial (Kalavan-1, Armenia)', *Antiquity* 90 (2016): 953–972.
35 M.V. Andreeva, 'Pre-adult and adult burials of East Manych catacomb culture' in *BRIPP:* 149–160.
36 A.V. Polyakov & Y.N. Esin, 'Horn figurines from an Okunev burial on Lake Itkul, Khakassia, southern Siberia', *Archaeology, Ethnology and Anthropology of Eurasia* 43 (2015): 43–57; www.livescience.com/53167-rattles-found-in-prehistoric-infant-grave.html
37 Whittle, *Europe in the Neolithic*, pp. 96–97; T. Higham et al., 'New perspectives on the Varna cemetery (Bulgaria) – AMS dates and social implications', *Antiquity* 81 (2007): 640–654.
38 Y. Boyadžiev & M. Gurova, 'Mobilier funeraire de nouveau-nés et d'enfants: cas d'étude de la Bulgarie' in *BRIPP*: 87–94.
39 T. Mishina, 'A social aspect of intramural burials' analysis: the case of EBA Tell Yunatsite, Bulgaria' in *BRIPP*: 137–146.
40 E. Rega, 'Age, gender and biological reality in the Early Bronze Age cemetery at Mokrin' in *IPP*: 229–247.
41 C. Marangou, 'Social differentiation in the Early Bronze Age: miniature tools and child burials', *Journal of Mediterranean Studies* 1 (1991): 211–225.
42 McGeorge, 'Intramural infant burials', p. 2.
43 Whittle, *Europe in the Neolithic*, pp. 72–73; Scott, *Archaeology of Infancy*, p. 99.
44 J. Sofaer Derevenski, 'Age and gender at the site of Tiszapolgár-Basatanya, Hungary', *Antiquity* 71 (1997): 875–875.
45 S. Shennan, 'The social organization at Brančc', *Antiquity* 49 (1975): 279–288; Scott, *Archaeology of Infancy*, pp. 103–5.
46 E. van Rossenberg, 'Infant/child burials and social reproduction in the Bronze Age and Early Iron Age (c. 2100–800 B.C.) of bentral Italy' in *BRIPP*: 161–173.
47 Van Rossenberg, 'Infant/child burials', p. 165, citing Damiani et al.
48 E. Alarcón García, 'Social relations between adulthood and childhood in the Early Bronze Age site of Peñalosa' in *CSI*: 59–74.
49 R. Aliaga Almela et al., 'Infant burials during the Copper and Bronze Ages in the Iberians Jarama River Valley' in *CSI*: 243–261.
50 Aliaga Almela et al., 'Infant burials', p. 254.
51 A. Malgosa et al., 'A dystocic childbirth in the Spanish Bronze Age', *International Journal of Osteoarchaeology* 14 (2004): 98–103.
52 M. Simón et al., 'The presence of nuclear families in prehistoric collective burials revisited: the Bronze Age burial of Montanissell Cave (Spain) in the light of aDNA', *American Journal of Physical Anthropology* 146 (2011): 406–413.
53 S. Bergerbrant, *Bronze Age Identities: costume, contact and conflict in Northern Europe 1600–1300 BC*, Stockholm: Bricoleur Press, 2007, pp. 107–117.
54 Bergerbrant, *Bronze Age Identities*, p. 108.
55 Bergerbrant, *Bronze Age Identities*, p. 114–115.

56 K.M. Frei et al., 'Tracing the dynamic life story of a Bronze Age Female', *Scientific Reports* 5 (2015): 10431: Supplementary information.
57 P. Garwood, 'Vital resources, ideal images and virtual lives: children in Early Bronze Age funerary ritual' in *CCS*: 63–82.
58 Garwood, 'Vital resources', pp. 69–71.
59 Scott, *Archaeology of Infancy*, p. 92, citing H.S. Green.
60 D. McLaren, 'Where have all the flowers gone? Bronze Age children's burials in South East England: initial thoughts' in *RLA*: 85–99.
61 M.E. Lewis, *Bioarchaeology*, p. 91–92; D.J. Watts, 'Infant burials and Romano-British Christianity', *Archaeological Journal* 146 (1989): 37–83.
62 K. Hladíková, 'Perception of children in Villanovan period in southern Etruria' in *CCLA*: 41–74.
63 M.J. Becker, 'Etruscan infants: children's cemeteries at Tarquinia, Italy, as indicators of an age of transition' in *RLA*: 24–36, pp. 28–29.
64 Hladíková, 'Perception of children', pp. 60–61, citing Bonghi Jovino.
65 P. Xella et al., 'Phoenician bones of contention', *Antiquity* 87 (2013): 1–9; J.H. Schwartz et al., 'Skeletal remains from Punic Carthage do not support systematic sacrifice of infants', *PloS ONE* 5 (2010): e9177.
66 R. Karl & K. Löcker, 'Thrown out with the bathwater or properly buried? Neonate and infant skeletons in a settlement context on the Dürrnberg bei Hallein, Austria' in *RLA:* 37–46.
67 Karl and Löcker, 'Thrown out', p. 42.
68 D. Krausse et al., 'The "Keltenblock" project: discovery and excavation of a rich Hallstatt grave at the Heuneburg, Germany', *Antiquity* 91 (2017): 108–123.
69 M. Chmiel, 'Children in the Wielbark culture societies' in *CCLA*: 89–112.
70 Welinder, 'The cultural construction'.
71 B. Tibbetts, 'Infant burials in Iron Age Britain' in *BRIPP:* 189–194.
72 Lewis, *Bioarchaeology*, p. 31, citing a conference paper by M.E. Lewis & R. Gowland.
73 R. Fleming, *Britain After Rome: the fall and rise 400–1070*, London: Penguin, 2010, pp. 46–47.
74 B.R. Hartley, 'The Wandlebury Iron Age hill fort, excavations of 1955–6', *Proceedings of the Cambridge Antiquarian Society* 50 (1957): 1–28, p. 26.
75 Wiseman, *Hide and Seek*, p. 97.
76 S. Salvatori & D. Usai (eds), *A Neolithic Cemetery in the Northern Dongola Reach: excavations at Site R12*, BAR International Series 1814, Oxford: Archaeopress, 2008.
77 L. Krzyżaniak, 'Early farming in the middle Nile Basin: recent discoveries at Kadero (central Sudan)', *Antiquity* 65 (1991): 515–532.
78 K.A. Bard, 'The Egyptian predynastic: a review of the evidence', *Journal of Field Archaeology* 21 (1994): 265–288; A. Stevenson, 'Social relationships in predynastic burials', *Journal of Egyptian Archaeology* 95 (2009): 175–192, p. 184.
79 S. Duchesne et al., 'Le rôle des parures dans les cérémonies funéraires au prédynastique: l'exemple des sépultures d'enfants à Adaïma', *Bulletin de l'Institut Français d'Archéologie Orientale* 103 (2003): 133–166.
80 H. Dabernat & É. Crubézy, 'Multiple bone tuberculosis in a child from predynastic Upper Egypt (3200 BC)', *International Journal of Osteoarchaeology* 20 (2010): 719–730.

81 R.K. Power & Y. Tristant, 'From refuse to rebirth: repositioning the pot burial in the Egyptian archaeological record', *Antiquity* 90 (2016): 1474–1488.
82 M.A. Tafuri et al., 'Mobility and kinship in the prehistoric Sahara: strontium isotope analysis of Holocene human skeletons from the Acacus Mts (southwestern Libya)', *Journal of Anthropological Archaeology* 25 (2006): 390–402.
83 D.N. Edwards, 'African perspectives on death, burial, and mortuary archaeology' in L.N Stutz & S. Tarlow (eds), *The Oxford Handbook of the Archaeology of Death and Burial*, Oxford: Oxford University Press, 2013.
84 M.B. Lynch & L.H. Robbins, 'Cushitic and Nilotic prehistory: new archaeological evidence from north-west Kenya', *Journal of African History* 20 (1979): 319–328; T. Russell & P. Kiura, 'A re-consideration of the rock engravings at the burial site of Namoratung'a South, northern Kenya and their relationship to modern Turkana livestock brands', *South African Archaeological Bulletin* 66 (2011): 121–128.
85 G. Connah, 'The Daima sequence and the prehistoric chronology of the Lake Chad region of Nigeria', *Journal of African History* 17 (1976): 321–352, pp. 332, 347; G. Connah, *Three Thousand Years in Afric*a, Cambridge: Cambridge University Press, 1981, p. 151, fig. 7.3.
86 C. Meister, 'Remarks on early Iron Age burial sites from southern Cameroon', *African Archaeological Review* 27 (2010): 237–249.
87 P. de Maret, 'Tea party toys? Classical Kisalian grave goods from the Upemba (D.R. Congo)', *Journal of African Archaeology* 14 (2016): 19–32; P. de Maret, 'Bones, sex, and dolls: solving a mystery in Central Africa and beyond', *Journal of Field Archaeology* 41 (2016): 500–509.
88 M. Steyn & W.C. Nienaber, 'Iron Age human skeletal remains from the Limpopo Valley and Soutpansberg area', *South African Archaeological Society Goodwin Series* 8 (2000): 112–116.
89 Details of such pot burials and a valuable discussion of the ethnographic analogies are in J. Boeyens et al., 'From uterus to jar: the significance of an infant pot burial from Melora Saddle, an early nineteenth-century African farmer site on the Waterberg Plateau', *Southern African Humanities* 21 (2009): 213–238.
90 N.B. Vinogradov & N. A. Berseneva, 'Intramural burials of children at Bronze Age sites in the southern Urals (early 2nd millennium BC)', *Archaeology, Ethnology and Anthropology of Eurasia* 41 (2013): 59–67.
91 N. Berseneva, 'Child burials during the Middle Bronze Age of south Urals (Sintashta culture)' in L.V. Dammasnes et al., *Situating Gender in European Archaeologies*, Budapest: Archaeolingua, 2010: 161–180.
92 ancientexplorers.com/ancient-explorers/bronze-age-necropolis-unearthed-in-siberia
93 N. Berseneva, 'Women and children in the Sargat culture' in K.M. Lunduff & K.S. Rubinson (eds), *Are All Warriors Male? Gender roles on the ancient Eurasian steppe*, Lanham, MD: Altamira, 2008: 131–152; N. Berseneva, 'Archaeology of children: sub-adult burials during the Iron Age in the Trans-Urals and western Siberia' in M. Georgiadis & C. Gallou (eds) *The Archaeology of Cult and Death*, Budapest: Archaeolingua, 2006: 179–192.
94 Berseneva, 'Women and children', pp. 143–144, citing Pogodin.
95 E.M. Murphy, 'A biocultural study of children from Iron Age south Siberia' in *BRIPP:* 175–187.

96 P. Sellier, 'Hypotheses and estimators for the demographic interpretation of the Chalcolithic population from Mehrgarh, Pakistan', *East and West* 39 (1989): 11–42.
97 Sellier, 'Hypotheses', p. 25.
98 For a discussion of the problems of research priorities in the region see K.A.R. Kennedy, 'The uninvited skeleton at the archaeological table: the crisis of paleoanthropology in South Asia in the twenty-first century', *Asian Perspectives* 42 (2003): 352–367. One recent find, from the 1st millennium BC, is child in an urn containing further pottery, from near Nadapuram in Kozhikode district: www.thehindu.com/news/cities/kozhikode/Bones-of-child-found-in-megalithic-urn/article16927874.ece
99 M. Oxenham et al., 'Childhood in late Neolithic Vietnam' in *BRIPP*: 123–136; M. Oxenham et al., 'Health and the experience of childhood in Late Neolithic Viet Nam', *Asian Perspectives* 47 (2008): 190–209.
100 Oxenham, 'Childhood', p. 195.
101 Oxenham, 'Childhood', p. 201.
102 S.E. Halcrow, N.Tayles & V. Livingstone, 'Infant death in late prehistoric Southeast Asia', *Asian Perspectives* 47 (2008): 371–404.
103 J.C. White & C.O. Eyre. 'Residential burial and the Metal Age of Thailand', *Archeological Papers of the American Anthropological Association* 20 (2010): 59–78, pp. 61, 65.
104 A.-S. Coupey, 'Infant and child burials in the Samon valley, Myanmar' in J.P. Pautreau et al. (eds), *From* Homo erectus *to the Living Traditions: choice of papers from the 11th International Conference of the European Association of Southeast Asian Archaeologists*, Bougon: European Association of Southeast Asian Archaeologists, 2008: 119–125.
105 Coupey, 'Infant and child burials', p. 124.
106 D.J.W. O'Reilly, A. Von Den Driesch & V. Voeun, 'Archaeology and archaeozoology of Phum Snay: a late prehistoric cemetery in northwestern Cambodia', *Asian Perspectives* 45 (2006): 188–211.
107 www.reuters.com/article/us-taiwan-fossils-idUSKCN0XN1WI: an announcement of the find by Chu Whei-lee, a curator in the Anthropology Department at Taiwan's National Museum of Natural Science.
108 L. Giliazeau, 'La mort des tout-petits dans l'archipel Japonais durant la période Yayoi: une esquisse' in E. Portat et al. (eds), *Rencontre autour de la mort des tout-petits: actes de la 2e rencontre du groupe d'anthropologie et d'archéologie funéraire*, Saint-Germain-en-Laye, France: Gaaf, 2016: 31–37, p. 32. This draws on her University of Paris I thesis *Le rôle et l'influence du continent asiatique sur les sociétés de l'archipel japonais durant la protohistoire à travers les pratiques funéraires: du Yayoi moyen au Kofun ancient*, online at 1drv.ms/f/s!AvzBT_oW7Bi3gmez4OTgMt4LKCZc
109 Giliazeau, 'La mort', pp. 31–32.
110 K. Mizoguchi, *The Archaeology of Japan: from the earliest rice farming villages to the rise of the state*, Cambridge: Cambridge University Press, 2013, pp. 146–148; K. Mizoguchi, 'The child as a node of past, present and future' in *CMC*: 141–150.
111 Giliazeau, 'La mort', p. 35.
112 H.R. Buckley, 'Subadult health and disease in prehistoric Tonga, Polynesia', *American Journal of Physical Anthropology* 113 (2000): 481–505; R.A. Farah

et al., 'Physiological insult or the burial environment: differentiating developmental defects from post-mortem stained enamel in deciduous dentition from the Chiefdom Period of Tonga, Polynesia' (2016) online at sciencematters.io/articles/10.19185/matters.201605000005

113   E.g. N.A. Rothschild, 'Introduction' in *CPPS*: 1–13, p. 6; J.D. Bengtson & J.A. O'Gorman, 'Children, migration and mortuary representation in the Late Prehistoric Central Illinois River Valley', *CitP* 9 (2016): 19–43; J.W. Gruber, 'Patterning in death in a Late Prehistoric village in Pennsylvania', *American Antiquity* 36 (1971): 64–76.

114   S.M. Whittlesey, 'The cradle of death: mortuary practices, bioarchaeology, and the children of Grasshopper Pueblo' in *CPPS*: 152–168, p. 158; G.C. Baldwin, 'Excavations at Kinishba Pueblo, Arizona', *American Antiquity* 4 (1938): 11–21, pp. 18–19.

115   See for example contributions to *CPPS*. Work before 2001 is reviewed by B.E. Roveland, 'Archaeological approaches to the study of prehistoric children: past trends and future directions' in H.B. Schwartzman (ed.), *Children and Anthropology: perspectives for the 21st century*, Westport, CT: Bergin & Garvey, 2001: 39–56.

11
PROGRESSING
The future of childhood's deep past

This book has reviewed what we can see of children and childhood in prehistoric societies, with examples drawn from a broad range of times and places. The sources cited in the notes to each chapter show the active work that has been undertaken by many researchers, from archaeology, bioanthropology and associated fields, and data from field and laboratory studies which contribute to our understanding of prehistoric childhoods. Perspectives on children's lives (and deaths) in prehistory can provide insights for those whose interest in childhood comes from other disciplines and standpoints.

But this survey also suggests how little we still know, and how great is the potential both for new research and for new thinking across a substantial field of enquiry. Children and childhood in prehistory have remained under-represented in the literature of archaeology, as discussed in Chapter 1, even though, at the time of writing, scholars have recently celebrated 25 years since a pioneering article on the topic.[1] If archaeology deals with all of human life and society, these include birth, infancy, childhood, adolescence, the years of full adulthood and old age. Most work and narratives by convention focus only on the final two categories, though with relatively little on the last.

Conservative paradigms and narrow approaches to the scope and goals of archaeology and related disciplines have been challenged and eroded over time. The study of social processes replaced an emphasis on ethnic identities, interest in social elites expanded to cover all ranks in society and, in more recent decades, awareness and studies of women in the past consciously grew to complement and replace a male-focused tradition. If elitism and sexism have faded, ageism remains one of the frontiers still to cross. Archaeologists put time and resources into the study of topics far more obscure than the younger half of society.

As stated a few times in this narrative, if archaeology is seen as a social and humanistic science, then studying childhood is a core part of understanding past societies. Family relationships, family economies and family values (visible not least in the treatment of those who die before adulthood) are central to society. Culture and tradition, without which prehistory would just be a jumble of minor facts, are learned, transmitted and sometimes challenged during the earlier years of life. The younger half of society, and the earlier years of life when knowledge and culture are acquired, form a core element of what we can consider and investigate.

In the current stage of research and interpretation, prehistoric 'children' are still finding their place in academic work without much gender distinction. This will change. Images in rock paintings, finger daubs or footprints do not tell us the sex of a child. Assumptions have sometimes been made about the sex of a child from the associated grave goods (e.g. weapons implying a boy, weaving items implying a girl), which leads in turn to circular arguments about childhood activity. While it is difficult to distinguish between sexes when looking at the skeletons of younger children, studies of their DNA can allow sex determination. Such applications to new and existing finds will allow us to develop beyond a prehistory of children to a prehistory of boys and a prehistory of girls. We will be able to differentiate between the developmental, social and economic lives of male and female children as far as the bioarchaeological and archaeological evidence can allow, as has been done in Old World literate cultures and in studies of pre-Columbian civilisations of the Americas.[2]

The unearthing of prehistoric childhood can be kept in mind during any excavation of a settlement – whether a hunter-gatherer home base or an animal herders' camp, an early farming homestead or the advanced village of a metal-working community on the brink of urban civilisation.

We find the right answers only when we ask the right questions: questions suggested by the examples spread through this book. New research projects can include in their design and programme the presence and activities of the younger half of society, and interrogate the data to address this perspective.

In any settlement, where were the living areas of mothers and infants? Could an apparently random distribution of objects be a sign of child's play? Are individual artefacts toys or possibly part of children's games: even sticks, vegetable matter and isolated bones? Are clay and stone figures of animals and humans children's dolls or from the adult world? Are specific miniaturised items part of a ritual deposit, or designed as children's playthings or for burial with the dead? We know the children were probably about half the population, so where are they located in the archaeological record of the site?

The search for apprentice and juvenile learner craft has provided some rewarding results, as discussed in Chapter 6. If childhood is a period of

Petroglyph of a family from the Mojave desert, Nevada, USA

learning, the material remains of individual crafts can be examined for signs of trial and apprentice work. Many millions of stone artefacts have been plotted from tens of thousands of prehistoric sites, yet relatively few zones of unskilled and semi-skilled work from young learners have been recognised. These may be identified from the distribution of artefacts – places where the stone tool preparation is less skilled than the norm. The exhaustive process of refitting flakes to cores can show techniques at different levels of competence. In pottery, small finger marks and poor unfired work can bring us to the presence of children. A panel of rock painting may have small finger marks from a child participating with adults in its creation.

While the research design for new excavations and site surveys can include consideration of the 'hidden half' of society, revisiting the wealth of older research could be equally rewarding. Where artefacts have been carefully plotted, or where assemblages are available for restudy, the localised presence of children may emerge. And of course a review of finds with a fresh eye might identify toys, dolls or items from children's games that had previously been ignored or classified quite differently. Not every inexplicable item is a 'ritual object', but not every miniature item is a child's toy.

Some older excavation reports of cemeteries may have paid little attention to the burials of children, and merit revisiting. Conventional archaeological studies of burials in settlements and cemeteries remain invaluable: to show us material culture of clothing, ornamentation and other grave goods rich and poor, to demonstrate the social and family status of infants, children and adolescents, and indicate the beliefs and rituals associated with childhood death. But the collaboration of multidisciplinary teams is allowing rewarding directions for study and interpretation, with bioarchaeologists and bioanthropologists increasingly active in the study of children and in applying newer techniques to consider old and new questions.

Studies of the skeletal remains of children of different ages contribute more than demographic information. Examination of their bones for signs of disease and malnutrition is rewarding: after all, these are the bodies of those who did not survive into adulthood and we need to ask why. A prehistory of health is based on a study of those whose health failed. Signs of violence on a skeleton are more immediately obvious, but still require distinction between the results of an attack, the impacts of an accident, or a practice such as child sacrifice.

As well as providing sex identification, DNA studies can indicate whether and where biological relationships exist in a group of children and adults – studies which usefully extend back into finds of deep prehistory.

Isotope studies on skeletal remains have been used to show dietary patterns and use these for broader interpretations: the age of weaning, the regions where a person spent their childhood, the comparison of a childhood diet with an adult diet. The skills and resources of bioarchaeologists are thinly spread across remains recovered from all periods, places and ages at death, but in the study of prehistory, where we lack written records to complement our image of childhood, their contribution is especially crucial. The biological examination of children's remains needs to be interpreted and amplified in the context of archaeological and environmental studies and the taphonomic evidence of the deposits themselves, as interdisciplinary work contributes more than the sum of its parts.

This book has drawn especially on material from Europe, the Middle East and Africa, together with examples from the Americas, Asia and Oceania. In North America, the interpretation of evidence for children and childhood activities in prehistory requires linkages to the patterns seen in the ethnographic observation and historic record of Native Americans. The complex narratives in South and Central America include the development of the special roles and evidence of children in the high civilisations of the Americas, going well beyond familiar topics such as the sacrifice of children. Burials, artefacts and visual representations all offer rich resources. A full survey of children and childhood in the archaeology of the New World is overdue.

In discussing early hominin evolution we rely on the work of palaeoanthropologists, environmental scientists, archaeologists and others.

Anatomy can take us only so far. The attention now paid to parents and offspring in primate studies is bringing new insights that can inform us of aspects of our early hominin ancestors, including motherhood, infancy and the acquisition of skills; some of these have been discussed in this book.

Questions we ask about prehistoric childhood can be stimulated by accounts and discussions of ethnographic accounts: descriptions of those societies whose scale and economic basis had features parallel to some in the prehistoric world. By definition, the accounts we have were of communities who had already encountered the 'modern' world and any new field studies are of groups even more part of a global economy. Nevertheless, the debates of social/cultural anthropologists about children and childhood can feed into our discussions of prehistoric childhoods – and, indeed, the reverse is also true.

Studies of prehistoric childhood add significantly to our understanding of the development of society through the full stretch of human history. As we uncover more details of variability and change we can see contrasts to the assumptions and images we take from periods dominated by written sources: urban civilisations and the historical narratives than have dominated many ideas of childhood's past. No 'history of childhood' is complete without considering the archaeological and bioarchaeological evidence within historic periods, and the range of material from prehistoric eras.

There is a further argument for the interest and importance of studying prehistoric childhoods. As implied in David Lancy's magisterial survey *The Anthropology of Childhood*, our modern western urban models of children's lives, learning, development and roles are in marked contrast to those seen elsewhere in the world in the recent past and (by extension) in the distant past.[3] Lancy suggests that in modern western society a 'neontocracy' has replaced a 'gerontocracy', by positioning the child at the pinnacle of society.

The vast area of discussion of children by behavioural and social scientists, with applications in education, psychology and beyond, is too often circumscribed by 'presentism', an analysis restricted in time and space. Understanding the nature and variation of infancy, childhood, adolescence and the roles of the young through the long past takes us beyond these limitations, with archaeology contributing the extra dimension of time to the study of humanity. Concepts of birth and motherhood, family structures, the raising of infants, the nature of play and learning, social interactions and the roles of children in family and society are all areas of active study where presentism risks biasing and limiting scientific perspectives. Kathryn Kamp wrote in a 2001 survey article that, for archaeological interpretation, 'the most difficult task will be to cast aside our own perceptions of the meaning of childhood'.[4] If that is difficult for archaeologists it may be much for difficult for those in other social sciences.

It is not yet possible to create a survey of prehistoric childhoods as definitive as David Lancy's contribution to anthropology. But in a growing field it will be surprising if the present book is not rendered well out of date by new research in very few years' time, and that would be very welcome indeed.

In the chapters of this book I have outlined evidence for aspects of childhood across time and space in prehistory. I have indicated both the kinds of research methods that help answer questions about children in the deep past, and some of the broader framework of debate where prehistoric childhood may complement or even significantly modify assumptions in subject areas within and beyond the historical sciences.

The topic of childhood in prehistory stimulates and engages with a wide range of questions. These may be about motherhood and infant care, fertility, infanticide and family. They can address diet, health, clothing, personal decoration, apprenticeship, play, inter-group and intra-group conflict, and sacrifice. Large issues include the transformation of life stages, economic life, social status and belief systems. This survey was intended to raise questions and show potential, rather than to adopt and advocate for positions in these many important and complex debates. Different readers will see different implications when children are given a greater place in the study of the deep past, and when the deep past is included in studies and our understanding of children and childhood.

NOTES

1   *TCIN.*
2   R.A. Joyce, 'Girling the girl and boying the boy: the production of adulthood in ancient Mesoamerica', *World Archaeology* 31 (2000): 473–483.
3   Lancy, *Anthropology* 2ed.
4   K.A. Kamp, 'Where have all the children gone? The archaeology of childhood', *Journal of Archaeological Method and Theory* 8 (2001): 1–34, p. 26.

INDEX OF PLACES

Abbekås 114
Abu Hureyra 81, 87–88
Adaima 115–116, 249
Aegean *see* Greece
Africa, Central 98, 132, 160
Africa, Southern xxiv, 9, 17, 19, 20, 30n.56, 48, 62, 63, 67, 80, 82–84, 100, 133–134, 142, 160, 182, 218–219, 221–223, 250
Africa, sub-Saharan 9, 200, 249–250
Ain Mallaha 217
Ak Alakha 191
Alabama, USA 188
Alaska, USA 83, 133
Alepochori 236
Alepotrypa 236
Alfriston 245
Algeria 60
Amazon 48, 66, 133, 223
Anatolia *see* Turkey
Ancon 189
Arctic 140, 165, 183, 223
Arcy-sur-Cure 138
Arene Candide 103–105, 216
Argentina 109, 117, 183, 220
Aria 236
Arizona, USA 85, 89, 145–146, 188
Arkansas, USA 188

Armenia 112, 240
Arroyo Hondo 187
Asia, Southeast 20–21, 35–36, 200, 251–253
Aşıklı Höyük 86
Asparn Schletz 185
Atapuerca 180, 208
'Atele 253
Australia 7–8, 16, 19, 20, 58, 62, 65, 68, 83, 98–99, 118n.1, 134–135, 136, 141–142, 222–223
Austria 87, 103, 112, 185, 215, 246
Avdeevo 46

Balkans 168, 185
Barma Grande 46
Belas Knap 185
Belgium 86, 213
Bettelbühl 113, 246–247
Black Mesa 89
Borsuka 109, 215
Bossou 22, 126–127
Branč 243
Brazil 64, 160
Bredsätra 247
Britain 7, 68, 88, 90, 187, 244, 248
    see also England; Scotland; Wales
Bruniquel 129
Bulgaria 112, 162, 165, 167, 237, 242
Buret' 46, 102–103

Bury 238
Byblos 237
Byneskranskop 219
Byzantium 6

California, USA 68, 85, 164, 183
Cambodia 253
Cameroon 63, 144, 161, 250
Camino de las Yeseras 243
Canada 86, 140, 146, 163, 165, 183, 191, 220, 223
Caserio de Perales 243
Castellón Alto 187
Çatalhöyük 48–49, 56, 112, 235
Çayönü Tepesi 86, 186
Central African Republic 64
Cernavoda 237
Chauvet 58
Chen Chen 117
Chenque 109, 183, 220
Chickamauga 188
Chile 109, 117, 183, 220
China 9, 25, 34
Choga Mish 116–117
Choga Sefid 116–117
Colorado, USA 90, 187–188
Congo 20, 36, 64, 160, 169–170, 250
Cosquer 141

INDEX OF PLACES

Côte d'Ivoire 126–128, 204
Coulelerach 139
Cova Negra 212
Croatia 23, 163, 180, 212
Cromagnon 216
Crow Creek 188
Cuevas del Engarbo 7
Cyprus 117, 235
Czech Republic 81, 102, 163–164, 180, 187–188, 215

Daima 250
Danube 86, 108, 236
Dederiyeh 211
Denisova 208
Denmark 113, 139, 182, 189, 218, 244
Devnja 162
Dickson Mounds 89
Dikika 207
Dolní Věstonice 81, 102, 214–215
Dongola Reach 114–115
Doune 191, 245
Durankulak 242
Dyrholmen 182
Dzudzuana 102

Ecuador 117
Egtved 113, 244
Egypt 49–50, 60–61, 81, 88, 115–116, 214, 249
El Castillo 141
El Cerro de las Viñas de Coy 243
El Sidrón 56, 80, 212
El Wad 109
Engare Sero 60
England 5, 9, 56–57, 86, 88, 137, 163, 169, 185, 187, 191–192, 200, 209, 216, 238, 244–245, 247–248
Ethiopia 206–207, 214
Etiolles 139
Eulau 185
Ezero 237

Felsställe 237
Finland 189
Flores 25, 208

Fontanet 58
France 46, 57–59, 81, 87–88, 105–106, 129, 138–139, 141–142, 185, 191, 200, 212, 214, 216, 238
Franchthi 236

Ganj Dareh 116–117
Gargas 58–59, 141–142
Georgia, Republic of 102
Georgia, USA 90
Germany 46, 67, 87–88, 163, 182, 184–185, 187, 189, 237, 246
Gerza 249
Gilgil 250
Godedzor 240
Gombe 37, 78, 127–128, 158, 203
Gomolava 236
Gøngehusvej 182
Gönnersdorf 67
Gough's Cave 216
Grasshopper Pueblo 89, 188
Greece 112, 117, 146, 164, 167–168, 218, 236, 242
Grimaldi 46
Grootebroek 164
Grosser Ofnet 182
Grotta dei Fanciulli 107, 181, 216
Grotta delle Fate 212
Grotte du Prince 46
Guinea 22, 126–127
Guinea Bissau 170

Hadar 206
Ħaġar Qim 47
Hainburg-Teichhal 112
Hallstatt 113, 132
Happisburgh 56–57, 209
Hattoridae 138
Hayonim 181, 217
Head-Smashed-In Buffalo Jump 163
Herto 214
Hierakonpolis 87
Hoëdic 81
Hornish Point 248
Hove 245
Hungary 242

Ileret 56
Illinois, USA 50, 89, 183, 188
India 7, 260n.98
Indian Knoll 219
Indonesia 140, 208
Indus Valley 163
Ipswich 137
Iran 116–117
Iraq 211, 239–240
Ireland 139, 162
Irian Jaya 140
Isleham 191–192
Israel 109, 121, 186, 211, 217, 239
Italy 46, 103–105, 107, 112, 114, 143, 181, 191, 212, 216, 243, 246
Itkul 112, 164–165, 240–241

Japan 20, 109, 138, 166, 219, 253
Jebel Irhoud 214
Jebel Qafzeh 211
Jebel Sahaba 181
Jungfernhöhle 185, 237

Kadero 249
Kalala Island 98
Kalavan 112, 240
Kamennyi Ambar 146–147
Kamirishirataki 138
Kanenokuma 253
Kayhausen 189
Kazibaba 189
Kemerton Camp 187
Kenan Tepe 239
Kentucky, USA 88, 219
Kenya 23, 52n.35, 56, 136, 144, 181, 208, 249
Kephala 236
Khirokitia 235
Khok Phanom Di 252
Knight Mound 50
Knossos 236
Koonalda 141–142
Korea 219
Kori 166
Kostenki 45–46, 105, 214
Koster Mound 188
Kovačevo 237

Kowalewko 246
Krapina 23, 180, 212
Krems-Wachtberg 103, 215
Kuelpa 189
Kuriyama 253

La Ferrassie 212
La Madeleine 105–106, 216
Laetoli 40, 206
Lagar Velho 103, 216
Lake Itkul *see* Itkul
Largo Gallina 187
Larson Village 183
Las Chimeneas 141
Las Cogotas 147
Laugerie Basse 46
Le Caprine 243
Le Moustier 212
Lebanon 237
Lepenski Vir 217–218
Lerna 236
Libya 249
Lindängelund 189, 238
Lokomotiv 47
Lomekwi 23, 136
Lorraine 219
Lough Boora 139
Lucio o de Gavidia 42

Maastricht-Belvédère 138
Madagascar 160
Mahale 22, 37, 78, 158, 203
Makapansgat 180
Makotřasy 188
Malapa 206–207
Malta (island of) 47
Mal'ta, Siberia 46
Man Bac 252
Maningrida 20, 65, 68, 134–135
Mariupol 112
Maszycka 180, 215
Mata Menge 208
Matjes River 82
McDuffee 188
Mehrgarh 252
Melkbosstrand 182
Menneville 185
Mesoamerica 85, 117
Mexico 143

Middle East 24–26, 87, 109, 116, 129, 169, 209, 235, 237–240, 245, 250
Middle Park Station 62
Milton Keynes 244
Modder River 182
Mokrin 143, 242
Morocco 213
Mouanko-Lobethal 250
Moundville 188
Mouzon 191
Myanmar 252

Nagaoka 253
Namibia 62
Namoratunga 249
Nariokotome 208
Nataruk 181
Nazlet Khater 214
Nea Nikomedia 236
Near East *see* Middle East
Netherlands 138, 164, 238
Nevada, USA 140, 264
New Mexico, USA 50, 145, 187
Ngogo 78
Niaux 58
Nigeria 250
Norris Farms 183
Norway 189

Ocoee 188
Öland 87, 114
Olduvai 208
Osipovka 109, 218
Ostrovul Corbulei 185
Ostuni 216
Otzing 185
Ovčarovo 167
Ovnigi 112

Pakistan 252
Paloma 220
Papua New Guinea 66
Paraguay 67, 221
Pavlov 102
Pecos Pueblo 145
Peñalosa 113, 243
Peq'in 239
Peru 84, 90, 109, 117, 189, 220
Pete Klunk 188

Philippines 83, 221
Phum Snay 253
Pincevent 139
Pinnacle Point 80
Platia Magoula Zarkou 167–168
Poland 86, 109, 180, 215, 246–247
Portugal 103, 216, 238
Poundbury 247
Prague-Střešovice 164
Prague Vinoř 164
Předmostí 180, 215

Quoin Point 182

Rakitovo 237
Ramsautal 246
Rhenen 138
Rising Star Cave 209
Roc de Marsal 212
Romania 185, 237
Romito 216
Rouffignac 141
Russia 45–46, 105, 107–108, 112, 146–147, 164–165, 214–215, 240–241, 251
see also Siberia

Sahara 60
Salisbury 163
Salts Cave 88
Sand Canyon 90, 187
Sanga 169–170
Sannai Maruyama 219
Saunaktuk 183
Scandinavia 162, 233
see also Denmark; Finland; Norway; Sweden
Scania 244
Scotland 139, 191, 245, 248
Serbia 108, 143, 217–218, 236, 242
Sevilla 61
Shanidar 211
Shiqmim 186
Siberia 20, 46, 47, 67, 102–103, 134, 165, 191, 208, 251–252
Sima de las Palomas 212

INDEX OF PLACES

Skateholm 218
Skhul 211–212
Sleeping Ute 188
Slovakia 243
Solvieux 139
Souphli Magoula 236
South Africa 61, 80, 82, 180, 182–183, 204–207, 209, 219
South Dakota, USA 183, 188
Southwest USA 9, 69–70, 85, 88–89, 111, 145, 169, 254
see also individual states
Spain 7, 42, 56, 60, 80, 113, 141, 147, 180, 187, 208, 212, 243–244
Sterkfontein 206
Stonehenge 88, 169, 238
Stovepipe Wells 164
Strizhevo 251
Strøby Egede 238
Sudan 88, 114–115, 181, 248–149
Sunghir 107–108, 214–215
Surskaja 112
Sweden 87, 114, 139, 189, 200–201, 218, 238, 244, 247
Switzerland 163
Syria 81, 87–88, 112, 211, 239

Tågerup 218
Taï Forest 126–128, 203
Taiwan 253
Takarkori 249
Talheim 184
Tanzania 20, 22, 37, 40, 60, 63, 78, 127–128, 158, 203, 206, 208
Tarquinia-Pian di Civita 246
Tassili n'Ajjer 60
Taung 204–105
Tell Abada 240
Tell Abu Husaini 239–240
Tell Hazna 112, 239
Tennessee, USA 69, 188
Tepe Gawra 240
Teshik-Tash 201–202, 211
Téviec 81
Thailand 252
Tierra del Fuego 20, 98
Tiszapolgár-Basatanya 242
Titriş Höyük 186, 239
Tochibora 219
Tollense 187
Tonga 253
Torres Strait 30n.55, 134
Trans-Urals 146–147, 251
Troisième Caverne, Goyet 213
Trollesgave 139
Tuc d'Audoubert 57, 142–143

Turkey 48–49, 56, 86, 112, 186, 235, 239

Uganda 78, 134
Ukraine 109, 112, 218
USA 20, 85, 143, 169
see also Southwest USA; individual states
Uzbekistan 189, 201–202, 211

Varna 112, 242
Vedbaek 182, 218
Velim 187
Vengerevo 165
Vietnam 168, 252
Vilnjanka 112
Vlasac 108, 217

Wadi Amud 211
Wadi Kubbaniya 81
Wadi Sura 60–61
Wales 62, 191
Wandlebury 248
Warandebergen 138
Wetwang Slack 86
Wilczyce 109, 215
Willandra Lakes 5

Yoshitake Takagi 253

Zambia 98
Zaraysk 46
Zauschwitz 237
Zimbabwe 62

GENERAL INDEX

Aborigines (Australian) 7–8, 16, 19, 20, 65, 68, 83, 98–99, 118n.1, 134–135, 136, 222–223
Ache 67, 221
Acheulean *see* Palaeolithic, Lower
adolescence (human) 4–7, 10, 38, 83, 124, 138, 148, 160–162, 178, 214, 217
adulthood (human) 4–7, 21, 42, 55, 61, 135, 140, 221
  see also initiation
agriculturalists *see* farmers
Agta 83, 221
Ainu 20
Aka 64, 132, 160
Akwe-Shavante 133
Aleut 133
Anasazi (Ancestral Puebloans) 69–70, 89, 145, 164, 187–188
Andronovo 251
Anglo-Saxon 6, 173n.27
anthropology xviii, xxiv, 9, 15, 16–21, 63–66, 82–85, 130–135, 160–162, 220–223, 266
  see also Lancy, David
apes *see* primates
apprenticeship *see* learning
archaeological theory xix–xx, 10, 28n.36
Archaic period (North America) 140, 220
Ardrey, Robert 180
Ariès, Philippe xxvi n.4
art *see* plaquette; rock art; sculpture
Australian Aborigines *see* Aborigines (Australian)

Australopithecines 22, 23–24, 39–40, 79, 100, 180, 201, 204–207
Aztec 179

Bailey, Douglass 168
Baka 63, 161
Balák, Libor 105, 108, 144
Basketmaker culture 69–70, 85, 111
basketry 68, 131, 164, 242
Baxter, Jane Eva 10
beads *see* ornamentation
Beaker culture 68, 88
Berseneva, Natalia 146–147
Binford, Lewis 53n.52
bioanthropology 5, 13, 201, 264–265
  see also DNA studies; isotope studies; sex determination; weaning
bioarchaeology *see* bioanthropology
biological anthropology *see* bioanthropology
Birdsell, Joseph 223
birth 33–50, 60
birth rates *see* fertility
body shaping 117–118
Bofi 132, 160
bog bodies 91, 189
bonobos 21–22, 35, 76, 128, 158, 204
Bordes, François 138
bow and arrow 161, 190–191
brain (human) 5, 25, 39, 41–42, 80–81, 130, 150n.35, 202, 205, 216
Bronze Age 26, 68, 86–88, 90, 112–115, 143, 146, 164–165, 186–187, 191, 238–245, 250

burial 198–224, 233–267 and *passim*
Bushmen *see* San

Cambridge, University Museum 13, 137
cannibalism 56, 180–181, 183, 187–188,
  203–204, 208–209, 213, 215
Chalcolithic 26, 112, 116, 118, 147, 186,
  238–243, 250
chimpanzees 21–22, 36–38, 51n.24,
  77–78, 125–128, 157–159, 179,
  203–204
Chinchorro 109, 183, 220
Classical xx, 7, 14, 189, 246
clothing 47, 97–116, 134, 161, 165, 167,
  169, 215–216, 242–244, 247
conflict 176–192
cradle 46, 66–67, 70, 240
cradleboard 68–69
Cree 83

Dart, Raymond 180, 204–205
Darwin, Charles 33, 98, 204
de Maret, Pierre 169–170, 250
dental studies 42, 56, 75, 80–81, 85, 86,
  90–91, 187, 202–208, 215, 252
diet
  human 5, 16, 39, 42, 66, 75–91, 199,
    219, 252, 265
  primate 36–38
disease 13, 66, 85, 88–91, 189, 206, 215,
  221–222, 235, 248–249, 252–254,
  265
DNA studies 13, 21, 185, 202, 208, 215,
  263, 265
dolls 46, 134, 159, 165–166, 168–171, 240,
  250, 263–264
Dowaya 144

economy 8, 15–16, 84, 89, 131, 156, 234
  see also farmers; foragers
Efe 64
Epipalaeolithic *see* Mesolithic
Ertebølle 238
ethnography *see* anthropology
Etruscan 246

fabric *see* textiles
farmers xxiii, 26, 44, 50, 66, 68, 84–91,
  110–116, 143–147, 162–165,
  167–170, 184–189, 190–192,
  233–261
  see also Bronze Age; Chalcolithic;
    Iron Age; Neolithic

fathers (human) 8, 40, 55, 63–64, 125,
  131–132, 156, 160, 163
feminism 12, 40, 48, 179
fertility 9, 27n.20, 34, 44, 48, 64–65, 67,
  84, 86, 90, 200, 209, 221–223,
  235, 243, 252
figurines *see* sculpture
finger marks *see* flutings; pottery
Finlay, Nyree 136
flutings 141–142
food *see* diet; weaning
footprints 24, 40, 52n.35, 56–60, 62,
  141, 143
footwear 101, 102, 113
foragers xxiii, 16–21, 47–48, 63–68,
  78–84, 100–110, 132–135,
  160–161, 165, 180–183, 204–224
  see also Palaeolithic
Fossey, Dian 22

Gamble, Clive 10
games 130, 157, 160–163, 165, 169, 171,
  191, 263–264
Gat, Azar 177
gibbons 21, 35, 76
Gimbutas, Marija 48
Goodall, Jane 22, 158, 203
gorillas 21, 35, 76, 125, 157, 203
grandparents 6, 41, 55, 63, 64, 68, 83,
  132, 210, 221
Gravettian 103–105, 214–215

Hadza 20, 28n.21, 63, 82–84, 134
hair 111, 244
Hallstatt culture 113, 163–164, 246
Hammond, Norman 171
handprints 58, 62, 141
Harappan 163
Hayashi, Misato 127
health *see* disease
Hewlett, Barry 17, 64
Hiatt, Les 19
Hirata, Satoshi 126
Hirschfeld, Lawrence xviii
history 5–6, 12, 14, 48
Hodder, Ian 28n.36
hominins 12, 22–24, 38–43, 79–80,
  129–130, 204–213
Homo antecessor 24, 56–57, 208
Homo erectus 24, 32n.85, 41, 56, 79, 100,
  137, 208–209
Homo floresiensis 208
Homo habilis 24

Homo heidelbergensis 24, 137
Homo naledi 209
Homo neanderthalensis see Neanderthals
Hopewell 50, 188
Hopi 169
hunter-gatherers *see* foragers

Ik 134
Inca 117, 179
infanticide 8, 14, 48, 190, 201, 203–204, 212, 220, 222–223, 234–235, 237, 250, 252
Ingold, Tim 66
initiation 57, 61, 135, 169, 185
injury *see* trauma
Inuit 20, 165
Iron Age
    Africa 98, 169–170, 249–250
    Europe 26, 87–88, 90, 114, 132, 143, 147, 162–164, 169, 187, 189, 191, 245–248, 251–253
    see also Hallstatt culture
Iroquois 146, 169
isotope studies 75, 79, 81–82, 85–86, 88, 91, 244, 249, 265

jewellery *see* ornamentation
Jomon 109, 219, 253
Jones, Nicholas Blurton 134

Kamp, Kathryn 10, 267
kaross *see* sling
Keeley, Lawrence 178
!Kung *see* San

labour *see* economy; work
Ladygina-Kohts, Nadezhda 158
Lamb, Michael 17
Lancy, David xx, 15–16, 48, 84, 131, 156, 266–267
language 25, 33, 43–44, 71, 124–125, 129–130
Later Stone Age (Africa) 25, 61–62, 82, 101, 142, 182–183, 218–219
learning 2–3, 44, 77–78, 102, 123–148, 156–157, 160, 190, 234
Lee, Richard 67
life expectancy 90, 200, 207, 209, 219, 221, 223, 232n.144, 233
Lillehammer, Grete 10, 13, 27n.3
Linearbandkeramik 86, 184–185, 191, 237

Lovejoy, Owen 38–39
Lubbock, Sir John 18
Luo 144

Magdalenian 46, 57–58, 139
Mansi 67, 134
marine foods 80–81, 219
marriage 6–8, 19, 133, 145, 185
Martu 83
Matsuzawa, Tetsuro 127
Maya 85, 179
Mbuti 221
medieval 5, 27n.1
Mellaart, James 50
Mellars, Paul 138
menarche 5, 47–48, 61
Meriam 134
Mesolithic 25, 42, 47, 62, 81, 86, 108, 139–140, 181–182, 217–218
metalworking 143, 145–146, 238–239
Middle Stone Age (Africa) 24, 80, 100
midwives 33, 39, 40
Mikea 160
Mimbres 50
Mississippian 90
Mithen, Steven 43, 124
modern society xx, 8–9, 14–15, 33–34, 44, 48, 124, 128, 132, 177, 191, 266
    see also anthropology
monkeys 38–39, 125, 204
mortality rates (human) 8–9, 44, 89–91, 199–200, 207, 209, 213, 221–223, 233, 235, 242
mothers (human) 33–50, 55–71, 98, 124–125, 131–132, 134, 143–145, 156, 160, 165, 213, 217, 220, 222, 235, 250
    see also fertility; weaning
Mousterian *see* Palaeolithic, Middle
mush 81
music 43, 124–125, 159, 161, 164

Natufian culture 109, 181, 217
Nayaka 7
Neanderthals 8, 23, 24, 41–43, 56, 79–80, 100–111, 129–130, 138, 201–202, 207, 209–213, 224, 228n.77
Neolithic 15, 26, 81, 86, 88, 112, 114, 116–117, 139, 144, 162, 167–169, 184–186, 188–190, 217–218, 234–238, 248–249, 252
    see also Linearbandkeramik

Netsilik 223
Ngadadjara 65
Nielsen, Mark 8, 129

ochre 100, 103, 107, 114, 141, 182, 215–218, 220, 237–238
Oldowan 23
omega-3 fatty acid 25
orangutans 21–22, 35, 76, 125, 203
ornamentation 97–116, 182–183, 215–216, 217–218, 219–220, 236, 239–240, 242–243, 249–254

Paiute 9, 20
palaeoanthropology *see* hominins
Palaeolithic
   Lower 24, 129, 137, 208
   Middle 24, 100, 138, 180, 209–213
     see also Neanderthals
   Upper 3, 25, 43–46, 57–60, 80–81, 101–109, 138–139, 141–142, 159, 180–181, 207, 213–217
     see also Gravettian; Magdalenian
Parakana 64, 160
Paranthropus see Australopithecines
Pettitt, Paul 212
Piaget, Jean 124
plaquette 46, 67
play 38, 156–172, 179
porotic hyperostosis 88–89
pot burials 239, 250, 253
pottery 50, 87–88, 111, 163–165, 236–245, 250, 251–255
   pottery making 143–147
predynastic Egypt 49–50, 115–116, 249
Primate Research Institute, Kyoto 127
primates xxi, 21–22, 34–38, 76–78, 125–128, 157–159, 203–204
puberty (human) 5–7, 111, 202
Pueblo 111, 145, 254
   see also Anasazi
Pygmies 19, 20, 221

Rice, Patricia 44, 200
rock art 7, 25, 42, 57–58, 60–62, 111, 135, 141–143, 250, 263–264
Roman 48, 90, 110, 163, 189, 200, 245, 248
   see also Classical

sacrifice 179, 182, 186, 189–190, 192, 215, 235, 240, 246, 251

San xxiv, 9, 17, 19, 20, 30n.56, 48, 62, 63, 67, 82–84, 133–134, 160, 218–219, 221–223
Sartre, Jean-Paul xviii
sculpture 3, 25, 44–50, 57, 102–103, 107, 112, 116–117, 145–146, 159, 164–165, 168–169, 171, 215, 235, 240–241, 250
scurvy 90–91, 252–253
Scythian 251
sewing 101–102, 112, 134, 143
sex determination 13, 236, 202, 236, 263
Shea, John 137
Shoshone 9, 20
Sinagua 145–146
Sintashta 146–147
skills *see* learning
slavery 131–132
sling 17, 63, 66–68, 101, 109
Solecki, Ralph 211
speech *see* language
stillbirths 201, 203, 235, 249, 250, 252, 254, 265
stone artefacts 23–25, 56, 79, 81, 86, 101–102, 107, 125, 127–128, 136, 159, 182, 184, 188, 212–218, 239, 242, 249–250
stone bowls 235–236, 239
stone tool making 136–141, 159, 190

Takakura, Jan 138
Tanner, Nancy Makepeace 12, 40
Tasaday 83
tattoos 98
teeth *see* dental studies
textiles 102, 109–110, 112, 143, 189, 237
Thule 165
Tiwanika 117
Tiwi 83
tool making 38, 125–141
   see also pottery; stone tool making
Toth, Nicholas 128
toys 11, 70, 137, 145–146, 157, 159, 161–165, 167, 169, 173n.27, 190–191, 263–264
trauma 13, 176–193, 206, 212, 219, 237
trephination 188–189
Turnbull, Colin 134
twins 47, 48, 215, 222, 235, 250
Tylor, Edward 18

Ubaid period 239–240

Villanovan 245–246
violence *see* conflict

weaning 35–38, 48, 75–91, 207, 265
weapons 133, 159, 178, 180–181, 185–186, 190–192, 220, 249, 251–252
Wielbark 114, 143, 246–247

Wileman, Julie 13, 167
Woodland 85, 88, 90
work 15, 44, 113, 131–132, 145

Yanomami 48, 223
Yayoi 166, 253
Yora 84